D1526151

Plato's Cosmology and Its Ethical Dimensions

Although a great deal has been written on Plato's ethics, his cosmology has not received so much attention in recent times, and its importance for his ethical thought has remained underexplored. By offering integrated accounts of *Timaeus, Philebus, Politicus,* and *Laws* X, the book reveals a strongly symbiotic relation between the cosmic and the human sphere. It is argued that in his late period Plato presents a picture of an organic universe, endowed with structure and intrinsic value, which both urges our respect and calls for our responsible intervention. Humans are thus seen as citizens of a universe that can provide a context for their flourishing even in the absence of good political institutions. The book sheds new light on many intricate metaphysical issues in late Plato, and brings out the close connections between his cosmology and the development of his ethics.

Gabriela Roxana Carone teaches at the University of Colorado at Boulder and is a Fellow of the Harvard University Center for Hellenic Studies.

Plato's Cosmology and Its Ethical Dimensions

GABRIELA ROXANA CARONE

University of Colorado at Boulder and
Harvard University Center for Hellenic Studies

CAMBRIDGE UNIVERSITY PRESS

CAMBRIDGE UNIVERSITY PRESS
Cambridge, New York, Melbourne, Madrid, Cape Town, Singapore, São Paulo

Cambridge University Press
40 West 20th Street, New York, NY 10011-4211, USA

www.cambridge.org
Information on this title: www.cambridge.org/9780521845601

First published 2005

Printed in the United States of America

A catalog record for this publication is available from the British Library.

Library of Congress Cataloging in Publication Data
Carone, Gabriela Roxana.
Plato's cosmology and its ethical dimensions / Gabriela Roxana Carone.
p.   cm.
Includes bibliographical references and index.
ISBN 0-521-84560-2
1. Plato.   2. Cosmology, Ancient.   3. Ethics, Ancient.   I. Title.
B398.C67C37   2005
113′.092–dc22   2005046970

ISBN-13   978-0-521-84560-1 hardback
ISBN-10   0-521-84560-2 hardback

A Rosa Mazzini,
en mi recuerdo

Contents

Preface   *page* ix

1   Introduction   1
   I. Why Cosmology and Ethics?   1
   II. Plato's Cosmology in the Context of the Dynamics of
      Plato's Thought   7
   III. Plato's Cosmology and the Interpretation of
      Plato's Dialogues   13
   IV. The Plan of this Book   18
   V. The Order of the Dialogues   22

2   Demiurgy in the *Timaeus*   24
   I. Introduction   24
   II. The Philosophical Meaning of the Demiurge   29
   III. The Ontological Status of the Demiurge   42
   IV. Conclusion   51

3   Cosmic God and Human Reason in the *Timaeus*   53
   I. The Cosmic God as a Model for Human
      Reason   54
   II. Divine and Human Demiurgy   62
   III. The Ethical Function of Astronomy   68
   IV. Conclusion   78

4   Creating Mixtures in the *Philebus*   79
   I. The Dialectical Prelude and the Context for the
      Cosmological Discussion   81
   II. Cosmology and the Fourfold Classification   85
   III. Conclusion   102

5   Happiness in the Universe of the *Philebus*   103
     I. *Pleasure, God, and Human Life*   104
     II. *Happiness for All Humans: The Socratic Revival and the*
         Philebus' Educational Suggestions   116
     III. *Conclusion*   122

6   Reversing the Myth of the *Politicus*   124
     I. *Understanding the* Politicus *Myth: Why does It Matter?*   125
     II. *Some Gaps in the Traditional Interpretation*   129
     III. *The States of the Cosmos Successively Presented in the Text* 132
     IV. *Autonomy and Divine Guidance*   141
     V. *Conclusion*   144

7   Cosmic and Human Drama in the *Politicus*   146
     I. *The Cosmological Significance of the Myth*   147
     II. *The Ethical and Political Meaning of the Myth*   153
     III. *Conclusion*   160

8   *Laws* X: First Causes and the Origin of Evil   162
     I. *The Priority of Soul over Body*   164
     II. *What is the Evil Soul? Some Questions*   170
     III. *The Scope of "Soul" at* Laws *896e–897b*   172
     IV. *The Status of an Evil Soul at a Cosmic Level*   174
     V. *Humans, Evil, and Teleology*   178

9   Conclusion   189

Notes   197
Bibliographical References   265
Index Locorum   281
General Index   305

Preface

This book is the result of many years of thought and research, and has
taken on several different shapes before reaching its final version. It
started as a project based on (and soon took off beyond) my Ph.D. thesis,
written between 1992 and 1995. My research on Plato's cosmology goes
back somewhat further, and I am happy that, as this book is coming to
fruition, my *La noción de dios en el Timeo de Platón*, originally published
in Buenos Aires in 1991, is due to appear in its second edition for a
Spanish-speaking readership. Proper acknowledgements were made in
both those productions to scholars and institutions, in Argentina and in
England, which contributed to my research then. But I would like here to
thank David Sedley and Richard Sorabji for their keen criticism early on.
I am also grateful to Christopher Shields and Raphael Woolf, who com-
mented on different chapters of the book, and to the anonymous refer-
ees for Cambridge University Press for their helpful suggestions. It is my
pleasure to thank, in addition, the National Endowment for the Human-
ities for generous financial support, and the Center for Human Values at
Princeton University, which has allowed me to finalise the manuscript in
optimal research conditions and in an excellent collegial environment.

Previous versions of sections of this book have appeared as follows:
Chapter 2, Section II.2 is based on Carone (2004c); Chapter 3, Section
III is based on Carone (1997); parts of Chapter 5, Section I are based
on Carone (2000); Chapter 6 is based on Carone (2004a); parts of
Chapter 7 are based on Carone (1993); and parts of Chapter 8 are
based on Carone (1994). I am grateful to the editors of those outlets for
permission to reprint this material.

Princeton, February 2004

Plato's Cosmology and Its Ethical Dimensions

Introduction

I. WHY COSMOLOGY AND ETHICS?

This book is a study of Plato's late cosmology and its relation to Plato's ethics. The combination might strike one as odd. Indeed, it might seem far from obvious, first, that Plato has any coherent cosmological story to tell; second, that even if he does, it would deserve any special attention beyond historical curiosity, still less as a necessary background for understanding his ethical thinking. In the modern literature, it has in fact been quite common to investigate Plato's ethics, but much less common to delve into his cosmology. At any rate, these two undertakings have usually been carried out in isolation from each other. Thus, for example, Terence Irwin's extensive treatment in *Plato's Ethics* contains no section on the *Timaeus*, and virtually no allusion to Plato's cosmology and theology. Even more striking in this regard is Christopher Bobonich's recent book on Plato's later ethics and politics, *Plato's Utopia Recast*, which, despite occupying more than 600 pages of exegetical treatment, does not for the most part consider it necessary, for its purposes, to take a stand on cosmological issues.[1]

Certainly, some fresh air has been brought to these topics in a few recent contributions, though an extensive treatment of Plato's late cosmology in relation to his ethics is lacking to this day. Julia Annas, for example, devotes a chapter of her *Platonic Ethics, Old and New* to the issue of assimilation with god, but does not do much in terms of integrating this aspect of Plato with other aspects of his ethical thinking, and is at any rate quite comfortable with the thought that Plato's ethics can be understood independently of his metaphysical commitments.[2] And, more generally, even when the issue of assimilation with god has been addressed,[3] it has been somewhat detached from an examination of what Plato means by "god" in those cases, and of how such an issue may relate to his wider views about nature.

Let us now turn to the cosmology itself. This side of Plato's thought has received rather little attention compared with the stress placed on his ethics, metaphysics, and epistemology in recent decades. But even when scholars have dealt with the cosmology, it has been in a fairly self-contained way, with little or no emphasis on how this piece might fit into the overall picture. One can think here, for example, of the works of Luc Brisson (1974), Gregory Vlastos (1975), Eric Ostenfeld (1982), Richard Mohr (1985), and T. M. Robinson (1995). The present book has often gained from a critical engagement with their arguments; yet not much heed is paid in these works to the question of what bearing Plato's cosmological speculations might have on his ethical views, and vice versa.[4]

This is not to say that the late dialogues in which one finds a treatment of cosmological issues have not been studied. But here there has been a temptation to downplay the properly cosmological side of these dialogues, or turn it into something else (such as ethics). Thus, for example, when M. M. McCabe considers the *Politicus* myth, which contains a picture of cosmic reversals, she affirms that its main message is not cosmological, but ethical.[5] This, so to speak, "reductive" approach may seem attractive; yet it risks, as I shall argue, depriving us of a richer picture. Let us first, though, try to understand what may motivate the prevalent attitude.

The neglect that Plato's cosmology as such has received in the last few decades may be due to several assumptions: first, that it is intractable (as much of it is written in the form of myth, and myths seem resilient to philosophical analysis); second, that it is contradictory (the *Politicus*, for example, appears to tell us that there is no god ruling our present universe, contrary to the story of the *Timaeus*); third, that it is an isolated compartment, or even a digression, in the context of Plato's philosophy as a whole, with little or no bearing on other aspects of it and on the way that we should live.

And yet – at least for those who have understood the main message of the *Republic* – it would seem alien to the Platonic spirit that philosophers should be occupied in abstract study unless such study is put to helping them and others lead better human lives. This also gives us a *prima facie* reason to be suspicious of the presumption that there might be loose elements, such as his cosmology, in Plato's thought that would not, directly or indirectly, connect with his other interests, and particularly with his ethical concerns. This book is rather an attempt to prove the opposite. Indeed, I believe it is in his late dialogues – particularly *Timaeus, Philebus, Politicus* (or *Statesman*), and *Laws* – that we find Plato most fully developing his theory of nature and his insights about the relation of humans to the universe. (For this reason, apart from reasons of space, I shall focus on the cosmology of the late dialogues, although references to other dialogues will also be made where relevant.) It is my aim to show that we actually need Plato's cosmology in order to make sense of his late ethics, and that the cosmological background is even necessary for an understanding of some of his late epistemological and metaphysical preoccupations, which are in turn inextricably linked to ethical ones. It is also my goal to demonstrate that we ought to look at Plato's cosmology as something continuous with, and not disconnected from, the motivations that urged him in dialogues such as the *Republic* to give an answer to questions about human happiness and the best means to attain it. If it is true, as we shall see, that the meaning of human life cannot for Plato be adequately determined unless one inserts it into a larger picture, then the universe, I contend, provides in the late dialogues an inescapable point of reference.

Now, one might say, to be fair to the contemporary tendency to neglect or downplay the cosmological passages in Plato's dialogues, that they are somewhat bizarre, or outmoded. In this regard, it may be harder to extract philosophical inspiration when reading the astronomical passages of the *Timaeus* than when, for instance, analysing the various puzzles concerning knowledge in the *Theaetetus*. In one sense, the complaint is just: why should it matter, philosophically, whether or not Plato, for example, believes the demiurge of the *Timaeus* to be a separate god in his structure of reality, or whether he thinks the planets err or revolve predictably? Even if it could be proved – as I shall attempt to do here – that some of his late ethical views rely on weighty cosmological assumptions (for example, that the study of astronomy will make the masses happy) it may be hard to make any sense of this, and the reader may choose to distance herself or himself from these passages and label their thoughts as outlandish.

Arriving at such conclusions too hastily, however, threatens to deprive us of the chance of seeing what larger philosophical motivations may have underpinned those particular views that we find odd, motivations that may, in addition, represent an important link, to this date perhaps still somewhat hidden, in the comprehension of later developments in the history of philosophy. After all, it is an incontrovertible pillar of Aristotelian ethics that nature is normative, so that one ought to act in accordance with it;[6] and the way in which Stoic ethics is made directly to rest on larger cosmic views is much discussed these days by classical scholars.[7] The thought that to know oneself one should know the larger universe of which one is a part goes back at least as far as the Presocratics; and Heraclitus' contention that "all human laws are fed on a single, divine Law" is well known.[8] The relation between law (*nomos*) and nature (*phusis*) was indeed a hotly debated issue at the time of the sophistic movement, and Plato's dialogues contain invaluable responses to that debate mainly by way of trying to supersede what had become in his eyes a largely unjustified divorce between these two notions. In this regard, it can be said that his cosmology is the best example of an attempt to reconcile them, by showing us how normativity is to be grounded on the workings of nature.[9]

For some, the appeal to ethical naturalism that is so common in philosophers of antiquity may appear ill advised, particularly given modern critiques that have denounced this procedure in terms of what has become known as the naturalistic fallacy, the supposed fallacy of inferring values from facts.[10] At the same time, however, the issue is still a matter of dispute,[11] and Virtue Ethics, a movement that has its roots in the ancient philosophers (particularly Aristotle) and is making a significant comeback in contemporary ethical theory, is often sympathetic to the idea that ethics is very much about realising one's human nature to the fullest – and, as late Plato and many after him would add, one's human nature cannot be understood without in turn understanding the way it is part of nature. Even the extent to which role models are important in ethics is these days much discussed[12] (remember Aristotle's insistence on virtue consisting in a habit of choice "as the wise (*phronimos*) person would determine it" in *N.E.* II 6). It seems ironic, nevertheless, that so little attention has been paid to the possible Platonic roots of this philosophical way of thinking, even though Plato, or so I shall argue, presents in a surprising way no less than god, or the universe, as the most admirable role model for ethical enquiry.

Now, why "god or the universe"? One of my contentions in this book is that, despite apparent evidence to the contrary, there is for Plato no god over and above the universe itself. And by "god" here I mean an intelligent living being – a notion that may make us wonder whether Plato is not getting carried away. Why should we relate at all to such a view, except as a poetic, or perhaps Romantic, albeit inaccurate, way of picturing nature? However strange it may seem at first sight, some modern environmentalists (such as deep ecologists) may, or at least should, regard Plato as an ally, and I have elsewhere discussed this issue.[13] But my point here is rather different. Even granting that it *is* odd to claim that god is some kind of intelligence immanent to the universe, or indeed that the universe itself is an intelligent living being, the claim may start to look more interesting when we examine it not in isolation, but as a consequence of Plato's overall approach to the mind-body relation in his late dialogues. For now I shall say a brief word about this issue, which will occupy pertinent sections of the book, to illustrate another aspect of the cosmology whose philosophical and historical interest has tended to be overlooked and to which I hope to make the reader more alert.

In modern discussions of the mind-body problem it has been common to refer to Aristotle as a healthy historical alternative to either robust dualism or reductive materialism. Plato has been largely disregarded, either because he was assumed to endorse the "robust dualism" side of the story (as opposed to Democritean materialism),[14] or because no definite view could be seen to emerge from his writings. And yet there is reason to suspect, as I hope the following treatment will suggest, that many of the merits that are attributed to the Aristotelian outlook nowadays in fact owe much to Plato, so that Aristotle himself may have been influenced by Plato's late writings. In particular, I shall try to demonstrate how, in late Plato at least (and whatever his former views may have been), the mind is the kind of thing that cannot exist independently of the body (and this will have not only metaphysical but also ethical and practical implications, if, as we shall see, the cultivation of an appropriate balance between mind and body will be particularly stressed). But if so, then we shall need to change, or at the very least qualify, our traditional stand on the "Platonic" view of the metaphysical status of the soul and its historical importance in understanding the modern debate.

It is precisely on the issue of god that Plato's late views are arguably more provocative than those of Aristotle. Whilst the modern relevance of hylomorphism has been much discussed, Aristotle's postulation of an active intellect, or *nous poiêtikos*, in *De Anima* III 5, has been seen as the exception to the rule. Whether that separate (or separable, *chôristos*) *nous* is taken to stand for an individual *nous*, or for the *nous* of god (as in Alexander's interpretation),[15] it seems clear that Aristotle's theory cannot be counted as one that *excludes* the possibility of separate existence for the mind, or one part of the mind. Even his god is depicted as a separate *nous* which is totally immaterial (*Metaph.* XII 7, 1073a3–7). Of course, this latter circumstance need not contradict modern stands on the mind-body relation. For it is often conceded that the discussion is restricted to our actual world and the way things are as far as the human mind is concerned, without this excluding that in other (possible) worlds things may be different.[16] Even modern physicalists may not disagree that dualism is logically possible; they may just argue that it is not the way *we* are made up. In that regard, discussion of the mind-body problem is often limited to what status the mind (our mind) *does* have in relation to the body, as opposed to what status a mind can in principle have; and so it may be thought no harm for a theory of the human mind as nonseparate that there may be other minds (such as possibly god's) that are not. I hope it will emerge from what follows that Plato's late claims about the nature of the mind are much stronger, as they can be seen to include both the human mind and the mind of god. I shall also show how he views these two entities (or possible entities) as isomorphic, so that there is no room left for a separate *nous* in Plato's scheme of things – unlike Aristotle's. Thus, even if the thought that god is immanent to the material universe may strike us as odd, the philosophical motivation behind it is, at the very least, an intriguing one.

Now, how does all this relate to Plato's ethics? The postulation of the universe as an intelligent living being carries with it many implications. In the first place, it functions *teleologically*, that is, with some good purpose; and this purpose is given by reason. This contention is supposed to do some explanatory work: to tell us why things are the way that they are;[17] but it is not exempt from problems. For one thing, it raises the need to account for the problem of evil; and so it is perhaps no accident that the dialogues containing the most detailed treatments of one issue should also contain the most daring suggestions on the other. Plato does think that it is the rationality governing the planets and stars that ensures that they do not err in their path; and he seems to be a firm believer that it is the rationality pervading the universe that establishes the foundation for a system of natural justice on which humans can rely. But the fact that he also considers another element in the constitution (and explanation) of the universe, which he calls "necessity" and which imposes limitations on intelligent activity, presents an interesting challenge for those who may think that his appeal to teleology is naïve. Indeed it is not, if his theory is, as I shall argue, that rationality is not completely successful in governing the universe, and that it is perhaps in the human sphere above all where things have been left unfinished. In this way, humans themselves are given a fundamental role in improving the goodness of the universe, even though one is made painfully aware that they also have the capacity to make things significantly worse.

In a sense, making the universe intelligent and divine may seem to "depersonalise" god and show its workings to be much more automatic than the craftsman metaphor, for example in the *Timaeus*, may suggest; but there are many senses still in which the universe behaves like the ideal human being. Take the unerring behaviour of the stars. Plato refers to it in relation to their "thinking always the same things about the same things" (40a8–b1), just as in the *Gorgias* Socrates is himself portrayed, by contrast with the erratic procedures of the rhetorician, as always "maintaining the same things... about the same things" (490e9–11, cf. 491b5–8), and deems it shameful to engage in politics when one is never "thinking the same things about the same things" (527d7). As I suggest here, what Plato finds admirable (however remote this thought may seem to us) in the behaviour of the stars is performative consistency, that is, consistency not only among one's thoughts, but also between one's thoughts and one's deeds. And this represents a continuation of, rather than a break with, his ethical preoccupations in the early dialogues.

Now, there is also another sense in which the cosmology of the late dialogues resumes Socratic themes, and it is what I shall argue is their more populist conception of happiness, as opposed to the elitism of the middle dialogues. If we recall, it was Socrates in the *Apology* for whom the unexamined life is not worth living, and no one, not even the craftsman or the stranger, was regarded as exempt from such a challenge.[18] This may contrast with dialogues such as the *Republic*, where philosophical examination and (one could argue) autonomous human fulfilment seem to be reserved for very few. It is worth reviewing this turn, so as to show how, in his later period, Plato may have felt a certain dissatisfaction with some aspects of his middle-period ethics, to which the cosmology represents a response. This will further help us see how the late cosmology, far from being a loose cannon in Plato's philosophy, may indeed prove to be quite central to an understanding of its development. I shall offer next a preview of this issue.

II. PLATO'S COSMOLOGY IN THE CONTEXT OF THE DYNAMICS OF PLATO'S THOUGHT

In the *Gorgias*, Socrates can already be found telling Callicles: "the wise men say, Callicles, that both heaven and earth, and gods and humans, are bound by communion, friendship, orderliness, temperance and justice;

and that is why they call this whole an order (*kosmos*),[19] and not a disorder (*akosmia*) or unrestraint (*akolasia*)" (507e6–508a4). The insistence on an order that pervades the universe is particularly relevant in a context where lack of order or consistency (*homologia*) in one's beliefs threatens to dissolve the unity of the subject (cf. 482b–c). The friendship and harmony that holds the universe together as one already functions as a paradigm, we may say, of the internal unity that is desirable for the person.

Beyond this allusion, however, we do not find much about cosmology in Plato's early dialogues. Later on, in the *Phaedo*, Socrates refers to the ordering *nous*, or *nous diakosmôn*, of Anaxagoras (also mentioned at *Cratylus* 400a), and expresses initial enthusiasm about a mind that could account for the good arrangement of the totality of things, which is professed to be "the way things are now" (99c1–2). But this possible course of explanation is not pursued, given Socrates' disappointment at the mechanical way Anaxagoras proceeded to explain each individual phenomenon (cf. 98b–c).[20] Nonetheless, soon in the *Republic* we find allusions to a craftsman or demiurge (*dêmiourgos*) of our sight (VI 507c), who is also responsible for the heaven – and things in it – being arranged "in as beautiful a way as is possible" (VII 530a5–7). This is a designing agent who would have taken care not only of the universe as a whole but also of individual phenomena. Plato does not expand on the cosmological significance of this *dêmiourgos*; we shall have to wait till the late dialogues for that. They will also provide the detailed teleological explanations that Socrates had failed to find in Anaxagoras. However, the notion that cosmic order and beauty has its foundation in some sort of design starts becoming explicit here; and it may be no accident that, at least as far as the *polis* is concerned, the philosopher ruler is called a demiurge (*dêmiourgos*) of virtue, who orders the state, the citizens, and himself according to goodness (VII 540a8–b1, cf. VI 500d). Some parallelism between the ideal *polis* and the *kosmos* is thus suggested, even though they are kept distinct. To what extent the *kosmos* itself may later on stand for or replace, for many, that ideal *polis* of Plato's dreams is a matter that will concern us presently.

Indeed, while scholars have tended to neglect Plato's late cosmology, there is no controversy about the relevance of the *Republic* for an understanding of Plato, even though the theories set out there do leave problems that have not escaped its readers. Thus, I shall now focus on certain ethical issues in the *Republic* so as to show how this central work contains gaps and flaws demanding a solution that, I argue, is to be found at least partly in the late cosmological passages. I am for this purpose assuming that the *Timaeus, Philebus, Politicus,* and *Laws* are chronologically posterior to the *Republic*. This assumption can for now rely on scholarly consensus, though I shall in any case be referring to the chronological issue later.

Together with the *Phaedo* and the *Symposium,* the *Republic* is considered to encompass Plato's middle-period metaphysics, in which he postulates imperceptible and unchanging entities called Forms as the foundation of the world of change that we perceive, and also as the foundation of his ethics. Such entities are the highest object of human knowledge (this represented at its summit by philosophy) and also the highest goal of human aspiration. There is throughout these dialogues a deep concern for the happy or self-fulfilled life expressed in a state of well-being, or *eudaimonia*.[21] The *Phaedo,* with its other-wordly tones, reserves the possibility of *eudaimonia* strictly speaking for the philosopher, as something to be attained once he is freed from the chains of the body (80e–81a). Philosophy, then, is there regarded as the only means of salvation, and confined to a small group of initiates such as Socrates and those in his circle. The *Republic* can be seen as an attempt to extend happiness to the whole of society,[22] but now such happiness seems to assume one of the following two forms: either (1.) you are again a philosopher, having direct and infallible knowledge of the Forms, from which you get enlightenment about the nature of the truly good and happy human life;[23] or (2.) you are under the rule of a philosopher, in those cases where you lack a philosophical nature. But even here you are capable of attaining happiness if you follow strictly the rule of the philosopher: he or she, possessing the infallible knowledge that you lack, will be able to impart to you right opinions about the best way to conduct your life in a harmonious community.[24] In all cases, virtue is a necessary prerequisite for happiness: If you are happy, you have the wealth of a good life, and this presupposes wisdom and justice (VII 521a, I 354a).

The picture in the *Republic* might then seem quite promising compared with the *Phaedo*. First, Plato is showing concern for the happiness of a community, not just a few individuals, and second, he is inscribing individual happiness in the context of a happy society (*polis*). He is saying that if you want to find a means to self-fulfilment you cannot ignore your immediate social background. Rather, you should start by considering yourself part of that whole and discover that it is by promoting the latter's well-being that you will find the rewards of personal well-being. In this case the main virtues to be furthered in the community will include sound-mindedness (*sôphrosunê*), that is, the modest recognition of whether you have the right nature to rule others or rather be ruled; and

justice (*dikaiosunê*), the limiting of yourself to the role that you are supposed to perform in order to promote the good of your society.[25] It seems,
however, that these two virtues cannot exist without wisdom,[26] a virtue
possessed by the *polis* thanks to those, namely the philosophers, who rule
and enjoy knowledge of the true nature of the good (the Form of the
Good): these are the ones who will tell you accordingly what your role in
a good society is. Without wisdom, then, justice and sound-mindedness
do not seem liable to be preserved (cf. IV 443e, 442c–d). Nor indeed
does courage, the virtue consisting in holding to a right opinion about
what should be feared (IV 429b–c), given that such opinion is imparted
through education by those who already possess knowledge (ibid.). So
having a professional army preserve that opinion will make the *polis* coura-
geous, as long as they follow the instructions of the philosophers who are
in power and know what is best for the whole community.

Now, if this is the case in the *Republic*, it is not hard to see how the very
same postulates that seem to allow for human happiness can become a
great limitation on it. If happiness lies in virtue, and preeminently in wisdom, then it is only the philosophers who will have autonomous grounds
for happiness. This is fine for them, who can rely on the unshakeable
motivation for their behaviour given by their own reason. In the case of
the rest, though, their share in happiness will to a great extent be parasitic
on the rule of a philosopher. If they need someone to tell them what is
good so that they can do it,[27] then their happiness is, to use a Kantian
term, heteronomous, not autonomous, that is, it stems from the rule of
others rather than from one's own self-rule. But what if the ideal person
on whose existence and rule the happiness of the majority depends does
not exist? In addition, even if that person did exist, a lot of control would
need to be exerted on the majority if they are to follow the philosophers'
prescription. For it seems that if they do not have internal stable reasons
for the parameters that they accept as good, their opinions might easily be shaken by the wind.[28] (Note that, except for the military and the
ruling class, the great mass of people in this society does not have access
to education.)[29] Evidently, Plato himself concedes that the rule of the
philosopher is only an ideal. Though not impossible, it is really very hard
to realise, but it does at any rate provide a model that might orient human behaviour.[30] Maybe Plato is still influenced by the striking paradigm
of Socrates as a case where philosophy is put to foster the good of a
community: If we were to have one of those rare philosophers around,
their example would be so inspiring that we would either wish to subject
ourselves to their care, or it would at least be beneficial for us even to

be obligated to do so. How should we cope, however, with the actual messy world in which we live, and what are we supposed to do if the social conditions under which the rule of the philosopher will flourish cannot be implemented?

There is an easy answer that one might give to this question. We might draw attention to Plato's later political work, and to his insistence on our subjecting ourselves to laws as strictly as possible in case the charismatic personality of the philosopher-ruler is missing. In this sense, his approach has become more realistic, by appealing to laws as a second best. This seems to be the main story in the *Politicus* (294c ff., 297b ff.), and also in the *Laws* (IX 875c–d). Now, the *Politicus* presents laws as second bests without specifying exactly the content of such laws; the *Laws* undertakes at painful length the latter enterprise, creating again the problem about the feasibility of enacting such a legislative system if one were to expect from it an immediate solution for human happiness. As the *Politicus* suggests, it is better, of course, if the laws have been settled in a knowledgeable way; but even if they have not (which is very likely to be the case in most societies) sticking to them is better than having no laws at all (297c–301e). This is, then, the alternative path that is left for us if we want to take immediate action, but does such a path by itself guarantee any human happiness?

It seems not. Sticking to laws in a society in which the laws are not made on the basis of knowledge can at most guarantee temporary survival, not the self-fulfilled happy human life (cf. *Pol.* 301e–302b), for which the addition of something much more substantial seems to be needed. Now, I do not think Plato ever abandoned his conviction that such a life can only be realised against the supportive background of a wider context. In this sense, he never abandoned his ideals about how to bring about the best possible society. Thus, even when he proposes laws as second best in the *Politicus* and *Laws* he still maintains that the "first best" would be the rule of a wise expert whose superior skill would be capable of doing without legislation, and who would conduct the whole state most happily.[31] However he still has to face the problems with which the *Republic* left us, namely:

1. Given that the rule of the wise is an ideal at least difficult to realise, is a political framework of such a nature still *necessary* in order for the individual to attain virtue and happiness?
2. Can *happiness for the many* be secured in a way that makes it rely on sufficiently stable inner grounds, independently of whether there

is a philosopher in charge, and even if the surrounding social world is a mess?

In this book I argue that it is in Plato's late cosmology that we shall find an answer to these questions.

1. First, the late cosmological work shows us that, even if there is no ideal human model for others to look at as a guide for their behaviour, there is a real model, and that is the universe itself. (And here, as I shall show, we can find a clear Platonic root for the later Hellenistic notion of humans as "citizens of the universe".) So, say you do not live in ideal political conditions, nor have laws founded on the basis of knowledge. Still, you can not only preserve your life but indeed attain at least some level of self-fulfilment, or happiness, by imitating the orderly cosmos[32] that surrounds you. For such a cosmos has a mind[33] (not dissimilar to the mind of the ideal philosopher ruler though even superior to it) that *does* grasp the nature of objective goodness and implements it in the natural surrounding world. In this regard, it becomes crucial that Plato should show that there is order in the universe, and that it is indeed a uni-verse, that is, a single whole bound by structure and purpose, if it is to function as a model for the organic unity, structure, and consistency that characterises in his eyes the self-fulfilled human life.

2. Whereas the *Republic* limited education to only a small part of society, there is a move in the late dialogues dealing with cosmology to extend it, at least to some reasonable degree, to every individual. It will still be true that not everybody can attain philosophy in the high-powered sense of grasping Forms over and above the perceptible universe. (After all even in the *Republic* that was only the result of an extremely long process of education, which was pretty much unavailable to most people.) But at least they can study the perceptible universe itself (without even needing to attain the utmost accuracy; *Laws* VII 818a1–2), and thereby achieve some initial level of justification of its orderly nature that will make them familiar with the very nature of order and consistency as a guiding pattern for their behaviour, and as a means towards attaining personal fulfilment. In short, it will be possible, by studying the universe, to attain happiness without necessarily knowing the Forms or being dependent on one who does.

If, then, Plato's ethical preoccupations centre around how to secure human happiness, and if the latter question (at any rate in the late dialogues we are considering) cannot be answered without taking account of the sensible universe, it will become clear that cosmology is the indispensable background for ethics. So, according to Plato, either you live under the right political conditions, with the rule of a gifted sage, or you do not. If you do, even your ruler will need to follow the more immediate model provided by the universe. If you do not, you might still be recommended, at least in principle, to stick to human-made political laws; although they do not constitute the best example of rationality and order, you should not, however, despair. For, even in that case, the universe is still there to offer a paradigm for your behaviour, and, as we shall see, a framework of rational laws, which the *polis* so often fails to provide.

Now, my remarks to this point might give the erroneous impression that the universe is something that Plato considers to be statically good, and therefore stands simply as a model to be imitated. If this were the case, then the impact of human intervention on our natural surroundings would be limited, if not altogether annihilated. This has in fact been one of the charges that some modern thinkers have raised against teleological conceptions of the universe in general.[34] Contrary to this assumption, I wish to show how, if one looks closely at Plato's late cosmology, there is actually a story to tell of the way in which the emphasis moves from the cosmos as ethical paradigm for humans (e.g. in *Timaeus* and *Philebus*) to an increasing stress on the cosmic import of human actions (e.g. in the *Politicus* and particularly in the *Laws*). In this regard, I shall argue that Plato's notion of cosmic teleology is complex enough to admit also of first bests and second bests. Plato's suggestion is that we should aim at attaining a first best cosmic teleology and that the only way to do so is to have humans actively using their reason in harmony with the universe. He will even propose (at one point in the *Laws*) that human greed is responsible for most, if not all, sublunary natural disorders. If this is the case, then Plato's cosmological dialogues will be presenting, in overall perspective, a strongly symbiotic picture of the relation between humanity and the cosmos. This picture is one that encourages us to become aware of the large-scale effects of human actions, and to know ourselves as parts of a broader universe, which is the common origin and home of all humans.

III. PLATO'S COSMOLOGY AND THE INTERPRETATION OF PLATO'S DIALOGUES

So far we have been talking as if there were a set of views to which we can refer as "Plato's late cosmology"; but how can we be sure of Plato's cosmological views when much in them is expressed in a mythical medium? One may also raise the more general question about what kind of consistency can be expected from Plato's dialogues. Given the dialogue form and the apparently different views expressed in the dialogues on similar issues (or indeed, sometimes within the same dialogue), one might think that maybe Plato was not really interested in presenting well worked-out positions of his own, but was simply experimenting with a variety of hypotheses in a noncommittal way. Let us consider each question separately.

1. Argument and Myth

Of the four dialogues with which we shall be dealing here, no less than two of them, the *Timaeus* and the *Politicus*, deal with cosmology by way of myth. That is to say, they present cosmological issues in the context of a story or narration (*muthos*) rather than, it seems, a rational argument or *logos*. And these narrations include settings and items that are unverifiable, such as events placed in a remote past or the afterlife, and superhuman anthropomorphic figures. These elements have been taken as criteria distinctive of Platonic myths.[35] Thus, the *Timaeus* tells us about the world having been created by a provident god from chaos, and the *Politicus* resumes this motif while adding a picture of the recurrence of chaotic cosmic periods. Poetical images abound throughout, in a way that makes the philosopher at points indistinguishable from the artist. Why should Plato resort to those images, which are shrouded in ambiguity, when he is otherwise so capable of presenting neat, straightforward arguments? Shouldn't philosophical readers simply skip those pages where Plato seems to be indulging in his literary hobbies?[36]

There has indeed been a tendency in analytic philosophy to look down on myths as irrelevant to the comprehension of an argument. Gallop was only an example of the tendency to ignore myths when alleging that "they do not lend themselves to logical analysis".[37] In recent years, this tendency has been balanced out by an increasing emphasis on trying to understand the relation between the form of Plato's work and its content, and by studies that seek to reconcile the threads of philosophy and literature in the dialogues,[38] though little work of this kind has focused on the cosmology. The approach that I submit here will suggest that it is simply false to assume that myths have no philosophical importance, or can contribute little or nothing to the understanding of an argument.[39] On the contrary, I wish to show how Plato's myths can indeed help us grasp the point of an argument, and how philosophical arguments can in turn help us interpret a myth.

Are those scholars who have looked down on myths really to blame? After all, Plato himself, as an arguing philosopher, gave sufficient hints in the *Republic* of an ambivalent attitude towards myths and artistic expression in general. Art appeals primarily to the nonrational aspects of one's personality and can therefore have a strong effect on one's emotions.[40] But this can be good or bad. It is bad in the case of the traditional myths, such as those passed down by the epic poets and tragedians, because they have no commitment to a content of truth[41] – which is ultimately tested argumentatively.[42] However, if art follows the prescriptions dictated by philosophy, it can be a powerful means of educating one's personality, particularly given that we are not just rational beings: so myths can constitute the starting point of the individual's upbringing, and prepare him or her to welcome reason when it arises, thus promoting harmony between the emotions and the intellect.[43] It is in the latter respect that we find Plato setting down through argument, as a philosopher, the "patterns of theology" that any writer of myth should follow (II 379a), and even claiming that there is some content of truth in his own myths (376e–377a).[44]

Now, there are certainly many criteria that one might use by which to judge myth. Some of them may be more or less arbitrary, or simply based on one's philosophical or exegetical taste. Instead, I propose here that judging Plato's myths by his own criteria[45] can give us a better understanding of what his own purpose may have been. Thus, myth should not be privileged above rational argument, which provides the ultimate test of truth;[46] but it should not be totally ignored in favour of argument, since it can complement it by illustrating or delivering a philosophical point differently.

This is, then, the approach that I shall adopt in this book, along lines that are congenial with some recent scholarly suggestions. Whereas Plato is far from endorsing the literal truth of every or indeed of any myth, he does seem to create myths and self-consciously use them for his own philosophical purposes, so that they too can convey truth. Not only does he tend to state overtly the purpose of his myths[47] (in a way that a traditional popular myth does not), but also, such myths are frequently rich enough to display a significance that goes far deeper than their *prima facie* lesson; a meaning that can still be discovered with the help of the discursive context of the dialogue.[48] In this respect, I agree with Julia Annas that myths written within a philosophical framework, as opposed to the popular myths that Plato criticises, do lend themselves to philosophical analysis.[49] The relation between myth and rational or argumentative discourse (*logos*) should then be seen as one not of antagonism but of complementarity: each can help us in interpreting and understanding the other.

We should note that myths are a symbolic kind of discourse, whose richness lies in lending themselves to different interpretations.[50] However, it still seems to be the task of the philosophical reader of Plato to see which of these interpretations makes most sense with regard to the overall argument or context in which it is inserted, and maximises the philosophical coherence of the thoughts expressed in them. I propose then that, if certain details in a myth contradict views argued for and not refuted in argumentative contexts, then those mythical details should not be saved at the expense of the results reached by argument. In this sense, again, *muthos* should be subordinated to *logos*.

But *muthos* can in turn illuminate *logos* to the extent that it makes vivid, through the use of images, points that are the subject of more abstract argumentative justification in the same or other dialogues. Accordingly, if we see Plato in a myth employing some notions that will also appear in nonmythical and more argumentative discourses, then we should not underestimate the philosophical importance of these notions even if they occur in a mythical context. This will be particularly pertinent in the case of the *Timaeus* myth, which is referred to both as a "likely account" (*eikos logos*, 30b7) and as a "likely story" (*eikos muthos*, 29d2), and which more than any other myth introduces passages that resemble *logos* in a strict sense (as argumentative discourse), by appealing to statements that for Plato are verifiable or susceptible of demonstration.[51] If so, then we should be entitled to take some parts of a myth more seriously than others (particularly when we would otherwise find contradictions within the same myth). This will be, for instance, one reason for taking the notion of a "cosmic soul" more seriously than the image of a provident creator god separated from the world in the *Timaeus*. But we shall have plenty of room for discussing this matter in due course.

2. Coherence and Interpretation

We come now to a second issue in the interpretation of Plato: Why should one even try to bring Plato's points in a myth into agreement with his arguments? More generally, should we expect Plato to be a coherent philosopher at all? I agree here with the view of some modern hermeneutical studies that a presupposition of intelligibility is indispensable for any interpretation of a text.[52] However, intelligibility presupposes coherence, and this is not far from Socrates' recommendations that our thoughts should accord with one another (cf. *Gorg.* 482b–c). If having or fostering a consistent set of beliefs was one of Socrates' main preoccupations, it would then be odd not to expect from each Platonic dialogue the same ideal, particularly when the dialogue form chosen by Plato seems itself to stress the importance of constantly subjecting any views one may have to the questioning and examination of others.

But now, precisely because Plato chose the dialogue form and not a more straightforward way of setting down views in the first person, the question arises whether there is anything like "Plato's views" that we can trace in the dialogues. Responses to this question by current scholars vary from radical scepticism to moderate optimism. After several centuries when it was just customary to speak of "Plato's doctrines" as if he had been an enlightened preacher, and when the dialogue form was mostly seen as an empty device, the radical scepticism represented by, for example, Michael Frede has been a healthy reaction.[53] Yet we find that those scholars who adopt the agnostic or sceptical attitude end up sooner or later attributing some views to "Plato", in a way that threatens their claims and shows that, deep down and to a greater or lesser extent, we cannot help thinking that after all Plato did have his own position on many questions that he raised in the dialogues.[54]

In this respect, I tend to side with the moderately optimistic view expressed by scholars such as Terence Irwin and Richard Kraut.[55] If the characters in a dialogue pose questions and give answers, they are certainly aiming at some truth (cf. *Phil.* 14b),[56] and I shall here talk of "Plato's" views as those submitted, agreed to, and not further refuted within a dialogue. The situation will be all the better if we find agreement on certain issues across various dialogues. So if, as we shall see, the views expounded and not further refuted in one dialogue coincide with those expounded and not further refuted in others, then this should provide enough material for us to think that such views most probably come from Plato. An example would be the critique of crudely materialistic theories of nature, which Plato seems to maintain through the mouths of different main speakers, such as Timaeus in the *Timaeus*, Socrates in the *Philebus*, the Eleatic Stranger in the *Sophist*, and the Athenian Stranger in the *Laws*.

This procedure is not meant to ignore any dramatic, philosophical, or chronological differences between the dialogues, and attention to such differences will be drawn as they arise. But it does presuppose that if we see one view being defended in one dialogue, and *prima facie* a different view on the same subject being defended in another, then we have to account for such differences (e.g. by postulating difference of emphasis or aspect, chronological developments, difference of intended audience, and so on).[57] The procedure also aims to be independent of the familiar discussion about whether one should be a unitarian or a developmentalist in the interpretation of Plato. It would certainly be inadequate to impose *a priori* any rigid expectations on our interpretation of the text; the ideas we form of Plato should only come as conclusions, after careful examination of the evidence. It is true that, as an arguing philosopher, Plato is likely to have revised his views (as I contend he did with regard to ethics in his late period), and to this extent "development" should come as no surprise; on the other hand, one should also resist the temptation of seeing dissimilarities too quickly between various dialogues or assuming that there was not a "voice" behind them, the voice of a single philosopher who was preoccupied by the issues that he raised.

The dialogues present large intellectual challenges. In seeking to meet them, and to provide coherent interpretations, we can consider ourselves as responding to their invitation always to think matters over a little further (*Prot.* 361c–d; *Phil.* 67b). But this procedure also grants that Plato himself saw the importance of giving an answer to these questions, and that he may have formed well-grounded beliefs about certain issues, which he was nevertheless always ready to expose to argumentative testing.[58] It is only by giving some answers that you can ask more questions, and, in this respect, I hope that, through my treatment of Plato's cosmology, the reader will find enough material to stimulate reflection on her or his own life and its place in the wider world.

IV. THE PLAN OF THIS BOOK

It is my aim in this book to maximise not only the coherence but also the organic unity of each dialogue.[59] This is important given that Plato's late work dealing with cosmology has often been charged with failing to meet one or both of these conditions. What are we to make, for example, of the Demiurge in the *Timaeus* sometimes being mentioned as a provident cause of the universe, sometimes being ignored in summary accounts of its ontology?[60] Or how are we to deal with the cosmology of the *Politicus*, and especially with the apparent "unclarity of the myth's point in the dialogue"?[61] Questions may also be raised about the relevance of the *Philebus* cosmology to the ethical discussion of the dialogue, or about whether the *Laws* succeeds in presenting more than an incomplete and fragmented theology.[62] In all cases, I shall attempt to show that many of the apparent contradictions can be dissolved, and that the cosmological passages show more care in their composition and fit better in their respective contexts than has sometimes been assumed.

This study is divided into seven main chapters dealing with the *Timaeus*, the *Philebus*, the *Politicus*, and the *Laws*. In each case I start by analysing the larger metaphysical or cosmological accounts contained in each dialogue and then pass on to examine how they bear on ethical issues.

Chapter 2 tries to pin down the philosophical meaning of the demiurge in the *Timaeus*. Is it just a metaphor, or is Plato making some substantive philosophical claim? I argue that appeal to the demiurge allows Plato to make an important point about teleology. I analyse how Timaeus identifies the demiurgic action with one kind of cause, namely primary cause, and how he sees the relation between teleology and mechanism in his explanation of the universe. In that context, mind (*nous*) is presented as a teleological agent that works by relying on material conditions. The demiurge is described as a mind; if the mind is the kind of entity that cannot exist independently of space, nor operate independently of a body, then even the mind of god must be seen as immanent to the universe, despite some passages suggesting that the demiurge is a separate god. Thus, I argue, it makes more sense to take the demiurge in the *Timaeus* as a symbol of the rational workings of the soul or mind of the universe itself (= the "cosmic god"). This presents a picture of all mind, including god's, which is far removed from Cartesian dualism, and which has, in turn, important repercussions from a practical perspective.

Chapter 3 explores the ethical consequences of this conclusion. I argue that, in the *Timaeus*, god is presented as a model for human beings in various ways. First, god is offered as an ideal example of the excellent relation and balance between mind and body that a living being can attain. Second, god functions as an example of how to impose intelligent purpose on given recalcitrant materials; in the case of humans, such material includes not only certain aspects of their physiological makeup, but also, and more generally, the events arising through "luck" that they do not cause. How can one turn putative bad luck into good luck, obstacles into allies? Here god's interaction with "necessity" in the *Timaeus* provides an important role model for human virtue (a line of thought that is in turn pursued in the *Timaeus*' unfinished sequel, the *Critias*). Finally, I contend that the *Timaeus* presents the study of astronomy, or the movements of the cosmic god, as a route to happiness that is in principle available to all human beings, even in the absence of a good political constitution. In this regard, I analyse the issue of "assimilation with god" in the *Timaeus* in a way that highlights the practical application of this invitation, contrary to recent studies that have seen it merely as a call to philosophical contemplation.

Chapter 4 deals with the difficult cosmology and metaphysics of the *Philebus*. Does Plato keep a commitment to middle-period Forms in this dialogue? If so, does that entail an underestimation of the value of the sensible universe? I show how, even if the first question is answered positively, the *Philebus* nonetheless presents an "elevated" account of the sensible world as a kind of "becoming", in Plato's words, that can be rendered intelligible, and is thus a "being" in some sense. I argue that this elevated account is one that endows nature with intrinsic value thanks to two factors: first, its exhibiting a mathematical structure; second, its possession of an organising mind that must be viewed as immanent, and not transcendent, to the universe itself. In doing so, I try to mediate in a long-standing discussion that has taken place between "revisionists" and "unitarians" in the interpretation of this dialogue. In addition, I demonstrate, against some conceptions, that the *Philebus* suggestions do not contradict the main tenets of the cosmology and metaphysics of the *Timaeus*.

Chapter 5 analyses how the cosmological treatments of the *Philebus* are directly relevant to answering the main ethical question of the dialogue, namely: what is the place of, respectively, pleasure and knowledge in the happy life? As to pleasure, recent studies have taken it that Socrates' aim in the *Philebus* is to downplay its role, or even to present a wholehearted antihedonistic attack. I take issue with this interpretation and argue, instead, that at least some pleasures are in the *Philebus* raised to the status of "being", and thus endowed with intrinsic value in a way that is in line with the dialogue's elevated account of the phenomenal world. Even more, I contend that the life of god, which is presented in the *Philebus* as embodying the ideal of happiness, is one that *combines* pleasure with knowledge. In this regard, then, god is a model of the purity of the pleasures that are to function as a standard in our own choice of pleasures. Further, the chapter examines the dramatic and philosophical importance of the revival of the early Socrates in the dialogue, with its consequent emphasis on a more populist conception of knowledge. While it is granted that the professional philosopher will still have access to the most accurate form of study, the chapter argues against the view that in the *Philebus* it is only the philosopher who can lead a happy life.

Two chapters then follow on the *Politicus* myth. In Chapter 6, I try to make sense of the letter of this text, which has standardly been read as suggesting that our current cosmic era is one deprived of god. I take issue with this reading, and argue that, on the contrary, better sense can be made of the text if we take it as suggesting that our current era *is* under the governance of god, even though the form of such a rule and its relation to human autonomy is more complex than has usually been recognised. But why is deciding this issue relevant? Certainly, it helps us see that Plato need not here be contradicting, for example, the story of the *Timaeus*. But, more importantly, I argue that my reading makes much better sense of the function of the myth with regard to the overall political argument of the *Politicus* itself. Thus, I show how it is crucial for Plato to insert the discussion of political affairs in a cosmic context that offers hope for progress rather than being doomed by the fated prospect of deterioration.

Chapter 7 explores further why Plato may have chosen the idiosyncratic picture of opposite cosmic cycles in the *Politicus*. From a cosmological perspective, some affinities are found with the myth of the *Timaeus*, especially insofar as both myths seems to depict dynamically the successive rule of opposite factors (such as intelligence and the corporeal) that in fact interact in our actual universe. But some features are peculiar to the *Politicus* itself. What are we to make, for example, of Plato's exaggerated description of the universe as an almost human creature, which runs occasional risk of chaos and destruction? I argue that Plato has projected, in his depiction of the universe, some distinctively ethical and political preoccupations. In addition, I show how the rule of Cronus in that myth should be taken as a paradigmatic example for the political expert, and even for individuals, who are thus encouraged to take charge of their own spheres of influence and work for a world that better resembles the ideal environmental conditions of that age. Cosmic drama, then, is shown in the *Politicus* to stand for human drama, and the universe to represent not only the stage but also a symbol of individual and political behaviour.

Chapter 8, on the *Laws*, continues and furthers this line of thinking, by addressing Plato's particular response to the problem of evil in book X. First, it analyses the Athenian's account of the priority of soul to body, and shows that Plato's approach is consistent with a view of mind and body as necessitating one another: on this basis, the universe itself is seen as suffused with life and design. But this, however, raises the question of what the cause of evil (including natural evil) may be. Several scholarly answers, in this regard, are rejected, in order to show, however strikingly, that Plato in *Laws* X holds only human beings responsible for evil. Is this a mean-minded response, to the effect that "it is all your fault"? I argue not. Indeed, Plato's claim here is much deeper. By emphasising human responsibility even for what might appear to be natural disorders, Plato is making a point about the large-scale effects of human actions within an interconnected universe where whatever happens to a part affects the whole. Precisely because the universe is organic, the apparently narrow effects of human actions have in fact repercussions throughout the whole system, and for this reason humans are allotted responsibility in the administration of the entire universe. In this way, the *Laws* can be seen as the culmination of the story about the relation of humans to the cosmos that started at least with the *Timaeus*. While the *Timaeus* and the *Philebus* stress the universe's role as a model for human behaviour, the *Laws*, continuing the theme of the *Politicus*, shows the other side of the question: a universe whose order can be enhanced by the right behaviour of humans, who are in turn part of the *kosmos* and need to contribute to its perfection.

In advancing this picture of Plato's cosmology, I hope to show how the late dialogues allow us to extract a great cosmological vision, one that has remained underrated or unnoticed both in itself and as an important precedent for later historical developments. While it exceeds the purpose of this book to study the evolution of ancient thought after Plato, students of Hellenistic ethics, for example, may be motivated to appreciate the extent to which Plato's late dialogues are forerunners of the Stoic idea that humans are citizens of the universe; a thought the Stoics developed hand in hand with the notion that our soul is an "offshoot" (as in the *Philebus* and *Timaeus*) of the ruling cosmic soul, with which we should live in agreement.[63] Even the suggestion that humans should "live contemplating the truth and order of the totality of things, helping establish it as far as possible",[64] should strike the reader of this book as familiar. I hope in this regard that my study may also represent one step in a larger project for classical scholarship.

V. THE ORDER OF THE DIALOGUES

I make no essential claims about the chronology of Plato's works, but rest content with the widespread consensus that *Phaedo*, *Symposium*, and *Republic* are to be taken as middle dialogues, coming before the *Parmenides*, while the *Theaetetus*, *Sophist*, *Politicus*, *Philebus*, *Timaeus*, and *Laws* are late.[65] Which dialogue comes before which in each group, especially the latter, is not a particular concern here. Rather, I wish to show that there is, in the last four dialogues mentioned, some closeness in spirit that could be supported by, or support, closeness in date.

We do know, however, that the *Politicus* (284b) mentions the *Sophist*, so that it seems intended to be read after, or at least with reference to, the latter. Aristotle, for his part, reports the *Laws* as postdating the *Republic* (*Politics* II 5–6, 1264b24–9), and in fact there is general modern consensus – which corresponds to the ancient tradition[66] – that it is the work that occupied Plato till more or less the end of his life. Now, the relative dating of the *Timaeus* was the subject of fierce controversy some decades ago, centered on Owen's proposal that it antedates the *Parmenides* and Cherniss' riposte.[67] Since then, however, there have been few defenders of Owen's thesis,[68] and there now seems to be general agreement that the *Timaeus* belongs among the late group of dialogues. The *Philebus*, too, is nowadays generally regarded as late.[69]

So, I shall talk of Plato's late cosmology without assuming any special chronological ordering between the four dialogues mainly treated here. I shall, though, be presenting the issue in a rather developmental way, which might be a useful reading guideline, and might also, in the best of cases but not necessarily, be taken as an argument to support a certain chronological order. In any case, I wish to show here that the four dialogues to be studied can illuminate each other at least as far as certain cosmological themes are concerned, and that they can collectively strengthen our understanding of Plato's late thoughts on cosmology both in themselves and as a framework for human life.

2

Demiurgy in the *Timaeus*

I. INTRODUCTION

What kind of universe do we live in? How can we coherently explain a world where there is room for both beauty and ugliness, good and evil? In what way do these factors interact, and to what extent do they affect our own lives? The *Timaeus* will utilise a rich conceptual apparatus, anchored in the notions of intelligent design and recalcitrant necessity, to make sense of these issues, which will occupy us here and in the next chapter.

The leading image the *Timaeus* employs for this purpose, that of an intelligent craftsman or "demiurge" coping with difficult materials, may raise suspicions about its philosophical meaning, particularly in a work that offers such a difficult medium for the interpreter. Two questions in particular need to be addressed at the outset: First, how much of the *Timaeus* should be considered mythical, and how much as pertaining to the realm of argumentative discourse? Second, what is the relation, if any, between the various speeches that compose it? Let us start with the latter question.

Notably, Socrates is *not* the main speaker (that role is allotted to Timaeus, an expert astronomer from southern Italy). Yet the *Timaeus* starts with an allusion by Socrates to his speech "given yesterday" concerning the best kind of constitution (*politeia*, 17c), which seems to be reminiscent of the content of the *Republic*.[1] It is puzzling, though, that little is said in these pages of the *Timaeus* about the long philosophical curriculum established in the *Republic*; yet the interlocutors agree that they are omitting nothing of importance (19a–b). Socrates then momentarily hands over the speech to Critias, who proposes to depict this ideal state "in motion" (b–c), and so presents a preview of the Atlantis story, which will be deferred to the unfinished dialogue named after him (20d–26e). In the meantime, the narrative is delegated to Timaeus, as we are promised an account that will start with the birth of the universe and end with the nature of humans (27a5–6). This marks the beginning of the cosmological myth, which occupies the bulk of the *Timaeus.*

Such a structure and succession of speeches may look like little more than a random aggregate. Why should the *Timaeus,* which is mostly about cosmology, start with a supposed, though incomplete, allusion to the *Republic?* Why should we next be given a programmatic account of a legendary old Athens that defeated an Atlantis empire full of arrogance? It is certainly not immediately clear how all this might be of relevance to cosmology. Yet, I contend, the first two short sections of the dialogue anticipate and introduce core themes to be treated in Timaeus' cosmological account. The initial allusion to an ideal state such as presumably that of the *Republic* indicates that the *Timaeus* will revisit some of the issues presented in that work – for example, what kind of education is to count as appropriate for the achievement of human happiness. Further, it suggests that now even political issues are meant to be dealt with against a wider cosmological background. Critias' preview of the Atlantis story, for its part, introduces vivid and dynamic examples of what one might easily count as natural evil (and as pertaining to "the works of necessity" in the cosmological section): that is, periodic destructions of humans and things on earth by fire, water, or cosmic cataclysms (22c–d, 23a). But it is suggested at the same time that these are sent by the gods (22d), which introduces the question, to be addressed by the rest of the *Timaeus*: in what ways does teleology interact with necessity in the explanation of natural phenomena? Finally, it is left up to the reader to explore a connection between the *hubris* of Atlantis and its dramatic end (24e–25c). On one level, the *Timaeus* will tackle the theme of "cosmic justice" as one of the aspects of cosmic teleology. At the same time, the fact that such an ostentatious empire would end up being defeated starts to suggest the unavoidable responsibility that humans have as demiurges of their own destiny, and hints at a connection between virtue and flourishing that reappears not only in the cosmological myth (42b) but in the subsequent *Critias* (112e).

A further difficulty concerns the very status of Timaeus' account of the universe, which is described as "likely" (*eikos*). What are we to make of this? At first blush, Timaeus merely seems to mean that his account borrows its character from the nature of its subject matter: it is likely (*eikos*), we are told, since its object, the sensible world, is a copy (*eikôn*) of intelligible realities. Thus, our discourse about the changeable universe cannot claim to have the same accuracy, stability, and epistemic force that discourses concerning the Forms have (cf. 29b–c). But matters seem to become more complicated with his introduction of the word *muthos* (29d2). What does it mean to say that the *Timaeus* is – mostly – a myth? Should such a myth be taken on an equal footing with other Platonic myths?

Certainly, this raises some larger questions of interpretation, to which I have referred in Chapter 1. Brisson has suggested that a feature characteristic of Platonic myths is their appeal to items that are unverifiable and not susceptible of rational demonstration.[2] The *Timaeus* does contain sections that look more argumentative, or nonmythical, according to these criteria; but the Demiurge's construction of our souls out of the remnants of the mixture used for the world-soul is not, for example, available either to the senses or to the intellect – and thus is not "verifiable" according to Platonic standards of verification. To this extent, the *Timaeus* shares features common to many other Platonic myths, such as its appeal to events placed in a remote past, or to supernatural anthropomorphic figures.[3] Is the Demiurge then a merely fanciful figure (as Aristotle seems to have taken it),[4] or is it supposed to do some important philosophical work in the description? Is it even particularly relevant that it should be wrapped in mythical clothing?

No wonder that the similarities between the mythical Demiurge of the *Timaeus* and the God of *Genesis* have made this dialogue a favourite in the Judeo-Christian tradition.[5] Yet one still needs to decide what motivation may underlie Plato's presentation of his god in mythological form, and to what extent he is committed to such a picture. In the *Euthyphro*, Socrates insinuates that he does not believe in the gods as traditional religion portrays them (as, for example, committing reprehensible acts, 6a–c).[6] In the *Republic*, it becomes clear that one reason why many stories from Homer and Hesiod should be rejected is that they convey the wrong moral message. As an alternative, Plato has Socrates propose certain patterns of theology by which myth-makers should abide; patterns that he in turn tries to justify through argumentative discourse (II 378e ff.). These myths perform an important function in the education of children, and will conceivably preserve their usefulness in front of adult audiences who are still prone to be affected by such pictorial representations of reality. We read, for instance, that if the citizens are told about the gods doing this or that, they will be liable to imitate them: that is why a "young person should not hear it said that he would be doing nothing remarkable in committing the most extreme injustices, and again in punishing in every way an unjust father, but instead doing what the first and greatest gods do" (II 378b).

How the characters portrayed in myths lend themselves to imitation is the core concern here. For, if one is to have one's personality shaped after certain role models, we had better make sure that they are of the right kind. It seems, in this regard, especially relevant that Plato should in the *Timaeus* resort to myth, and not surprising that he should describe the Demiurge in the *Timaeus* in the way he does: this god is essentially benevolent, knowledgeable, and its main activity consists in promoting the good. That is, god in the *Timaeus* will, on one level, be an illustration of what the human condition can be at its best, and in that respect the mythological imagery can function as a model for human activity.

But, of course, any investigation of god has to face the *problem of evil*. Thus, we are told in the *Republic* that, if god is good and never bad, he can only be beneficial, that is, the cause of only good things, and evils must be found "other causes" (379c). What these other causes may be we are not immediately told. And yet it is this answer that is required of any account of god that hopes to be even minimally convincing. This problem, one that was left pending among others from the *Republic*, figures among the many that the *Timaeus* now sets out to address. Indeed, one of the main assumptions on which the atheist's criticism usually rests is the thought that *omnipotence* is one of god's essential properties. But if *goodness* is too, how can god not stop the existence of evil in the universe? Thus, the atheist concludes, the very notion of god makes no sense.

The *Timaeus* is noteworthy for its view that while goodness and rationality can be taken as essential features of god, omnipotence needn't be. If so, then evil may have another cause, irreducible to, and existing side by side with, god; one that the *Timaeus* will call "necessity". God on this view might seem too fragile for some: what is the use of a god who could not have prevented the famine that plagues so many impoverished countries, or the very fact of death? Perhaps, though, it is not god's fragility as such, but the resourcefulness given such fragility that offers itself as worthy of admiration, and even imitation. As we shall see, it is precisely the intelligent way in which god deals with "necessity", or the given, unavoidable circumstances that one often has to encounter and that one does not generate, that erects the former as a model for us.

In this regard, the *Timaeus* will deliver an ethical message by portraying mythically how god managed to make most things work for the best given the initial constraints on his activity. If we succeed in dealing with "luck" in the way this story shows god dealing with necessity, making the best out of it, we are probably very close to understanding and embodying the notion of "virtue", which is at the core of Plato's ethics. This, I believe, is a point worthy of the reader's attention, whether or not he or she is a sceptic about god. Plato in fact is not, as he believes that there is indeed an entity in the structure of reality that we may call by the name of god, even though that entity is less anthropomorphic than his mythical descriptions suggest, and is ultimately an inherent aspect of life and intelligence within the universe itself: its cosmic soul (or world-soul). This cosmic soul, we shall see, performs in his system the function of securing goodness given the other restraints, a function that we may call *teleological.* In this regard too, god is a model for humans, for whom virtue consists also at least partly in an activity of apprehending and pursuing good ends.

In the following pages I shall focus on the metaphysical assumptions on which the picture just outlined ultimately rests. Thus, this chapter sets out to elucidate the meaning and status of god as "principle" of the universe, as this appears in the figure of the Demiurge. Later, in the next chapter, we shall see what consequences Plato's views on god have for an understanding of the place of humans in the universe, and what suggestions the *Timaeus* can now offer with regard to many issues surrounding human happiness that were left pending from the *Republic.*

I shall argue that Plato uses the image of the Demiurge to underscore the presence of teleology, which pervades the universe and explains the organisation of it and its parts from the large to the small scale. With this, Plato is not making merely an epistemological point, or emphasising "reasons" that may be invoked in our understanding of reality with no strict ontological correlate.[7] For he believes, I wish to argue, that there is an entity that is the *cause* of the intelligibility of the universe in its teleological structure, and that such an entity, symbolised by the Demiurge, should not be sought over and above the universe itself. Indeed, such an entity is none other than the mind or principle of organisation of the universe, which does not exist independently of it but rather necessitates a body, as I contend every intellect and every soul does in Plato's late work. In this regard, delving into these questions should be of interest not only as a way of clarifying Plato's cosmological commitments but also insofar as these cosmological issues are inserted into a broader psychological and metaphysical picture that they help illuminate. So I shall start by investigating the philosophical meaning of the Demiurge and afterwards proceed to elucidate its ontological status.

II. THE PHILOSOPHICAL MEANING OF THE DEMIURGE

1. The Demiurge Takes the Stage

Let us begin by focusing on the letter of the myth to see what kind of hints it offers about the nature of the Demiurge. This will serve as a platform for a deeper exploration of its role as a creator, and its philosophical import.

The *Timaeus* presents the Demiurge as the cause of the universe (29a6), according to the demand that everything that undergoes becoming, or generation (*genesis*), does so necessarily by virtue of a cause (cf. 28a4–5, c2–3).[8] He creates it not *ex nihilo*, but from a preexisting state of disorder, trying to make his product resemble the eternal model of the Forms (29a, 30a). We can characterise the Demiurge's activity as comprising different stages: (1.) He looks to the Forms (29a, 39e); (2.) he wishes that everything should be good, or as similar to the eternal model as possible (30a, b, 30d, 31a8–b1) – this is the purpose or design that guides his work; and (3.) he acts accordingly, after reflecting upon the most suitable means to attain his end (cf. e.g. 30b, 32c–33b).[9] In other words, the Demiurge has not only a *theoretical* function, by which he apprehends the intelligible order of the Forms, but also a *practical* one, by which he sets about imposing this order upon the sensible realm and thus creates a universe as a true *kosmos*. The notion of intelligent purpose or design is recurrently emphasised in the myth, as when we are told that the universe itself "is a result of design" (*ek technês* 33d1) and through the constant use of terms connoting rational intention.[10] Let us note, however, that the Demiurge in the mythical description does not just limit himself to producing the world as an orderly whole, but also legislates (41e–42d), governs (48a2), and commands (41b–d).[11]

We can already see how the Demiurge appears as a mediator between the immutable Forms (those stable paradigms that serve to direct his purposive activity) and our sensible and changing realm. He is presented as the efficient cause, or principle of becoming and order (cf. *geneseôs kai kosmou . . . archê*, 29e4),[12] that organises the sensible world by imposing on it regularity and structure according to the model that it contemplates. This is how the Demiurge can give the universe a teleological orientation, thus enabling the Forms to have an actual influence on, or connection with, the visible domain. The goal pursued by the Demiurge is the good (*to eu*, 68e5; *to ariston*, 46c8, 68e1–2) of the universe, which he tries to

frame (*tektainomenos*, 68e5) or fulfil (*apotelôn*, 46d1). But how are we to
understand goodness here?

This goodness, as we have seen, is recurrently described in terms of
order (particularly telling in this regard is *Tim.* 87c: all that is good is fair,
and what is fair is not exempt from measure). But this order must in turn
be understood in terms of mathematical proportion bringing about unity
in its constituents. Thus, at 68e the Demiurge is said to have constructed
the good (*to eu*) in all the things generated, and this is subsequently
rendered as introducing proportions (*summetriai*) in each thing, both
with respect to itself and to the others (69b). Similarly, at 31b–c we are
told that a fair combination of the four bodies (fire, air, water, and earth)
in the body of the universe is achieved by proportion (*analogia*), which
produces unity most perfectly in the things it binds.[13] Time itself, which
goes according to number, is created so that the universe could resemble
the eternity of the model that abides in unity (37c–d, 38b–c). So, despite
the fact that our sensible realm is one of multiplicity and in that sense
departs from the unity of a Form, the closest approximation to the latter
can be achieved by producing order in this multiplicity, making all its
various elements friendly and harmonious with each other.

The emphasis on teleology recurs in the description of the creation of
plants and the framing of mortal parts of living creatures, and now the
aim can be summarised, concretely, as helping, as much as possible, the
ruling of reason in the individual within the limits imposed by necessity:[14]
plants were created for the aid and nutrition of the mortal body (77a) –
and a living being is not fine if its soul is joined to a body that is weak
(87d); spirit (*thumos*) was especially located between the midriff and the
neck so that, subordinated to reason, it could, if required, restrain the
appetites by force (70a); the intestines were framed in spiral in order that
the food should not pass through too quickly and so compel the body
to need more, making the human race unphilosophical and uncultured
(73a).[15] And sight was given so that by contemplating the movements of
heaven we could stabilise our thought, something in turn indispensable
for philosophy (46e–47c). Thus, teleology seems to be at work in these
microcosmic examples in facilitating a life of reason, a life that will parallel
that of the macrocosm, in which intellect rules. Why is so much stress laid
on reason? As we shall see, Plato's point when emphasising the rule of
reason at all levels (both macro and microcosmic) is precisely that it is
the task of reason to apprehend the overall good and implement it: in
this way, when humans conform to reason, they will be contributing to
the teleological arrangement of the universe.[16]

In principle, the myth describes some division of labour: the Demiurge himself will generate the immortal parts of the universe, while the gods generated by him will be demiurges of the mortal parts. But in practice, once the lesser gods have been created and as the mythical account proceeds, the initial theatrical distinction between a singular major God, creator of the immortal, and several lesser gods concerned with the mortal parts of the universe is increasingly blurred, so that the terms 'god' (*theos*), 'gods' (*theoi*), and 'the divine' (*to theion*) start to be used interchangeably.[17] This situation, I propose, should not lead us to focus on the question (perhaps anachronistic, and in any case misguided) whether Plato was a monotheist or not.[18] Instead, it encourages the view that the Demiurge does not seem to have such a distinct personality, and perhaps we should consider not so much his anthropomorphic appearance as the abstract and more impersonal "demiurgic function" that he seems to represent in the universe, namely that of intelligent causation aiming at an end.

2. Creation and the Demiurge

To this extent, we have reason to doubt that we should take literally every detail of Timaeus' story. But what about the very description of the Demiurge as a creator of the universe? If Plato is not so interested in maintaining a picture of god as a *personal* creator, in what sense is god a creator at all? Does Plato's universe even have a temporal beginning? This is indeed a vexed question, and the discussion seems to have reached a stalemate. Typically, "literalists" have been inclined to answer "yes", while "nonliteralists" have affirmed the contrary.[19] Much turns on what status, whether mythical or not, one gives to the lines that lead to the conclusion that the Demiurge is the creator of the universe. Let us briefly review the argument, not with the purpose of helping perpetuate the terms of the discussion by taking sides, but with an eye to bypassing the discussion altogether with the proposal that it may rest on a false dichotomy. It may be, after all, that there are merits to both outlooks that we want to reconcile.

The specific argument for the generation of the universe is presented in the following form: (1.) The universe is tangible and visible and possesses body: it is thus sensible; (2.) all sensible things are in process of becoming and generated (*gignomena kai gennêta*); (3.) therefore, this cosmos has come into being (*gegone*), 28b7–c2. This, for Hackforth, constitutes an "unadorned logical argument" and T. M. Robinson writes: "Whatever

Plato may have meant, he certainly speaks of the beginning of the world as though it took place in time".[20] Literalists often insist that this argument is presented before the start of any mythical account (the word *muthos* being introduced only later, at 29d2), so that it would be unsound to take it figuratively.[21]

Contrast this with nonliteralists such as Cornford, who argues that the word "becoming" (*genesis, gignesthai*) is ambiguous, and can mean either (a.) coming into existence at some time; or (b.) being in process of change. In the latter sense, "it is true that in such becoming something new is always appearing, something old passing away; but the process itself can be conceived as going on perpetually, without beginning or end". According to Cornford, (b.) best fits the use of *genesis* at *Tim.* 28b7–c2, since the whole argument is introduced in the context of a twofold distinction of entities, where "that which is always, and has no *genesis*" is contrasted with "that which always becomes (*to gignomenon aei*) and never is" (27d6–28a1). For Cornford, "the application of the premiss to the visible world must mean that the world belongs to the lower level of existence as described". Cornford in turn follows ancient interpreters in understanding the expression "it has come into being" (*gegone*) in terms of the possession of "a derivative and dependent existence which is not self-sufficing".[22]

Thus, this line of argument advises us to take the *gegone* at 28b7 as pointing to the more general concept of *genesis* as process of change. In principle, we can immediately see its attractions. For there are those passages where the world itself is connected with the realm of becoming (*genesis kai to pan tode*, 29d7–e1; *genesis kai kosmos*, 29e4) soon after we are told that, "as being (*ousia*) is to becoming (*genesis*), so is truth (*alêtheia*) to belief (*pistis*)" (29c3). If so, *genesis* would pertain to the world, or indeed be coextensive with it, at least in the sense that the sensible world is in a process of constant change in some or other respect.[23]

Now literalists have traditionally complained that, with regard to the argument at 28b4–c2, "no metaphorical or figurative language infiltrates this sequence of propositions":[24] the text does seem to conclude that the world "has come into being" (*gegone*), and not just that it is a thing that becomes, or *gignomenon*. Thus, to judge by the way these two interpretations have been posed, it would seem that they are irreconcilable.

Yet there is no need to take one side or the other. Instead, a *via media* is possible between these two opposing interpretations. Let us readily concede that it is possible to read the *gegone* at 28b7 as *literally* meaning "has come into being", and not just as metaphorically standing for "it becomes". But "has come into being" does not exclude the possibility that generation is a perpetual process instead of an isolated event at the beginning of time. In fact, *gegone* literally means "has come into being" rather than "came into being", as literalists sometimes mistranslate.[25] This opens up room for taking the process of generation to be still ongoing, or indeed perpetual,[26] as suggested in turn by *Tim.* 38c1–3:

> Whereas the model (*paradeigma*) exists in all eternity, the former [= the universe or *ouranos* at 38b6] *continuously for all time has come into being* (*dia telous ton hapanta chronon gegonôs*), exists and will exist.

Once more, then, the use of the perfect tense (as opposed to the aorist) here at 38c3 (*gegonôs*) – as much as at 28b7 (*gegone*) – plus the adverbial expression "continuously for all time", seem to indicate that the coming into being of the world did not occur "once upon a time", but is a continuous process.

In addition, there are some other passages where creation by god is depicted not merely as having taken place in the past, but also as occurring *in the present*, something that would again support the view of creation as a perpetual process. Thus, for example, in the middle of the description of the creation of time, we find the use of the words "makes" (*poiei*, 37d6) and "contrives" (*mêchanatai*, 37e3) – in a passage where, interestingly, Plato is talking specifically about tense (37e4 ff.), so that one would expect him to be particularly careful about the tenses he is using.

My interpretation, I contend, has the advantage of exempting us from overimaginative solutions to problems posed by the text: we do not need, as Cornford does, to stretch the meaning of *gegone* at 28b7, and to this extent we do not need to side with the traditional nonliteralist. But neither do we need to postulate, with Vlastos (and with ancient literalists), a precosmic time in which chaos would have taken place before creation by the Demiurge. Other problems, too, beset the traditional literal interpretation,[27] but I shall here briefly focus on the intriguing issue of time in the *Timaeus*, and why Vlastos's valiant attempt at making his literal view compatible with it ultimately fails.

Time is presented in the *Timaeus* as generated by god together with the orderly universe, and as related to measurement. It is an image of eternity "which circles in accordance with number" (38a7–8); we are also told that "days, nights, months and years did not exist before the heaven came into being, but were contrived at the same time as it was framed" (37e1–3; cf. 38b6). But if this is so, there seems to be no room for a

Demiurge creating the universe from a *temporally* previous state of chaos. Vlastos sees this difficulty, but replies, mostly based on arguments from silence, that it is still possible to postulate a "precosmic time" understood as irreversible succession of past and future, which however cannot be measured.[28] What is problematic about Vlastos's account is less its lack of textual evidence (as might be required for such a large claim) than its misreading of portions of the text. For even past and future are described as "generated *kinds* of time" (*chronou gegonota eidê*, 37e4), which would thus mean that past and future themselves are the product of the orderly action of the Demiurge. Vlastos would like to take past and future simply as "attributes" of time (as a rendering of *eidê* at 37e4), which could, *qua* attributes, exist independently of cosmic time.[29] But "*eidos*" cannot mean "attribute", but rather means "kind" of time. Thus, as we are told that time was generated together with the universe, it would follow that any kind of time was generated together with the universe. In addition, Timaeus explicitly links past and future to the measurability of time when he says at 38a7–8 that they are "kinds of time . . . which circles in accordance with number". This suggests that simple duration is insufficient for time, which instead requires orderly sequence.

Let us also think a little about the trait of goodness that defines the Demiurge, and his desire to make things good as far as possible (29e–30a). Such features seem incompatible with the thought that the Demiurge should have remained inactive, apparently for no good reason, while the precosmic chaos occurred.[30]

But if this is so, what shall we make of the "Creator" (*poiêtês*, 28c3)? On the surface, this description may have served Plato's attempt to meet, on their own ground, opposing materialist theories, which would tend to describe the universe as generated from aimless forces.[31] But, on close examination, it has become apparent that the Demiurge should be called "creator" not so much in the sense of a god who anthropomorphically created the world "once upon a time", but, rather, insofar as he is the efficient cause that is perpetually generating and in that way *sustaining* order in the universe. Thus, the precosmic chaos may well have counterfactual value: it helps us see how the universe would be *if* aimlessness prevailed. In any case, the artisanal metaphor, suggesting a definite product and different steps of the work starting and developing in time, has proved a most useful way for Plato to highlight the teleological arrangement of the world, like any good product of art, which is made not at random but with a definite purpose (cf. *Gorg.* 503e–504a) seeking to fulfil an end through a chain of means.[32] The universe, however, is not an inert product of craftsmanship, but a living being itself (30d, 32d, 92c), whose life is constantly being renewed (cf. *Politicus* 270a3–5), and whose order is the result of continuous intelligent rule over its necessary tendencies (*Tim.* 48a, 53a8–b4). As a matter of fact, there may be more than one layer to this teleological picture: for, just as the Demiurge imposes order upon disorder, so does Timaeus (albeit with more difficulty) try to impose order upon random modes of speaking (cf. 34b–c).[33] (After all, the best form of discourse is in the *Phaedrus* [264c] described as a *zôion* – like the universe in the *Timaeus* – and in the *Philebus* [64b] a complete or accomplished argument is described as a *kosmos.*) To see the world being created by a benevolent god out of chaos is to see Timaeus' discourse in the making (which he self-consciously admits participates in chance, cf. 34c2–4); what the result shows us, however, is that the universe as such is less subject to randomness and chaos than human ways of speaking may suggest, and instead provides a paradigm for anyone wishing (through discourse or in their actions) to create a *kosmos.*[34] It is, then, to this teleological arrangement of the world in the *Timaeus* that we should now turn our attention, by investigating further the philosophical meaning of the Demiurge.

3. Intelligence and Causation

We have seen that the Demiurge in the *Timaeus* is a cause (*aition*, 28c2, 29a6) in the sense that it has the function of generating order (cf. 29e4). Now if, as I have argued, this generation is perpetual, then god must also be in charge of keeping the cosmos in good order. This in turn corresponds to the function of *governing* that the myth allots to him (cf. 48a2, 41a–42e, 71d). Despite its usual description in the past, this governance should also be understood as present if the world is to continue being orderly, as we read that everything behaves without plan and measure (*alogôs kai ametrôs*) whenever god is absent from something (*hotan apêi tinos theos*, 53a8–b4), in a context where "god" must allude to the Demiurge.[35] So, if the world is good and fair (as is affirmed at 29a5, 92c), that is, orderly (cf. 87c4–5), it is implied that god must be constantly present in it to sustain it.

The functions of ordering and governance of the cosmos are often attributed to intellect (*nous*) or to god in the dialogues;[36] and the *Timaeus* is no exception. The Demiurge himself is described as a *nous*, which has both a theoretical role (contemplating the Forms) and a practical one (organising the sensible world). Thus, on the one hand, we have

numerous allusions to intellectual activities of the Demiurge;[37] on the
other, the works of this god are called "the things demiurgically framed
by *nous*" (*ta dia nou dedêmiourgêmena,* 47e4), and the Demiurge is pictured
as a *nous* that rules over necessity by persuasion (48a2). So god presents
the essential feature of rationality and – inextricably – goodness (cf. 29a,
e), since his producing good or orderly effects is based on his knowledge
of the Forms as a paradigm of order. In what follows, I shall analyse the
particular mode of operation of this *nous* in the universe, with special
reference to its causal role.

3.1. Intellect (Nous) and Necessity. We can then ask ourselves: How does
this causation of *nous* operate upon the world? And how successful is it?
Timaeus seems to be quite aware that his praise of the organisation of
the present universe has to be balanced out by the recognition that the
universe is not perfect. But god, or *nous,* is not to blame, for the simple reason that he is not omnipotent. Once more, artisanal metaphors
become useful here. Take the example of a human craftsman who has
the purpose of creating a table. Certainly, he is, in one sense, limited by
his goal: realising a table according to a certain form or pattern. But he
is also limited by his preexisting materials, which can offer obstacles to
the achievement of his purpose. The craftsman, in our example, might
want to create a table as perfect as possible, but the wood is brittle. Similarly, the Demiurge is limited, first, by the Forms or the Ideal pattern
(the "Perfect Living Being" 31b1, cf. 30c, 39e1) that guides his work
and that he must follow if he is to instantiate goodness in the world.
Second, and most importantly, he is constrained by a given factor in the
material constitution of the world, which, like the Forms, he does not create either and which precedes the production of the world. This factor
the *Timaeus* calls "necessity" (*anankê,* 47e5–48a5) or "necessary cause"
(68e–69a).

At 48a–b, necessity is related to the nature of fire, water, air, and earth
and the attributes (*pathê*) that they possessed before the generation of the
universe: thus, necessity seems to be a property inherent in the materials
that fill in space.[38] Further, it represents a potential source of disorder
and imperfection within the universe, so that the constant task of *nous*
consists in checking, insofar as it is possible, this tendency to disorder and
making it subservient to its own purposes (this is represented mythically
as the "persuasion" that *nous* exerts over necessity, 48a). Thus, "necessity"
in this context carries the meaning of something inevitable, on the one
hand (insofar as the Demiurge cannot change certain inherent properties

of his materials), and that of something instrumentally necessary, on the other (as the means without which a goal cannot be fulfilled).

Take again the example of a human *dêmiourgos* or craftsman, in this case a charioteer, who uses horses as helpers or auxiliaries. He would like to drive his chariot from Athens to Sparta, but in doing so he has constantly to guide his horses according to his purpose, as these horses, if left to themselves, might go in any direction. Similarly, "necessity" describes a material that the Demiurge needs to carry out his purpose, but which can produce undesirable and random effects if uncontrolled by him.[39] Or take the example of rain: if we leave the elements to themselves, and the water follows its own mechanical path, it can rain so much that it floods the area, spoils other parts of nature, and causes various kinds of natural disorder. However, human resourcefulness, guided by intelligence, can try to build a dam and orient that same water, which if left to itself might lead to destruction, to help areas that need moisture: in this case, we have turned that element, which by itself would cause chaos, into a cooperative or subservient cause to one's purpose.[40] This is exactly the way *nous* works on necessity on a cosmic scale: what preexists the intelligent activity of god are some traces (*ichnê*, 53b) of the elements themselves, with their mechanical tendencies to produce certain effects (e.g. the watery to moisten, the fiery to heat, 52d–e); what the god does is to deprive those traces of their tendency to disorder insofar as it is possible and use them in framing a uni-verse, that is a cosmos bound by a single purpose of goodness and unity, where all parts work interconnectedly for that goal (cf. 53b ff., 69b–c). So we find that *anankê* is an ambiguous concept in the *Timaeus*:

1. If (or when) *anankê* is undirected by *nous*, or left to itself, it becomes tantamount to randomness or chance (*tuchê*) as cause of disorder.[41] Under these circumstances, *anankê* (46e2) is related to those "causes which, if/when deprived of intelligence, always produce random and disorderly effects"[42] (46e5–6). In this respect *anankê* is a "wandering cause" or "errant cause" (*planômenê aitia*, 48a),[43] and is responsible for the disorderly motion that is depicted to have taken place in the precosmos. Thus, at 48a–b the errant cause is said to "produce motion by nature" (48a7), and referred to the properties of the bodily before the generation of the cosmos (48b3–5).

2. Under the guidance (or "persuasion" – to put it mythically) of *nous*, *anankê* becomes an orderly sequence of bodily causes and effects

arranged according to, and serving, the good purposes of *nous* (cf. 46c7–e2, 47e5–48a5, 68e1–69a5). In this respect *anankê* becomes a "co-cause"[44] or subservient or auxiliary cause[45] for the latter, something necessary in the sense of the means without which an end cannot be fulfilled.[46] We can call this chain of means mechanism, insofar as we can explain each link in it by way of antecedent conditions. However, as we have seen, this mechanism does not seem to become truly orderly except by the intervention of *nous*, which for the most part deprives those bodily traces of their tendency to disorder (cf. 47e ff., 53a–b, 69b–c). Thus, we can see how teleology subordinates mechanism but at the same time relies on it for its achievement, so that the relation between the two is not one of exclusion but of complementarity.[47] Furthermore, Plato carefully stresses that necessary or secondary causes should be sought for the sake of primary (46d8) or "divine" causes (68e7–69a5) in the fulfilment of the good.[48]

Along these lines, the same phenomenon such as vision can admit of both a mechanical and a teleological explanation: at *Tim.* 45b–d its mechanism is explained by appeal to the theory of "collision" between fires, that stemming from the eye (the visual current), that stemming from the sun (daylight), and that stemming from the object (its colour). This mechanical order, however, is introduced by the gods (45b4–6) and has no greater function (*ergon*, 46e8) than to enable human beings to contemplate the undisturbed motions in heaven so as to correct the wandering motions of their intellect (47b–c) and, by learning number, to acquire philosophical wisdom (47a4–b2).

3.2. Primary and Necessary Causes. Thus, the *Timaeus* presents us with two kinds of causes, which it calls necessary (or secondary) and primary respectively (the latter pertaining to the action of *nous*, 46d–e, 68e–69a). We can call these two kinds of causes "efficient" insofar as both of them produce certain effects.[49] In the second case, efficient cause has also a teleological constituent[50] in the sense that it is said to produce "*good* effects" (46e4); in the first, it may or may not have it according to its subordination or not to primary causes, since necessary causes are by themselves blind to any goal. Both necessary and primary causes seem to be necessary conditions for the fulfilment of teleology, and one could wonder what it is that makes the latter "primary". It doesn't seem satisfactory to adopt the criterion of "saliency" that Fine uses as regards the *Phaedo* to mark off the real cause from its necessary material conditions,[51] since the question might then arise: by what criterion do we call it salient? It seems rather that primacy lies in *initiating* a causal chain, a primacy that is given in addition an axiological import by its being purposively oriented towards a positive goal. Thus, in the *Phaedo* Socrates exclaims that his bones and sinews would be somewhere else if he thought that it was best to escape (98e–99a). Likewise, in the *Timaeus* (46c7–e2) Plato characterises secondary causes as those that are both moved by other things (e1) and devoid of any plan or intellect (d4), unlike primary causes, which would then suggest that primary causes are both intelligent and principles of motion.[52]

Now, where does all this talk about causation leave the Forms? Unlike previous dialogues (cf. e.g. *Phaedo* 100b ff.),[53] the *Timaeus* never explicitly applies the word "cause" to them.[54] Yet treating *nous* as primary cause does not mean that the Forms have no causal role. Borrowing Aristotelian concepts, one could say that in fact two kinds of causality would be implicit in the Platonic concept of "primary cause": the efficient one (exerted by *nous*) and the final one (corresponding to the Forms to which *nous* looks).[55] Thus, Forms could be final causes in the *Timaeus* insofar as they are goals or models of intelligent activity, in a way that makes them, if not efficient causes, at least relevant in the explanation of this kind of efficient causation.[56] If this is so, the causation exerted by *nous* would not deprive the Forms of a causal role,[57] but would rather presuppose it – inasmuch as they are the model to which intelligence must look so as to order the sensible in resemblance to the former. At the same time, the causality of *nous* makes it possible to fulfil an end through a chain of mechanical means, thus attenuating the gap or *chôrismos* that would otherwise exist between Forms and sensibles.[58]

3.3. Is Nous' Control Complete? From our reflections on creation in the *Timaeus*, it emerges that it only belongs to the *literary* form of the narration to represent the wandering cause as left to itself, reigning in a precosmic state of disorder. But even if we take it that *nous* is *always* in control, where does that leave the action of necessity? For we could still wonder whether necessity in the first sense described in section 3.1 (i.e. left to itself as a cause of disorder) is just an abstraction or has a real presence within the ordered cosmos under the rule of *nous*. This issue has, again, received heated discussion, and more recently Lennox has proposed that the triumph of *nous* over *anankê* is complete, so that "necessity is *always* a servant of intelligent ends".[59] Evidence from the text, however, inclines us towards the opposite conclusion. For Plato has Timaeus repeatedly use restrictive expressions when alluding to the operation of intelligence upon necessity. So, for example, we are told at 48a2–3 that *nous* rules over *anankê* "by persuading her to lead towards the best the majority (*ta pleista*) [and not "all", *ta panta*] of things that take place";[60] and at 46c7–d1 god makes use of auxiliary causes "when fulfilling, so far as possible (*kata to dunaton*) the form of the best". These qualifications would suggest that there is always a random residue of necessity left in the cosmos upon which *nous* could not settle with absolute control, so that the "instrument" could occasionally become an "obstacle".[61]

That residue of *anankê* would be particularly present not so much in heaven, where *nous* seems to prevail to such an extent that the heavenly bodies are called gods, but in the earthly and mortal domain. We read in the *Theaetetus* (176a5–8) that it is necessary that "evils wander about the mortal nature and this realm", not among the gods. And it is precisely as regards our mortal domain that the *Timaeus* myth gives the specific examples of the resistance that *anankê* opposes to *nous*. We can note this in certain properties of the materials on which the deity works, which are not so docile for its purposes,[62] such as the hard constitution of the bones, which has the advantage of serving for the protection of the brain and marrow, but the concomitant disadvantage of making the bones brittle (cf. *Tim.* 73a–74b); or in the fact that the deity has to compromise in the construction of the human head, abundance of flesh (which would protect the head and thus enable us to live longer and more healthily) not being compatible with acute perception (cf. 75a7–b1). In choosing a sharper intelligence over a longer life, the deity chooses a greater over a lesser good, but it is nonetheless implied that higher propensity to disease, and shorter lives, are a necessary but less than ideal consequence of such a choice (75b–c).

In this way, we have spelled out one reason why god is not to blame for the imperfection of the universe: there is a given factor in the ontological makeup of the sensible that is as primordial as intelligent causation in the explanation of the natural realm.[63] This is still consistent with the description of the universe as "the most beautiful of things generated" (29a5), or, we may say, materially possible, even though the universe is not the best one imaginable or logically possible.

3.4. The Demiurge as Primary Cause. I have argued so far that both *nous* and *anankê* are causes, and that the Demiurge corresponds to the first kind of cause. I have illustrated in what ways, and within what boundaries, *nous* can take control of *anankê*, and how both kinds of cause interact for the fulfilment of teleology in the universe. Indeed, it should be clear by now that the relation between *nous* and *anankê* is identical with that between primary or divine causes, on the one hand, and secondary or necessary causes, on the other (as presented in the twofold causal scheme of *Tim.* 46c–e and 68e–69a). For we have seen that *anankê* corresponds to necessary cause, and we can likewise expect *nous* to correspond to the primary or divine kind of causation. This is precisely what seems to be suggested by the *Timaeus* definition of primary causes, since these are said to belong to an "intelligent nature" (*emphrôn phusis*) at 46d8[64] and called "those causes which, by using *nous*, are artisans of fair and good effects" (*aitiai hosai meta nou kalôn kai agathôn dêmiourgoi,* 46e4).[65] There are two key words here: *nous* and "artisans" (*dêmiourgoi*), which strongly suggests that, at a more abstract or conceptual level, the Demiurge is a symbol of this function of primary causation, both intelligent and efficient, which is responsible for the fulfilment of teleology in the universe.[66] Can we be sure of demythologising the Demiurge this way? As I suggested in Chapter 1, it is a good sign if Plato maintains, even within a so-called "mythical" description, elements that he is ready to keep in more argumentative contexts. This is the case as far as the distinction between two kinds of causes is concerned (see e.g. *Pol.* 281d–e, *Laws* X 895b), which gives us reason to suspect that Plato is committed to such a distinction above and beyond any mythical images he may choose to represent it.

This hypothesis is in turn supported by the fact that, in the two passages dealing with the distinction between primary and secondary causes, it is at first god or the Demiurge who is introduced as "taking over" (*parelambanen,* 68e3) or "making use of" (*chrêtai,* 46c8) necessary causes as "cocauses" towards the fulfilment of the good (46c7–d1, 68e4–6), whereas immediately afterwards the text passes on to speak of primary or divine causes as opposed to the necessary or secondary ones (46d1–e6, 68e6–69a5). We can see here how, even though these passages start with a mythological allusion to the Demiurge, his functions are subsequently put, in a more abstract way, in terms of primary causation, something that encourages us again to take the former as a symbol of the latter. That the Demiurge corresponds to these divine or primary causes[67] is supported by the very beginning of the myth, where he is called "the best of causes" (29a5–6).

In the light of this, we can conclude that the Demiurge is the mythical counterpart of the notion of one kind of causation, namely primary

causation. By these means, Plato has explained the teleological arrangement of the universe, and how teleology is fulfilled by subordinating and
at the same time depending on mechanism. Here, I have argued, lies the
main philosophical point served by the image of the Demiurge.

III. THE ONTOLOGICAL STATUS OF THE DEMIURGE

We have seen that the Demiurge is or performs the functions of a mind
or *nous*. But what kind of *nous* is it? More generally, is intellect in the
Timaeus the kind of thing that can exist independently of any material
or spatial medium (as most readers take the *Phaedo* to suggest)? If Plato
is comfortable with this kind of metaphysical dualism (which some have
compared to Cartesian dualism),[68] it might be no wonder that he conceives of god along the same lines. Or perhaps he thinks that, while god's
intellect does not necessitate a material embodiment, human intellect
does. I shall show, however, that Plato's claims about the nature of intellect in the *Timaeus* concern intellect as such, that is, as a genus of which
both human and divine intellect are kinds. So that, if he doesn't (any
more?) believe that intellect is the kind of thing that can exist independently of some material embodiment, we should expect this conclusion
to apply to god's intellect as well.

Now, the relation between what Plato calls intellect (*nous*) and what
he calls soul (*psuchê*) also needs elucidating. In the *Republic*, for example,
intellect had been treated as one part of the soul (*psuchê*), which also has
other parts, and which may not have *nous* at all (V 436b ff., VI 494d).
From this it would seem that *nous* necessitates soul (but not vice versa).
Is this the case, though, as far as god's intellect is concerned, or should
it be seen as separate from any kind of soul? Analysing these questions
will give us some grasp not only of what Plato's views about god may have
been, but also what kind of relation to the body he envisages for the mind
in the *Timaeus*.

1. What Kind of *Nous* is the Demiurge?

This is indeed a vexed question. Interpretations have varied from taking
the Demiurge as a *nous* that is separate not only from the world, but from
any kind of soul,[69] to granting that the Demiurge may be an ensouled
nous. Here again, there has been disagreement as to whether he is to be
regarded as separate from the universe (and from the universe's soul)
or not.[70] Let us take a brief look at this array of views and see whether

any decisive arguments can be invoked to settle the matter. All of them, in a sense, may be responding to ambiguities in the text; yet I believe it is more economical, and indeed more interesting, to suppose that god is not separate from the universe, but tantamount to the world-soul. In addition, this view, I shall argue, better helps preserve the internal consistency of Plato's text.

The fact that Timaeus describes the Demiurge as creating the world-soul and individual souls has led some to take him literally as a personal god, and to believe that the Demiurge himself, as the creator of soul, does not have a soul. Thus, Hackforth argues for "discriminating *nous*, as an ultimate principle, from *psuchê*, as a derived principle".[71] Yet a tension immediately becomes apparent: if the Demiurge embodies *nous* and is taken to create all soul, then the Demiurge should be a *nous* separate and ontologically prior to soul. At the same time, defenders of this claim often endorse the view that soul is the only principle of motion,[72] and even grant that *nous* partakes of motion (*Tim.* 34a, cf. *Laws* X 897c ff.),[73] which seems to imply, whether they are aware of it or not, that soul should be ontologically prior to *nous*.[74] Clearly, these two conclusions cannot be maintained at once. But there is no need to incur this awkwardness, as nowhere does the myth say that the Demiurge creates all kinds of soul. Further, that *nous* partakes of motion is a thought that recurs in a variety of texts, which gives us reason to believe that Plato does not mean this claim as mere mythological fancy.[75]

This conclusion can be backed up by several passages pointing to the dependence of *nous* on soul (30b3, 37c3–5; cf. *Phil.* 30c9–10, *Soph.* 249a). Upholders of the contrary view commonly allege that these texts refer only to one kind of *nous* (e.g. the intellect that belongs to the world-soul), not the *nous* of god, which could still exist independently. Yet the evidence is underdetermined and could arguably be invoked in defence of the opposite conclusion. In fact, we tend to find *nous* described not as an entity different from soul or separate from it, but rather as a state or faculty of soul, namely soul's power of knowing the Forms (*Tim.* 37a–c; cf. *Rep.* VI 508d4–6). For example in the *Timaeus* (37a6, c1–3) we read that, when soul is in contact with the indivisible, and its discourse deals with the Forms, then "intellect and knowledge of necessity is achieved" (*nous epistêmê te ex anankês apoteleitai*). It is true that, in the context, Timaeus is speaking of the cosmic soul, but he adds a clause that makes the point general: "But if anyone should ever say that it is in any of the things which exist, except soul (*psuchê*), that these two states come about, he will be saying anything but the truth" (37c3–5). In addition, at

Tim. 30b3 we read that "it is impossible for intellect to belong to anything separately from soul" (*noun d'au chôris psuchês adunaton paragenesthai tôi*). We are here most naturally led to believe that the text is making a general point, as valid for *anything* (*tôi*);[76] and it is by virtue of this general validity that the claim will then be applied to the specific case of the *nous* in the world (that is why god "framed *nous* in soul, and soul in body", *Tim.* 30b4–5).

Those who would like the Demiurge to be a soulless *nous* might argue that *genesis* is not to be predicated of him (as it seems to be predicated of ensouled *nous* e.g. at 30b3, 37c3–5).[77] However, it is less than clear that the Demiurge, *qua nous*, should not belong to the realm of becoming or change (*genesis*), or even be a self-generating kind of entity, as we shall see soul is in the *Laws*.[78] After all, in a summary account of the *Timaeus* ontology, at 52d, we are told that three things existed before the generation of the universe: being, space, and *genesis*; no mention is made of the Demiurge as a separate entity (despite his being alluded to e.g. at 53b4). Even though it might be tempting to include him in the realm of being (which preeminently belongs to the Forms), this possibility is precluded by the fact that such a realm is immutable (38a3), while *nous* is in motion.

Focusing on the motion of *nous* will also help us settle other matters. So far I hope to have shown that we may plausibly believe that in the *Timaeus* all *nous*, including god's, should be ensouled. But whether that soul is immanent or transcendent to the universe still needs to be examined. Again, it has been tempting here to preserve the image of the Demiurge as a personal god, closer to the Judeo-Christian view, by arguing for the latter possibility. I shall start by presenting one brief but important argument for believing that there is, on close examination, no room left for transcendence; afterwards I shall pass on to consider further arguments and objections.

We have seen that if the Demiurge is a *nous*, he is in motion. Thus, at *Tim.* 34b, rotatory motion is mentioned, among all motions, as "the one that maximally belongs to *nous*;"[79] and in *Laws* X we are told about the "motion and revolution of *nous*" (*nou kinêsei kai periphorai*, 897c5–6). Even when scholars have seen this point, they have standardly missed the importance of a second, independent point, namely that *motion presupposes space*. That this is the case for *nous* is already implied by *Tim.* 34a, where the motion of *nous* is described as rotation in the same [place] (*en tôi autôi*).[80] This point is not peculiar to the *Timaeus*. For it is stated in *Laws* X 893c1–2 that "whatever moves [including psychic motion] . . . moves in a place". Let us here add that, in turn, space implies body, since there is no void in Plato's universe (*Tim.* 58a). Thus, a spatial or material medium seems to be a necessary condition for the motion of *nous* itself.[81]

In principle, one could still think that those material conditions for god could be exterior to the world-body.[82] However, this seems implausible, for in the *Timaeus* there is nothing outside the world-body; rather there is just one single material universe (*Tim.* 31a, 32c–33d). Indeed, if the motion proper to *nous* is rotation, and god exerts his influence over the whole cosmos, it becomes most natural to identify this motion with the motion that is manifested in the axial rotation of the universe upon itself, whose origin the *Timaeus* in turn remits to its intelligent soul (34b, 36b ff.) – as a matter of fact, the world-soul, like *nous*, is said to "revolve upon itself", 36e3–4. These considerations lead us to identify the Demiurge with the world-soul.

Certainly, it could be objected that assimilating the Demiurge to the world-soul would threaten the notion of the ontological dependence of the world, which the postulation of a separate god seems rather to highlight quite explicitly, thus making such a god nonredundant. My point here, however, is not to deny the ontological dependence of the world, since it transpires from the myth that the universe has a derivative existence and is not the ultimate reality (cf. 28b, 41a–b).[83] Rather, it is to show that in order to ensure and even explain such ontological dependence we do not need two kinds of entity above it (the Demiurge and the Forms) but one is sufficient (namely, the Forms, as the ultimate principle of order of this *kosmos*), particularly after we have denied that the Demiurge should be allotted a role as creator of the present universe in the mere past. Even though the Demiurge is not itself equivalent to the Forms,[84] it does perform an actual function of grounding the orderly nature of the universe on the latter; yet, as we shall see, in Plato's structure of reality it is the world-soul that can be counted on as fulfilling this teleological function, and as the efficient cause or principle on which the universe depends, a principle that will turn out to be immanent to the universe (as its self-generating principle of motion and order) rather than extrinsic to it.

One could wonder, though, how "nonmythical" the cosmic soul itself is: how can we be sure that Plato is not joking or being lighthearted when attributing a soul not only to humans, but also to the whole world?[85] From a hermeneutical point of view, perhaps we can call it nonmythical strictly in the sense by which we previously demarcated mythical elements from nonmythical ones: while the former are unverifiable and are not the subject of rational argumentation and demonstration, the latter Plato believes to be so. Thus, in the *Timaeus* he explains how we can learn, through astronomy, the motions of the world-soul in the heavens (*Tim.* 47b–c, 90c–d) whereas in other contexts he will try to prove the existence of a world-soul by making use of distinctive arguments (cf. e.g. *Phil.* 28e ff.; *Laws* XII 966d–967a with 967e1 and Chapter 4, Section II.4. and Chapter 8, Sections I–IV). In the next chapter we shall see, in addition, that apprehending the world-soul constitutes one stage in the ethical and epistemological ascent of the human soul towards the Forms, whereas the Demiurge occupies no such distinct place in that ascent (except perhaps in the form of an image from which the mind must move away). But most importantly, as we shall see, by "soul" Plato does not here mean any ghost in the machine, but the principle of organisation of the body. And, given his insistence on the "unity" of the material universe (32c), he must believe that such unity cannot be due to matter (which is intrinsically scattered, *Tim.* 53a–b) but must obey a principle that holds it together just as our soul does in the case of individual organisms (a line of thought explicitly developed in the *Philebus*).[86] In fact, what makes up "body" is mathematical proportion (cf. 53c ff., 31b–32c), in turn remitted to the agency of "divine" or "primary" causes (68e–69b, 46e), which, as we shall see, belong to the domain of soul (46d).

2. The World-Soul as Primary Cause

Indeed, we should be struck by the fact that the Demiurge and the world-soul are presented with parallel functions in the text, which again suggests that we identify them. In the first place, we have seen that the Demiurge appears as having a *mediating role,* insofar as it connects the heterogeneous domains of Forms and sensibles (29a, e ff.). Forms are invisible and immutable (*akinêtôs, Tim.* 38a3, cf. 52a1–3), whereas our realm is mutable and visible. Yet the *Parmenides* had already presented the objection: If Forms exist in a separate realm of their own, how can they have any influence or power (*dunamis,* 133e5) on our realm (133c–134e)? How can participation be possible at all? Similarly, Aristotle criticises Plato on the grounds that the Forms, being immutable, cannot really be efficient causes or principles of motion (*aitia kinêseôs*) of the sensible (cf. *Metaph.* I 9, 991a8–11, 991b3–5). The *Timaeus* emphasises, perhaps more than any other dialogue, the ontological gap between Forms and sensibles.[87] So can the gap be bridged by the notion of a Demiurge, or, for that matter, a world-soul?

Arguably, their use is to fulfil precisely the role of "efficient cause" or "principle of motion" that Aristotle rightly did not find in Plato's Forms. In the late dialogues, it is not the Forms,[88] but soul that is explicitly called "principle of motion" or "cause of motion",[89] and the same suggestion can be found in the *Timaeus* itself (37b5, 46d–e).[90] Further, it is specifically *nous* that, in addition to having a productive aspect, is endowed with the role of ordering.[91] This is the case at a cosmic level with the *nous* of the Demiurge, who is called, as we have seen, the principle of becoming and order (*geneseôs kai kosmou . . . archê*, 29e4). It is precisely because of this efficient and mediating power that the demiurgic *nous* can connect the heterogeneous realms of Forms and sensibles, and this *nous* can do so by having properties akin to both: like the Forms, it is invisible or intelligible; like the sensible domain, it is in motion. At the same time, however, the text allots the same mediating role preeminently to the world-soul, whose ontological constitution is described in the *Timaeus* as intermediate between the indivisible or intelligible and the divisible or sensible,[92] being therefore *partly* akin to the Forms and *partly* akin to sensible things (35a1–b1). And so, by virtue of its twofold nature, it can act as a bridge between these two realms and connect them. But how can such bridging actually occur?

The craftsman metaphor, let us recall, was useful insofar as it suggested how, in the first place, it is important for the productive agent to have an intellectual grasp of a stable model if the product is to be fair (28a–b); on the other hand, the Demiurge had also, together with intellectual functions, a practical role of ordering the sensible world according to his plan. But these same functions seem allotted by the text to the world-soul itself: the world-soul has an *intellectual knowledge* of the Ideal order (cf. 37a–c), but, being itself in orderly motion (37a–b),[93] it can rule the universe (34c). In this way, it can project the Ideal order onto the sensible realm.[94]

In this regard, it is no surprise that the world-soul itself should embody the function of *primary cause* despite other passages where the Demiurge was seen to point to that notion. At *Tim.* 46d–e, if we recall, a distinction is drawn between two kinds of causes, primary and secondary. The latter is said to have to do with bodies, and the former with rational planning and *nous*, because "among entities (*tôn ontôn*), soul is the only one for which it is appropriate to possess *nous*" (46d5–6). That is, it is now soul that turns out to be the entity suited to the function of primary causation that we had previously seen the Demiurge symbolise.

This view is in turn developed in *Laws* X, which, speaking of primary and secondary motion instead of primary and secondary causation, describes the motion of soul as the primary cause of all the other kinds of motion. This primary motion, associated with *nous*, makes use of (*chrômenê*) the secondary motions of bodies in order to guide everything rightly and happily (cf. 895b, 896e–897b). Thus we can see that it is the teleological action of soul, *qua* rational, which leans on mechanism and subordinates it by using it as a means towards an end, just as we saw the Demiurge rely on mechanical or secondary causes in the *Timaeus*. All this suggests that it is soul, and particularly the cosmic soul,[95] that performs the role of primary causation mythically allotted to the Demiurge.

3. Reason and the World-Soul

Now, what exactly is the relation of the cosmic soul with *nous*? As we have seen, soul need not be exclusively rational: a good example of this is the human soul. Does the world-soul possess any irrational faculties? Even though this thought has tempted some, it is implausible.[96] For the cosmic soul is described as having the same nature as human individual reason, only with a greater degree of purity (41d). Along the same lines, the world-soul as a whole is said to have an "intelligent life (*emphrôn bios*) for the whole of time" (36e4–5). Further, the motion with which soul moves the body of the universe is often characterised as the motion of *nous* in the heavens (34a, 47b7, 89a1–3, 90c8–d1), in a way that seems to treat the world-intellect indifferently from the world-soul. For this same reason, it is no wonder that in many passages it is soul that is ascribed the functions that we have seen belong to *nous*, such as governing (*Tim.* 34c, *Laws* XII 967d, as well as that of imposing order, *Laws* X 898c, 899b, cf. *Crat.* 400a).

In a narrow sense, though, the world-soul can be said to have *nous*, by which it grasps Forms, as opposed to opinion or *doxa*, by which it grasps sensibles.[97] But not even this *doxa* can be said to be "irrational", as it is not only true, but also stable (37b8).[98] Presumably, it is precisely that doxastic acquaintance with the realm of change, which is nonetheless backed up by intellectual knowledge of the Forms, that enables the world-soul to perform the function of ruling the world-body (as at 34c), in a way reminiscent of the rule of the philosopher-king in the *Republic*, who is best suited to rule in the cave insofar as he knows "the images and of what they are images" (VII 520c). And these two functions seemed to pertain in the myth of the *Timaeus* to the Demiurge himself, who, while characterised as a *nous*, not only knows the Forms but also "rules" and "persuades" necessity.[99]

4. The Immanence and Corporeality of God

Assimilating the Demiurge to the world-soul, I contend, also serves to present a more cohesive reading of the text, one that helps us bypass certain problems that would arise if instead we suppose that the Demiurge (whether ensouled or not) exists independently from the sensible universe. One problem is *duplication*: If we have two *nous*, that is, that of the Demiurge, and that of the world-soul, we seem to be duplicating entities.[100] For both of them would be performing the same functions of contemplating the Forms on the one hand and ruling over the universe on the other hand. It seems rather more economical to suppose that there is just one *nous* in the structure of reality, and that the mythical image of the Demiurge can be subsumed into the (nonmythical) *nous* in the world.

Another problem is *separation*: If we admit that the Demiurge is a link between independently existing Forms (which are immutable, 38a3) and our sensible moving world, we meet a real paradox if we make this *nous* as separate as those Forms it tries to connect to our world. In other words, god's *nous* would itself exist separately (*chôris*), independent of our world, instead of filling in the gap or *chôrismos* between Forms and sensibles. If this were the case, we would then have to re-ask the question: What is the relation of this separate *nous* to the world and its soul? Rather than providing a way out of the problem of separation, as the Demiurge initially seemed to, we would thus be duplicating it. On the other hand, as we shall see in the *Politicus*, the separation or *chôrismos* from god seems to be the state when god is not governing the cosmos (*Pol.* 273c–d: if or when the universe is separated from god, increasing disorder takes place; a point also suggested at *Tim.* 53b). All of this indicates that, if one of the properties of god is to rule in the cosmos (cf. *Tim.* 48a), and if such a rule is to occur effectively, god should not be separate. Instead, we have shown that *nous* cannot exist without motion, motion presupposes space, and space presupposes body.

This is, indeed, an extraordinary suggestion; one which seems to incline Plato towards a view of the mind-body relation that does not exempt even the mind of god from the need for space and body, and which

couldn't be further removed from Cartesian dualism.[101] Instead, the remarks we have made about the nature of *nous* lead us to posit what we
might call, in a qualified manner, the "corporeality" of god. I mean this
in the sense that, even though the motions pertaining to *nous* do not
seem to be of the same order as its body (at least insofar as at *Tim.* 36e
and 46d soul is said to be distinct from body as the invisible from the
visible)[102] they still manifest themselves, or make themselves "visible"
(cf. 47a–c), through a spatial body that acts as their vehicle. Why the
mind (any kind of mind) should need the body as a vehicle should now
come as no surprise. For, as we have seen, it belongs to the mind to be a
teleological agent, but teleological agency necessarily relies on mechanical conditions. In this regard, the body provides the mechanical means
without which teleology cannot be fulfilled. Thus, the world-soul is inseparable from the world-body, while grounding the latter's intelligibility and
unity.[103]

However striking the dependence of soul (including god's soul) on
body might seem to a reader only accustomed to Plato's middle dialogues (recall particularly the seemingly sharp mind-body dualism of the
Phaedo), we must here note that the description of god as requiring a body
as instrument does in fact represent an overall, and arguably distinct, tendency in Plato's later work. Thus, in the *Phaedrus* (245c ff.), an account
of soul is introduced as self-mover and "principle of motion" (c9), which
seems to imply that soul is the principle of the motion *of something*. And
even though soul can be the principle of its own psychic states (such as
those mentioned in a similar context in *Laws* X 896e8–897a4), the union
of soul with body (as its principle of motion) is nonetheless stressed, particularly at 245e4–6: "all body . . . which itself by itself has motion from
within is animate, since this is precisely the nature of soul" (*hôs tautês ousês
phuseôs psuchês*). That is, *the very essence of soul* seems to consist in animat-
ing a body through the motion that it imparts to it from within.[104] By this
appeal to soul as *archê kinêseôs*, or principle of motion, Plato appears to
advance a more friendly relation between soul and body that will in turn
recur in other later dialogues, so that, rather than an obstacle (*empodion
to sôma*, *Phaedo* 65a10, cf. 66c1) the body will become mainly a vehicle
(*ochêma*) for the soul (cf. *Tim.* 41e2, 69c7),[105] not only as the instrument
of the purposive action of intelligent souls,[106] but also as its place of
residence. In that regard, it is noteworthy that, in the *Timaeus*, human
reason (which is said to be of the same nature as the world-soul, 41d) is
not separate from a body even in the most pure state it can achieve. For
in the latter case the reward consists, according to the myth, not in the

detachment from all body but, conversely, in going to dwell in the incorruptible body of a star (41d–e, 42b2–5, cf. 90a). Further, the ethical consequence of a less than virtuous life is described as reincarnation, which means that the soul will exist in some inferior sort of body (90e–92c). If this is so, then the corporeality of god would be no odd conclusion but quite congenial with Plato's overall way of tackling the mind-body relation in his later dialogues.

IV. CONCLUSION

In this chapter I have argued for two theses:

  1. The Demiurge is a symbol of the function of primary causation.
  2. The Demiurge is a symbol of the cosmic soul.

These theses are in principle logically distinct. I hope, however, that my treatment of the subject makes it clear that by his analysis of "cause" in the *Timaeus* Plato not only means to supply us with teleological *explanations*, but also, and inextricably, with a grasp of an actual *entity* in his scheme of things that is responsible for the world being ordered as it is. From this perspective, far from being mutually exclusive,[107] 1. and 2. can be seen as different aspects of the same thesis. For 1. merely alludes to a function that in turn calls for an agent to perform it, which is found in 2. Or, in other words, 1. corresponds to the philosophical and abstract meaning of the figure of the Demiurge, but this meaning cannot be fully understood unless we refer it to the entity that embodies it. The correspondence between these two levels is made evident, for example, in *Laws* X (895d–896b), where we are told that "the motion with the power to move itself" – which has the function of primary causation, 894b ff. – is the definition (*logos*) that "refers" (cf. *prosagoreuomen*) to the same entity (*ousia*) that we call "soul". If we recall, the *Timaeus* too emphasises soul as the only *entity* that can have *nous* – and therefore operate as primary cause – in contrast with causes that are devoid of all wisdom (46d–e). From this perspective, 1. and 2. are wholly complementary and go indispensably together. Thus, we may conclude that the Demiurge is a symbol of the teleological function of primary causation that is preeminently fulfilled by the cosmic soul in Plato's structure of reality.

Analysing the myth has, in this way, helped us discover how important it is for Plato in the *Timaeus* to postulate even on a macrocosmic scale (and not just on a microcosmic one, as he had done in the *Republic*) a mind that, by being in contact with the Forms, can ensure the highest possible degree of participation of the sensible domain in goodness and order. Remember that, in the *Republic*, the philosopher had been presented as the mind that would be able to order the city-state after the pattern of the Forms: "By seeing the Good itself and using it as a paradigm, they must order (*kosmein*) the *polis*, the citizens and themselves" (VII 540a8–b1); in this way the philosopher is called a *dêmiourgos* of virtue in his fellow-citizens – and thus of the goodness of the whole city (cf. VI 500d). Now, by the time of the *Timaeus*, we find god as the ultimate philosopher-king, who has not just one parcel but the whole cosmos under his care. Even though it suits Plato to present such a god as a personal Demiurge, after the model of human craftsmanship, we have found, on reflection, that the Demiurge is the world-soul that suffuses the whole universe with purpose. This however does not mean that we should regard the Demiurge's personal guise as otherwise insignificant. The extent to which god is meant to function as a role model for humans is to occupy us in the next chapter.

3

Cosmic God and Human Reason in the *Timaeus*

In the previous chapter, we examined Plato's conception of god in the *Timaeus* as the teleological agent *par excellence,* and showed how that agency relies on bodily conditions, so that god turns out to be immanent to the universe. Now, why should this matter from an ethical perspective? What, if anything, are we to learn from this god, both through its mythical description and through the more rigorous study of astronomy?

I shall argue that Plato thinks we have indeed much to learn. In the course of my treatment, it will also become clear in what ways the *Timaeus* can be seen as a response to the *Republic* (and in that regard it may be no accident that the dialogue should start with an account reminiscent of that work). However, rather than claiming, as has been done recently, that the *Timaeus* keeps "the basic ethical and political ideology of the *Republic*",[1] I set out to show how the *Timaeus* can, to a large extent, be seen as an attempt by Plato not just to resume but also to move *beyond* some important *Republic* conclusions.

In particular, I shall emphasise how Plato's ethics in the *Timaeus* takes us away from the elitism of the *Republic*, presenting instead an independent way to happiness that is available to everyone. How is that possible? It is possible, I argue, precisely because everyone can share the universe as a common paradigm, and internalise its order. What the study of astronomy does for us, I contend, is not simply (as some have suggested)[2] to prepare a few for the highest level of study (of a philosophical kind). It also transforms our lives in a practical manner, in a way that is available to all, and does not even require the rule of a philosopher or a good political system in general. To understand the magnitude of this proposal we need to insert it in the context of a larger concern about role models that runs through Plato's ethics, and we shall see how the threads of myth and rational discourse are interwoven around this issue in the *Timaeus*.

I. THE COSMIC GOD AS A MODEL FOR HUMAN REASON

1. The Cosmic God

Someone who reads the *Timaeus* for the first time may be struck by the fact that so many things in this work are called gods. Not only is the Demiurge called a god; so is the universe and the heavenly bodies, as well as the traditional gods. As I have argued elsewhere,[3] this is not just a random way of speaking; in fact, there is a fine correspondence between the mythological description under which Plato sometimes chooses to present god and his more technical approach. Thus, for example, the relation Demiurge-lesser gods parallels, in mythical terms, the ruling role of the world-soul over the heavenly bodies from an astronomical perspective, which in turn mirrors the ruling role of Zeus over the other gods in the traditional religion.

Indeed, we concluded in our previous chapter that the Demiurge must stand for the world-soul. But the fact that the world-soul does not exist in isolation, but in a perceptible body (30b4–5), results in the divinity of the universe itself, which is thus called "a sensible god, greatest and best and most fine and complete" (92c7–8). So the universe turns out to be, in Plato's own structure of reality, the major god,[4] at a singular level of divinity. There is also a plural level, namely the individual heavenly bodies, which, we are made to think, share the same nature as the world-soul.[5] This is what Timaeus describes as the "heavenly class of gods" (*ouranion theôn genos*, 39e10), in a passage that makes successive allusion to the fixed stars (40a2–b6), the planets (40b6–8, cf. 38c ff.), and the Earth, which is called "the first and most venerable of the gods born in the universe" (40c2–3). From now on, I shall refer to the universe and the heavenly bodies collectively as "the cosmic god".

How are the individual heavenly bodies subordinate to the world-soul? Delving into their astronomical relation will help elucidate this point. At 35b–36b, Timaeus describes the composition of the world-soul according to harmonic intervals (which, as we shall see, will measure the relative distances between the heavenly bodies). He then moves on to divide it according to two Circles: that of the Same and that of the Other (36b–d). Basically, the Circle of the Same describes the orbit of the fixed stars, which are placed at the periphery of the universe, whereas the Circle of the Other is divided into seven circles corresponding to the orbits of each of the planets (36d), the Earth in turn being placed at the centre. In one sense, the motion of the stars at the periphery coincides with the axial rotation of the whole universe, so Timaeus often refers to the motion of the world-soul as the motion of the Same. Further, since both the Circles of the Same and of the Other are said to be "joined" (36c1), the motion of the Same carries with it the planetary orbits inscribed in the Circle of the Other, even though they also go in the opposite direction (36c): this results in what Timaeus calls the "ruling" role of the Circle of the Same over the Circle of the Other (36c7). It is this astronomical hierarchy that results also in a specific hierarchy between various levels of divinity in Plato's cosmology.

Thus, in the same way as the Demiurge was said to give orders to the young gods (cf. 42d, 41a ff.), and to have a ruling role that can be seen as the prevailing of a unitary teleological design in the whole universe, so is the world-soul (or the Circle of the Same)[6] said to "prevail" over the motions of the heavenly bodies (see *kratos* 36c7, cf. 39a1–2, 40b2),[7] apart from the overall governance that it exerts on the sensible or the world-body as such (34b10–35a1). In this way, the structure of the cosmos itself shows relations between its different levels of divinity that are analogous to those that were initially depicted demiurgically.[8]

Even the individual heavenly bodies share the basic features of the world-soul. For the stars are called "divine and perpetual living beings" at 40b5, and attributed thought (*dianoein*) at 40a8–b1. The planets, in their turn, are said to have life and soul (their bodies having been bound with psychic bonds, 38e5), and their possession of intelligence is implied by their learning (*manthanein*) what was prescribed to them (38e6) – surely their own celestial motions, in the light of 36d4–5. It is, then, again their possession of *nous* that we can take as the foundation of their divinity, and the constant exercise of *nous* is manifested in regular behaviour: Each star moves "in the same place and regularly, thinking always the same things for itself about the same things" (*peri tôn autôn aei ta auta heautôi dianooumenôi*, 40a8–b1).[9] Thus, we can see that not only the world-soul, but also the heavenly bodies perform the twofold functions of having *intellectual* contemplation, on the one hand, and inextricably *moving* in an orderly fashion.

What we have just said applies even to the "planets", which the Greeks (as shown in the etymology of the word) used to refer to as "wanderers". Although Timaeus uses the word *planên* at 40b6, presumably keeping to the traditional denomination, the text seems far from suggesting that they divert from their route. On the contrary, it appears to stress that, despite the complexity of their motions (and their variations of speed), they all follow the route of the different orbits into which the Circle of the Other was divided.[10] The protest against thinking that planets "wander" is explicitly found in *Laws* VII 822a, the reason being adduced that "each of them traverses the same route, i.e. not many but always one single route in a circle" (a6–8). With this we confirm that whatever order we observe in the heavens, including that of the motion of the planets, is due to and evinces the presence of *nous*. And given their properties of intellection and motion (cf. 38e, 40a–b), which they share with the world-soul, it is no surprise that the heavenly bodies can also act as primary causes.

We must note in this respect that the gods to whom the Demiurge delegates the task of framing the mortal parts of the universe are those generated by him, that is, *the heavenly bodies themselves* (and also the traditional gods, probably as their counterparts, 41a3–6).[11] Even though they appear in the myth with an *anthropomorphic* role of "creation" (*dêmiourgia*, 41c4–5) of mortal beings – and also "nurture" (*trophê*, 41d2), making grow (cf. *auxanete*, 41d3) and ruling or piloting (*diakubernan*, 42e3) – that role could be interpreted more astronomically in the sense of the active role that the heavenly bodies – and particularly the Sun – have in the generation, growth and nurture (*genesin kai auxên kai trophên*) of life on the Earth (*Rep.* VI 509b2–4), thus ruling (*epitropeuôn*) and being the cause (*aitios*) of things there (*Rep.* VII 516b9–c2). Similarly, at *Tim.* 40b–c the Earth is called "our nurse" (*trophon*) and "guardian and demiurge (*dêmiourgon*) of day and night".

It is indeed no accident that both the cosmic god and the traditional gods are made to fulfil the teleological function that we have seen to be characteristic of god in the previous chapter. Thus, for example, at one point *the Muses* are mentioned as donating harmony to humans for the sake of promoting order in their souls (47d). Even the traditional gods can be seen as a personified version of the cosmic gods, if we take into account, for example, that "heaven" and "earth" appear in a double aspect, first as constituents of the universe generated by the Demiurge, and then, more anthropomorphically, as the first links (*Gaia* and *Ouranos*) of the genealogy from which the rest of the traditional gods proceeds.[12] This kind of presentation may well be seen as an attempt by Plato not to exclude but to incorporate the traditional gods within his own cosmic religion.[13] It seems, then, that Plato is seeking to unify his manifold allusions to god under the common denominator of an efficient cause that is responsible for the intelligent organisation of the universe. And this, in turn, can be read as a redefinition of the nature of god, which contrasts with the traditional images of Homer and Hesiod, criticised as immoral in previous dialogues (cf. *Rep.* II 377d ff.).

2. God and the Forms

Now, if this is so, it seems clear that Plato is trying to present the reader of the *Timaeus* with various ways of approaching god, ways that appeal to the imagination as well as one's reasoning abilities. Even when it turns out that the image of a Demiurge as separate from the universe may be false, there is still "something true" about the mythical description, as with every Platonic myth (cf. *Rep.* 377a), such as the goodness and rationality of god. As we shall see, more argumentative passages in the *Timaeus* make the same point rather differently. Thus, our intellectual powers too will be stimulated, through the study of astronomy, to discover god's intelligence and goodness.

But what, then, are we to make of the Forms? They are certainly the most self-sufficient reality in the *Timaeus*.[14] Even the Demiurge depends on them for the fulfilment of his teleological and intelligent activity;[15] but the Forms themselves do not depend on anything. To this extent, we may think of the Forms as the ultimate level of the divine, the supreme reality. But if so, why not call *them* "god"?

The characterisation of god as an intelligent living being offers a reason for not applying this name to the Forms.[16] Even when the Forms are intelligible,[17] they are not intelligent. Instead, the *Timaeus* seems to postulate two distinct sorts of entity to embody features that tend to be combined in the Judaeo-Christian conception of "God":[18] on the one hand, being the ultimate and absolute reality, and on the other, the creator and source of life and movement. In the *Timaeus*, only the latter corresponds to what Plato calls god, as a superhuman *nous*. The Forms, however, are called "divine", in a more impersonal manner.[19]

Now, choosing to call "god" not the entity most remote from us and from the sensible universe, but rather that universe itself as a living and intelligent being (thus capturing the aspect of mental activity that is often associated with the concept of god), is not simply a matter of terminological preference on the part of Plato. In point of fact, it is a central feature of his moral theory, which is based on the proper cultivation of the self as the key to happiness, that one should have appropriate role models. In the *Republic*, a first approach is made by way of the attempt to purify the traditional conception of god in the stories that one tells the young (in books II and III). But later, finding the theoretical underpinnings for the intended reform becomes a much more sophisticated affair, and great emphasis is placed on how communion with the Forms could have the effect of transforming one's whole life. Thus, one would not have the leisure "to be filled with envy and ill-will by fighting people" if one "looks at and contemplates things that are in order and always in the same state, and do not commit or suffer injustice from one another, but are all in a logical arrangement", and thus one "imitates them and emulates them as far as one can . . . Then the philosopher, by communing with what is divine and orderly . . . becomes himself orderly and divine as far as that is possible for a human being" (VI 500b–c). Yet, for the many, this model is unavailable; and even for the philosophically inclined soul who is not yet at the summit of understanding, this might turn out to be a model too abstract and remote to follow, and too difficult to grasp without some propaedeutics. In that regard, "god", as he appears initially through the mythical guise of the Demiurge (which is depicted as essentially good and experiencing no envy, 29e), and later in the actual face of the cosmic god (as an embodied being, also presented as an exemplar of virtue and happiness, 34b8, 92c, cf. 37a2), will in the *Timaeus* turn out to provide a model that is closer to us and available to all.

3. Human Reason and Necessity

Certainly, the suggestion just made is not exempt from difficulties. For it is not immediately clear how *the universe* may turn out to provide any less remote a model than the Forms. We can perhaps understand what it would mean to imitate Peter Pan or Abraham Lincoln. But in what way can one imitate the universe? Perhaps it is precisely in this respect that wrapping Plato's god in the mythical robes of the Demiurge might provide some point of reference, as anthropomorphic images seem to be easier for us to relate to. But it is also important to understand what Plato means by our imitating the *astronomical* universe, however strange this thought may appear at first blush.

The universe is described as an immortal, ageless, self-sufficient living being, possessing a body which does not create for it any needs (33a–d). It is a real friend to itself (34b7–8), and is called "most excellent" and "happy" (92c8, 34b8); we are made to reflect on how its rational soul, suffused with wisdom, is the source of its excellence (34b–c, 36e). If, as we shall see, virtue consists in the invariable exercise of reason and in the harmony of a living being, the universe embodies just that. However, to grasp what force, if any, there is in this suggestion we must look more closely at the similarities and differences between us and the universe.

In some respects, the human soul is analogous to the world-soul. It is made up, like the latter, of the circles of the Same and the Other (cf. 42c, 43d), having by nature the same intervals as the world-soul (43d, cf. 35b–36b). As in the world-soul, so in the human rational soul the revolution of the Same (by which the soul apprehends the intelligible) is meant to have a ruling role (cf. *archousa, hêgemôn*, 44a4). This would guarantee both, from a theoretical perspective, true judgements (even about sensibles, 44a) and, from a practical one, the mastering of one's own passions (cf. 42c–d), just as the cosmic *nous* has the ability both to grasp truth on a theoretical plane and to rule over its body on a practical one.

But if the human soul mirrors so closely the world-soul, why aren't we on a par with god? Plato never calls human reason god, even though it is called divine, immortal, and a *daimôn* (that is, some kind of divine entity).[20] Our main difference with god, however, is that it is possible for humans *not* to follow the rule of reason; instead, there is in our domain an element of necessity that we *ought to* harness, just as *nous* actually does on the cosmic scale. So we need to analyse what role "necessity", as a factor that also operates on a cosmic level, plays in human life. This will in turn be important in understanding how virtue itself can be seen as the capacity to deal with necessity, and how god is a model in that regard.

Both the universe and the heavenly bodies are immortal with respect to their soul (36e, 40b) and their body (33a, 43a). The human being, by contrast, is not immortal in all the elements of his composition. For human reason is conjoined with a corruptible body, which will be returned to the four elements (cf. 42e–43a), plus another two psychic faculties, adapted to that body (cf. 69c ff.), which are equally mortal. Thus, *Tim.* 42a3–b1 makes it clear that affections (*pathêmata*) like spirit (*thumos*) (which will be treated as one part of the soul at 70a) and erotic love (*erôs*) mixed with pleasure and pain (as would be experienced by the lowest part of our soul) supervene inevitably, or "by necessity" (*ex anankês*), when the immortal soul is implanted in bodies to which things come in and from which they go out. In this way, the existence of passions and affections of various sorts in the individual represents in him an element of necessity that may remain uncontrolled. And it is because our mortal body is not self-sufficient (unlike the immortal body of the universe) that, for example, the desire for food exists. In this way, whereas the cosmic god seems to be completely comfortable in his body (a real friend to himself, 34b) which doesn't create for him any needs, for us the body may constitute, in our earthly life, a potential source of limitations on rational activity (cf. 86b ff., 87e, 88a–b).

Further, it is precisely because of the soul's association with a corruptible body that all kinds of distortions are likely to affect the circles of the soul and prevent them from ruling, which explains the origin of false judgement (43e–44a). And so we are shown how that element of "necessity" in our human constitution, represented by irrational affections, can act as a wandering cause. Recall that in Chapter 2 we saw how "necessity" has the twofold aspect of constituting, on the one hand, a possible hindrance to intelligence (thus acting as a random or "wandering cause", *planômenê aitia*, 48a7), and, on the other, an indispensable instrument for intelligent design, thanks to the transformative effect of the latter. How necessity, if left by itself without the rule of *nous*, causes disorderly motion becomes vividly clear in the "erratic" behaviour of the infant soul (*planômena*, 43b4), which moves in all directions before intelligence takes over. This situation is not confined to the infant; it can easily pervade adult life, especially if the right education is absent (44b–c). So we can see here that, whereas, in the cosmos, *nous* rules over necessity "for the most part" (48a3), in the case of the mortal being, by contrast, necessity seems to be capable of prevailing over *nous* if one does not master one's passions. But to what extent are we just victims of our physiological constitution?

It is emphatically suggested that it is up to us whether reason rules or not in actual practice, as god is not to blame (*anaitios*) for any wickedness (*kakia*) in individuals (42d, e, cf. *Rep.* X 617e4–5). But *Tim.* 87b might be taken as a challenge to this notion of human responsibility, as we are there told that all the wicked are wicked involuntarily, and that "one must always blame the begetters *more than* the begotten, and the educators *more than* those educated". Yet (as one can see from the words I have italicised) this does not mean that the educated and begotten should not be blamed at all. In fact, the passage goes on to say that one must strive, as far as possible, through one's endeavours and studies, to escape evil and pursue the opposite (ibid.). Thus, even though it may be true that no one does wrong willingly in the sense that one would never do or be evil if one had the proper education and the right psychosomatic balance (86d–e) – hence the importance of trying to secure those conditions in those under our care – one is still responsible for one's actions and one's choices (including the choice of the right sort of practices and education to promote goodness). And this is perfectly consistent with *Tim.* 42e3–4 making it clear that gods govern humans except where they are responsible (cf. *aition*) for their own evils.[21]

In dealing with our physiological constitution, then, we must turn the potential obstacle into an instrument, and here we can be aided by imitating the cosmic *nous*. In this way we shall be, like the latter, primary causes that are "demiurges of fair and good effects" (46e). Indeed, the body, which as we saw could act as a potential source of disorder, is, instead, meant to have for us precisely the role of an instrument or vehicle (*ochêma*) for reason (44d–e, 69c, cf. 41e); this is the place that it has been allotted in a teleological universe. Likewise, the lower parts of the soul, we have seen, are presented as a necessary result arising from the fact that we have a mortal body (42a–b, 69c–d). But even that element of necessity that is capable, as such, of hindering our rational activity if neglected or overindulged, can conversely be used to facilitate it. Take the case of our desire for food, which belongs to the lowest part of our soul. On the one hand, it would be unwise to lead a life that revolves around the satisfaction of that kind of desire: the *Timaeus* describes that situation as "becoming mortal", as if the immortality that pertains to reason were itself a challenge or open task for us rather than a given (90b–c). On the other hand, such a desire is natural (cf. 88b1–2) and fulfils a teleological role. Thus, we should satisfy it not only with the aim of fulfilling a physiological need (70d7–8), but also for the sake of cultivating the appropriate balance between body and soul without which virtue is impossible (87c–d). Similarly, the irascible element of our personality, *thumos*, can and should be used as an ally of reason in securing appropriate self-control in the soul and for the sake of the person's participating in bravery and fighting injustice (70a–d).

Thus, a life of virtue will include giving the passions their appropriate place and allowing them to perform the role for which they are meant in the person as part of a teleological universe. As a consequence, the *Timaeus* does not advocate the elimination or suppression of the lower parts of one's soul, but rather, the proportionate interaction between all parts (90a1–2). Even when, as we have seen, the cosmic soul is entirely rational and so has no irrational faculties,[22] the goal in the individual, by imitation of the latter, is to use his subrational faculties in such a way that he too is free from false judgement and irrationality in the undesirable sense of the word, as conflicting with reason.[23]

Now, the *Timaeus* not only emphasises that the soul as a whole should be proportionate; it should also have a harmonious interaction with the body. In fact, "no proportion or disproportion is more important for health and disease, virtue and vice, than that existing between body and soul themselves" (87d1–3); in this way we are recommended to

cultivate the required balance through gymnastics and general education
(87c–88e). Why should it be so important to cultivate psychosomatic balance for the attainment of virtue? This should come as no surprise if, as
we saw in Chapter 2, *nous* cannot exist independently of material conditions, nor can it exercise its activity without a bodily medium. In this
regard, god is no exception to mind-body interdependence; rather, being
itself alive, it is the best example of the kind of balance that is desirable in
any living being (87c5). That is why, when we read about the friendliness
and harmony that already exists between the cosmic soul and the body
of the universe, we are encouraged to think that this god is presented
as the model of virtue (*aristos*, 92c, cf. 34b–c). Even gymnastics, which
already figured in the *Republic* as part of an individual's upbringing, is
here treated as a case of imitating the spatial movements of the universe
(88d–89a). And so the *Timaeus* ends with praise for the universe as the
"most excellent and most complete ... living being" (92c), having earlier
emphasised its self-sufficiency and immunity to disease (33a, d, 34b). If,
as we shall see, even these latter features form part of the goal for humans
in the *Timaeus*, we can start to understand why the universe is presented
as the highest expression of a happy life.[24]

II. DIVINE AND HUMAN DEMIURGY

1. The Form of Timaeus' Speech Revisited

We might, however, need to comprehend more vividly, perhaps by way
of example, how we can be teleological agents. For to follow role models
involves the possibility of asking oneself: what would the model do in a
particular case? To reply that the universe is a combination of necessity
and *nous* where *nous* triumphs over necessity might still be a little too
abstract, to say the least. The same may be true of any description of the
universe as a happy and virtuous living being. But it is here that mythical
descriptions become usefully illustrative. Let us step back and consider
for a moment the dramatic structure of the *Timaeus*.

Even though Timaeus' presentation is famous for the remarkable absence of dialogical exchange, there is still an audience there when he
delivers it. Critias describes Timaeus as the one among them who most
knows astronomy and the universe (27a), so the latter has to face the
challenge of addressing his discourse to those less versed than him. In
this regard, it may be part of Timaeus' strategy to start by presenting
god in the mythical guise of a Demiurge who brings order from chaos.

It has been suggested that, in general, Plato's mythical description of the gods portrays the divine at the level of *eikasia*, or imagination, which, if we recall, is the lowest section of the line in the *Republic*.[25] The *Critias* confirms that it is always easier to deliver speeches in the form of *mimesis* and *apeikasia* to ignorant audiences, particularly when those speeches concern unfamiliar topics such as god (107a–b).

In trying to relate his account to the line allegory of book VI of the *Republic*, it has also been argued that Timaeus' treatment of astronomy and related mathematical sciences better fits the level of *dianoia*, or scientific discourse, in the line.[26] It may well turn out that, as we ascend in our education, we move, as in the line allegory, away from mere images towards more rigorous understanding, presumably once we get formally trained in astronomy. This study may thus reveal to us the real nature of god, but the latter may be impossible to communicate to the uneducated masses, and is anyway difficult to find (28c). In this context, appeal to the image of the Demiurge, *qua* image, may have a place in Timaeus' discourse and in our epistemological access to this complex issue. We are bound to discover, at the end of that journey, that the images employed in the course of our first approximation to the topic were inaccurate; and the *Critias* asks for indulgence in a similar respect (107d–108a; cf. *Tim.* 29c). But to grant that they are inaccurate is very different from claiming that there is no likeness whatsoever between them and the original.[27] As already noted, even after one strips away the Demiurge's mythical clothing, it remains true, for example, that god is essentially rational and good.

Myths have, in addition, the power to elicit one's emotional responses.[28] If it is a matter of inspiring us to pursue virtue, it may be irrelevant, at least in the beginning stages, whether the story we read or are told literally corresponds to the facts or not. In principle, one may be moved and transformed just as much (if not more) by reading *King Lear* as by reading a forensic report. In this regard, Plato may be situated within a historical tradition (starting from Homer) where story telling plays a fundamental role in shaping our conception of the virtues.[29] In this context, the mythical image of a Demiurge serves us well, as does the story presented by the *Timaeus'* immediate successor, the *Critias*. To this I shall now turn.

2. Luck and Virtue

The Demiurge, we have seen, is not omnipotent; yet his core task consists, as a *nous*, in persuading necessity, or the recalcitrant nature of his materials, and turning it into a cooperator for his purposes. We also saw how necessity, in abstraction from *nous*, is equivalent to chance (*tuchê*): thus, necessary causes are those that, without *nous*, produce their effects in a random (*tuchon*) and disorderly manner (46e). For example, the builder of a dam may know how to orient the water to produce beneficial results; left to itself, however, the same water may cause a flood and other natural disturbances.

Now, there is certainly an ambiguity of scope in the word *tuchê*, which should not escape us. For *tuchê* can not only mean "chance" on a cosmic scale, but also "luck" as it might affect human life. "Luck" connotes the realm of events that one does not cause, but inevitably has to encounter, just as necessity is for the Demiurge a "given" that he has to cope with. As we have seen, necessity can be good or bad depending on whether intelligence succeeds in using it for its purposes or not. Likewise, it is suggested that "chance" events (or events arising by "luck") are not intrinsically good or bad, but can become good if they are used with intelligence to fulfil its goals.

Here again the comparison between human and divine demiurgy becomes appropriate. Take the Demiurge: his creation, the universe, is said to be a combination of necessity and *nous*. Yet we explained that his success consisted in persuading necessity for the most part, even though there is always a residue of chance over which the Demiurge does not have complete control. What can we do about it? This is where human intervention may be quite relevant. So, for example, when we do not understand why certain things happen that we do not apparently cause, several explanations seem available. One of them is to say that we may, after all, be responsible for them, as is the case with the Atlantis empire, which fell not just as a mere historical and geographical contingency but also due to the "bad luck" that its citizens' *hubris* attracted. Another (nonexclusive) avenue is to say that we are here faced with that residue of imperfection in the universe for which neither we nor god are directly responsible; but maybe it is with regard to that residue that our intervention becomes most important, to the point that our own happiness and virtue may well be described as the art of dealing with luck successfully. I shall explore each avenue in turn.

At *Critias* 120e ff. we are told of a phase in the history of Atlantis when its rulers ranked virtue above everything else, and also prospered in external goods, with the recognition that "these things grow thanks to friendship and common virtue". This is described as a situation in which the "divine nature" prevailed in them. By contrast, when this divine nature was corrupted, they were no longer able to discern the true life as far as happiness is concerned. Thus, being full of *hubris* and power, they were only *believed* to be supremely fine and happy. It is at that point that Zeus decided to punish them, "so that they would become more orderly and restrained" (121b–c). This is not an arbitrary and exceptional occurrence in the order of events. On the contrary, it can be seen as an example of "cosmic justice". Thus, the Demiurge in the *Timaeus* settles the law that virtue is necessary and sufficient for happiness (42b–d) – so that, if humans turn out to be liable for their own evils (as suggested at 42e3–4) they will accordingly have to face the consequences.

Can humans, however, be counted as responsible for all bad things that happen to them? While Plato may like to say that lack of virtue brings "bad luck" (as in the *Critias* story) it is not immediately obvious that all bad luck is directly the result of vice. Examples abound in history and in our daily experience of the contrary situation, where good people are exposed to defamation, illness, and all kinds of obstacles that might threaten to hinder their flourishing. Similarly, the Demiurge is not responsible for abundant flesh in the head not being able to coexist with acute perception, and thus he is not responsible for the fact that the human race cannot live as long as it would if those two properties had admitted to coexist. It is *anankê*, necessity, that prevents this coexistence (75a7). Yet god still makes the best of the situation, on the assumption that a better quality life is always to be preferred to one that is longer but of lesser quality (75a–c). In so doing, he provides us with an example of what a good choice is in the imperfect world in which we live: that is how our craftsmen decided that "*everyone* should in every way prefer a shorter and better life to a longer and worse one" (75c).

And it is in this latter respect that god is particularly paradigmatic for humans. After all, practical virtue (specifically, justice) is described as "control" over the element of necessity in us (in this case, our passions, 42a–b). That is, human virtue involves dealing with necessity (and its otherwise "random" effects) in the way the cosmic *nous* (which the Demiurge represents) deals with necessity too (48a). As we saw, human *nous* is not excluded from the realm of primary causes, those which, "by using *nous*, are artisans of fair and good effects" (46e). In another passage Plato suggests that happiness (*eudaimonia*) itself consists in having one's reason in good order (90c), which implies that reason will be in its natural position of ruling rather than being ruled and of apprehending truth rather than judging falsely. But if the practical task of reason for humans consists in dealing with "necessity", and necessity includes not only the corporeal and irrational elements of their constitution but also the unpredicted elements of luck (*tuchê*) in their lives, then virtue also comprises the use by humans of their intelligence in dealing with luck.

A good example of the importance of this practical attitude and how god can be of help is in turn provided in the *Politicus* myth, where our current era (the age of Zeus) is described as one that does not enjoy the very best environmental conditions: one in fact where life can present itself as particularly hostile. In this regard, humans might seem resourceless when faced with this element of necessity for which they are not responsible (274b–c). Yet it is here again that gods come to our assistance and teach us how to be resourceful (274c). In the *Timaeus*, this teaching is done directly by the metaphor of the Demiurge, which illustrates how that god applies deliberation and thoughtfulness to the challenges that necessity may impose on his purposive activity. Similarly, when this Demiurge tries to "persuade" necessity and turn it into an ally (48a), we are given an example of the artful way in which we can deal with luck in our lives.

Now, there is another dimension to the relation between virtue and happiness, which the *Critias* illustrates rather vividly. It is a debated issue in Platonic scholarship whether and to what extent Plato endorsed the so-called Sufficiency Thesis, that virtue is sufficient for happiness. The *Timaeus*, as we have seen, does seem to express an endorsement of the thesis, insofar as it guarantees that, *if* a person is virtuous, then he lives well and is happy (42b). Philosophically, this question may seem problematic because of its allegedly absurd consequences. We may remember in particular Aristotle's famous complaint: "those who say that the victim on the rack . . . is happy if he is good, are, whether they mean it or not, talking nonsense".[30] Now, does Plato mean in the *Timaeus* (and the *Critias*) that a person's virtue cannot protect him against the kind of luck that he encounters, as Aristotle's critique seems to presuppose?

From the elements that the text has provided so far it is clear that the answer should be no. First, we have seen that virtue comprises at least partly reason's ability to deal with luck, so that one can turn hostile circumstances, or "bad" luck, into the best possible instrument for our purposes.[31] Second, and even more provocatively, it could be argued (and I think Plato indeed wishes to argue in his late dialogues) that the person who is virtuous will also, *a fortiori*, attract good luck. Such "good luck" is not only the right desert that awaits the just after death in the mythological description (42b). It is also, we are now told, what follows *on earth* from a life of virtue properly cultivated. Thus, in the *Critias*, the original uncorrupted race of Atlantis receives praise insofar as, first, "they applied gentleness with wisdom to the strokes of fortune (*tuchas*, 120e5) that are bound to occur"; by contrast, the perverted race is characterised as unable to deal with their external circumstances. (A similar suggestion is found early on, in the talk of the virtue and simplicity of old Athens and its ideal environmental conditions, 110c–111d.) Second, they did not make mistakes by getting drunk with luxury on account of wealth and failing to rule themselves. Rather, they clearly recognised that external goods of this sort are promoted by common friendship and virtue and that, if one pursues the former as the final end, one will miss both them and virtue. Thus, all these things prospered as they reasoned in this way (120e–121a).

The *Timaeus* in turn provides further examples of how virtue produces "good luck", that is, how virtue will generate outcomes that might otherwise seem beyond our control. Take the case of a disease. We are prone to thinking that this is the kind of thing that might befall even a virtuous person. Yet the *Timaeus* appears to believe that certain practices are sufficient to prevent illness (88b–e, and cf. *Laws* VII 788c ff., 789c–d, 797e–798a, 807d). Indeed, virtue and vice, health and sickness, are treated as closely connected pairs, and Plato is clearly adapting the Homeric ideal of the person who is "good-and-beautiful" in his conception of human excellence or virtue (87c–d, 88c).[32] In the *Timaeus*, as we have seen, "virtue" describes not only a state of the soul, but a state of the whole person including her harmonious interaction with her body (87d). By contrast, asymmetry between body and soul, and the overexercise of one at the expense of the other, causes disease and prevents one from being justly called fair and good (87d–88b). In fact, the proper care of the body that helps to secure the desirable psychosomatic balance is part of what we can count as a "life according to reason" (89d) and therefore as a life of excellence overall. If, as we explained, Plato's views on the mind-body relation in the *Timaeus* stress union and codependence rather than the mere juxtaposition of two independently existing substances, it is no wonder that his ethical system should accordingly view virtue not just as the flourishing of one part of the person (her soul) in isolation from the rest, but of the person as a whole (*holon*, 87d7; cf. *sunamphoteron*, 87e5–6), including her body (87d–88c).

This, then, shows elements in the *Timaeus* and *Critias* pointing to the notion that virtue and good luck go very much hand in hand. The *Laws* (829a), in turn, will carry this thought further, by contending that "perfect virtue" comprises the power to fight injustice in such a way that one does not suffer the kind of unfair defamation and treatment at the hands of others to which Aristotle refers when trying to ridicule the Sufficiency Thesis.[33] In this regard, we shall be perfectly virtuous when we imitate the way god (Zeus, for example, in the *Critias* story, 121b–c, or the Demiurge in the *Timaeus,* 42b–d) succeeds in implementing justice on a cosmic scale. Thus, in the *Critias* god decides to punish those who, filled with excess, were far from living the true life of happiness, and merely appeared to be perfect and happy. This punishment, however, is not brought about through zeal for vindictiveness, but is intended to make them "more orderly and restrained" (121c). Similarly, in the *Laws* the perfectly just person is the one who not only has the virtues for herself, but can and does communicate them to others (730d–e), fighting and vanquishing vice (731b–d). This in turn finds illustration in the Atlantis story, which correlates the excellence of Old Athens with its ability to defeat the *hubris* of the former empire (*Tim.* 23b–c, 24d, 25b–c, cf. *Critias* 112e). These passages only confirm the thoughts of the *Timaeus* cosmological myth about humans being responsible agents and cooperators with god in diminishing the degree to which *ananke,* as brute irrationality (including the irrationality of others), can in various ways manifest itself in the world.

III. THE ETHICAL FUNCTION OF ASTRONOMY

Now, beyond these narrative illustrations, we may still be concerned about how to achieve the order in our soul that is necessary for virtue. It will not be sufficient to be exposed to stories of the sort we have just discussed. Useful though they may be as a first step, they are ultimately cognitively inadequate for a full grasp of the issues at stake.[34] Instead, a more rigorous training seems to be necessary. The *Timaeus* itself is a good example of a mix of fiction and rigorous discourse, and I turn now to this latter side of the account, in particular its recommendation of the study of astronomy. Strange as this recommendation may seem, we shall see both that and why it carries a great deal of philosophical weight in Plato's theory. After all, reason is a capacity that human beings should fulfil for the sake of attaining happiness (*eudaimonia*), so we need to investigate in more detail how in the *Timaeus* Plato thinks they can manage to do so. Do we still need a political context such as that found in the *Republic,* and the guidance of a gifted ruler with access to the Forms to give us norms of action? I believe not. Plato's alternative answer, I contend, will consist in postulating the cosmic god as a model by studying which humans can attain happiness. In addition, I shall explain how this constitutes a step forward with regard to the views on *eudaimonia* expressed in the middle dialogues insofar as happiness becomes available to the many (and not just to a minority of people) in a more autonomous way.

I shall tackle the issue by addressing three questions:

1. If it is now god who is the model for the human being, what has happened to the Forms? Remember that, in the *Republic*, the Forms were the ultimate model to be apprehended in order to lay the foundation of a virtuous community and even a virtuous personality. Does Plato still believe in this dialogue that human beings can have access to the Forms, or is it now only god who can do so?

2. If, as I shall argue, Forms are still accessible to a privileged minority of people, how can this access be achieved?

3. What avenue is left for persons other than philosophers in order to be happy?

I wish to argue that it is basically astronomy, or the intellectual study of the movements of the cosmic god, that provides an answer to both 2. and 3. And I shall further explain why Plato should place so much importance, from an ethical perspective, on our imitating the movements of the cosmic god.

1. The Human Soul and Knowledge of the Forms

Certainly, one could start by querying whether humans can have access at all to the Forms in the *Timaeus*. This question would be particularly provoking if one supposes that the *Timaeus* postdates the *Parmenides*, where it is aporetically suggested that, if Forms are indeed separate, they would not have any actual influence on the sensible world at all (133c–134a), nor be knowable by us who are in the sensible world: rather, it would seem that they would only be knowable by god (134b–c). And, as a matter of fact, it has been contended that in the *Timaeus* Plato reduces philosophy to a mere study of the "nature of the universe" (47a7, cf. 41e2),[35] with the implication that he abandons the conception that the ultimate goal of the philosopher is the Forms.

Is this right? The dialogue does stress the relation of the *nous* of god (rather than that of human beings) with the Forms (cf. 29a, 37a–c). Thus, whereas, for example, in the *Republic* dialectic was reserved for would-be philosopher-rulers, in the *Timaeus* we see god performing the functions of a dialectician, as the paradigm of the philosopher on a cosmic stage. So, at 39e, we find god distinguishing the different species comprised in the Form of Living Being (*ho esti zôion*), and providing an example

of the proper method of division or *diairesis* in that those divisions are
performed not arbitrarily, but according to nature: in this way, living beings are not divided between humans and animals, but between aquatic,
terrestrial, aerial, and heavenly kinds (*Tim.* 39e–40a), a point that Plato
will independently emphasise in the *Politicus* (262a ff.).

Does all this, however, mean that god is the *only* possible dialectician or
knower of the Forms in the *Timaeus*? A close reading of the text indicates
not. For at *Tim.* 51e it is asserted that "of true opinion (*doxa alêthês*) one
must say that all men partake, whereas of *nous* only gods and a small class
of people". This claim is made in a context where *nous* appears precisely
as the cognitive correlate of the Forms whose existence the whole passage
in question (51b7–52a4, cf. esp. 51d3–5) argues for. So we can see that,
even though it is now god preeminently who is put in relation to the
Forms, Plato still allows that possibility for a small minority of human
beings, who would naturally be the philosophers.

2. Astronomy and Contemplative Fulfilment

Now, as this very passage at 51e seems to suggest, knowledge of the Forms
is very hard to achieve for humans. And so we find, in the *Timaeus*, an
attempt by Plato to bridge the gap between us and the Forms (which
is in a sense an example of the more general gap between Forms and
sensibles). The key concept, in this respect, is the cosmic soul. We have
seen that, from a metaphysical perspective, and because of its ontological
constitution, it serves to mediate between the indivisible and the divisible,
that is, Forms and sensibles (cf. 35a1–b1): insofar as the cosmic soul
partakes of the indivisible, it knows the Forms; insofar as it partakes of
the "divisible which becomes in the case of bodies" (35a2–3), it moves
in an efficient fashion using the whole cosmic body as a vehicle, and
thus imparts the order that it contemplates to the sensible domain. We
have also seen that this cosmic soul (or the universe that it animates)
is a god, itself has a mathematical structure (35b ff.) and rules over the
motions of the divine stars and planets. And it is precisely these motions
of the whole universe and the heavenly bodies which, from an ethical
perspective, human beings are encouraged to learn.

As in the *Republic* (VII 528e–530c), this learning of astronomy involves
mainly the exercise of intellectual functions.[36] Vision is, of course, in the
Timaeus a necessary condition of astronomical research, for without it no
inquiry into the heavens is possible (47a). But Timaeus also implies that it
is wrong to suppose that the firmest proof about the heavens is obtained

through the sense of sight (91d6–e1). Rather, he makes it clear that we must participate in the reasonings or calculations (*logismoi*) of the universe (47c). At 90c–d, again, we are encouraged to follow and learn the "*reasonings and revolutions* of the All" (*hai tou pantos dianoêseis kai periphorai*, 90c8–d1), that is, not just the physical visible motions of the corporeal universe but the intellections in which the motions of its soul consist. And this is done by *thinking*, which is assimilated to the object of thought (cf. *tôi katanooumenôi to katanooun exomoiôsai*, 90d4). Such learning of astronomy is based on the apprehension of mathematical relationships[37] (such as those governing the relative distances between the heavenly bodies, cf. 35b ff., 36d2–3),[38] and will constitute in the *Timaeus* again, as in the *Republic*, the possibility of an intermediate step towards the knowledge of Forms. So, at 47a4–b2, we read that the observation of days, months and years has given us the notion of number and time, and the possibility of researching the nature of the universe, from which we have derived philosophy, the greatest good that has been gifted to mortals by the gods.

At 90b–c, in turn, we are told that "whoever has devoted himself to love of knowledge and true thoughts... must of all necessity think (*phronein*) things immortal and divine, if he be in contact with truth (*alêtheias ephaptêtai*)," participate in immortality (as far as is possible for human nature) and be happy. What, in this passage, are those "things immortal and divine" (*athanata kai theia*) that one must think? On the one hand, "*athanata kai theia*" is an expression that Plato uses in previous dialogues for the Forms (*Phaedo* 80b1, 81a5, cf. 79d–80a; *Rep.* X 611e2–3); and "being in contact with truth" at 90c1–2 immediately recalls a similar expression in the *Symposium* (*tou alêthous ephaptomenôi*, 212a5), where the allusion is to a Form. But, on the other hand, the heavenly bodies have been called "divine and everlasting" (*theia kai aidia, Tim.* 40b5), and the universe a god as we have seen. And so "*athanata kai theia*" could also here (at 90b–c) include – as well as the Forms – the "harmonies and revolutions of the All" which, some lines immediately below (90c–d), we are recommended to learn and intellect, thus "assimilating that which thinks to the object of thought" (90d3–4). The openness of the passage is suggestive, since, by allowing that the human mind can have access to the divine either in the form of the cosmic god, or the Forms, Plato would be allowing that human beings can be happy in either way, and therefore without necessarily being philosophers, but just by studying astronomy. Further, if, as I have argued in the previous chapter, intellect in heaven belongs to the order of the primary or "divine" causes, it becomes

clear why, at 68e7–69a2, it is recommended that we should "search for
the divine kind of cause in all things in order to acquire a happy life
(*eudaimonos biou*) as far as our nature permits".

But *why* does astronomy contribute to human happiness? Whereas in
the *Republic* the ethical consequences of the study of astronomy were not
particularly highlighted,[39] they are in the *Timaeus*: We should learn astronomy, or the unperturbed revolutions of intellect in heaven, in order
to correct the wandering revolutions of our thought (47b–c, cf. 39b4–
c1), which underwent perturbations at our birth (43a–e). These perturbations prevail in the infant soul but can also continue in adult life, thus
being the cause of diseases and evil for the soul, though "one must strive,
as much as one can, through nurture and one's practices and studies to
escape evil and choose the opposite" (87b6–8). Only if the revolutions of
our soul are working properly can those revolutions rule (44a–b). And
in the *Timaeus*, as we have seen, Plato makes happiness, or *eudaimonia*, lie
in a life based on the rule of reason: thus, at 90c5–6, the meaning of the
word *eudaimôn* is derived analytically from having one's *daimôn* – that is,
one's reason – in good order.

We can see, then, that the astronomical universe will provide a proximate model for human behaviour. This, in turn, has two kinds of consequences: nonimmediate, for the philosopher; and immediate, for every
kind of person.

For the philosopher, astronomy will serve a most important function in
the attainment of knowledge of the Forms. For studying astronomy makes
our rational soul orderly, that is, it helps it regain its own mathematical
proportion (43d–44c)[40] in accordance with that of the universe (see also
47b–c). And only if the revolutions of our reason are working properly
can we have access to truth at all (44a–b), be it concerned with sensibles
or, particularly for present purposes, with Forms as the object of knowledge (*epistêmê*) and *nous* (37b3–c3). That is why, at 90b–d, the only way
we could know the Forms would be through learning the harmonies and
revolutions of the whole celestial system. If this is so, astronomy would in
the *Timaeus* be an indispensable step towards philosophy proper.[41] The
propaedeutic character of astronomy was certainly indicated in the *Republic* (VII 528e ff.), but now it clearly presents a religious function, the
whole astronomical universe itself being god. We should thus "assimilate
that which thinks to the object of thought" (90d4), and having assimilated it (*homoiôsanta*, d5), achieve the goal of the best life that the gods
put before humans (which will presumably include, for those capable of
intellecting them, knowledge of the Forms).

In this regard, it is noteworthy that, whereas the middle dialogues tended to stress the relation of affinity and similarity between the human being and the Forms,[42] the *Timaeus* stresses the affinity or similarity between the human being and god.[43] This similarity with god, or *homoiôsis theôi*,[44] is specifically conceived in the *Timaeus* in terms of communion with the god of the universe (cf. *tou pantos* 90c8, d3).[45] Microcosmic reason has been made in the *Timaeus* to have the same kind of motion and share the same nature as the macrocosmic one (and to proceed from the same mythical source, 41d) and this entitles the former to be called "of the same name as the immortals" (*athanatois homônumon*, 41c6). It is then by virtue of this kindred nature (cf. *Tim.* 47b8, 90a5, c8 for *sungeneia*) that we can become similar to god (*homoiôsanta*, 90d5), participate in him (*metaschontes*, 47c2), or imitate him (*mimoumenoi*, 47c2) as the model of behaviour that human reason should follow (47c, 90d). But, in turn, the Forms are the model that is imitated by god, not only in his demiurgic presentation (29a, 37c–d, 39e), but also by the universe and the heavenly bodies, whose motions constitute time (39d1) and which would, like time, imitate so far as possible, through their regularity, the ummovable paradigm of eternity (37c–38b; 39d7–e2).[46]

And so god would here have a mediating role in enabling humans to participate in the Forms.[47] In that case, its mediation would be both epistemological (since only by knowing god in its mathematical proportion – and thus becoming orderly – can our reason get to know the Forms) and ethical (as a step towards the happiness of a philosophical life). The macrocosm, in its constant regularity, would provide us with the pattern that we should follow in the first instance in order to become truly just and wise. And whereas a life of justice (42b2) – which, as we shall see, in principle doesn't seem to require dialectical apprehension of the Forms, but does require proper education through astronomy – is already sufficient to guarantee a "happy" life (*bion eudaimona*, 42b4), it appears that the further stage of theoretical communion with the Forms grounds a kind of life suitable for the philosophically inclined, a life which wouldn't be "distinctively happy" (*diapherontôs eudaimona*, 90c5–6) or "the *best* life" (*aristou biou*, 90d6) available to them unless they realise their capacities to the fullest.

In this way, the human ascent towards the Forms would involve several intermediary levels: Whereas human reason is a *daimôn* that connects the terrestrial side of our nature with the celestial gods (cf. 90a), god in turn would be a link between human reason and the Forms in a first level of paradeigmatism, which would facilitate the ascent towards the second level.[48]

3. Astronomy as Popular Therapy

At the same time, the study of astronomy provides immediate results, since an orderly intellect serves to make us act rightly. We have already seen the importance of astronomy in supplying the appropriate education (*paideia*) to straighten the revolutions in our head, which were distorted at our birth,[49] thus preventing our reason from ruling (47b6–c4; 43a–44c, esp. 44b8–c2; cf. 86e1–2, 87b). It is indeed by forming true judgements and having reason rule in our lives that we shall develop the appropriate ways of dealing with "necessity" after the mythological model provided by god. Accordingly, we find the *Timaeus* promising that if a person uses the rational part of his soul to rule over his passions (as education through astronomy would allow) he will be just and happy and free from reincarnation (42b2–5), though it predicts transformation into lower animals for those who haven't studied astronomy properly – either they did it with their senses, or they didn't do it at all (91d–e). In this way, the study of astronomy, which is recommended as one and the same "therapy" (*therapeia*) for everybody (*panti mia*, 90c6; cf. *hekaston dei* at 90d1),[50] would seem an indispensable means of securing a kind of happiness for any individual.

If this is so, then Plato's views in the *Timaeus* would seem to contrast with those expressed in his middle dialogues, and present a distinctive and arguably new tendency in his late thought. Let us remember that, in the *Phaedo*, happiness – and liberation – properly speaking belonged to the philosopher (cf. 80e–81a), and did not seem available to the ordinary person. Certainly, the *Republic* can be seen already as an attempt to extend happiness to the whole of society, given Socrates' emphasis that the state founded there pursues the happiness not only of the guardians but also of the rest of the *polis* (IV 420b, 466a). But this happiness seems in the end parasitic on the ideal conditions established by the rule of a philosopher. So, at I 354a the *just* person is said to be happy, and at VII 521a the happy person must have the wealth of a *wise* and virtuous life. Further, at IV 443c–d we learn that justice in the soul lies in each part of the soul doing its own, thus bringing about self-mastery and internal order: a just action will be that which helps to preserve this condition of the soul, and wisdom (*sophia*) the science that supervises (*epistatousan epistêmên*) that action (443e). But, strictly speaking, wisdom based in *epistêmê* does not seem to lie within every ordinary individual, but just in the philosopher. For it is only thanks to the smallest group, which rules, that a *polis* can be said to be "wise as a whole"; and it is the knowledge of the ruler that is the only true wisdom (IV 428e–429a). So, for example, a soldier in the ideal city has right *opinion* about the things that he has been taught to fear (IV 429b–c), but it is only the philosopher who can both justify and impart that right opinion in the light of his particular knowledge (cf. VII 520c). Without the latter no happiness seems in the end guaranteed for either the individual or the *polis* in the *Republic*. And this means that it is only the philosopher who has autonomous grounds for his own happiness, the happiness of the others being reliant on his rule.[51]

By contrast, astronomy in the *Timaeus* seems to provide a means to happiness in principle independent of philosophy, or of any ideal rule that might be exercised by the philosopher. What is emphasised, instead, is that each individual should grasp and understand the nature of order (at least as evinced in the motions of the universe) so as to be his own self-ruler as far as orderly and just behaviour is concerned; and this is an important move from heteronomy to autonomy. Of course we still need in the *Timaeus* a good kind of education, but the novelty is that this could exist within a bad form of government as a way of counteracting it. Thus, at *Tim.* 87b we are told that we become evil when "the forms of government are bad and bad discourse is made in the cities privately and publicly, and *when, furthermore (eti), no lessons (mathêmata) that could be curative of those* [i.e. those bad forms of government and discourse] *are learned from childhood*."[52]

If this is so, then Plato's views in the *Timaeus* would come closer to those expressed in other late dialogues, such as the *Philebus* and the *Laws*. In the *Philebus*, Plato is concerned with a mixed life of knowledge (*epistêmê*) and pleasure that would make *every* human being happy (cf. *anthrôpois pasi*, 11d5), and which is said to include self-knowledge and proper understanding of the nature of things (63b–c). The *epistêmê* at stake here embraces not only the precise knowledge of the Forms – a sense however that it keeps (as the "truer", 61d10–e4)[53] – but is given also a broad sense (cf. 59b7, 61d10–e3),[54] which allows everybody to participate in it. The same applies in this dialogue to the use of the terms "intellect" (*nous*) and "wisdom" (*phronêsis*).[55] In like manner we can find some uses in the *Timaeus* of the term *philosophia*, in a wide sense that covers fields other than the Forms: so for example, at 88c, "all philosophy" (*pasa philosophia*) and general culture[56] are advised to be exercised as a counterpart to gymnastics in order for *anyone* to deserve being called "fair and good" (*kalos kai agathos*).

The *Laws*, for its part, stresses the importance of people understanding the grounds for their moral behaviour, including the grounds on which atheism should be condemned and a belief in the cosmic god endorsed (cf e.g. VII 821c–e, X 890b ff.). Thus, unlike the *Republic* (where mathematical studies appear as indispensable only in the curriculum of those who are candidates to be guardians of the state, VII 521b ff.), the *Laws* makes explicit the need for every citizen to study astronomy (and mathematics in general): Among other benefits,[57] astronomy will reveal to them the marvellous calculations in heaven, which are a manifestation of intelligent design (XII 966e–968a); it will also help them "become divine" (*theios genesthai*) and attain their best state (VII 818c) – presumably by making them exercise the divine element in them, namely reason. Further, the *Laws* distinguishes two kinds of astronomy: a less accurate kind (to be learnt by the majority)[58] and a more accurate one (this would be compulsory only for the guardians of the state, cf. XII 966c ff., esp. 967d4–968a4).[59] Even though the *Timaeus* does not distinguish between these two kinds of astronomy, it at least highlights its importance for general education in a way that anticipates the more detailed treatment of the *Laws*.[60]

4. Astronomy and Consistency

Now, what can the modern reader make of Plato's emphasis on one's following the movements of the universe? Julia Annas points out the strangeness of the suggestion, and briefly puts forward a view of it as an invitation to reason "which takes people beyond their particular and personal viewpoints and gets them to think from the point of view of the universe".[61] But we still need to understand what is so special about adopting the point of view of the universe that studying astronomy should transform our lives, and even have a therapeutic function. I submit that the answer to this question is closer to home for a student of Platonic ethics than it might seem at first blush, and it rests again on the paradigmatic role that Plato means to allot to the astronomical universe.

From his very earliest dialogues, Plato presents a concern with rational consistency, understood not only as consistency among one's beliefs, but also as consistency between what one thinks or says and what one does. Thus, for example, in the *Laches* Socrates is praised as a man who "harmonises words and deeds" (188d). In the *Gorgias* he expresses his concern to Polus about having one's life set right "both in deeds and in words" (461c), and concludes by remarking to Callicles how shameful it is for people to engage in public business "who never think the same things about the same things" (527d). Internal consistency among the beliefs of all the parts of the soul is in turn pivotal in the *Republic*, and results in actions that accord with it (IV 442c–d, 443c–444a).

If this is so, then it is no oddity that the main reason why the universe should be held up as a proximate model for everyone is precisely because it embodies the ideal of logical and performative consistency. The stars, as we have seen, are described as "thinking always the same things about the same things" (*Tim.* 40a8–b1); accordingly, they follow always the same regular path. The astronomical universe is a perfect example of what it is to be a rational being whose behaviour conforms to its thoughts, and can thus be, so to speak, predicted. The universe is never subject to akratic behaviour; never 'errs' or 'wanders' in the way an irrational being does. The movements of the universe are focused in the way we would expect the sage to be in conducting his life: thus, if the sage believes that promoting justice is the right thing to do, he will never divert from that path in his actions. Rather, we can count on the sage always doing what reason dictates. So in the *Republic* Plato complains of the erratic behaviour of tyrannical souls who are unlucky enough to be in charge of a state.[62] When Plato is adamant in affirming, then, that the planets do not "err", it is not just an astronomical but an ethical point that is at stake. For god is now a model for human behaviour, and it is in our thoughts and deeds that we should imitate the consistency of the universe.

To focus the mind on the study of astronomy, then, is to divert it away from the scattering stimuli that bombard one whose life is excessively devoted to the deliverances of the senses. By studying astronomy, the soul gains acquaintance with order, even becoming similar to what it studies,[63] if the soul is driven to that study by the love of it (*Tim.* 90b6) or desire for it (88b1–2) and like is friend with like,[64] in a way that will inspire one's own actions and help one move with structure and purpose in the phenomenal world. Seen in this light, gaining order is in fact regaining it, as assimilation with the object of thought occurs according to the "original nature" of the soul (90d5), which Plato believes to be as uncorrupted as that of the universe. Studying astronomy would then be a means for the soul to rediscover itself as a harmonious entity and supersede the deformations and inconsistencies that it has acquired through exposure to confusing external stimuli from birth: hence the "therapeutic" function of this kind of process. Plato's insistence on our studying the astronomical universe becomes intelligible when we realise that it is not so much the object as such, but the features of the object (its harmonious structure) that merit our love. In this regard, then, to adopt (in Annas's phrase) the perspective of the universe is nothing more mysterious than to adopt the perspective of rational consistency, both in word and in deed, that Plato has been emphasising from the start of his career.

IV. CONCLUSION

In sum, we can find in the *Timaeus* a Plato who, on the one hand, retains the belief of the middle dialogues that the Forms are the highest goal of the philosopher,[65] though, on the other hand, he is now more worried, first, about bridging the gap between us and the Forms and, second, about offering some internal guarantee of right behaviour and therefore happiness for every kind of person (even independently of political support). And in both respects the study of astronomy – that is, the intellection of the cosmic god – proves to serve a most important ethical function. God can either be the only model for human behaviour, or a step towards higher goals. And in the latter sense we have seen how god turns out to be a mediator not only at a metaphysical level, by connecting the sensible realm in general with the Forms, but also at an epistemological and ethical level for human beings. Further, even though god appears mythically as a personal Demiurge (which helps to make vivid the way human themselves can deal with necessity or luck), we have seen how that mediation is in the cosmos actually fulfilled by the world-soul and the heavenly bodies, for whose status as gods the text supplies plentiful evidence. And *this* is, in the end, the kind of god that can be seen, learned and argued for, and hence the one that deserves a place in Plato's structure of reality.[66]

4

Creating Mixtures in the *Philebus*

The *Philebus* is known as a dialogue on pleasure. Its central issue is "the good", or happiness, for humans, and where it is to be found. Is it in pleasure, knowledge, or a mixture of both? At the outset of the dialogue, Philebus and Protarchus are presented as two supporters of hedonism, advocating the first view. Socrates appears, at least initially, defending the second one, even though they agree that if a life is found that is superior to both, that candidate wins (11d–12a). The question will then concern the status of a mixed life of pleasure and knowledge with respect to happiness, and what the role of those components is within it.

Now, if this is so, and if the purpose of the dialogue is fundamentally ethical, it might seem *prima facie* surprising that so much of it is spent on taxonomy, or dialectical classifications of kinds of pleasure and knowledge. In particular, it might seem disturbing that the interlocutors should devote a whole section (14–31) to dealing with a pair of notions that stand out as especially obscure in Plato's writing. These are those of limit (*to peras*) and the unlimited or indefinite (*to apeiron*),[1] whose interpretation has raised unending controversy. As we shall see, they are introduced not as mere technicalities, but with the hope of shedding light on difficult logical (or dialectical) and metaphysical issues. But why should dialectic and metaphysics matter to a hedonist? As the dialogue progresses, it becomes evident that whatever stand one takes on ethics presupposes or implies some specific metaphysical (and even cosmological) commitments. Let us begin by looking briefly at some dramatic aspects of the dialogue, as this may help us see how its various topics are interrelated.

Philebus is the recalcitrant hedonist. He is so recalcitrant that he is not even willing to pursue philosophical discussion, and instead dogmatically asserts: "it seems to me and it will continue to seem to me that pleasure wins, at all costs (*pantôs*)" (12a7). Protarchus' position is more moderate: he will in fact become the main spokesman for hedonism after Philebus' early withdrawal from the dialogue. Neither of these two hedonists seems aware of the full implications of the positions they defend, and so the rest of the dialogue can be seen as an elenctic attempt by Socrates to make the positions initially submitted by them self-consistent.[2]

The hedonists fluctuate between two views. First, they would like to understand the good as *momentary feelings* of utmost enjoyment (cf. 27e7–9, 55b1–c1). Second, they also agree with Socrates that they are concerned about the happy *life*, which would possess such a feature *stably* (11d4–6, e2). As part of this hesitation, hedonism is presented as flirting with two incompatible metaphysical pictures. On the one hand, the theory of radical flux: that is, the theory that "all things are always flowing up and down" (43a3), which would imply that there is no stability at all in the universe and thus there would be no point in seeking stability in any human life, if that life is immersed in the sensible universe. In such a universe, it would be the "unlimited" (*apeiron*), as the metaphysical principle that is "never at rest" (24d4), that would reign.

But, on the other hand, the hedonist Protarchus is also made to see the stable presence of a certain structure in all good products of art, and how intelligence is at the basis of them. He is even drawn to agree that it is rational planning and order that underpin the very workings of nature (28c–e, 30a–d). If we can view nature itself as endowed with structure and organic unity, then we are presenting the hedonist with a paradigm to follow when framing his own life. For, if he is to live in harmony with nature, then the goal will be, at least partly, to make one's pleasures share in such an order according to an intelligent plan. But that will mean imposing a "limit", *peras*, on one's unlimited desires, and thus it is the life of virtue and self-control, not the life of unrestraint, that is the key to happiness.

In this context, it will also be of the highest importance to decide which kinds of pleasure and intelligence are good candidates to form part of the happy life. For it may turn out that certain pleasures are after all not worth pursuing, and there is a question about what type or types of knowledge are required for an individual to attain happiness. This concern then justifies both a reflection on dialectic (14c–19b) and the practice of it, which occupies a large portion of the dialogue (23c–65a).

It is my aim in what follows to delve into the dialectic and metaphysics of the *Philebus* as a background for the ethical treatment that is to occupy us later. This will involve unravelling what Plato means by the notions of *peras* and *apeiron* in the various contexts in which they occur. My strategy will consist in showing how the *Philebus* lays the ground for two forms of dialectic that will enable both expert philosophers and nonphilosophers to participate in it; and how it also presents an elevated account of the sensible universe that provides the metaphysical foundation for the ethical discussion that will be the focus of our attention in the next chapter.

I. THE DIALECTICAL PRELUDE AND THE CONTEXT FOR THE COSMOLOGICAL DISCUSSION

We must, first, understand to what extent pleasure and knowledge are each both a plurality and a unity. For it may be a little confusing to call two opposite things (say, the pleasure of the temperate and that of the dissolute) by the one single name of "pleasure", if we do not also understand certain distinctions; without this, in addition, we shall not be able to reach an answer to the question whether pleasure (or only one kind or certain kinds of it) is good. And the same applies to knowledge (cf. 12b–14b). To this effect, Socrates introduces a reflection on the very method of division, which will show how "the many are one and the one is many" (14c8). But, contrary to what Protarchus would expect, the concern is not simply with phenomena that come into being and pass away; rather, Socrates aims to tackle the one-many problem in the realm of "the one which is not among things that are generated and corrupted". Thus, he focuses on claims such as Human is One, Ox is One, or Beautiful or Good is One (15a). Various puzzles (*aporiai*) are posed in connection with these "monads". For example, the question is raised how the same monad can be in many generated things without either having become many and scattered or totally separate from itself (*Phil.* 15b1–8, cf. *Parm.* 131a–e).[3]

As a way of dealing with these questions, Socrates introduces a "method" or "path" (*hodos*, 16b5) of which he is a lover (*erastês*, b6)[4] claiming that through such a path "all the things participating in art (*technê*) ever discovered have become manifest" (16c2–3). It is, we are told later, the method of dialectic (17a), and we must use it hand in hand with the notions of *peras* and *apeiron*, which are here presented as a gift from the gods through a certain Prometheus:[5]

The ancients, who were better than us and lived closer to the gods, passed down this claim, namely that the things that are always said to exist consist of one and many and naturally have in themselves limit and infinitude (*ex henos men kai pollôn ontôn tôn aei legomenôn einai, peras de kai apeirian en hautois sumphuton echontôn*). (16c7–10)

Socrates goes on to recommend the following as the proper method: one should postulate a form for everything, and then seek two, or otherwise three or some other number, until we can see that "the original one is not only one, many and infinite, but also how many it is" (16d). Similarly, one must not apply the character of infinitude to multiplicity until one has seen the intermediate number between the infinite and the one. And it is precisely this attention to the intermediate stages (*ta mesa*) that is the mark of dialectic (17a). By contrast, "eristic" methods of discussion (as those employed by the sophists) overlook those intermediate stages by dealing with the one and many too quickly or too slowly – and so, for example, one may be misled into thinking that pleasure is the good on the basis that one finds some pleasures good.[6]

What is this whole passage about? What are the "ones" or "monads" at stake, and what work is supposed to be done by the notions of *peras* and *apeiron*? In principle, it would seem that, with many scholars,[7] we may reasonably take the passage at 14c–19b to be a reflection on the process of division (*diairesis*, 15a7, cf. *dielôn* 14e1), which still puts the emphasis on the Forms, or those monads that are beyond generation and corruption (14d ff., esp. 15a–b). The point would be to show how each generic monad contains a limited number of kinds mediating between it and the indefinite quantity (*apeiria*) of sensibles into which it appears to be ultimately "dispersed" (cf. 15b). Each initial monad, we can say, would then be limited in itself and in the number of kinds falling under it. In this regard, each Form would contain *peras* (1.) insofar as it is one, that is, specifically determinate and distinct from any other Form, and (2.) insofar as there is a limited number of Forms (to be brought to light by the method of division) mediating between it as genus and the infinite sensible things. In a different sense, it may at the same time be said to contain "indetermination" (*apeiria*), mainly as the capacity to be shared by an infinitude – as indefinite number – of sensibles (cf. *Rep.* V 476a, *Phil.* 15b).[8] In this way, the notions of *peras* and *apeiron* govern the understanding and the practice of the method of division.

There is, however, much debate over whether the monads, or "ones", of this passage are middle-period Forms (I refer to these with capital F). In principle, it would seem that the characterization of dialectic as a *method* (*hodos*, 16b5) is intended to include more than that, as we are told that through it *all the arts* have become manifest or clear (*phanera*): that is, the method is said to be applicable to all disciplines (*hosa technês echomena*, 16c2–3). If the Forms are regarded as the most difficult object of knowledge, and as the subject matter of one specific art, Waterfield may be right that "the passage is best read, then, simply as a recommendation of scientific analysis in general".[9] It is conceivable, for example, that in order to be a medical doctor Socrates is not demanding that a person should have any high-powered knowledge of Forms, although he is demanding that she should be able to have some grasp of phenomena under the aspects of unity and multiplicity that help organise our understanding of reality.[10] And the examples provided by Socrates of the dialectical method confirm this point: a grammarian, for instance, will not need to be a philosopher to know how to divide "sound" articulately and exhaustively into subkinds (vowels, consonants, and semiconsonants) so as to make sure that all the letters are properly classified; but it is in any case clear that doing this will help one deal scientifically with the otherwise intractable phenomenon of the unlimited multitude of instances of sound.[11]

But if the method at stake can be applied to *all* the arts or branches of knowledge,[12] and there is one explicitly concerned with the Forms, then there is no reason to exclude the Forms from this passage.[13] It is interesting to note, in this respect, that dialectic in the *Philebus* is presented in a twofold way, first, as we have seen, as a general *method* of inquiry, and second, later on (at 57e–58c) as an art (*technê*) characterised in terms of a specific object, which one would naturally associate with the Forms. For such an object features as the eternal, true, and identical being (58a2–3, cf. d5), by contrast to things that become (59a–b); likewise, the *Philebus* postulates divine objects of knowledge independently of their sensible counterparts (61e–62a).[14] If by "Forms" we understand a realm of entities that is eternal, stable, divine, apprehensible by the highest form of knowledge and irreducible to the realm of *genesis* (cf. 57e–58a, 59c–d, 61e–62a), it would seem, then, that we can, in principle, talk of Forms in the *Philebus*. (I say "in principle" because the discussion will occupy us at greater length, in the next section.) The concern in this case may well be how such entities interact with the realm of becoming (without falling into the puzzles mentioned at 15b). In this regard, the notions of *peras* and *apeiron* can again prove quite useful, if we apply them now to our understanding of the sensible realm. For, as I shall argue, it is precisely to the extent that sensible things contain "limit" in them that participation in the Forms is realised; but insofar as the limit that they contain is not itself the Forms, the latter need not be scattered, or mixed, in the sensible realm that they ground.

This, however, requires us to move from the dialectical to the cosmological section of the dialogue, and to analyse to what extent the notions of *peras* and *apeiron* retain, respectively, their associations with number on the one hand, and indefinite quantity on the other, that they exhibited in the dialectical passage, despite differences of application.[15]

The shift from the former to the latter is, I think, coherent. Socrates reminds us that it is all related to the initial question about intellect and pleasure and which of them is preferable, and says it is important to determine how many and of what sort (*hoposa kai hopoia*, 19b3) are the kinds of pleasure and wisdom. In this respect, the divisional search proves to be vital and will be extremely useful in the second part of the dialogue (31b ff.). But we can also see, Socrates remarks, that neither a life of mere pleasure nor a life of mere knowledge would be self-sufficient (*hikanon*, 20d4, cf. *autarkeia* 67a7) and therefore the truly good life, desirable and complete for everyone. For nobody would choose a life of intellect, or a life of pleasure, in isolation from each other (20e–21e). In this way *a mixture* of pleasure and *nous* seems to be a better way of living. Now, the question is whether, as Socrates contends, *nous* is still more akin than pleasure to the cause of the goodness of that mixed life (22d). It is precisely in order to clarify this point that he introduces a fourfold classification of everything in the cosmos into *peras*, *apeiron*, the mixture of these and the cause. The purpose of this division is to show that the good life corresponds to the kind of the mixture, unrestrained pleasure to the class of *apeiron*, and intellect to the class of the cause.

Against this background, I turn now to the passage at *Phil.* 23c–31a and its fourfold classification. I shall start by arguing that the passage under discussion is in fact cosmological, by which I mean that it is concerned with the sensible universe as a whole (including both its body and soul) or with entities within it. In that context, I propose to analyse the four genera of the *Philebus* and the place and role of *nous* within the classification. In the course of this treatment, we shall see that Plato is able to present an elevated account of the sensible universe thanks to its possessing an intelligible mathematical structure, and thanks to the postulation of an organising mind that must be viewed as intrinsic to the universe itself. We shall also see how his theory presupposes an isomorphic relation between the human being and the universe, in a way that will prepare us for the ethical discussion in the next chapter.

II. COSMOLOGY AND THE FOURFOLD CLASSIFICATION

At *Phil.* 23c4–5 Socrates suggests dividing "all the things that now exist in the All" (*panta ta nun onta en tôi panti*) "into two, or rather, if you wish, into three [classes]". These are *apeiron*, *peras*, and the mixture of the two, to which he will afterwards add a fourth: the cause. What kind of reality is Socrates classifying in this passage? The meaning of "the All" in his expression might in itself seem unclear, since it could in principle be thought to apply to the whole of reality, including the Forms.[16] However, it is clarified by the context in which the classification is inserted (23c–31a), where "the All" (*to pan*) is consistently used for the sensible universe.[17] If this is so, the "now" (*nun*) in the expression would make good sense, as Socrates would be referring to objects of our actual experience that admit of temporal denominations.[18] Thus, we can take the passage as cosmological, that is, as concerned with the sensible universe or entities within it, and the fourfold classification here introduced as directly relevant for an understanding of the structure of the physical realm.[19]

But, if this is so, then a puzzle seems to arise: Why should Plato in the *Philebus* avail himself of notions that seem altogether different from the ones he used to analyse the sensible world in the *Timaeus*? It might indeed look a little irritating to the reader who has gone through the effort of disentangling the intricacies of the *Timaeus* cosmological theory that the *Philebus* should now drop that conceptual apparatus for a new and seemingly quite different one. This, however, will appear less surprising when we consider that the specific context of the *Philebus* does justify talking in these terms; in particular, *apeiron* is the kind of notion that, by admitting of degrees on a continuum (by contrast with *peras* as definite measure) is especially suitable for a discussion of pleasure and its role both in immoderate and moderate lives. Yet this is very different from saying, as some have argued, that the fourfold classification in the *Philebus* is merely "*ad hoc*".[20] I shall start by focusing on the *Philebus* as a self-contained dialogue, but as we proceed shall draw appropriate comparisons with the *Timaeus* so that the reader will be able to appreciate the continuity and complementarity (rather than the inconsistency that has sometimes been found)[21] between these two approaches.

Establishing a comparison between these dialogues will be useful as long as we also keep in mind their differences: for one thing, whereas the *Timaeus* is framed more mythically and narrates how the universe came into being out of a preexisting chaos, the *Philebus* is more discursive and just analyses the *actual* world of our experience into its constituents (cf. *ta nun onta en tôi panti,* 23c4).[22] But precisely because of its discursive style, the *Philebus* proves an invaluable source for understanding more deeply what Plato's thoughts may have been beyond the mythical way in which they were presented in the *Timaeus.* So, if the comparisons stand once we move beyond mythical imagery, we have a further good reason for taking his cosmological suggestions seriously. Let us then pass on to analyse the four kinds and what explanatory role, if any, they fulfil in the cosmology.[23] On each occasion, I shall start by laying out the textual evidence, and on that basis build a case for a view according to which Plato furnishes the sensible universe with intrinsic value in a manner that is still consistent with the postulation of transcendent Forms.

1. *Apeiron* and the Imperfection of Sensibles

We are told that a distinctive mark of the nature of the unlimited or indeterminate (*apeiron*) is to admit of more or less (25c10–11); "indeter-minate" are things that "appear" to become more and less (24e7–8). It includes contraries such as hot-cold, violent-gentle, quick-slow, dry-wet, great-small, acute-grave, pleasure-pain (cf. 24e–25a, 25c–d, 26a, 27e), since we can conceive indefinitely of "colder" or "hotter" and so on. Things falling under this genus therefore possess the property of not having a beginning, middle, or end (31a). They are "incomplete" or "imperfect" (*atelê,* 24b8) – that is, they lack a precise quantity, *poson* (cf. 24c–d). We read further that unlimiteds such as hot and cold "are always progressing and never at rest" (*prochôrei kai ou menei . . . aei* 24d4), which in turn suggests lack of fixity and discrete quantity. We could then say that *apeiron* is related to a *continuum* that extends indefinitely in either direction (e.g. temperature), and each opposite in a given pair refers to a direction in the continuum (e.g. hot-cold).[24] So we can take *apeiron* in this context to mean quantitative indeterminacy, or indeterminacy in degree, which is to be found on a scale of opposite qualities.

If this is so, then the difference in application of *apeiron* in this context from its occurrence in the dialectical context with regard to the sen-sible domain becomes clearer. In the dialectical context, we have seen *apeiron* applied to a discrete series of sensibles, the number of which is indeterminate; whereas here *apeiron* means whatever admits of more and less on a continuum. Each of the infinite possible degrees in a continuum can, in addition, have an indefinite number of discrete instances. Nei-ther of these features implies the other. For example, there could be only three hot things in the universe and still temperature would be *apeiron* as a continuum. Conversely, there could be an indefinite number of oxen in the universe without the property of being an ox admitting an infinite number of degrees. This does not preclude that one thing can be *apeiron* in both senses, for example pleasure, which is *apeiron* "both in quantity and in degree" (*kai plêthei kai tôi mallon*, 27e); and sound (cf. 17b ff., 26a).

What use is this notion from a cosmological perspective? We have seen that Socrates characterises *apeiron* as incomplete or imperfect (*atelê*), so, conceivably, *apeiron* can be seen to relate to the imperfection of the sensible universe. It has been argued that compresence of opposites is one main source of the imperfection of sensibles in Plato's middle dialogues.[25] If we pursue such a line of argument, we find the *Philebus* developing distinct conceptual resources to account for that imperfection. For here *apeiron* appears as a metaphysical element of the universe allowing not only for a thing's tendency to exhibit opposite properties, but also for the tendency of the sensible realm, if left to itself, to resist intelligibility. The examples of *apeiron* in the *Philebus* are mainly things that appear (cf. *phainêtai*, 24e7) through our sense perception or *aisthêsis* (hot-cold, wet-dry, violent-gentle, etc). Thus, *apeiron* has to do with phenomena, and seems to provide the material that stimulates our senses, but also puzzles them and so requires intellect for our understanding of the sensible world (cf. *Rep.* VII 523b ff.). We already find in Philolaus that all things would be unknowable if they didn't have number (44B4 DK). Similarly, at *Philebus* 55e we read that if arithmetic, measurement, and the like were removed from all arts, we would be left with something poor, namely guesswork and the use of perceptions by experience and habit (cf. also *Gorg.* 503d–e for nontechnical practices proceeding at random). This procedure is full of unclarity and instability. For, if stability relies on certain ratios or proportions, any approach to the world that does not take account of them is bound to throw us into confusion and perplexity. Thus, instability in an ontological sense, pertaining primarily to *apeiron*, conveys unintelligibility in an epistemological one. However, the *Philebus* also suggests that the sensible world can and indeed does participate in some stability and intelligibility thanks to limit (*peras*), as we shall see in the next section.

Now, the question about the imperfection of the sensible universe also cropped up when we discussed the *Timaeus*. To account for it, we saw Timaeus resort to another notion, that of necessity (*anankê*). We said that *anankê* is that "given" and recalcitrant aspect of the universe that behaves in a disorderly fashion without the guidance of *nous* (as conveyed in the metaphor of the chaotic precosmos, which is described as "not being at rest but moving with disharmony and disorder", 30a4–5). Upon this, the Demiurge of the *Timaeus* works by imposing geometrical determination, thus turning it into an auxiliary cause for his purposes.[26] Despite his adoption of different denominations, it is possible that Plato may be choosing complementary descriptions for similar phenomena. For *apeiron* in the *Philebus* too is described as being in motion and not at rest (24d4), and the conflict of these opposites is made to cease by the introduction of number, which makes them proportionate and harmonious (24c1–d7, 25d11–e2). In the *Timaeus* the "necessary" properties of the precosmic traces (such as hot-cold, rare-dense) seem to be dispersed or divided before the activity of the cause (cf. 52d–53a), which harmonises them in order to achieve "friendliness" and unity in the world-body (32c–33a, 31c). Similarly, in the *Philebus* to *apeiron* is in a state of disconnection and division as long as it is not "bound by limit" (*hupo tou peratos dedemenôn*, 27d9).[27]

2. Peras

Let us now turn to the role of *peras* in the *Philebus* cosmology. This genus is closely related to quantity (*poson*) and measure (*metrion*; cf. 24c–d) and includes all those "things which do not admit of these things [sc. more or less] but everything that admits of the opposites of these things: first the equal and equality, and after the equal the double, and *everything that is number (arithmos) in relation to number or measure (metron) in relation to measure*" (25a6–b2).[28] (For example, equality is the relation 1:1; the double is the relation 2:1, etc.). More generally, *peras* is "whatever stops opposites being different from one another, and by introducing number, makes them proportionate and harmonious (*summetra kai sumphôna*)", 25d11-e2. Limit is that with which measure is imposed (26d9). Law and order (*nomon kai taxin*) would then be examples of "things having limit" (*peras echonta*, 26b).[29] We are told that, in contrast with *apeiron*, "quantity" (conveyed by *peras*) "stands still and has stopped advancing" (*to poson estê kai proion epausato*, 24d5).

As we can see, *peras* is strongly connected with the mathematical proportion that is introduced in the continuum characterised by *apeiron*; in this sense, *peras* can be seen as providing some stability in contrast with the unceasing motion or progression of *apeiron*. Thus, for instance, when proportion is introduced in the pair "hotter-colder" a definite temperature results; when introduced in the pair "higher-lower" it produces the interval of a fifth, and so on. In general terms, we are told that it is through the imposition of *peras* upon *apeiron* that "all fine things in our realm" (*hosa kala panta hêmin*) have come into being, such as the seasons (26b1–2), which points to *peras* as one explanatory factor of the goodness of the cosmos. We do not live in a universe of chaos (as would be the case if *apeiron* prevailed) but one of order, and this order is at least partly due to *peras*. The universe, then, is a mixture of *peras* and *apeiron* where the former prevails over the latter. But how can *peras* perform its explanatory role? In order to elucidate this point, we first need to understand what relation, if any, *peras* bears to the Forms.

2.1. Peras and the Forms. The treatment of *peras* in the fourfold classification has added heat to the debate about whether or not we should take Plato in the *Philebus* still to maintain his commitment to transcendent Forms in the way they are presented in his middle dialogues and in the *Timaeus* (which appears to keep the paradeigmatism of the middle period, cf. 29a, 48e).[30] For some interpreters, *peras* is just another name for the Forms, which would show that Plato means to give the Forms an important role in his cosmology, as he did in the *Timaeus*.[31] For others, *peras* cannot possibly stand for transcendent Forms, and must thus indicate that Plato has abandoned his commitment to them in the *Philebus* or lowered them in status: this is the position standardly endorsed by revisionists.[32] I think that neither of these views is correct, and propose to mediate in the discussion by showing that *peras* cannot stand for transcendent Forms, but that this does not require us to believe that the latter have been abandoned in the *Philebus* nor that they are irrelevant to its cosmology. Why, then, can *peras* not stand for transcendent Forms?

First, in the *Philebus peras* is mixed with the unlimited, whereas the Form in the *Timaeus* "neither receives anything else into itself from anywhere else nor itself goes into anything else anywhere" (52a2–3). At the end of the *Philebus* the Forms are called "utterly unmixed" (*ameiktotata echonta, Phil.* 59c4, cf. *Symp.* 211e1), which seems to indicate that even within the dialogue Plato is willing to maintain a differentiation between *peras* and the Forms.

Secondly, the Forms are ungenerated in the *Timaeus* (cf. 52a1–2) as well as in the *Philebus* (where "the things which always are" – *ta onta aei* – are opposed to things that become or undergo generation – *gignomena* – at 59a7). By contrast, *peras* is said to be created (the verb is *apergazesthai*, 26a, d), and "introduced" in the unlimited;[33] which seems to suggest that *peras* is regarded as something that is brought to the mixture and then becomes part of the mixture. This introduction of *peras* creates *peras* in the mixture, and one could wonder what it is that effects that introduction.

The obvious answer would seem to be the cause, even though Socrates does not mention it explicitly in these passages since here he is discussing the third kind and hasn't yet started considering the fourth.[34]

Likewise in the *Timaeus*, we read that the Demiurge "produces" (cf. *apergazêtai*) the form (in the sense of an inherent property or character, *idea*) of something looking to a model (28a8); and in general Plato recurrently speaks of the Demiurge with the function of creating (*apergazesthai*) the world or its parts (cf. 29a1, 30b6, 37c8-d1, 40a3, etc.). So *peras* in the *Philebus* would be nearer to the immanent form that the Demiurge produces in something than to the model he looks to in the *Timaeus*.

But can one assume *separation* for the Forms in the *Philebus*? Even if Plato keeps "Form talk" along the lines of dialogues that postulate transcendent Forms, one may worry about the apparent silence in the *Philebus* with regard to this issue; contrast here, for example, *Tim.* 39e, which presents the Forms as capable of existing and being apprehended before (i.e. independently of) the existence of their sensible counterparts.[35] And so the treatment of *peras* as immanent or created in the *Philebus* might resuscitate revisionist doubts. However, as has been noted in the literature, at *Phil.* 62a Plato conceives of the possibility of someone knowing the divine Circle without knowing human circles – something that would be impossible if that divine realm were merely immanent or abstractable from sensibles.[36]

Further, even though, unlike the *Timaeus*, the *Philebus* makes no mention of Forms as paradigms for the activity of the demiurgic cause, it could be argued that recourse to some paradigm is required by the postulation of an artisan (cf. *to dêmiourgoun*, 27b1).[37] In this way, the Forms would be relevant to the cosmology of the *Philebus* while at the same time distinct from *peras*. We suggested before that the Forms are alluded to in the dialogue as the stable, unmixed, and immutable being opposed to generated realities (cf. 15a, 58a, 59c, 61d-e). It would then seem that it is the Forms that provide – in their identity and eternity – a parameter of stability or *bebaiotês* (59b-c). Thus, any stability and intelligibility conveyed by *peras* or mathematical proportion (cf. 24d4–5, 25d11–e2), as would be manifest most of all in the case of the universe, could reasonably be thought to be ultimately reliant on the Forms. For the latter are the object of *nous* in its strictest activity (cf. 59c-d) and *peras*, as we shall see, is imposed through the efficient agency of some intelligent cause.

2.2. Peras *and Goodness.* Now, to what extent can *peras* itself lay claim to some causal role, if after all it furnishes an important principle of explanation for the goodness of the mixture? The closing pages of the *Philebus* provide rich material for this discussion. There Socrates wonders again about the cause (*aitia*, 64d4) of the mixed life that makes it good, and now finds the answer in measure and proportion (*metron kai summetron*), which is in turn inseparable from beauty and excellence (64d-e). Plato's concern here is with the cause as it figures among the elements of the mixture (cf. *tí... en têi summeixei... aition*, 64c5–6). So one should suppose that the cause at 64d4, taken as measure and proportion at 64d9, corresponds not to a transcendent Form, but to *peras*, which would now be considered as *formal* cause of the mixture, that is, as the structure that makes it a mixture rather than (in Fowler's words) an "uncompounded jumble" (*akratos sumpephorêmenê*, 64e1).

Whether or not Plato wants to postulate, in addition, a Form of the Good over and above the mixture,[38] it seems clear that the text speaks of the good as *at least immanent* to the mixture. This would be a good (*agathon*) that can be grasped in the threefold aspect of measure, beauty, and truth (*alêtheia*, 65a),[39] as we are told in a context that regards these elements as included in the mixture (64d-e). Along those lines, Socrates makes an allusion to "the best (*to ariston*) *in* humans and gods" at *Phil.* 65b1–2, echoing the antecedent concern with "discovering *in the mixture* what is good, both in humans and in the universe" at 64a1–2.[40]

Now, if in the *Philebus peras* is connected with measure and proportion (25e-26a, 26d9), and these are in turn aspects of the good at 64d-65a, we can see that *peras* has a strong teleological import. In this respect, *nous* as an efficient cause would be responsible for the actual fulfilment of teleology insofar as its imposition of limit upon the unlimited involves giving a good arrangement to the materials upon which it works.[41] More precisely, *peras* would correspond to the *mathematical structure* that is introduced into the indeterminacy of *apeiron*, and creates harmony between otherwise opposing elements, such as hot and cold (25d11-e2). Likewise in the *Timaeus*, the "good" that the Demiurge frames in things (68e) is rendered in terms of the "proportions" (*summetrias*) introduced by god when everything was in disorder (69b), and the universe itself is described as a "mixture".[42] Does this description also apply in the *Philebus*? An analysis of the third kind should help answer the question.

3. The Mixture

Socrates calls the third kind in his fourfold classification "the mixture (*summeixis*) of both" *peras* and *apeiron*, "the offspring of both" or "a

communion" (*koinon*) of both (23d7, 26d8, 30a10). He also alludes to it
as a "mixed and generated reality" (*meiktê kai gegenêmenê ousia*, 27b8–9) or
"a generation that comes into being (*genesis eis ousian*) from the measures
produced with limit" (26d8–9).

3.1. Are All Mixtures Good? Now, we may wonder whether Plato thinks of
the mixture as (1.) *any* combination of the unlimited with mathematical
determination or (2.) as the *right* combination of those two factors (which
would in turn imply that *peras* is not any kind of mathematical ratio but
the right mathematical proportion grounding the goodness and beauty
of something).[43] In principle, Socrates praises the "right combination"
(*orthê koinônia*, 25e) of *peras* and *apeiron* as being brought about by the
causality of *nous*, which might be taken to suggest that there are combi-
nations that are not right.[44] However, as we have seen, towards the end of
the *Philebus* measure is treated as one mark of the good, so *peras* must be
intrinsically good as the formal cause of goodness in the mixture (64c–
65a, cf. section 2.2). If this is the case, we have reason to believe that
Socrates may be putting things loosely at 25e and that a mixture strictly
speaking is a *good* mixture, that is, one whose elements are properly combined. This is confirmed at 64d9–e1, where we are told that "any mixture
which does not encounter the nature of measure and proportion must
destroy its ingredients and first of all itself: for it is not a mixture (*krasis*),
but a disjoint misfortune (*akratos sumpephorêmenê*)".

Socrates mentions many examples of this third kind. Health exists by
virtue of the right combination of *peras* and *apeiron* (cf. 25e7–8); music is
created when limit is added to the acute and the grave, the quick and the
slow, which are unlimited (26a2–4); the seasons arise when measure and
proportion are brought about out of the illimitation of cold and warm
(26a-b). And, naturally, we have the example of the good life as a mixed
life of pleasure and order (cf. 26b). But all these examples and many
others (such as beauty, physical strength, etc., 26b5–6) represent particular cases within the more general framework of the universe (*ouranos, to
pan*, cf. 30a9-c7), whose constituents are said to be marvellously beautiful
(29c2–3, 30b7) and which also and primarily exists by virtue of a mixture
of *apeiron* and *peras*. Indeed, the world-body is said to be ensouled (*empsuchon*, 30a6), and all ensouled things (cf. *to empsuchon eidos*), we read at
32a9-b1, arise as a result of *apeiron* and *peras*. Thus, it appears that *apeiron*
and *peras* are properly combined not only in individual things[45] but also
in the cosmos as a whole.[46] And because *peras* is the formal cause of goodness in a mixture, we can see how the universe has goodness from within,

in a way that begins to account for the dialogue's "elevated" view of the sensible world.

3.2. *Being and Becoming.* But where does all this leave the Forms? I have argued for a reading of the *Philebus* that not only does not exclude separate Forms, but also finds some evidence for their presence. However, whatever results we may have reached on this issue seem to encounter a new threat, coming this time from Plato's explicit allusion to the mixture as a "mixed and generated reality" (*meiktê kai gegenêmenê ousia*, 27b8–9) or "a generation that comes into being (*genesis eis ousian*) from the measures produced with limit" (26d8–9). From Owen onwards, revisionists have suggested that these expressions point to the dissolution rather than the maintenance of the middle-period contrast between becoming (*genesis*) and being (*ousia*), if one bears in mind the apparently sharp distinction between those two notions, for example, at *Rep.* VII 534a. And if the *Timaeus* is seen to uphold middle-period metaphysics together with that same contrast (cf. 27d-28a), then the *Philebus* would seem to break away from the *Timaeus* too. In what follows I shall argue for consistency between the *Philebus* and the *Timaeus* on this issue, in a way that will deepen rather than jeopardise our understanding of the "elevated" account of the sensible universe that I contend the *Philebus* provides.

Owen has seen in *Phil.* 26d8 and 27b8–9 a sign of Plato's abandoning the theory of transcendent Forms insofar as these passages "help to supersede the assimilation of *ousia* and *genesis* to a pair of incompatible properties" of the sort found in the *Timaeus.*[47] Likewise, Teloh suggests that, while in the *Timaeus* and the middle dialogues "phenomena are and are not, in contrast with being" (cf. *Rep.* 477c ff.), *Phil.* 26d and 27b "clearly describe, in a distinctly theoretical context, the mixture as simply generated being", which therefore implies that being is now part of becoming and doesn't exhibit any separate ontological status.[48] We should note, however, that Plato is not committed to this conclusion simply from the fact that he combines *genesis* with *ousia* in those expressions alluding to the mixture. Two points are worth highlighting in this context.

In the first place, it has often been pointed out that an examination of Plato's vocabulary throughout the dialogues shows that *ousia* (as well as the infinitive "to be", *einai*) is not always used to allude to the Forms, but can have the wider, nontechnical sense of "reality" or "existence", being therefore applicable to any kind of being,[49] which is still quite consistent with Plato's maintaining in the *Philebus* a metaphysical distinction between Forms as real being, and becoming. Indeed the being-becoming distinction is made explicit at *Phil.* 14c–15a and, despite the *aporiai* posed at 15b, it is restated at the end of the *Philebus* (58e–59a, 61d–e).⁵⁰ But is this all there is to say to justify Plato's combining *genesis* and *ousia* when referring to the mixture in the *Philebus*?

Answering "yes" would fail to do justice to the complexity of Plato's enterprise in his late period. For I would also like to suggest that, without abandoning the metaphysical distinction between being and becoming, Plato is, at least in the *Philebus* and the *Timaeus*, ready to bridge the gap between those opposing categories at a cosmic level, by positing some intermediate reality which partakes of both.⁵¹ In the *Timaeus* this will be the world-soul (or the cosmos *qua* having a soul), which has a constitution intermediate between that of the Forms and that of sensibles (35a); and *genesis* is used to describe both the chaotic becoming out of which the universe is made (cf. 52d3–4) and the sensible and orderly ensouled universe itself (e.g. at 29d7–e1 and 29e4). The former, insofar as it is severely lacking in stability, is in fact directly opposed to changeless *ousia*; and the contrast would still stand for the present cosmos, at least insofar as the latter is always changing in some way or other. However, Plato makes it clear that the actual sensible universe also shares in some stability that is intelligently imposed (such as, in the *Timaeus*, that of the ratios that structure the world-soul and the world-body, cf. 31b-32c, 35b ff.). It is, then, *analogia* or mathematical relations that seems to do the work; and thus, for example, the *Timaeus* explains how the structure of fire is governed by certain ratios between its geometrical components, and so too with the other basic bodies (*Tim.* 53b ff.), despite their constant apparent transformations.

In the same fashion, one can distinguish in the *Philebus* between "mere becoming", strictly speaking corresponding to *apeiron*, and "becoming towards being" (*genesis eis ousian*), which characterises genuine mixtures, and results when *apeiron* is given an adequate teleological orientation through *peras*. That "becoming" in one sense should correspond to *apeiron* can be seen from the fact that things of this class are called "things that become" (*gignomena*) at 24e7–8⁵² and said to progress always and never rest (*prochôrei kai ou menei… aei* 24d4), as if suggesting no stability at all. In a second sense, however, "becoming" alludes to mixtures such as the sensible universe, which exhibits fairly stable mathematical proportions; and in this latter sense the mixture is called a becoming (*gignomenon* or *genesis*) at 26d8, e3, 27a1, b9.⁵³ Thanks to *peras*, the universe becomes susceptible of scientific study, so that it is possible for us to know it with some degree of exactitude by focusing on its mathematical underpinnings (55e ff.). In this way the mixture is an intermediate entity between raw becoming (represented by *apeiron*) and the Forms as ultimate being (in turn instantiated through *peras*); its denomination as a generated reality betrays, therefore, Plato's "elevated" view of becoming and a somewhat broader notion of being.[54] I would like to argue further that "being" in this discussion is not only connected with stability (and therefore with intelligibity) but, inextricably, with goodness. How so?

The being-becoming contrast set up at *Phil.* 53c-54d supports the broader notion of being we have talked about, as the contrast now seems to include one between process and result, where the latter can be seen as a mixture that represents the goal of the process.[55] "Being" is here treated as an axiological notion, that is, as something that "pertains to the category of the good" (54c10); it is "that for the sake of which" (*to hou heneka*) generation takes place (54c9). But if *peras* is the formal cause of any value in mixtures (*axion*, cf. 64d4), we can understand why Plato's articulation of a teleological account for the sensible universe would motivate him to treat it as some kind of "being". Thus, the sensible universe has "being" not only insofar as it is stable in some sense (i.e. in its possession of a mathematical structure that underlies the appearances) and thus intelligible, but also insofar as such a structure and order constitute the basis of its goodness (recall the *Timaeus'* own treatment of goodness in terms of structural unity and mathematical proportion). If this is so, we can also see why not only beauty and proportion (cf. *Tim.* 87c), but also truth (or reality, *alêtheia*)[56] are treated as inseparable aspects of the good at the end of the dialogue.

Now, one may wonder whether the *Philebus* maintains a consistent view of the sensible universe as orderly becoming. For example, at *Phil.* 43a we are presented with the theory that "all things are always flowing up and down" (*aei... hapanta anô te kai katô rhei*). This could be taken as a claim of radical flux – that is, precisely the theory that phenomena change in all respects and in no respect rest. Some scholars, in their attempt to oppose revisionism, have thought that this is the view expressed in this passage, and invoked it as evidence that Plato maintains the traditional contrast between being and becoming.[57] But this is problematic. For in a universe of radical flux there would be no room indeed for any stable mathematical structure, and therefore – it would transpire from our analysis above – no room for teleology.

The worry, however, is dispelled as soon as we put the passage in context. For the claim at 43a is attributed by Socrates *to Protarchus* (who initially appeared as a supporter of hedonism), as if hedonism were committed to an ontological theory of flux. This is an argument, however, from which Socrates wants to escape (43a8), and which he concedes only for the sake of debate, in order to show how even on that premise they must come back to his original suggestion (42d–e, which the theory of flux seemed to threaten) that there is such a state as having absence of pain and joy in the body (43c–e).[58]

If this is so, then we are proposing a middle ground between those who have tried to defend Plato's maintenance of the being-becoming contrast in the *Philebus* at the cost of denying all stability to phenomena, and those who have been inclined to revisionism precisely because Plato seems to allot some stability to the sensible. Whereas a universe of radical flux, or raw becoming, appears to be mainly a hypothetical picture (one which Socrates wishes to shun, much as some hedonists might be endeared to it), a universe of orderly becoming does not in any case exclude the existence of transcendent Forms, but represents rather an intermediary level between raw becoming and pure being. In the latter regard, we have found reason to believe that it is the Forms that constitute the ultimate "being" underpinning the stability of the sensible universe in the *Philebus*, in a way not substantially different from the *Timaeus*.

4. The Cause

From our analysis so far, there is a basis for thinking that the sensible universe has intrinsic value, at least to the extent that the formal cause of its goodness (*peras*) is inherent to it and constitutive of it. This picture will be reinforced if we can show that another factor explanatory of the goodness of the universe, namely *nous* as *efficient* cause, should also be viewed as immanent and not transcendent to it. This is the category of the "cause" referred to in the fourfold classification, which concerns, in principle, both the human intellect and intellect on a cosmic scale.

The distinctive features of this *nous* will be both to produce good mixtures and to govern and preserve them.[59] These functions, when seen on a cosmic scale, might recall the *Timaeus*,[60] except that now the cause is described more impersonally – that is, as "that which makes" (*dêmiourgoun, poioun*, in the neuter)[61] instead of "the maker" (*dêmiourgos, poiêtês*, in the masculine).[62] Further, in the *Philebus* (unlike the *Timaeus*) the "cause" is made responsible only for the generation of individual mixtures within the wider context of the cosmos, with no clear or explicit allusion to the generation of the cosmos as a whole. Rather, the relation of *nous* to the orderly cosmos is presented as one of ruling (and of ruling always, *aei*,

30d8), which might suggest that in this discursive context Plato wishes to emphasise the role of the cause as one of *sustaining* order in the universe, over and above any creational images he may use in the form of myth. Thus, while *peras* can still be the formal cause of goodness in a mixture, *nous* would provide the efficient explanation for the structure of the cosmos. And we are told, as in the *Timaeus*, that this intelligent cause relies on some subservient conditions (*to douleuon*, 27a8–9, cf. *hupêretousai*, *Tim.* 68e4–5) which, we are drawn to infer, must be of a material nature (cf. *Phil.* 54c1–2). If so, we have reason to suspect some kind of mind-body interdependence even on a cosmic level, just as we argued that, despite appearances, the picture of mind, both human and divine, in the *Timaeus* left little room for a robust kind of dualism. Confirmation of this suspicion will occupy us next.

In line with his interest in placing the search for a happy life in the context of a cosmological discussion, Socrates highlights a parallelism between human and cosmic mind, in an argument often referred to as the macro-microcosm analogy. This argument has not been well received.[63] It is, however, possible to make some sense of it once we discern the premises implicit in its structure. In the analogy, Socrates is trying to argue for the existence of a cosmic mind. After prompting a kind of "physico-theological" argument, which purports to infer the existence of an ordering mind from the orderly nature of the universe (*Phil.* 28d–e), Socrates presents this cosmic *nous* in overt parallelism with individual organisms: Thus, as we acknowledge in each of us the existence of a body that is derived from the body of the universe, so too we must suppose that our souls are derived from a universal and superior soul (cf. 29a–30a). And it is by residing in this (cosmic) soul that *nous* always rules the universe (cf. 30c–d).[64] We can reconstruct the analogical argument in the following form:

 a. Fire, water, air, and earth exist both in the universe and in us.
 b. In the universe, each is marvellous in quantity, beauty, and power.
 c. In us, each is feeble, poor, and ignoble.
 d. [The ignoble and lesser of a kind must originate from and be nourished by the noble and greater of that kind, rather than vice versa.]

---

 e. Thus, each of the elements in us originates from, and is nourished by, that of the universe.
 f. A composition of those elements together forms a body.

---

g. Thus, our body originates from, and is nourished by, the body of the universe.

h. [What our body has must be generated from what the body of the universe has.]

i. Our body has a soul.

---

j. Thus, the body of the universe has a soul (from h. and i.).

Certainly, there is a banal way in which the argument will not work. Say, for example, I agree that the water in my pond originates from the water of the universe. Say also that I decide to throw Da Vinci's Mona Lisa in my pond. In that case, my pond can be said to "have" the Mona Lisa (in the same way as I "have" a coin in my pocket), but that does not mean that the water in the universe has that kind of thing, nor that the Mona Lisa in my pond originates from the Mona Lisa in the universe. Socrates cannot surely mean this absurdity. Rather, he must be referring to things (or properties) that a thing has *intrinsically*. Thus, the conclusion at j. does in fact seem to present the soul as no substance separate from the body and contingently associated with it, but as some kind of intrinsic property of the body, or as, indeed, the principle of organisation and unity of a body as a composite (*suntheton*, 29e2) which is "one" (*hen*, 29d) rather than as an aggregate of material elements. Note, in this respect, that at one point in the argument Socrates *identifies* the universe with its body: "it [the universe] would somehow (*pou*) be a body, composed of the same elements" (29e2–3), just as at the end of the *Philebus* the human being is referred to as an "ensouled body" (*empsuchou sômatos*, 64b7). While the *pou* might reflect Socrates' qualms about presenting his views as a plainly – or, as one might call it, "reductive" – materialist position (which he takes great pains to criticise elsewhere),[65] it remains true that this vocabulary would hardly be used by someone who considers the body as a mere adjunct to the soul, as some take Plato's middle dialogues to suggest. Rather, the macro-microcosm analogy would seem to stress the presence of soul in the universe primarily as a principle of its organisation, similar to the soul in us (to which the function of being an *archê* is said to belong at *Phil.* 35d).[66] We can see how all this takes us far from Cartesian dualism, and reinforces the picture presented in the *Phaedrus*, suggesting that it pertains to the essence of soul to animate a body from within (245e).[67]

Now, is a divine demiurgic intellect an exception to mind-body interdependence? When the *Philebus* talks, in a way reminiscent of the *Timaeus*, of a "cause" of the universe that is "demiurgic" (*to dêmiourgoun*,

27b1; cf. *aitia* at 30a10, c5, and *aition* at e1) we are drawn to wonder whether this might not be a *nous* over and above the cosmic soul and separate from it.[68] Let us look, in particular, at 30a9–b7:

For we do not believe . . . that the kind of the cause (which is in all things as a fourth class,[69] supplies soul in our realm and creates physical strength, as well as creating medicine when a body is ill and healing and arranging other things in other things) is called the sum of all wisdom and yet, while these same things [sc. fire, water, earth, and air][70] exist in the whole universe and in its biggest parts, and are, moreover, beautiful and pure, that the cause has not devised in them the nature of the most beautiful and noble things.

What are we to make of "the nature of the most beautiful and noble things" (*tên tôn kallistôn kai timiôtatôn phusin*, b7) that the cause has devised (*memêchanêsthai*) in the four elements? Some scholars have taken this nature to refer to the world-soul, and suggested therefore that the cause is over and above it.[71] It seems, however, problematic to infer that Socrates is positing an intelligence that is soulless and superior to soul and *nous* in the *kosmos*, particularly when he has just stated the dependence of *nous* on soul by declaring that wisdom and *nous* could *never* arise without soul (30c9–10).[72] And the problem could hardly be solved by inferring that there is one ensouled *nous* that is superior to and separate from the intelligence of the cosmos.[73] In either case, why did Socrates establish the analogy between macro and microcosm, and consequently the existence of a cosmic soul – and *nous* – in a context devoted precisely to enlightening the nature of the cause?[74] Any interpretation of the cause as separate from the world will overlook not only the thrust of the macro-microcosm analogy, but also the fact that Socrates previously emphasised that the cause *exists in* (*enon*) all things (30b1) – an expression he had used for the four elements as "existing in" (*enonta*) the composition of the universe at 29a11 – or *in* the universe (*en tôi panti*, 30c4), which tends to suggest the inherence of the cause rather than its ontological separation.

But we should notice that 30a9–b7 does not commit us to any of the undesirable consequences just mentioned. For *tên tôn kallistôn kai timiôtatôn phusin* appears to refer not to the world-soul, in the singular, but to plural entities. Thus, the literal allusion to "the nature of the most beautiful and noble things" must be a reference to the heavenly bodies' souls, whose bodies are those "biggest parts" of the universe mentioned at b5. If this is so, there is no difficulty in thinking that *nous* – as the world-soul, immanent to the universe – is the cause of the soul of the heavenly bodies (which in the *Timaeus* are ruled by and inserted in the circles of the

world-soul).[75] Thus, the *nous* Socrates is presenting as a cause of the mixture of the universe must be the intellect in the world-soul and therefore
the cosmic *nous*. In fact, after asserting that our body has received its
soul from the world-soul (a5–7), he passes on to say that "the kind of the
cause" (*to tês aitias genos*) gives to our bodies soul (a10–b2), so that this
passage should be taken as supporting rather than challenging the view
presented in the macro-microcosm analogy.

And we should not be surprised that Plato thinks of the cause either in
terms of *nous* or in terms of soul. For *nous* tends to be treated as a psychic
faculty (cf. *Phil.* 58d on *nous* as "a faculty in our soul", *tês psuchês hêmôn
dunamis*); and, as we have seen, *nous* cannot arise without soul (30c9–10),
that is, soul is implied in the existence of *nous*.[76] Now, certainly *nous* and
soul do not completely coincide in the case of human beings, who also
have other psychic capacities (cf. e.g. 35a–d). However, they do seem to
coincide in the case of the universe, and that is why Socrates alternates
between saying that the cause is *nous* and implying that it is the cosmic
soul. This identification is reinforced by the fact that the function of
arranging years, seasons and months, which in the *Philebus* corresponds
to the cause (*nous*, 30c5–7), is in the *Timaeus* performed by the circles of
the world-soul (39c). In this way, we find continuity between the *Timaeus*
and the *Philebus* in the suggestion that not only does *nous* depend on
soul, but soul depends on body in some sense, a demiurgic god being
no exception. The universe, then, has organisation *from within*, being
pervaded by rationality in a way that, as we shall see, erects it as a divine
paradigm for the goodness that humans are to achieve in their own lives
as mixtures of intelligence and pleasure.

5. Teleology versus Chance: From Cosmology to Ethics

If the function of this chapter has been both to clarify some metaphysical
issues in the *Philebus* and to pave the ground for the ethical discussion of
the following chapter, I would like to finish by drawing attention to the
contraposition between teleology and chance offered in the cosmological
passage. How does the contrast work on both a cosmic and a human level?

We have seen that, for Plato's "physico-theological" or "cosmological"
arguments, it is crucial to prove that order in the universe can only be
explained by intellect reigning in it as its cause. By contrast, disorder
is to be explained by lack of intelligence and planning, and this cause
is often characterised as chance (*tuchê*, cf. *Phil.* 28d5–9, *Tim.* 46e, *Laws*
889c). Thus, in the *Philebus* (28d–29a) Socrates asks whether we should

say that the universe "is governed by the power of the irrational and random and mere chance" (*tên tou alogou kai eikêi dunamin kai to hopêi etuchen*) or whether, on the contrary, "intellect and some wondrous wisdom order and govern it" (28d5–9). The answer is that the universe is not disorderly and therefore it is *nous* (and not chance) that rules in it. Does *apeiron* have anything to do with chance? If the absence of *nous* in the universe guarantees the absence of *peras*, we are made to imagine that in such a universe, which has here been described as being at the mercy of chance, it would be *apeiron* that reigns.[77] Indeed, this correspondence is supported by the fact that chance at 28d–29a is related to disorder (cf. esp. 28d7 with 29a4, *ataktôs*), which, as we have seen, is in turn a feature of *apeiron*. In this way, the action of the cause can be seen as imposing order upon the chaotic and random indeterminacy of the sensible.

Now, just as in the *Timaeus* necessity (*anankê*) could by itself constitute a hindrance if unchecked by *nous* (though for the most part it was liable to become a cooperative cause through intelligent persuasion)[78] so in the *Philebus apeiron* shows this tendency particularly in the microsphere. While it is still denied that the universe as a whole can be governed by chance, the text does not rule out that some randomness may affect the sensible domain, as perhaps suggested by the assertion that the universe contains *much apeiron* and *sufficient* limit (30c4). Thus, for example, pleasures attendant on the satisfaction of physical needs, which, as we have seen, are in principle unlimited or liable to excess (for example the pleasures of eating) can be made subservient to teleology, insofar as the good life for humans cannot be achieved without the restoration of the balance of an organism that these pleasures accompany. In this way that kind of life must include those inevitable pleasures (cf. *anankaiai*, 62e9).[79] But given that this life is posited as prescriptive for humans (cf. *dei*, 59e2), it becomes obvious that there also exist, in actual human lives, pleasures that exhibit the condition of *apeiron*, not subdued by symmetry. And a life ruled by them will proceed at random, lacking organisation and constantly at the mercy of occurrent desires that cannot guarantee any stable happiness, of the sort that concerns us in this dialogue (11d–e).

An important contrast becomes apparent here, when we observe how at a cosmic level the prevalence of *nous* over chance, necessity or the unlimited is a given fact, worthy of the aspect of the heavens (*Phil.* 28e). For human beings, conversely, this is no given; it is up to us whether we opt for an irrational life of excessive pleasure or else decide to govern it with our *nous* (cf. 45d–e). But how can we understand our own tendencies so that we can control them better? How can we attain stably happy human lives? It is for this kind of ethical problem that the cosmological passage we have been discussing serves to establish the appropriate background, since it is equally important to learn "what is good, both in humans and in the universe" (64a1–2).

III. CONCLUSION

In this chapter I have analysed the cosmic import of the concepts of *peras*, *apeiron*, mixture, and cause in the *Philebus*. *Peras*, or mathematical proportion, has appeared as the immanent formal cause of the orderly arrangement of the cosmos, which renders it intelligible and inherently good. In addition, as an efficient cause of such teleological arrangement, we have seen Plato not only postulate but also argue for a *nous* that should be regarded as immanent to the cosmos and as thus grounding the divinity of the sensible universe itself. An elevated account of the sensible universe has thus emerged from our analysis, one which does not, however, need to do away with the existence of transcendent Forms. In all these ways, we have shown that the *Philebus* offers much more than a merely "*ad hoc*" cosmology, but rather one that should be taken as seriously held in its own right. As we shall see in the next chapter, this does not dismiss, but rather complements, the particular contribution that the cosmological speculations of the dialogue provide in setting the framework for its ethical issues.

5

Happiness in the Universe of the *Philebus*

In the previous chapter we focused on the metaphysics of the *Philebus* and its fourfold classification. In this one, I propose to show how those results can be brought to bear on the ethical discussion, which occupies the bulk of the dialogue, about what seem to be two competing lives: the life of intellect and the life of pleasure. In this regard, the roles of both pleasure and knowledge in a happy life deserve further scrutiny, and each will be treated in a separate section. First, if pleasure is one of the main subjects of the *Philebus*, should we think that it is only by way of compromise that Socrates ends up including it as a component of the happy life? This is a particularly pressing question, given that contemporary interpretations have tended to downplay the role of pleasure in the dialogue (so that Plato, through the mouth of Socrates, is at heart on the side of the intellectualist in the discussion) or even contended that god embodies the ideal of the pleasureless life.[1] In opposition to these readings, I shall argue that in the *Philebus* Plato does mean to allot pleasure an indispensable role even in the best form of life. Accordingly, if god functions as a model for humans, it is not as an entity who experiences no pleasure but as the ideal of the happiest life understood as one that combines pleasure with knowledge. Later, in a second section, I shall offer some reflections on the overall educational programme of the *Philebus* and its relevance for the attainment of happiness. Is it targeted to everyone, or only to a few? We shall see that the *Philebus*, like the *Timaeus*, is preoccupied with extending happiness and education to all humans even outside of an appropriate political context; and we shall also consider what philosophical importance the revival of Socrates as a character in the *Philebus* may have in this regard.

I. PLEASURE, GOD, AND HUMAN LIFE

1. *Peras, Apeiron,* and Maximisation of Pleasure

How does the fourfold classification help us understand the nature of pleasure? In principle, it would seem that Socrates and Protarchus would like to classify it under the category of *apeiron*: pleasure seems inherently unlimited, fluctuating, and prone to excess.[2] But if, as we analysed in our previous chapter, *apeiron* is related to the imperfection of sensibles, one might think that it is only a mark of our imperfect human nature to be exposed to pleasure, much as its inclusion in the happy life may be inevitable. It would thus be no accident that a great deal of the contemporary downgrading of pleasure in the *Philebus* is based on the assumption that pleasure is treated there as a mere *apeiron*, or a mere becoming (*genesis*), lacking all stability. This picture, however, is at best incomplete, and I propose here to revise it.

I undertake to show that a raw state of indetermination (*apeiria*) or becoming (*genesis*) belongs at most to some pleasures, which Socrates identifies as "false" pleasures. By contrast, there is an array of other pleasures (both mixed and pure)[3] that can be seen as intrinsically proportionate and good. The cosmology in this respect provides an important clue, as does our discussion of being and becoming in the previous chapter. For, just as nature is endowed with intrinsic goodness (or "becoming" with "being") thanks to the fact that *peras*, as a good-making property, is a constitutive aspect of it, so will pleasure, if receiving *peras*, be able to be intrinsically good, even when forming part of the phenomenal world. In this regard, making some cosmological analyses available to the ordinary hedonist becomes a crucial part of Socrates' attempt to help him gain some understanding of the very nature of the pleasure that he cherishes; and this seems in line with Socrates' efforts at integrating rather than rejecting hedonistic tactics of argumentation in his description of the happy life. To start delving into these issues we first need to comprehend various ways in which pleasures can be "false".

1.1. False Pleasures and Apeiron. It is part of Socrates' main project to persuade the hedonist that many of the pleasures that he exalts are really not worthwhile and in that regard are "false". His use of the term "false" in this context has aroused great controversy. First, it is unclear that Socrates is using the term consistently and not equivocating.[4] Second, one would tend to think that one's feelings of pleasure and pain are incorrigible, and therefore could not be false. Who is to tell me that I don't feel pain in my finger? However, as has been remarked, much of the discussion of false pleasure in the *Philebus* treats pleasure not as an undiscriminated feeling, but as a propositional attitude, so that when we feel pleasure, we feel pleasure about facts or states of affairs under a certain description, and it is this propositional content that can be false.[5] But, if the object about which one feels pleasure is not incidental to it but constitutive of it, we can better understand how we can have false pleasures.

Thus, when my finger hurts I will feel a false pain if the intensity of the pain is increased by the (false) belief that feeling pain in the finger is the worst thing that could happen to anyone (or that it was inflicted deliberately by someone wanting to hurt me). Similarly, I have a false pain if I anticipate bad things that will never in fact happen; I have a false pleasure when I am relieved from a painful disease and take the resulting condition as the summit of pleasure (in this case, I am deceived about the nature of pleasure, which is not identical to the mere absence of pain). I may also have a false pleasure when I drink thinking that drinking gives me more enjoyment than it really does (as I discover next day with the hangover) and when I am attracted to the intensity of motorcycling, not realising that a lot of the intensity arises from the fear (that is the pain) that is concomitant to it. Given that, in all these cases, my pleasure or pain is associated with a belief that turns out to be false, it could be argued (though I shall not press the point here) that Socrates' theory can after all be understood within the coordinates of propositional truth, in our modern sense.

How can we then summarise these various types of experience? In essence, Plato has Socrates distinguish the following kinds of false pleasures: (1.) false anticipatory pleasures (32b–40e); (2.) false pleasures due to error in respect of their magnitude (41a–42c); and (3.) false pleasures arising from a misconception of the neutral condition (42c–44a). He thereafter discusses mixed pleasures (44a–50e), which some interpreters[6] group as a separate kind of false pleasure (namely, pleasures whose falsity arises from their admixture with pain), even though Plato doesn't explicitly call them false in that context. In one sense, it is eloquent that Plato should not call all mixed pleasures straightforwardly false, since his main criticism will concern only one kind of mixed pleasure, namely the most intense ones;[7] but at least it seems that we can add this one kind – that is, (4.) unrestrained mixed pleasures – to our list of false pleasures. In all cases, we shall see how it is the element of indetermination (*apeiria*) that is at the basis of what Socrates dubs their falsity.

How is *apeiron* related to false pleasures? Let us start with (4.) and (2.). As we have seen, individual organisms are treated, together with the universe, as pertaining to the class of the mixture of *peras* and *apeiron*. Now, by contrast with the universe, the natural harmony of living beings like us can be dissolved and provoke pain, such as thirst (31b–32b). This is the origin of what Plato calls mixed pleasures, those which come with painful lacks. It is indeed this element of lack that marks an important difference between humans and the cosmos, and which makes us prone, in addition, to experiencing an unlimited desire for replenishment. This is how, under one description, mixed pleasures are characterised by their tendency to excess (52c). Thus, intense unrestrained pleasures (45a ff.) constitute a clear example of *apeiron* not subdued by proportion: they belong to the foolish and arrogant, who have failed to understand the meaning of the Delphic call to moderation and self-knowledge (45d–e).

Further, their admixture with pain often causes us to oversize the pleasures derived from the fillings of those lacks, since we fail to subtract, in our calculation, the negative quantity introduced by the accompanying pain. This is how, since "both pleasure and pain admit of the more and the less and belong to the class of the unlimited" (41d), often "the pleasures seem greater and more intense by comparison to pain, and vice versa with regard to pains in comparison with pleasure" (42b). In that way, the element of *apeiron* in mixed pleasures and pains explains not only their tendency to excess, but also their tendency to deceive us about their net hedonic magnitude, by appearing larger or smaller than they are. They are *apeira* insofar as they appear to us not in their absolute magnitude, or insofar as we judge them in relation to an absolute standard, but in relation to pain. It is then up to an appropriate art of measurement or calculation (as the *Protagoras* had suggested, 356a–e, see also *Pol.* 283d–e) to make sure that the incorrect appearance generated by that relative comparison should be removed (*Phil.* 41b–42c).[8] In this regard, Plato emphasises in the *Philebus* that evil (*ponêria*) can affect both the human body and the human soul (45e): not only can our body be assailed by diseases, but also our soul can mistakenly oversize the pleasure obtained from the relief of pain (42b–c).

Now, the element of *apeiron* can also be seen as the basis of (1.) and (3.). For it is common to mistake the real nature of pleasure for the mere relief from pain (42c–44a), and even to experience pleasures based on a mistaken conception of the facts about which one is allegedly experiencing pleasure (41a–42c). Also in these cases, it is the lack of intelligence and the guesswork (55e) that signals the absence of *peras* (inextricably connected with proportion, goodness, and truth, 25a–b, 64a–65a) that results in the predominance of *apeiron*, and this can be seen as the source of falsity, ignorance, and randomness in our lives.[9]

1.2. Pleasure and the Being-Becoming Contrast. But how justified are we in saying that *apeiron* pervades our experience of pleasure as such? In the previous chapter we established a connection between *apeiron* and raw becoming, and suggested that a state of predominance of *apeiron*, while largely hypothetical in the case of the universe, is a possibility that can easily be realised in the case of humans. The treatment of pleasure as a mere becoming (totally opposed to being) seems precisely the leitmotif of *Phil.* 53c–55a. There Socrates expresses gratitude to those who said that "pleasure is always a process of becoming (*genesis*), and there is no real being (*ousia*) of pleasure" (53c), and proceeds to criticise pleasure on the grounds that, whereas being exists itself by itself, becoming exists for the sake of something else (53d–54c). Thus, whereas the former pertains to the category of the good, pleasure, by contrast, "if it really is becoming, we shall be placing it correctly if we place it in a category other than the good" (54d). Does Socrates thereby mean to downplay all pleasure, or does he rather intend to restrict the target of his critique?

While the above characterisation of pleasure as a *genesis* has been taken to be definitory of all pleasure,[10] the hypothetical mode in which it is put should serve as a warning. As I have argued elsewhere,[11] it would seem that it is only intense mixed pleasures that Socrates wants to attack in the light of the above distinction (as generations or becomings in the crudest sense, lacking all stability), if those pleasures are defined in terms of a predominance of *apeiron*, and if predominance of *apeiron* marks all actual or hypothethical states of sheer becoming, with no participation in being or the good. Thus, insofar as *apeiron* is "incomplete" (*atelê*, 24b8, cf. 31a), Socrates points out that it would be ridiculous to attempt to find "completion" (cf. *apoteloumenôn* 54e2) in forms of generation; it is by contrast *peras* that achieves completion or perfection (cf. *teleôtata* 26a4). Yet it is at the same time clear that this is not all Plato has to say about pleasure, since he also allows for "pure", "true", or "good" pleasures.

By contrast with mixed pleasures, "true" pleasures are described as "those concerning what are called fine colours, and shapes, and most pleasures of smell, and those of [hearing] distinct sounds, and all those whose lacks are unperceived and painless, and provide perceived and pleasant fulfilments" (51b3–7, such as the pleasures of knowledge, cf. 52a–b). After expanding on these various kinds of pure pleasure,[12] and separating them from mixed or impure pleasures, Socrates points out:

> intense pleasures have disproportion (*ametria*), whereas the pure ones, on the contrary, have proportion (*emmetria*) ... And those which admit of the big and intense, and often or sometimes become such, we shall put into the class of that indeterminate (*apeirou*) which fluctuates more or less through both body and soul; the latter, by contrast, we shall put into the class of proportionate things (*tas de mê tôn emmetrôn*). (52c3–d1)

This passage explicitly inserts the current discussion of pleasure within the ontological framework of the earlier discussion at 23c ff., where the class of *apeiron* had been distinguished by its lack of limit or completion (24b8), and said to be always "becoming more and less" (24e7–8): it flows and "doesn't rest" (*ou menei*, 24d4), by contrast with the class of limit (*peras*), which, by introducing proportion or measure (*metron*, 25a6–b2), is "at rest" (24d5). And in this passage, again, we are told that it is *intense mixed pleasures* that are by nature unlimited.[13]

Instead, pure pleasures are characterised as those unmixed with pain; and insofar as they have proportion or *emmetria*, they have *peras* and therefore stability (cf. 24d5, 26d9, 25a6–b3, 26b2). Now, *emmetria* or *summetria* is precisely, at the end of the dialogue, one of the aspects in which the good is manifested: "For measure and proportion turn out to be everywhere beauty and excellence" (*metriotês gar kai summetria kallos dêpou kai aretê pantachou sumbainei gignesthai*, 64e6–7; cf. 65a). As opposed to intense mixed pleasures, which are mere "becomings", one can then treat pure pleasures as conveying a state of completion, thus enjoying a stability of internal structure or of object[14] and qualifying as a candidate for some kind of "being" (*ousia*).[15] And because of their stability they can be incorporated in the final mixture of pleasure with intelligence, as providing "secure" or "less risky" grounds (cf. 61d1–5) for the stably good life that even the hedonist is after (11d–e). In that regard, at least these pleasures will be capable of being intrinsically good, if, as Socrates argues, it is being, as the goal of becoming, that pertains "to the category of the good" (54c10).[16] Let us note also that pure pleasures are included in Plato's final ranking of goods (66c4–6).[17] If pure pleasures were considered as mere becomings or *geneseis*, then they could not figure in that list of goods, since – as we saw – "if pleasure really is becoming, then we shall be placing it correctly if we place it in a category other than the good" (54d1–2).

1.3. Pleasure and Goodness. What, then, do the metaphysical passages in the *Philebus* reveal when they are brought to bear on our analysis of pleasure? They help us see how we are now in a better position to counter the common interpretation of the *Philebus* according to which Plato denies that pleasure may be intrinsically good, or undertakes to reject hedonism altogether.[18] Despite Plato's lengthy focus on the nature of false pleasures, we should notice that his critique is not meant to apply to the whole of pleasure but rather to help delineate pleasure in its *true* form. For we have seen that the *Philebus* does allow for at least some pleasures to be regarded as intrinsically good. Now, we should notice further that these include not only, and especially, pure pleasures, but also mixed pleasures under one description. For the latter are not simply instrumentally good (cf. *anankaiai*, 62e) for a life of virtue and the attainment of pure pleasures, but can also become good and even inherently desirable by receiving the limit imposed by intelligence and thus forming part of proportionate mixtures (cf. 63a1–5, e4–64a2), if *peras* is indeed the formal cause of value in a thing (cf. *axia*, 64d4).[19] This means that the moderate person will enjoy mixed pleasures not *qua* mixed with pain, but *qua* having proportion and thereby helping to maximise the overall pleasurable and healthy state of her body and soul.[20]

But, if this is so, we can see that interpreters have not been quite fair to Plato when claiming, for example, that mixed bodily pleasures "are revealingly compared, all of them, to itching and scratching (46a, d)".[21] For one should note that such a comparison was used only in the context of presenting the antihedonistic argument from which Socrates explicitly distances himself (44c–d), and with the aim of illustrating pleasures arising from disease, not from health and virtue (45c–e). In the final mixing of kinds of pleasure and knowledge, as we saw, Socrates' main reason for selecting only certain types of pleasure was to guarantee a stable mixture, that is, one with the least risk (61d1–5). In that context, not only pure pleasures were included, but also "those which accompany health and moderation" and "those following the whole of virtue" (63e4–6). In general, one should welcome mixed pleasures as long as they are "beneficial" (*sumpheron*) and "harmless" (*ablabes*) (63a4). These, far from being in a raw state of *apeiria*, have become good mixtures by the proper introduction of measure.

Further, if ignorance was one main cause of falsity in our pleasures, such as those based on wrong anticipations or oversizings, as much as on incorrect beliefs about the real nature of pleasure, then knowledge and intelligence seem to prevent that defect. It would follow that, in a life ruled by intelligence, it is more likely that one will rightly experience pleasures of anticipation based on the true nature of things, and correctly estimate the net size of pleasure to be obtained from mixtures of pleasure and pain; likewise, one would be less prone to mistaking pleasure for the mere release from pain. This will be particularly so when one has experienced pleasures in their pure state and thus acquired the correct standards (cf. *krisis*, 52e3) to judge pleasurable experiences and even discern how much or how little pleasure there may be in otherwise confusing mixtures.

If this is so, then we have found good reason to view pleasure, insofar as it has *peras*, as at least one aspect of the human good. This is still different from claiming that pleasure is the good, or the only intrinsic good, which would leave the virtues as at most instrumentally good for the attainment of pleasure. Certainly, the virtues do bring about pleasurable consequences, and in this regard Socrates welcomes the pleasures "following" them (cf. *sunakolouthousi*, 63e6). Yet pleasurable consequences are not the only reason for pursuing virtues such as wisdom and moderation, since these are in fact said to share in the good for reasons in principle independent of pleasure, so that they must be honoured on their own ground (64c–66a, 59d1–2). In this respect, Plato may be keeping in the *Philebus* the intuition of the *Republic* that virtue is to be sought both for its own sake and for its consequences (cf. II 357b–358a).[22] In any case, it is clear that pleasure in the *Philebus* is still *one* of the desirable aspects of happiness, and even of virtue. Now, two things, say pure pleasure and pure knowledge, may each be intrinsically good and yet they may individually not suffice to constitute *the* good we are seeking when we talk about the happy human life.[23] This is in turn congenial with the repeated claim in the dialogue that pleasure must be an indispensable ingredient of the happy life, on the grounds that without pleasure even a life of intellect would not be desirable for a human being, nor complete or sufficient (21d–e, 60c–61a).

1.4. Pleasure, Hedonism, and Teleology. On this basis, we can see how, in the *Philebus*, Plato is trying to integrate hedonistic tactics of argumentation into a broader picture of the happy life, rather than reject them, as scholars such as Irwin have contended.[24] Even if one concedes that there are serious philosophical problems with a crude hedonism that is only concerned with seizing the most pleasure available at a given moment (as pointed out e.g. at *Phil.* 55b1–c1, cf. *Gorg.* 497d–499b), one should note that this is *not* (or at least not all there is to) the hedonism with which Socrates is confronted at the beginning of the dialogue, since it is also agreed that hedonists and intellectualists are each going to argue for a specific *state of the soul* (*hexis psuchês*) that can bring about the happy *life* (*ton bion eudaimona*), which would exhibit such a condition *stably* (*bebaiôs*, 11d4–6, e2).[25] If this is part of the hedonist's project, then it becomes easier to understand how Plato's criticism of false pleasures could be designed, at least partly, as a strategy to show the hedonist that, in order to be an optimal hedonist, or even a consistent hedonist, he or she should go for true, and not fake, pleasures, if after all pleasure is the object of their pursuit. But since neither maximisation nor recognition of the true nature of pleasure nor indeed stability can be achieved without intelligence (cf. 59c2–d2, cf. *Prot.* 356c8–e2), then the mixed life is to be accepted even by hedonists themselves (cf. *Phil.* 60d7–e1). This line of interpretation would in turn be confirmed by Socrates' pointing out that pure pleasures differ from intense mixed ones not only in truth and beauty, but also in quantity (cf. *hêdion*, 53b10–c2).[26]

But do not some texts indicate that some mixed pleasures are quantitatively larger than pure ones in the *Philebus*? If so, then Plato would appear to be dissatisfied with a quantitative criterion for the ranking of pleasures, and could not (contrary to what I have been arguing) be seen as trying to persuade the hedonist on his own grounds.[27] After all, such mixed pleasures are called "great" (*mega*) and "large" (*polu*) at 52d7, and even "the most intense" (45a1) and "greatest" pleasures (*megistai tôn hêdonôn*, a4–5). Yet Socrates also provides a clue to understanding in what sense he means "great": When criticising mixed pleasures, he contraposes supposedly small pleasures to those "so called" most extreme and intense (*tas akrotatas kai sphodrotatas legomenas*, 45a1–2), and at 45a7–b10 he points out that in cases of illness people "experience greater want, and have greater pleasures when they are fulfilled" (45b8–9). But it is here clear that "greater" (*meizous*, 45a7) applies only to "gross" pleasures, not to the lesser "net" pleasures that one actually obtains by subtracting the accompanying pain (see also 45e9–10 with 46d7–e3). Ultimately, it will become evident that these supposedly intense pleasures only "*appear* at the same time great and numerous, but are *in reality* all mixed together with pains and cessations of the greatest woes and confusion of body and soul" (51a6–9). It seems then that Plato is suggesting not that mixed pleasures have a bigger portion of genuine pleasure, but rather, that in

many cases the resulting mixture of pleasure and pain makes the pleasure look big precisely because of the admixture with pain. This is thus
perfectly consistent with his calling pure pleasure "pleasanter" (*hêdiôn*)
at 53b10–c2.[28]

If, then, the happy life in the *Philebus* is at least partly one devoted
to achieving the most pleasure, such maximum pleasure will in turn be
brought about by privileging pure, unmixed pleasures in our lives, together with any mixed pleasures (such as eating and drinking) that are
enjoyed insofar as they have a limit or *peras*, that is, insofar as they accompany health and moderation (62e, 63e). The latter two kinds of pleasure
have a share in truth that contrasts with the "false" pleasures enumerated
previously. This is how Plato can assert that "bad people generally rejoice
in false pleasures, and good people in true ones" (40c1–2). By contrast,
lack of understanding can lead humans to mistake the sources of pleasure
and condemn themselves to a life of greed and concomitant frustration
by letting the unlimited and unruly aspect of desire hold sway over them.
Such a life would be one of surrender to the desires of the moment.
It would lack and even hinder the planning and organisation needed
to postpone or resign certain apparently pleasurable situations for the
sake of greater ones. Thus, the "most intense pleasures" are said to be
"hindrances" to knowledge, disturb the soul and provoke forgetfulness,
thereby destroying knowledge (63d3–e3).

If this is so, then we can see how, while the teleological action of the
demiurgic cause at a cosmic level is characterised by design (30b6) and
guarantees the prevalence of order, it is clear that there is room for disorder in the universe at least insofar as it has its source in the unintelligent
souls of humans. But then it turns out to be most important that humans
should become themselves miniature demiurges of goodness in their
lives and, also, most eloquently, of the goodness of the lives of "those to
come" (11c2), if Plato thereby shows himself aware of the far-reaching
"beneficial" effects (cf. *ôphelimôtaton*, 11c1–2) of one's rational choices.
By opting for a life guided by intelligence, humans can thus exert, after
the cosmic cause, some rational planning in their lives, including their
pleasures. We are summoned, in this way, to make of our lives, subject to
the inevitable disruptions and fluctuations coming from the body, a mixture capable of preserving its goodness and escaping degradation and
corruption as far as possible. So, despite the fact that many people would
in ignorance prefer the most intense pleasures, thus choosing a kind of
life based on the instability of *genesis* (which however has the disadvantage that it brings with it decay as well – 54e–55a – and hinders thought,

63d–e), we are, in the *Philebus*, advised to go for stable mixtures in order to attain happiness: It is by discovering "the fairest and most restful mixture" (*kallistên . . . kai astasiastotatên meixin*) of pleasure and mind that we shall learn what is good (63e–64a).

But we have seen that it is *peras* – or, in other words, measure and proportion – which guarantees stability (cf. 24d); a proper mixture is a structured mixture and if it lacks proportion it is destroyed as such (cf. *apollusi*, 64d11). In that regard, moderation, which consists precisely in introducing *peras* into our pleasures, is a virtue to be sought hand in hand with intelligence, which has been presented as the efficient cause of *peras* (45d, 63e). Thus, when emphasising how *nous* is related to stability (59c-d), Socrates remarks that "*nous* and wisdom (*phronêsis*) are the names that we should honour above all". Most importantly, we are explicitly told that we should, *like "demiurges" or "artisans"* (*kathaperei dêmiourgois*) craft (*dêmiourgein*) the right mixture in our lives, combining certain kinds of pleasure with various kinds of knowledge: our good and happiness consist in that (cf. 59d10–e3; cf. 61b–c). With this choice of vocabulary, Socrates seems to be suggesting that we shall thereby be exemplifying the demiurgic action of the cause (called *to dêmiourgoun* at 27b1), which introduces limit to the unlimited. But this is an enterprise we ought to undertake (cf. *dei*, 59e2), by contrast with the *nous* in the universe, whose rule is a fact. And the mixture that is announced in words is only a prelude to the one we should achieve in actual practice.

2. God and the Mixed Life of Pleasure and Intelligence

Now, according to the interpretation I have submitted, a life of pleasure is to be welcomed in conjunction with a life of intelligence in the *Philebus*. This contention might again seem surprising for those, including some leading scholars in the field, who have thought that in the *Philebus* Plato rejects a life of pleasure as part of the ideal life, on the grounds that in this dialogue the life of the gods is a pleasureless one. Thus, D. Frede writes: "pleasure is at best a remedial good" and "the state of pleasureless imperturbability is actually preferable". This claim is in line with that of Gosling: "we get the suggestion that pleasure is only part of the good for *man*, and only because man is an inferior sort of being. It would be better to be a god, and so better to be able to live a perfect life without pleasure."[29] If this were so, we might think that, if god is supposed to be a model for humans, then a life of maximal pleasure is not part of the ideal human life. Alternatively, Plato would be presenting as a model (embodied in god's supposedly pleasureless life) something quite unattainable, enough to make us query the alleged value of the cosmology as a proximate paradigm for humans. Yet neither of these consequences need follow, if, as I contend, Plato is *not* denying that the gods may experience pleasure. I shall now proceed to defend this view.

2.1. God and Pleasure. Is it not the case that the *Philebus* does deny that the gods experience pleasure, and isn't the prevalent interpretation therefore correct? The following exchange between Socrates and Protarchus is illustrative in that respect:

Pro: It is at any rate not likely that the gods feel pleasure or the opposite.
Soc: Indeed it is not. The occurrence of each of them is something quite unbecoming. But we shall examine this question later on if it is relevant for our argument, and we shall make it a consideration in support of intelligence for the second prize, even if we cannot do so for the first prize.
Pro: Most definitely. (33b8–c4)

The apparent challenge introduced by this passage, however, disappears as soon as we situate it in its context, which is a discussion of *mixed* pleasures. For Socrates has just analysed cases such as drinking when thirsty, where pleasure arises from the restoration, and pain from the disruption, of the harmony of a living being (31e–32a); and he is about to consider pleasures and pains of anticipation (33c ff.). In any case, he has still a long way to go before he even reaches the point of analysing the nature of true pleasures (which he does at 51b ff.). Indeed, the whole passage is introduced with an explicit premise: "*if* what was just said is true, and pain consists in dissolutions, and pleasure is a restoration" (32d9–e2), then there might be a third life which is more divine. If this is so, we can then understand why it might be suggested that the gods do not experience pleasure or pain:[30] they do not experience mixed pleasure or pain, where each condition arises out of the preceding one. Furthermore, and interestingly, the denial that the gods feel pleasure-and-pain occurs in the *Philebus* precisely after the cosmological passage and the allusion to Zeus' soul as having a kingly *nous* at 30d1–2. Thus, it is likely that Plato is in the *Philebus*, as elsewhere, trying to redefine the nature of the Olympians and the very nature of god.[31] In that case, his main point will turn out to be that, contrary to the tradition, it is a prerogative of the gods not so much to experience mixed pleasures at their will (with their tendency to excess and to cause deception) but to enjoy pure, unhindered pleasure.

Indeed if, as we have seen, Plato conceives of god as a cosmic god that is essentially intelligent and in contact with the Forms, it is perfectly plausible to imagine that god's mind may share to the highest degree in the pleasures that accompany knowledge. As a matter of fact, the life of "purest possible thought" (55a7–8) belongs to "the most divine of all lives" (33b7), and Socrates points out that "divine kinds of knowledge", concerned with divine objects such as "the divine sphere itself" (62a8, b4) are typically accompanied by a pure pleasure (52b), while *Phil.* 63e3–4 confirms that pure pleasures are "pretty much proper" to knowledge. At the same time, he expresses a concern for the good life as one that would be "chosen by every living being" (22b5; cf. 60c-e), which must certainly include god, who has soul and mind (cf. 29a-30d, esp. 30d1–2).[32] And that the life of intelligence mixed with pleasure is a first best life (and not just a second best given our imperfect human condition) is emphasised by the use of the superlative when referring to the "most lovable life", which is said to include some pleasures, namely the pure ones (61e6–9). These pleasures, as we have seen, are also said to be intrinsically measured or limited (cf. 52c1-d1); and it is even suggested that they are quantitatively bigger (or "pleasanter", 53c1) than any mixed ones. All this indicates that in the *Philebus* gods, of all living beings, can be regarded as enjoying a happiness consisting in the most pleasure allied with knowledge. In that respect, the *Philebus* once more highlights the closeness between gods and humans rather than their ontological separation, and because of this closeness god can function as a proximate model for humans.

2.2. *God as a Paradigm for Humans.* Now, it is clear that, unlike god, humans are not wholly rational, nor do they possess an indestructible body, and thus their psychological and physiological makeup explains their propensity to experience mixed pleasures. Already in the *Timaeus*, pleasure-and-pain, together with the lower parts of one's soul, occur in a body into which things come and from which things go; by contrast, the body of the universe, which is unique and occupies the whole of space, doesn't therefore experience deteriorations or restorations due to an external agent.[33] Even though the *Philebus* does not explicitly mention the tripartition of the soul, both its spirited and appetitive capacities are alluded to insofar as some of their proper feelings, such as fear (*phobos*), anger (*orgê*) (in other dialogues attributed to the former part),[34] and *erôs* (often belonging to the latter)[35] are said to involve a mixture of pleasure and pain (47d–e, 50b–c).[36] Similarly, the pleasures of reason may be mixed insofar as they are accompanied by painful hunger for learning (51e–52a). Yet the text also suggests that it is possible for humans to experience pure pleasures, not only with regard to knowledge, but also in relation to the senses, such as the pleasures obtained from beautiful colours, smells and sounds (51b–52b), with the provision that the pleasures of knowledge are felt "not by the many but by the very few" (52b7–8). In this regard we can see how god would represent in the highest degree a possibility that is in varying degrees (culminating in the pure pleasures of a minority) available for humans.

If this is so, then we have seen many ways in which the setting of a macrocosmic background for human life in the *Philebus* is not accidental. For one thing, presenting proofs about the existence of god is no idle task: for as soon as we are made to realise the existence of design and intelligence in the cosmos, and shown that our souls are of like structure to the universe's, we are provided with a measure that can help us in our search for the best life. Microcosmic order should be a reflection and a part of the macrocosmic one. Understanding how the cosmic cause works, as bringing about order (*kosmousa kai suntattousa*, 30c5) – an order that in turn manifests beauty and goodness – can, accordingly, help us orient our lives towards the good. Further, if god's life is typically accompanied by pure pleasures, we are thereby given a criterion or standard (cf. *krisis*, 52e3) for our choice of pleasures in our search for happiness. In this way we can comprehend why the *Philebus* should treat "humans and gods" conjointly (65b1–2) when trying to establish what is good "both in humans and in the universe" (*en t' anthrôpôi kai tôi panti*, 64a1–2). As we shall now see, this initiation into cosmology to which Socrates subjects even the hedonist is part of a wider ethical project with deep metaphysical foundations.

II. HAPPINESS FOR ALL HUMANS: THE SOCRATIC REVIVAL AND THE *PHILEBUS*' EDUCATIONAL SUGGESTIONS

1. Socrates and the *Philebus*

Gregory Vlastos once put the difference between Socrates in Plato's early dialogues (SE) and Socrates in the middle dialogues (SM) with regard to their practice of philosophy in the following way: SE "has a mission 'to live philosophizing, examining [him]self and others' (*Ap.* 28e), those 'others' being 'anyone of you I happen to meet,...young or old, citizen or alien' (29d–30d). He believes that 'the unexamined life is not worth living by a human being' (*Ap.* 38a)." By contrast, SM's project in the *Republic*, where only "an exceptionally gifted, rigorously trained elite" practice philosophy "after they have completed their qualifying mathematical studies", would appear to SE to "condemn the great majority of its citizens...to a life 'not worth living by a human being'. In the whole history of Western thought no philosophy has been more populist in its outreach than SE's, none more elitist than SM's."[37] Now, assuming that Vlastos's description is accurate, then who is right, the Socrates of the *Apology* or Plato's Socrates in the *Republic?* Intuitively, it would appear that both of them have their share of truth. On the one hand, one could present worked-out reasons for the advantages of people pursuing their lives critically, no matter what their occupation or natural abilities may be; on the other hand, it seems reasonable to demand that philosophy as a profession can and should only be followed by a few.

Now, in addition to these two Socrates, there is also the Socrates of the late dialogue *Philebus*.[38] By contrast with other late dialogues, which often appeal to the authority of an expert as the main speaker (such as Timaeus in the *Timaeus*), it has been pointed out that one reason for Socrates' reappearance in the *Philebus* is the ethical nature of the dialogue, which recalls similar concerns – of Socratic spirit – about the happy life in early and middle-period works. Like the character of the early dialogues, the Socrates of the *Philebus* appears as deeply engaged in a conversation with an interlocutor who may well represent an ordinary man; like the one of the middle dialogues, he makes use of philosophical tools with the aim of arriving at some positive conception of the truth.[39] To this, I would like to add the observation that the Socrates of the *Philebus* represents a superseding of the early and middle Socrates with regard to the opposition between a populist and an elitist conception of happiness outlined in the previous paragraph. His new approach synthesises the possible merits of both outlooks.

I shall argue that the Socrates of the *Philebus* makes claims characteristic of the early Socrates while still maintaining some of the claims (though rejecting others) of Socrates in the *Republic*. In this regard, the *Philebus* can be seen as suggesting again (as in the *Timaeus*) a notion of happiness that will accommodate both expert philosophers and the many. At the same time, we shall see that the *Philebus* (together with the *Timaeus*, and unlike the *Republic*) offers a view of human happiness that is in principle independent of any political context, and analyse why this is so.

Certainly, the *Republic* could be seen as a qualified departure from the Socratic dialogues to the extent to which not everyone is encouraged to be philosophical about their lives. Justifiably so, it might be thought, if in the *Republic* "true philosophy" (VII 521c7–8) means not just examining one's claims and arguments but doing so in a very specific context, which requires the high-powered knowledge of the Forms and many years of scientific and logical training. It is my contention that, in late dialogues such as the *Timaeus* and the *Philebus*, Plato keeps *both* the middle-period claim that only a few can attain knowledge of the Forms *and* the early period suggestion that everyone should somehow be philosophical. How does he do this?

In the *Republic*, we had been told that "it is impossible that the majority be philosophical" (VI 494a4); by contrast, only a few (*oligoi*, VI 503b7, 491b4) were deemed to have a nature suitable for becoming a "complete philosopher" (491a9–b1), which includes the ability to contemplate true being. Likewise, the *Philebus* distinguishes between two kinds of art, even within the same field of study (such as arithmetic): that of the many (*tôn pollôn*) and that of the philosophers (*tôn philosophountôn*, 56d5–6). In this regard "dialectic", in the strong sense of apprehension of the Forms, is presented as the most exact and purest art (57e–58d), which, like the pure pleasures that accompany this kind of knowledge, would not be ordinarily available to people (cf. 52b). And this so far brings to mind the elitism of the *Republic*.

At the same time, Socrates appears in the *Philebus* as defending an outlook inherited from the early dialogues. This is shown in his encouragement of Protarchus – a fairly unsophisticated man who sympathises with hedonism – to pursue the *elenchos* for the sake of truth rather than victory (14b), to the point that Protarchus is made to exclaim: "It is a fine thing for the sound-minded person to know all things, but the second best is for a person not to be ignorant of himself" (19c2–3).[40] Plato, one might infer, has come to realise the dangers of not pursuing "the examined life" on an individual level, no matter how gifted that individual may or may not be intellectually (that is, no matter whether that person does or does not have the capacity to "know all things"). Along these lines, the dialogue *Philebus* itself can be seen as an attempt by Socrates to persuade the hedonist that, however much he may cherish pleasure, not even the pleasurable life can be securely achieved without introspection or self-knowledge (63c): that is, without some second-order reflection upon his own psychic states, including pleasure.

An equally "Socratic", optimistic view of human nature can be found in the assertion that everyone pursues the good, and wishes to catch and possess it (20d), even though it is always possible to choose other things (cf. *alla hêireith'*, 22b6; cf. also 55a5–6), much as this would be contrary to the nature of the truly choiceworthy and thus unwilling (*akôn*), done "through ignorance (*agnoia*) or some unfortunate necessity" (22b6–8).[41] But if we have an open choice as to what kind of life we pursue, but are liable to deception or confusion, how can we prevent ignorance and educate that choice? To this effect, reading the *Philebus* may itself prove instructive. Thus, Plato has Socrates himself assert, after scrutinising what exactly the good consists in: "the present argument appears to me to have been completed, like an incorporeal order that is to rule fairly an ensouled body (*kosmos tis asômatos arxôn kalôs empsuchou sômatos*)" (64b7–8).

2. Knowledge and Happiness

In this regard, it is illuminating that Socrates should – as we have seen in Chapter 4 – employ the term "dialectic" in the *Philebus* in a twofold sense: one, more broadly, as a general method of discussion (14a), which includes carrying out the right collections and divisions, and applicable to all disciplines (16b–17a); and another as the specific art concerned with the Forms as its proper object (57e–58a). One might imagine that it is in the first sense that Protarchus can, with the help of Socrates, perform or understand divisions between various classes of pleasure and knowledge in order to ascertain which ones form part of the happy life for all humans. That is to say, by the end of the dialogue we have come to realise why it is important for every person, including people who value pleasure above everything else, to engage in dialogue and some form of dialectic (at least in the broad sense of division of kinds, even though not everyone can refer those divisions to the Forms),[42] and thus use logic and classification to find out what deserves to be the real object of our choice. In this respect, neither the hedonist nor anyone else interested in their personal fulfilment should dismiss the dialectical treatment of the *Philebus* and the reflection on dialectic, based on the notions of *peras* and *apeiron*, undertaken at 14c ff.

Likewise, we saw in Chapter 3 that the *Timaeus* had used the term "*philosophia*" in one (broad) sense by which it was meant to be available to everyone. In addition, it had also presented astronomy as the study of the heavens by which happiness could thus become available to the masses. The *Philebus* too underlines the importance of mathematical studies, at least insofar as the very notion of *peras* (which pervades the dialectical and cosmological treatments with Pythagorean resonances) is associated with number and discovery of the right proportion. But if *peras*, or those mathematical proportions that underpin becoming, constitutes in the sensible domain the basis of its intelligibility, we can also understand why any person who were to apply herself to studying those proportions would raise her view above the mutable aspects of becoming towards a level that has a greater share in being.

Further, it is suggested that the truest parts of knowledge, including contemplation of true being, are associated with the "most lovable life" (*ton agapêtotaton bion*, 61e7–8). Even though the *Philebus* recognises that the possession solely of the highest forms of knowledge would not be sufficient to cater for all aspects of a happy human life, which must also inevitably include the practical ones (61e–62b), it would seem that such a life must include, among its "first disciplines" (*tas prôtas*, 62d2–3) not only (as some have taken it) apprehension of the Forms for the philosopher, but, in particular, mathematics and related studies for everyone.[43]

The importance of these studies for the happy life is made explicit at 55c ff. After the interlocutors have agreed that the happy life must include some knowledge, the question is to assess which kinds of knowledge should form part of the right mixture. In that context, mathematics is introduced as superior to other so-called arts or *technai* that do not rely on it: We are told that if arithmetic, measurement and the like were removed from all arts, we would be left with something poor, insofar as we would be confined to guessing by habit, through a procedure devoid of certainty (55e ff.). Instead, it is arithmetic and similar disciplines (57d6–7) figuring among the most exact arts (though still second to philosophical dialectic, 57e) that should be preeminently included in the mixed happy life. Two kinds of mathematical studies are distinguished with respect to accuracy: those of the many (as less exact) and those of the philosopher (which are more exact) (56d, 57c-d).

This passage certainly anticipates the section of the *Laws* (VII 817e–818a) where a more "exact" mathematics is going to be reserved for the study of a select few (namely the members of the Nocturnal Council), while it is still insisted that the many – for whom it is neither easy nor altogether possible to investigate these things with precision – should be educated in less accurate forms of the same discipline (including astronomy) if they are to live up to the divine (818c).[44] And even though *Phil.* 55c ff. does not explicitly mention astronomy, it must presumably include it among the "similar disciplines" following arithmetic and geometry that form part of a happy mixture (57d),[45] particularly after so much attention has been devoted to showing that there is in the universe and in its "biggest parts" (30b5; that is, the heavenly bodies) a divine *nous* that brings order to becoming (23c–30c).

3. Self-Knowledge and Humans as Citizens of the Universe

Can cosmology also help us know ourselves? We can see how initiating his interlocutor into this discipline (as he does at *Phil.* 23c ff.) constitutes for Socrates an important part of educating him about the happy life. For it is by apprehending the principles that are at work in the universe that he can gain a better understanding of his own place within it and of the factors to be integrated when designing his own happiness. Thus, in the *Philebus*, where the Socratic theme of self-knowledge is revived, it is now suggested that the key to knowing oneself is, at least partly, of a cosmological nature,[46] insofar as knowing one's source is part of knowing oneself. For, as our bodies derive from the world-body, so do our souls derive from the soul of the universe, whose constituents are said to exist in a manner which is "in every way finer" (*pantêi kalliona*, 30a, cf. 29b ff.). That is, all of our souls have the same nature, and are different only in degree of inferiority, but not in kind, from that of the universe (29a–30b). (The *Timaeus* in turn represents this fact mythically through the image of the Demiurge composing our souls out of the remnants left from the mixture used for the world-soul, 41d.) This means that the universe presents on the large scale a model for what humans would be at their purest. Furthermore, from the point of view of our origin, we are all the same and therefore kindred, in a way that may help us understand the more "populist" strand in this dialogue.

Let us remember that, from the beginning of the *Philebus*, we are presented with a concern about what will bring about the happy life *for all human beings* (*anthrôpois pasi*, 11d). We can now see how such a concern is justified if everyone can be shown to be capable of participating in both pleasure and intelligence (22a5); indeed, even plants – not to say animals – would be considered if we could show that they too are capable of choice (cf. 22b4–8). In this respect, recall that Socrates repeatedly states his concern for the happiness of every living being. But living beings include not only humans, but also animals and plants, which are, Plato believes, capable of pleasure (21c, 67b; cf. *Tim.* 77a–b). For that reason, he qualifies his concern at points as one about the happiness of every living being that can participate in intelligence and calculation

(11b7–c1) and be aware of the good (cf. *gignôskon*, 20d8). And even though it might be queried whether all living beings lower in the scale are capable of such awareness, we are, as a matter of fact, told that human life is, as much as that of god.

But if so, what are we to make of politics? Let us note that, together with its concern for the happiness of everyone, the *Philebus* makes no allusion to a *polis*. This certainly once more contrasts with the *Republic*, where, as we have seen, most humans were made to participate in intelligence only indirectly, through following the ordinances of their wise leader, who was there called a "craftsman" (*dêmiourgos*) of virtue and happiness for himself and for the whole city (VI 500d, cf. VII 519e). Instead, in the *Philebus* we are now offered a picture whereby humans are invited to be craftsmen of their own individual happiness, insofar as each person is expected to incorporate intelligence (*nous*) as the factor demiurgically responsible for their own mixtures (cf. 27b1, 59d10–e3, 61b11–c2). The *Timaeus*, if we remember, had alluded to the benefits that could be gained from living in a good *polis* (87a–b) but, notably, it had not presented those benefits as a necessary condition for happiness. Likewise, the discussion in the *Philebus*, detached from any political concern, seems instead more self-contained, as if combining certain forms of knowledge with certain forms of pleasure were indeed sufficient (*hikanon*, 20d4, 60c11, cf. 11d4–6) to attain happiness. Why is that? It is my contention that in his late dialogues Plato, while not abandoning the belief that happiness is to be realised against the supportive background of a wider environment, has come to see the cosmos itself as the ultimate *polis* that subsumes any forms – whether better or worse – of human association and brings all humans together. We are all thus ultimately seen as "citizens of the universe", our primary home whence we come.

III. CONCLUSION

In this chapter I have analysed various ways in which the cosmology of the *Philebus* provides an indispensable background for an understanding of the dialogue's main ethical issues. We have seen that, after the model of the universe, humans are advised to impose intelligence and structure on their lives to attain goodness, which means pursuing a life of moderation and wisdom allied with certain pleasures. Thus, it has become evident how the *peras-apeiron* distinction developed in the context of the fourfold classification proves important for discovering the true nature of pleasure. This has in turn led us to understand, despite some contemporary readings of the dialogue, how the main principles underpinning *eudai-monia* could be available even to a hedonist, as long as that hedonist is interested in the most pleasure securely attainable in one's life. In that same regard, we have seen god presented as the model for a mixed life of pleasure and intelligence, a model that stands out as the possibility of a life that is to some greater or lesser degree available to all. And even though such a life also requires every person to be familiar with certain forms of knowledge (and even dialectic), once more, as in the *Timaeus*, Plato is trying to ground happiness for the many in a way that does not require them to attain the exceptional and high-powered knowledge of the Forms, much as it does not exclude it either for the few. Further, Plato offers in the *Philebus*, as much as in the *Timaeus*, a way to happiness for humans that needn't rely on a good political system, but does rely on humans' having some understanding of the principles governing the universe in order to be able to be appropriate craftsmen of goodness in their own lives. Because we don't live in a universe of chaos, but one of order, a life "in harmony with nature" requires us to escape from chaotic indulgence in false pleasures and seek a good that is manifested in truth, measure, and beauty. This will indeed be attained through the efficient action of *nous*, which we share with the universe.

6

Reversing the Myth of the *Politicus*

So far I have argued that there is a tendency, in the late dialogues, to emphasise the teleological arrangement of the cosmos as one in which intelligence prevails. In this context, it is possible to see how the universe can provide a framework for the realisation of human autonomy, if now it is no longer expected, or required, that the individual should be under the rule of a gifted sage in order to attain happiness. Instead, by studying and imitating the rational consistency that pervades astronomy and mathematical disciplines in general, he can find and internalise models for his own behaviour, and be encouraged to explore his identity within that larger picture. This move towards the education of the many, who are no longer expected blindly to follow an authority, seemed to contrast with the *Republic*, and promised to pervade Plato's thinking in his later years as a mark of positive philosophical development. However, the *Politicus* confronts us with a problem in this respect – or, rather, with many problems.

First, it is not clear what the function of its cosmological myth is in relation to the overall political argument of the dialogue; at any rate the prevalent tendency has been to read that myth (by contrast with the dialogues we have so far considered) as suggesting that the universe is *not* under the control of god. But this is a good thing, it could be argued, because the picture we get in the *Politicus* when god is governing (here described as the golden "age of Cronus") is one where Cronus simply nurses a "tame and unthinking population";[1] and in this regard it has been no accident that pioneers of modern Platonic scholarship such as G. E. L. Owen should have seen a parallel between the age of Cronus in that myth and the rule of the philosopher-king in the *Republic*.[2] Instead, to be, and to realise that we are, in a universe without god where now *we* have to be the protagonists of our story and frame our lives, with no spoon feeding from above, gives us encouragement to take charge of our existence without, so to speak, waiting for Godot.

Certainly, the interpretative and philosophical reasoning that might underlie this preference for the prevalent interpretation may not ever have been put in quite these terms; yet, more or less implicitly, it can be extracted from many contemporary studies of the myth that also try to weigh its political implications. I believe, however, that this is the wrong approach. Of course it remains true that a view that promotes human autonomy rather than its obliteration under the rule of a superior is in principle a better view; but on my interpretation we do not need to sacrifice it. Rather, in what follows I propose to show that the two main assumptions behind the prevalent reading of the *Politicus* myth – first, that according to it our current universe is not one ruled by god, and second, that being ruled by god would entail the absence of human autonomy and independent thinking – are mistaken. In this respect, I intend to "reverse" the myth of the *Politicus* from the way it has standardly been read. It is my aim to show that the myth tells us that god *is* after all in charge of our universe; but also that, even if god, or an idealised past golden age, functions as a model, it is not at the expense of individual autonomy at all.

I shall start by presenting in a little more detail the state of the question, delineating briefly some problems with it from the point of view both of the internal consistency of the dialogue and the myth's relation to larger cosmological issues. This will help motivate the main body of the chapter, which is a rather close exegesis of the text of the myth devoted to proving my first point concerning the rule of god in our present universe. I shall conclude by returning to the issue of human autonomy and its relation to divine governance in order to show that it is more complex than has usually been recognised. This will help demonstrate how the results of my interpretation fit, rather better in fact than the traditional reading, into the overall context of the dialogue.

I. UNDERSTANDING THE *POLITICUS* MYTH: WHY DOES IT MATTER?

The *Politicus* myth speaks of periods in which god guides the world and those in which he does not, and so contrasts a golden age guided by him with a subsequent period when god abandons his governance of the universe, which moves in reverse until everything goes so wrong that god has to return to the helm and restore order. The human race at this new stage, however, is said to have to resort *on its own* to ways of surviving in a more hostile universe that contrasts with the one depicted in the Golden Age. On this basis, some renowned Plato scholars such as Cornford and Skemp, and with them the majority of interpreters of the dialogue, have taken the myth to suggest that we are now living in a reverse period when god is not exerting his governance.[3] This picture would seem particularly striking by comparison with cosmological suggestions in other late dialogues (such as the *Philebus*, the *Timaeus*, and the *Laws*), which rather tend to stress the existence of a divine *nous* that is responsible for the way our world is arranged, which is the best and most beautiful way possible.[4] On the other hand, Brisson has more recently challenged the traditional interpretation by suggesting a reading that makes our present era one that is governed by god.[5] Scholars, however, have continued to endorse the view that in the *Politicus* myth the present era is a godless one, and in that sense they have reverted to the traditional interpretation of the myth.[6] But why should this issue bear any weight in the context of the *Politicus* itself?

The *Politicus* myth has an explicit political function, which is to correct the first definition of statesmanship in the dialogue;[7] it thus paves the ground for seeking the correct account of statesmanship (as will be provided by the third definition, 292d ff.). Yet what politics has to do with a cosmological myth is not immediately clear. As a consequence, one may think that the myth is an unaccomplished piece of writing, one that is excessively long for the point it is supposed to convey.[8] I hope it will emerge from this chapter that the *Politicus* myth does, after all, possess a tight structure; and I shall have more to say in the following chapter about how its cosmology relates to ethics and politics. But some questions need to be addressed now. The most crucial one is why Plato should have chosen the picture of cosmic reversals. Precisely with regard to this, one might argue that the contrast with the ideal age of Cronus is meant to imply that politics takes place in a universe in which we are autonomous, and that this must therefore be a godless universe, where we are no longer directly nursed by a divinity.[9] But there is in this way of thinking a flawed assumption that I hope the following pages will expose.

Certainly, it would be quite puzzling (though not impossible) if Plato were trying to make a political point at the expense of either totally diluting a cosmological picture that he had emphasised in other dialogues, or sending a message that is opposite to it by now denying that we are living under god. One main question centres around whether or not the universe has a teleological nature, and whether we should expect it to provide a background for politics. Lane, for example, has recently granted that teleological concerns may bear some weight as far as an interpretation of the myth is concerned, but argued that teleology may be present in the godless cycles insofar as the universe has intelligence, and that the rule of such intelligence (even without god) is "quite impressive": thus, a world in reverse does not in fact undermine our hopes for human existence in the present era.[10] But on close examination we realise that we get a rather different picture in the text: Without god, things in the universe get worse and worse; the time when the universe's intelligence helps to run things optimally thanks to remembrance of god's teaching is extremely brief (273c5–6), and with the passing of time the state of disharmony "increasingly even rules" and eventually "flourishes" (273c7–d1) so that in the end the universe, "mixing together small goods with a great mixture of the opposite things, reaches danger of destruction of itself and of the things within it" (273d1–4).[11] So how can one look forward to the best kind of politics when the universe itself is on the path to decay?

This question becomes particularly pressing when we take into account that, according to the myth, "we imitate and follow the whole cosmos for all time" (274d6–7). That is, if Plato means to inscribe human and political occurrences within a larger cosmic picture, it would seem to be rather discouraging or indeed contradictory to be told, on the one hand (as many scholars recognise), that the perfect ruler of the third definition is a prospective ideal whose advent one must remain open to,[12] when, on the other, the standard reading of the myth suggests that things will necessarily go worse in the cycle in which we live. How can one then make sense of the possibility of human and political progress when the universe does not provide proper support? Of course, one answer could be the following: true, our cycle will get worse and worse, but then god will take pity and come back again. Thus, Rowe and Skemp read the text as promising a new age of Cronus.[13] But in such an age, if the structure of cosmic cycles is, as this interpretation seems to take it, repetitive, there would be no politics:[14] what is the point, therefore, of advocating the best kind of politics in the rest of the *Politicus*, if the myth suggests that the cosmos either prevents such an achievement in our current cycle or promises the abolition of all politics in a future one?

Thus, it is crucial for any interpretation of the political importance of the myth of the *Politicus* first to become clear about what exact picture the myth of cosmic reversals presents us with. In this chapter I wish to show that the traditional reading is wrong, or at least extremely problematic, not only for the philosophical consequences that would obtain as far as an interpretation of the whole dialogue is concerned, but, particularly, because it fails to do justice to the text of the myth itself. Therefore, we do not need to commit Plato to the difficulties on a political level that would result from that interpretation. Indeed, I wish to show that he believes politics, even the best kind of politics that humans are capable of, does take place in a universe under providential care so that it won't take us myriads of revolutions (that is, millions of years) for an upgrade in the quality of our human existence.

In what follows, I shall argue that even the evidence that has generally been used to support the traditional interpretation is insufficient to do so. Further, the traditional interpretation fails to preserve the consistency of the text on a literal reading, as I instead intend to do. To this extent, I agree with Brisson's basic suggestion that in the *Politicus* our era is one that is after all governed by god. However, I disagree on some points of interpretation of the myth and think that the issue deserves more thorough scrutiny, including a more detailed consideration of opposing points of view and their possible virtues and flaws. Thus, I undertake here to revive the debate and challenge the traditional interpretation by defending the thesis that, according to a literal reading of the myth, we are living in a period of guidance by god, and that such a reading, unlike the traditional one, helps to maximise the consistency of the whole myth as far as that is possible in this kind of literary medium.

As a matter of fact, the widespread view has seen the *Politicus* as dealing mainly with the opposition between two cycles, that of Cronus and that of Zeus, by taking the two as going in opposite cosmic directions and the latter as one of those periods of absence of god, when the universe is left to itself.[15] But curiously enough none of the adherents of this view seems to have attempted to sketch a reading that takes account of the evidence of the whole myth. They often tend to fasten on one or other passage of a much more complex myth that also contains counterevidence for their claims. Further, some particular details in the myth could be invoked against the alternative interpretation. In trying to account for this, I shall set out to defend a reading of the main body of the text as presenting a view of our actual universe as one ruled by god. I shall start by challenging the prevalent reading on some basic points of textual interpretation and afterwards proceed to propose my own reading of the text and my own answers to possible objections. This procedure is independent of any actual adherence to a literal exegesis of the myth or not.[16] Rather, becoming clear about what the text actually says is an indispensable preliminary step to any further discussion about the possible philosophical advantages or disadvantages of taking such a text literally. Nonetheless, one of the strengths of this procedure will be to show that, *even* on a literal reading (and whether or not one chooses to take other mythical details seriously) there is good evidence that god's designing mind prevails in our present universe. Finally, I shall suggest what consequences my interpretation has for the wider political argument of the dialogue.

II. SOME GAPS IN THE TRADITIONAL INTERPRETATION

The *Politicus* myth offers a picture of alternate cosmic cycles, which are referred to the agency of god and the universe respectively. The "law" (*themis*) governing these cycles is summarised at 269e–270a: "one must not say either that the universe turns itself always (*strephein heauton aei*), nor that, as a whole, it is always turned by god (*hupo theou strephesthai*) in two opposite revolutions, nor that, finally, two gods with opposite designs turn the universe. But ... the only remaining possibility is that, sometimes, the universe is guided by a different, divine cause ... and at some others, when it is released, it moves by itself ... backwards," deprived of divine intervention (cf. 269d–e).

Now, if this is so, the following pieces of evidence can be taken to suggest that Plato is intending to give a picture that makes our cycle one ruled by god.

1. Plato proposes to integrate ancient legends in the myth, among which there is the phenomenon concerning "the change in the setting and rising of the sun and the other stars, so that, from where it rises now, in that same place it set at that time, and it rose from the opposite place; and it was then when, bearing witness in favour of Atreus, the god changed it [i.e. the course of the sun and stars] to its present form" (269a1–5). Here it is *the god* (Zeus, more specifically, in the legend that is being referred to) who changes the course of the heavenly motions,[17] something that will be characteristic of god's action at the beginning of the cycles of god's guidance in the myth, as opposed to those in which he merely lets go of the universe when it is left to itself in its reverse march (cf. e.g. 270a, 273e).[18] The present form of the motion of

the universe would therefore have its cause in god and would be suggestive of his presence.

How has the standard reading dealt with the evidence of this legend that is incorporated in the myth? Rowe, for example, associates this phenomenon with what happens in the past age of Cronus (rather than the present age of Zeus).[19] This claim may square with his denial that god guides (and therefore rules)[20] the direction of our present cosmic cycle; however, the claim is directly contradicted by the evidence, which speaks of the *god* of the legend changing the heavenly bodies to their *present* form (269a4–5).

Some others, also defending the view that we are currently living in a period *without* the guidance of god, cannot but accuse Plato of contradiction[21] in the face of the evidence of the legend, which conversely shows god turning the universe to its present direction. Since that (traditional) interpretation suggests that the universe is guided by god in the *opposite* cycle to the present one, the picture of the legend becomes doubly contradictory, given that the text denies explicitly that two different gods with opposing thoughts turn the universe in opposite directions (270a1–2).

For my part, I shall show in due course that Plato maintains the point suggested by the introductory legend to the very end of the myth, where he tells us that the universe "was turned" (*strephthentos*, 273e6) to its present path of generation, after we read about god's actively turning (*strepsas*, 273e3) the universe when he comes back to the helm.[22]

2. At 272b2–3 the present era (*ton nuni*) is characterised as that of Zeus, in a way that conforms with 1. Can we, with the traditional interpretation, make anything of the fact that the Eleatic Stranger alludes to the age of Zeus as "this [life] which is said to be in the presence of Zeus" (*tonde d' hon logos epi Dios einai*), as if he were not himself endorsing that saying?[23] I believe not. For the strategy of the myth is to *incorporate* popular legends, not to reject them: "All these things, and also countless others . . ., arise from the same phenomenon, but because of the large amount of time [that has passed] some of them have been lost, and others are told scatteredly (*diesparmena*), each separate from the other. But which is the phenomenon that is the cause of all these things, nobody has said, and should now be asserted" (269b5–c1). In addition, it would not seem right to disbelieve those reports in this mythical context, since in this regard the Stranger complains about the fact

that many old stories "are, *incorrectly*, now disbelieved by many" (*logôn hoi nun hupo pollôn ouk orthôs apistountai*, 271b2–3).

The Stranger's apparent commitment to the view that we are in a period governed by god is in turn confirmed by the further assertion at 271d4, where we are told that in the age of Cronus god took care of the universe "as now" (*hôs nun*):[24] this is indeed the reading of all the manuscripts, so we do not need to amend the text as Burnet does.[25]

3. With its emphasis on the close connection between macro- and microcosm, the myth tells us that the direction of ageing of individuals follows the direction of the cosmos (271b7–8; cf. 273e11–274a1, 274d6–7). In the age of Cronus it is said that souls fall into the earth as seed (272e3), with the implication that they follow the normal process of growth and death, like a plant. Similarly in the age of Zeus there is normal conception, generation, and nurture of living beings (274a), which suggests that both the era of Cronus and that of Zeus follow the same direction of microcosmic events (from youth to old age) and so therefore should the macrocosm.

If this is so, then both the age of Cronus and that of Zeus would be opposed to periods involving a reversal of the ageing process, from old to young (as mentioned e.g. at 270d–e, cf. Section III.3). Such a reversal of the ageing process is mentioned as the biggest phenomenon accompanying the cycle opposite to the present one (270d–e, esp. 270d3–4). Those interpreters who, instead, wish to contend that our era follows and is opposed in respect of direction to the one of Cronus are therefore led to postulate that: (1.) in the age of Cronus people were born from the earth as old and then grew young,[26] or (2.) conversely, that the growing younger of the old belongs to our present era.[27] In both cases, however, they do so at the cost of overlooking the evidence mentioned in the previous paragraph.

Now, a defender of the traditional reading might perhaps attempt to push point (1.), by arguing that souls "falling into the earth as seeds" at *Pol.* 272e3 need not (contrary to my interpretation) suggest a normal process of growth from young to old, like a plant: if we imagine that we are in a reverse cycle (like a film played backwards), where people grow from old to young, couldn't the end of the process be described as "falling into the earth as seeds"? If so, the evidence would be insufficient to show that the age of Cronus is one where people grow from young to old, and therefore that our age, following the same direction of growth, should be one governed by god.

This suggestion, however, does not succeed. For, at the end of the reverse process, nothing would *fall into the earth as seed*. If we imagine, as the objection suggests, a film played in reverse, we wouldn't have a seed *falling* into the earth, but the baby plant gradually *disappearing* into the earth – for in the film played forward the baby plant will appear from the earth some time after development from a seed. (In fact it is the verb "disappear", *exaphanizesthai*, not fall, that the Stranger uses for the reversal of ageing at 270e8–9.) Thus, it appears that the language of "falling into the earth as seed" can only be interpreted one way, that is, as describing the normal planting of a seed at the beginning of a cycle where generation goes from young to old.

Let us add, in passing, that Plato has not invented the motif of people being born as old: in Hesiod, for example, we are told that the race of iron will be destroyed when humans are born with grey hair (*Op.* 181; cf. *Pol.* 273e10–11 on "bodies newly born from the earth with grey hair"), something suggesting a state of degradation that seems far removed from what is otherwise described as the ideal conditions of the age of Cronus (for example, god's close tendance of humans, mild weather, and spontaneous growth of things from the earth). If this is so, then our interpretation of the direction of ageing in the era of Cronus in the myth would in turn match its legendary background.

Having, not exhaustively, highlighted these as basic points against the standard reading, I now set out to offer my own reading of the structure of the myth and the overall picture of cosmic cycles that it presents. I shall proceed by following mainly the sequential order of the text and inserting my view into a description of the various stages of the cosmic history narrated in the myth.

III. THE STATES OF THE COSMOS SUCCESSIVELY PRESENTED IN THE TEXT

1. Creation of the Universe

God is described as the "begetter", "demiurge", and "father" of the cosmos (cf. e.g. 269d9, 270a5, 273b1–2), which indicates his creation of it, presumably after a precosmic state of disorder due to the prevalence of the bodily condition of the universe prior to its creation (cf. 273b–c).

2. Overall Description of the Alternate Cycles

At 269c4–d2 and 270a3–7 we are given a picture of the opposite cycles:

1. *sometimes* (*tote men*, 269c4, 270a3) god himself "guides and helps the universe revolve as it goes", 269c4–5; that is, the universe "is guided by a different, divine cause", 270a3.
2. *at some other times* (*tote de*, 269c5, 270a5) he lets the universe go, so that it "spontaneously goes back round in the opposite direction (*palin automaton eis tanantia periagetai*)", 269c5–7; this is described as a reverse march (*anapalin ienai*, 269d2). The universe is said to "go itself by itself (*di' heautou auton*), released at such a moment as to go backwards (*anapalin poreuesthai*)", 270a5–7.

In view of these expressions suggesting backward motion when the universe is released, we can call the cycles described at 2. the "reverse cycles", in the sense that the universe moves in a reverse direction. So we shall call "forward" those periods guided by god, and "reverse" those in which the universe is left to itself, without the guidance of god. In any case, what is crucial is not to speak in terms of forward or reverse (since either one is opposite to the other), but in terms of cycles in which the world is or is not actively guided by god.

It is important to notice the role of god in the reverse cycles. He is not said to die or disappear, but to release control of the universe[28] and to leave it or go off to his place of outlook (cf. *apestê*, 272e5), so that he stops having any direction over the course of the universe (since there cannot be two gods nor the same god turning it in opposite revolutions, 269e8–270a2), and does nothing, except observing passively what is going on (272e5).

Now, at 270b7–8 the Stranger summarises the double picture, by saying "sometimes (*tote men*) the universe moves in the direction in which it *now* circles (*eph' ha nun kukleitai*); at some other times (*tote de*) it goes in the opposite direction (*epi tanantia*)." Here he does not define which cycle is reverse or which is forward (both are opposite as such), though, to go on with the order of exposition he has chosen above, at 269c–d and 270a, by which first (through the expression *tote men*) he presents the forward cycle guided by god and secondly (through the expression *tote de*) the reverse cycle, we may suspect that "the direction in which the universe now circles", mentioned at 270b, corresponds to the forward cycles, that is, the periods of god's guidance.

If this hypothesis is correct, then even the chosen mode of exposition would match the evidence we have already collected from the preliminary legend concerning this cycle being one guided by god. For there it is god who is said to change the course of the sun and the other stars to its present direction (269a1–5), and his turning the universe is a characteristic of those periods of god's intervention in the myth (cf. 269c5, 269e5–270a5). It is also important to recall that according to the legend the god in question is traditionally Zeus,[29] under whom, in turn, we are said to be living in the myth (272b2–3). Further evidence will help to confirm this.

3. Contrary Motion to the Present: Reversal of the Ageing Process – Accompanying Reversal in the Universe

Let us now see how the myth describes the cycle immediately opposite to ours. In fact the text at 270b10–271b3 goes on to say that, *in the motion contrary to the present one,* a lot of changes take place. First, there is *destruction of animals* (270c11–12), something that will afterwards be described as what immediately follows the release of the universe by god (273a3–4), and which can therefore suggest that the motion we are considering is one of reversal. Secondly, and most importantly, there is the *growing younger of the old,* until they disappear (270d–e). This reversal of the ageing process is said to accompany (*sunepomenon*) the reversal of the universe (*têi tou pantos aneilixei*), whenever the phase contrary to the one which is now established begins (*hotan hê tês nun kathestêkuias enantia gignêtai tropê*), 270d3–4. It is essential to bear in mind that in the myth the microcosmic events follow the same direction as that of the cosmos, as we can gather from the general rule at 274d6–7 that "we imitate and accompany (*sunepomenoi*) the whole cosmos for all time" (cf. 274a1: all other things "imitate and accompany the state of the universe", and 271b7–8: "generation circles back in the opposite direction to follow the revolution").

Further, it is suggested that, during this period, people were "born from the earth" (*gêgeneis*) as old and again grew young (271a2–b3). But, if there are earthborn during this age of reversal, which are born from the earth as old, they should be distinguished from the earthborn of the age of Cronus, since, as was shown in Section II, it is implied at 272e3 that the latter are born from *seeds* (*spermata*), and therefore follow the normal process of growth from young to old, like a plant.

How does the text describe a transition to the age of Cronus? Such a transition is rather understated, since the focus at 271a4–c2 seems to be to narrate the amazing phenomenon of people being born from the earth, even though we shall soon find out that the phenomenon has indeed taken place over a long span of time comprising opposite cosmic cycles. Nonetheless, the text seems to provide room for a transition to the earthborn of the age of Cronus at 271b3, where the Stranger admonishes us to consider "what comes next".

4. The Reversal of the Reversal

4.1. The Earthborn Race and the (Forward) Age of Cronus. We are told that "it follows (*hepomenon*) the old going to the nature of a child, that, from *those who are dead and lying in the earth*, there again people *are constituted and return to life*, as generation circles back in the opposite direction to follow the revolution" (271b4–8). We can wonder whether the coming to life again from the earth at 271b6–7:

A. takes place within the same period of reversal as 3. (as Brisson believes);[30] or
B. represents the start of a new period (namely, the forward age of Cronus, which will be mentioned more explicitly from 271c4 onwards).[31] In this case, being born from the earth after (or "following", *hepomenon*, 271b4) the growing young of the old constitutes a new cycle both for humans and also for the cosmos, as seems also suggested by the statement that "generation circles back in the opposite direction to follow the revolution" (271b7–8). And this process would then correspond directly to the age of Cronus and the earthborn mentioned there (271c ff.).[32]

My reading allows for either interpretation, since in both cases the direction of the age of Cronus (as shown by the direction of microcosmic events) is opposite to the motion where people are born from old to young; but, as this was in turn said to be opposite to the present one (cf. 270d4 and above, III.3.), then the conclusion stands that the age of Zeus follows the same direction as the age of Cronus.

My preference, nonetheless, is for interpretation B. First, since this reading presupposes the active presence of god during the time of the earthborn mentioned at 271b4–c2, it can make perfect sense of the allusion to god at 271c2, where we are told that some exceptional humans were taken by god (*theos*) to another destiny instead of being reborn from the earth (interpretation A., by contrast, leaves that allusion to god unexplained, if it takes it to occur in a reverse period). Second, interpretation B. would account for the Stranger's further reference to the age of Cronus as "the previous[ly mentioned] one" at 271d3, as we shall now see.

4.2. *The Contrast between the Ages of Cronus and Zeus.* But doesn't the text after all contain direct evidence for the traditional view? Following the reference to the earthborn race at 271a2–c2, Young Socrates asks whether the age of Cronus took place "during those turnings or in these" (271c4–5). To this the Stranger replies: "What you asked about the spontaneous birth of everything for humans least of all (*hêkista*) belonged to the present established revolution, but this also belonged to the former one (*tês emprosthen*)", 271c9–d3. This wording might seem to make it quite plain that the age of Cronus took place right before ours,[33] and is opposed rather than parallel to the age of Zeus.

My answer to this challenge consists in accepting that there is an actual contraposition between the ages of Cronus and Zeus. However, it needn't be one of direction of motion. First, it is conceivable that the allusions to "those turnings" and to "the former" or "the previous" revolution are *not* to an immediately *temporally* previous cycle to ours.[34] Rather (particularly if one follows interpretation B. above), it seems perfectly natural that the Stranger's reference to "the former one" (*tês emprosthen*, 271d2–3) should be to the era of the earthborn just previously mentioned *in the text* (271b–c) instead of the era of the earthborn immediately preceding our time.

Second, we must note the qualified way in which the age of Cronus is said to have "least of all" (*hêkista*) belonged to our era: it is "with regard to the spontaneous birth of everything for humans" (*peri tou panta automata gignesthai tois anthrôpois*, 271d1). And the text goes on to explain how, in this ideal age of Cronus, both humans and all the fruits sprang naturally from the earth; there was no need for agriculture; there were no wild animals, no wars, no families or states since all the parts of the universe were under the close care of gods; and there was a warm climate obviating the need for fire (271d–272b). It is, then, at most in all these ways that the age of Cronus is "least of all" the current revolution (cf. 271d1); but not in respect of the direction of the revolution.[35]

The Stranger then proceeds to ask which of the two ages was happier, whether that of Cronus or "this [life] which is said to be in the presence of Zeus (*epi Dios*)", which is "*the [life] of the present era* (*ton nuni*)", 272b1–4.

The suggestion that we are living under god matches our claim that the current period is one of those in which the universe is not just left to itself, and this will receive further support.

5. Reversal After the Age of Cronus: Increasing Cosmic Disorder and Reversal of Ageing

Now, if our previous interpretation is correct, and both the ages of Cronus and of Zeus go in a forward direction, we still need to postulate a reverse cycle between them, to follow the cosmic structure of opposite cycles laid out at III.2. The text in fact goes on smoothly to present this reverse cycle at 272d6–273d4. There the Stranger describes what happens at the end of the age of Cronus: "when the time of all these things was finished, and change was due to come about, and moreover all the earthborn race had by that time been consumed, since each soul had given all its births by falling into the earth as seed as many times as had been assigned for each, then *the pilot of the universe so to speak released the tiller and went off to his place of outlook, so that fated and inborn desire turned the universe backwards* (*palin anestrephen*)" (272d6–e6). This reverse cycle is characterised by initial cosmic convulsion and "another" (*allên*) destruction of animals (273a3–4) – parallel to that occurring at the beginning of the reverse cycle described at III.3. (cf. 270c11–12); restoration of order for the very briefest period after the release (273a5–7, c5–6),[36] and then increasing cosmic disorder which results in the danger of the destruction of the universe (273d3–4). And it is when the universe is on the brink of destruction that god intervenes to start a new era.

Typically, scholars have supposed that this reverse cycle immediately following the age of Cronus belongs to our age of Zeus (which is described at greater length at 273e6–274e1). However, we should note, first, that the text refers to the reverse cycle following the age of Cronus as completely in the past, as we learn from the remark that, with regard to the universe's remembering the teachings of its father, "at the beginning it did so more accurately, towards the end more dimly" (*kat' archas men oun akribesteron apetelei, teleutôn de ambluteron*, 273b2–3).

This circumstance, I claim, is not accidental, nor a simple manner of speaking. For we can also see that it is to this reverse cycle that we should attribute (as to the one at III.3) a reversal of the ageing process so that humans and other animals grow younger rather than older. Indeed, at 273e we are told that, when the universe was turned along the road towards its present generation (meaning the present age of Zeus), that "produced *new things opposite to the ones before. For those animals which were almost due to disappear through smallness grew larger, and those bodies newly born from the earth with grey hair again died and descended to the earth*" (e7–11). In this latter sentence the new things of this cycle are set against those happening before: the normal present process of growth is contrasted with the previous growing smaller and disappearing; as to the second clause, the text cannot mean that the earthborn belong to this period (for that is ruled out at 274a2–4), but they must belong to the previous age, following on the above-mentioned contraposition.[37]

This means that in the period previous to the age of Zeus animals were growing younger. And this situation again contrasts with the age of Cronus where, as we have seen from the image of the seed (272e3), the ageing process of the earthborn goes from young to old, like a plant, as does the ageing process in the age of Zeus (cf. 273e8–9, 274a, with the reference to conception, birth and nurture). If this is so, then we have earthborn not only in the forward age of Cronus but also, of a different kind, in the following reversal, which must be distinguished from the present age of Zeus.[38]

6. Forward Cycle: The Age of Zeus. The Appendix of the Myth and the Case Against

Let us now see how the text describes what happens when the universe is on the brink of destruction, in the cycle following the release of its control by god. We are told that at that very moment "god who ordered the universe, seeing that it was in trouble, and worried lest, having been storm-tossed and dissolved by confusion, it should sink into the limitless sea of dissimilarity, *sits back again at his tiller*, and after *turning* (*strepsas*) what was sick and dissolute in the previous period when the world was by itself, he *puts it in order* (*kosmei*) and, *setting it right again* (*epanorthôn*), *makes it* (*apergazetai*) *immortal and ageless*" (273d4–e4).

The action of god sitting back again at the tiller suggests the start of a new forward cycle, since his absence from the tiller was characteristic of the opposite period after the age of Cronus (272e4 ff.). In addition, god is here said to restore the world's immortality (cf. *athanaton auton kai agêrôn apergazetai*, 273e3–4), something that characterises god's action in the (forward) period when he guides the universe, as we learn from 270a3–5: "Sometimes the universe is guided by a different, divine cause, acquiring life again and receiving restored immortality (*lambanonta athanasian episkeuastên*) from its creator; at other times it is let go".

What age does this new forward cycle correspond to? Contrary to the standard view,[39] I think we can preserve the consistency of the text if we take all this description to allude to the start of our present age of Zeus (cf. *epi Dios, ton nuni* at 272b2–3). Thus, when we read that the universe "is turned" (*strephthentos*) along the road towards its present generation (*tên epi tên nun genesin hodon*, 273e6–7), we are made to think that this was indeed done by the very action of the god who turned it (*strepsas*) at 273e3,[40] so that we should read the passage that follows (273e–274e), and which we can call the "appendix" of the myth, as continuous with this one and within the age of Zeus.

Now, if this is so, some immediate problems seem to arise. For the text goes on to describe the hardships that humans had to encounter at the beginning of this cycle, "deprived of the care of the god that possessed and tended us" (274b5–6). Doesn't this support the traditional view that we live in a period of absence of god? As an answer to this challenge, Brisson remarks that the point of the passage is to indicate that, "contrary to the age of Cronus, we are no longer tended by daemons" or lesser gods. According to Brisson, we can understand the age of Zeus as one where god still takes care of the revolution of the whole universe, even though we no longer have secondary deities taking charge of their respective regions.[41]

To say that in the present cycle we are deprived of the care of the regional gods, but not of the overall care exerted by god in the universe, can in principle make sense of the greater part of the text of the myth (269c–273e) and the actual suggestions of god's care in our era. However, the appendix can also be seen to contain some counterevidence for this kind of interpretation. Let us quote the most challenging text in that direction:

And everything that contributed to human life arose from those things, once the care of the gods, as has now been said, left humans, and they had to lead their own existence and take care of themselves by themselves (*di' heautôn*), like the whole cosmos (*kathaper holos ho kosmos*), which we imitate and accompany for all time ... (274d2–7)[42]

According to this, it would be hard to say that only humans are deprived of their caring gods but not the universe; the text just quoted rather suggests the contrary (and might even remind us of the "care and rule" – *epimeleia kai kratos* – that the universe has of itself "by itself" at the beginning of the reverse cycle at 273a7, cf. 270a5). Now, to this one could certainly reply that the text establishes an analogy between human beings and the cosmos only in respect of the care of themselves that they have to have, not in respect of their being left by the gods.[43] However, it also seems fair to suppose that there must be some kind of symmetry between the situation of parts of the universe and the universe itself, particularly if one follows closely the macro-microcosm parallelism emphasised throughout the myth.

This apparent difficulty, however, is eased when we put those passages in context. For after all it is not said that the gods withdraw every sort of care, not even for human beings, but only the care of each of the gods "tending us" (*nemontos hêmas*, 274b5) during the age of Cronus (cf. 271d6–e1). The gods are still present as bestowers of gifts like the arts (*technai*) to humanity, which are granted together with the "necessary teaching (*didachês*) and education (*paideuseôs*)" (274c6–7).[44] "Teaching" was exactly the kind of thing given by god in the periods when he guides the universe and which the latter has to remember when left to its own (cf. 273b2). Indeed, the presence of lesser gods must imply the presence of a ruling god, since we read at 272e–273a that, no god being at the helm of the universe, there are no longer lesser gods having intervention.

So, if the gods are still present, though more detachedly, in the present era by giving us gifts, teaching and education oriented towards facilitating a more independent life on the part of human beings, one should expect god to be in charge of the universe with a similar function. Going back to 274d2–7, then, "what has left humans" as much as the universe is not divine care altogether but only the close divine care that they used to have in the era of Cronus. If this is so, it makes perfect sense to read that:

In the same way as the cosmos had been ordered to be the master of its own march (*kathaper tôi kosmôi prosetetakto autokratora einai tês hautou poreias*), so and similarly were the parts ordered to conceive, procreate and breed by themselves so far as it was possible, by similar guidance (274a4–b1).

In this passage, the notions of divine guidance and instruction are again to the forefront but portrayed as oriented towards making the universe and us more autonomous. We find a similar situation in the *Timaeus* when the Demiurge instructs (again, the verb *prostattein*, 36d4–7) the heavens how to move; this seems to be what the heavenly bodies learn (38e6) and they continue doing so even after, according to the mythical literal picture, the Demiurge ceases his direct work on the universe, and the world-soul and the heavenly bodies have to take up ruling functions in it (41a ff., 42d–e; cf. 34c4–5), so that the universe's orderly foundations end up being much more internal to it than the external figure of the Demiurge initially suggested.

IV. AUTONOMY AND DIVINE GUIDANCE

Why this emphasis on the more autonomous character of the whole universe and its parts in the era of Zeus in the *Politicus*? The whole idea this appendix seems to convey is that the present era of Zeus, by contrast with the earlier era of Cronus, is not characterised by the kind of divine care that would prevent the existence of societal self-rule. As we shall see shortly, Plato seems to be willing to suggest here that politics takes place neither in an ideal universe where god's *nous* would have so much power, nor in its opposite under the predominance of necessity (*anankê*), but in our *actual* world where *nous* and necessity coexist. Perhaps that is why in this era there are wild beasts, the weather is cold enough for humans to require fire (274b–c), and so on.[45] As Brisson has proposed, we can think of this era as a *synthesis* between the ideal order of the age of Cronus and the disorder that is depicted as prevailing in the reverse cycles,[46] in the same manner as in the *Timaeus* our actual world is said to be a synthesis (*sustasis*) of *nous* and *anankê* (47e–48a). And this circumstance would in turn explain why in the appendix to the myth of the *Politicus* we find such apparent tension between passages reminiscent of the reverse cycles on the one hand and passages suggestive of the opposite situation on the other.

But, just as in the *Timaeus nous* still rules over *anankê* and prevails within the composition of the *kosmos* (48a), here again we should think that god rules, since he is still at the helm of the universe (273e1), and exercises guidance (*agôgê*, 274b1). He also gives orders to the universe (cf. *prostattein* at 274a5 and a7), even though the universe is ordered to be independent (274a5). This suggests an active role for god and not just a passive one as in those reverse periods when he withdraws his hand from the helm (and literally leaves or lets go of the universe, 269c5, 270a5–6), limiting himself, at the very most, to observing what is happening from his place of outlook (272e). The same active role of the deity is suggested by the allusion to the *gifts* of the gods (such as fire, skills, and seeds) at 274c5–d2, who come and help the defenceless condition of humans, giving the necessary "teaching and education" (274c6–7),[47] in a way that is not so close to royal shepherding, but still provident enough and far from the passive role of god in the reversions. God is then present even though we are said to be deprived of the guidance of the particular gods who used to tend us in different parts of the universe (274b5–6 and d3–4, cf. 271d–e),[48] something that is however crucial to allow for politics in the sense of humans guiding themselves.

We see then that the structure of the forward cycles is not repetitive.[49] The age of Cronus depicts an ideal situation which contrasts with the real one. And it is important that these two ages, while both being ages of god, should have different characteristics in the context of the whole dialogue, since in the light of them Plato will criticise the first definition of the statesman given before the myth, that is, shepherd as breeder of human bipeds or the human flock[50] (a characterisation which rather belonged to god in the apolitical era of Cronus),[51] and put forward a new one in the light of the myth – statesmanship in terms of human concern, the latter being more adjusted to the facts (cf. 274e–275a, 276c–d).

At the same time, the advent of arts or crafts (*technai*) during the age of Zeus helps to present not only the need for politics as a *technê*, but the plurality of competitors with which it will have to deal when claiming to be an art of concern for humans (after all, farming and cobbling also show concern). It thus invites a further reflection (undertaken at 287b ff.) about what exact kind of concern is distinctive of politics by contrast with other arts and pseudo-arts.[52] On a cosmological plane, however, we can see how the myth shows us the development of the arts themselves: for the arts respond to our resourcefulness, which tries to impose order upon chaotic tendencies, and resourcefulness (as opposed to being without resources, *aporos*, cf. 274c5) is the kind of thing which one requires in an imperfect universe due to the restraints imposed by *anankê*: thus, the need for humans to organise themselves would be an example of those limitations (cf. *anankazein*, 274c4). In this regard, the way in which (under this interpretation) *nous* prevails over *anankê* on a cosmic scale in our cycle functions as a point of reference for humans if they are to be themselves teleological agents striving to create a political *kosmos*.

If so, god would still function as an exemplar for the politician to follow, and maybe this is at the back of the Stranger's mind when he later claims that the myth was framed in order to provide a paradigm for the king (277b3–5). Even the age of Cronus, removed as it is from us, can prove inspiring, insofar as it invites us to emulate, so far as possible, its ideal environmental conditions.[53] But it will now have to be the politician who will be mostly in charge of bringing about that state of affairs. He will do so, however, not by removing the need for the arts, as would appear to be the case in the age of Cronus, but by using the help of all the other arts and thus providing people with the desirable external conditions (such as proper food and shelter) that make the flourishing of the state possible.[54] At the same time, he will leave a certain autonomy in the field of each art, and among the citizens, thus allowing for differences between them while interweaving them,[55] just as in the era of Zeus the universe itself is autonomous and promotes autonomy among its members while at the same time encouraging collaboration.[56]

And while the degree to which we are left to ourselves is larger in this era, we are still reminded that happiness is something to be achieved by humans, as opposed to a mere "given", even in the most idealised era of humanity. For it is clear that in the age of Cronus the mere existence of favourable external conditions is not sufficient for humans to qualify as "happier" than those of our time. Instead, it is the exercise of philosophy and the pursuit of dialogue for the sake of the acquisition of wisdom that will make them happier (272c); but since this is stated as a possibility even for the nurslings of Cronus, autonomy is something that god would not want to eliminate altogether from humans even in that idyllic age.

This image is also suggestive in another way, insofar as it shows that it is possible to lead a philosophical life in which "philosophy" is conceived not as a profession but as an attitude of dialogue grounding happiness that has strong Socratic resonances (cf. *Ap.* 41b–c).[57] It is in this regard striking that all the nurslings of Cronus are given the possibility of philosophy, even if "philosophy" here probably means something less than the high-powered discipline (available only to a few) that crowns the educational curriculum of the *Republic*, and may not reach the "greatest objects" (*megista*) that are the ultimate goal of dialectic later in the dialogue (*Pol.* 285d4–286a7). In this way, the possibility of a "philosophical" mode of life for people under intelligent rule in the era of Cronus, and of their learning from a distinctively gifted individual (272c1–4) may foreshadow the *Politicus*' further suggestions on the divine bonds of true opinion (309c5–e8) that the large body of citizens will be able to receive under the rule of the ideal statesman. These, by appealing to *nous* as a divine or immortal element is us (309c1–3), and by being accompanied by stability, must involve some reasoned understanding rather than uncritical acceptance of what one is told.[58]

In this regard, the contrast between the ages of Cronus and Zeus becomes less sharp, and the invitation to philosophise (external conditions ideal or not) a key moral message of the story.[59] But if so, then the equation autonomy-godlessness (which so often lies behind the traditional interpretation) dissolves:[60] not only do we see contrasts, but also parallelisms between the ages of Cronus and Zeus, as we would expect if after

all the two ages run in the same direction. Thus, the point about autonomy turns out to be more complex than it seems: on the level of political
autonomy, it is true that the politician must be a human rather than a
god; on the level of individual autonomy, however, the age of Cronus is
no exception to the suggestion that the best form of life is something that
the person must choose for herself. And even on this issue, I contend that
my interpretation of the structure of cosmic cycles makes the best sense
of the text, as the opposite interpretation fails to account for how the age
of Cronus would leave open to its nurslings the possibility of growing in
wisdom (272c4) if after all they become younger and therefore eventually
less knowledgeable.[61]

   If things are as I am arguing, it appears that the traditional interpretation has tended to take the myth and its two main cycles pretty much
upside down: on the one hand, it has committed us (people under Zeus)
to a cosmic era of inevitable march towards chaos that seems to preclude
the possibility, however remote in the future, of the rise of, or advance
towards, the best kind of politics that the rest of the dialogue wants.[62]
On the other, it has frequently equated autonomy with godlessness – to
the point of denying or ignoring that even in a god-reared universe happiness is something that belongs to the individual; it has made people
in the era of Cronus go backwards in age in a way that robs them of the
opportunity, explicitly allowed in the text, to grow in wisdom;[63] and thus
it has missed important ways in which the myth, albeit helping refine and
criticise the previous definition of the statesman by differentiating ideal
from real conditions, may show a god-driven universe as paradigmatic for
a political search.

V. CONCLUSION

In sum, by following the movement of the text, I hope to have offered a
coherent reading of the letter of the myth of the *Politicus* according to
which the cycle in which we are living is an orderly one under the care
of god and not one of increasing cosmic disorder, as has usually been
assumed at the cost of implicating the account in unnecessary difficulties.
Our present cycle proved parallel and not opposite to that of Cronus in
respect of direction, even though some differences can be found in other
senses and are indeed required for Plato to be able to make his political
point by means of the myth at all. In this way I hope to have shown that,
even on a literal reading of the text, the mind of god can still be regarded

as the foundation of the present cosmic order, so that in this respect the *Politicus* picture need not conflict with similar claims in other dialogues.

Furthermore, we have seen how it is crucial that our historical dimension should not (*pace* the standard reading) be one of increasing cosmic and human deterioration, but a forward one that is yet distinct from the age of Cronus, if we are to take the statesman of the third definition as a practicable human ideal towards which we can progress, and thus make sense of the dialogue's message that one should strive for the ideal constitution or at least try to imitate it as best one can (297a–c, 300e–301a). Precisely in this respect, the Stranger complains of the many's mistrust that "anyone worthy of such government could ever arise, willing and able to distribute rightly what is just and pious to everyone by ruling with virtue and knowledge" (301c–d). If, then, Plato in the *Politicus* is no pessimist about politics,[64] I hope to have shown in this chapter how a proper reading of the cosmic cycles in the myth provides the larger framework against which one can understand why it is reasonable for us (as the imperfectly governed people living in the age of Zeus) to have hope.

7

Cosmic and Human Drama in the *Politicus*

The previous chapter argued for a view of the myth of the *Politicus* according to which, even on a literal reading, we are currently living in a period governed by god. In this respect, the letter of the text has been shown to be consistent with the cosmological accounts of other dialogues, which gives us good reason to suppose that Plato does after all mean to present our universe as one under divine guidance. And this, in turn, has enabled us to make better sense of the possibility of human and political progress as allowed in the rest of the *Politicus*. A further point to discuss now, however, is how literally the myth should be taken in other respects, and whether it does not still deserve other levels of analysis that could complementarily enrich and enlighten our understanding of its function in the dialogue. It is *prima facie* clear that the guise of the myth is cosmological, but how much cosmological significance does it have?

Positions on this point have often been extreme. Thus, the myth has sometimes been treated either as a digressive and separate piece of cosmological doctrine,[1] or as a rather lengthy tale fashioned for the political purposes of the dialogue but deprived of great cosmological importance.[2] In this chapter I wish to undertake a more integrated analysis, by stressing the cosmological content of the myth and, against that background, exploring further its ethical and political implications and its relevance to the general political purpose of the dialogue. I shall argue for the thesis that: (1.) despite the mythical device of creation and cosmic cycles, any allusion to disorder or cosmic drama in the whole universe should not be taken literally (though we shall see that the myth does contain some important cosmological suggestions); but (2.) these stand for human and social disturbances: in other words, it is mainly in human affairs that confusion and disorder arise.

I. THE COSMOLOGICAL SIGNIFICANCE OF THE MYTH

1. The Implausibility of a Literal Interpretation of Cosmic Drama

Let us start by summarising the picture of opposite cosmic cycles that we saw in more detail in the previous chapter. God is described as the creator of the universe, and there are times when he himself guides the world and makes it go in a forward revolution. But at some other times god lets the universe go and it turns backwards. This rotation in reverse starts by being regular, thanks to the world's intelligence and remembrance of god's instructions. But, as time passes and memory grows dim, the influence of the corporeal element of the world's constitution becomes greater and the motion of the universe becomes therefore increasingly disorderly, to such an extent that god has to come back to restore order (cf. 269c–d, 272e ff.). This picture, if taken literally, would suggest the idea of cosmic drama, which we can take as a conflict between good and evil, or their respective causes – that is, intelligence and the corporeal[3] – which not only coexist but seem also to prevail alternatingly in the whole universe, making it exhibit either purposive or random behaviour.[4]

If this is so, we may wonder whether Plato meant to present such a unique description of the universe seriously. As a matter of fact, some textual clues could be invoked as indicative that this picture of opposite cosmic cycles (of order and increasing disorder) should *not* be taken literally. First, we must be sensitive to the way the Eleatic Stranger introduces the story to Young Socrates: it is a *paidia* (268d8), a "game for children". He invites Young Socrates to listen to the story "like children, for you are certainly not many years removed from children's games" (268e5–6). It appears, then, that in this manner of presenting the myth, Plato is presumably not intending his readers to take the whole of this fiction as the facts. His playful tone, on the other hand, contrasts with the serious tone of the *Timaeus*,[5] where the narrator stresses the difficulty of finding the maker of the All (28c) and prays for the help of the gods in his big undertaking (27b–d, 48d–e).[6] Even if the *Timaeus* picture is, on different grounds, not to be taken literally in all its details either, it seems that in the "likely account" or *eikos logos* of the *Timaeus* Plato is engaging in a more serious enterprise than when "raising" in the *Politicus* a big mass of *muthos* (277b4–5) to illustrate the king.

This being so, and given the mythical character of the story, we are entitled to think that, if the picture of cosmic reversals does not appear in any other context, and furthermore is contradicted in more argumentative passages, then we have a *prima facie* reason for not taking it literally.[7] Successive complete cosmic reversals, in fact, do not appear elsewhere,[8] let alone ones that end in disorder. Furthermore, there seem to be positive reasons to reject the idea that Plato could have believed in them. In the first place, it can be queried to what extent an astronomer of Plato's day could have accepted the picture of a reversal of the heavens (which is in this case in addition increasingly disorderly). That he could has been denied,[9] and we can pose the question in the context of how Plato himself seems to understand astronomy in discursive passages.

In the *Republic*, for example, astronomy is conceived of as a strict intellectual discipline, and, despite the sensible aspect of the heavens that makes them fall short of the absolute stability of intelligible entities,[10] Plato nevertheless stresses that the heavens are "the most beautiful and accurate" of sensible things (529c8–d1, cf. 530a3–7) and must be used as an example (*paradeigma*, cf. 529d7) in understanding the intelligible proportions that govern the movement of the heavenly bodies. As Mourelatos has put it, "in the heavens we have the best visible concrete realization" of the abstract object of its corresponding science.[11] These heavenly bodies, however, could hardly serve as an example if their motions were liable to become disorderly in the radical way that the *Politicus* myth proposes,[12] nor would the fatal evils that end up prevailing in the universe during the reverse cycles in the *Politicus* befit Plato's appraisal of its extreme beauty and accuracy in the *Republic*. The *Laws*, for its part, stresses that the heavenly bodies follow *always* the same circular track (VII 822a7), and treats as impiety the contrary belief (821c–d).[13] Let us recall in this context that both in the *Republic* (VI 508a4) and in the *Laws* (VII 821b6, 821c7) the heavenly bodies are regarded as gods,[14] and that, according to the *Republic* (II 381b–c) any change of the gods to the worse would be viewed as contradictory to their goodness. So it seems clear, from the discursive treatment that astronomy receives in dialogues other than the *Politicus*, that Plato regards the sensible astronomical system as continuously orderly.[15] And, if there is consensus in situating the *Politicus* between the *Republic* and the *Laws*, it would seem unreasonable to suppose that Plato temporarily changes his mind by allowing the movement of the stars to pass from order into almost complete disorder in a dialogue where, furthermore, no discursive ground can be found for such a claim.[16]

Discursive evidence, then, seems not only to be silent about opposite cosmic cycles in the fashion of the *Politicus* but also to go against their postulation. We must also bear in mind that, in the rest of the *corpus*, where cyclical disturbances are mentioned at all, they are not referred to the whole universe but just restricted to Earth – in the form, for example, of fires, deluges, and catastrophes sometimes or periodically affecting nature and destroying civilization, particularly in Plato's late work (cf. *Tim.* 22c ff., *Crit.* 109d ff., *Laws* III 677a ff.); and even so, they appear mainly in legendary or narrative contexts. So, even if Plato is elsewhere thinking of cosmic cycles, it would be within those restrictions, that is, within our mortal domain, where that residue of "necessity" not completely controlled by *nous* seems to manifest its effects the most in the *Timaeus*.[17] In addition, these potential disruptions in nature could never compete against the more comprehensive order, so that in any case it is *nous* that reigns over the universe as a whole (cf. e.g. *Tim.* 48a, *Laws* X 903b, 904b).

2. The Philosophical Meaning and Status of God

On this basis I do not think that the "cosmic drama" in the *Politicus*, or the opposition between directions of the universe determined respectively by *nous* and the corporeal, should be taken literally as serious cosmological doctrine. This, however, does not mean that the *Politicus* myth lacks elements of cosmological importance. On the contrary, we can find here notions that prove to be the subject of more detailed or argumentative analysis in other dialogues. Thus, for instance, the universe is conceived of as a "living being" (*zôion*), with a body and an intelligence of its own (*Pol.* 269d1; cf. *Tim.* 30b4–5, *Phil.* 29e–30a). In addition, god appears as a "divine cause" (*theia aitia, Pol.* 270a3) that accounts for whatever order, goodness and beauty exist in the universe (cf. 273b–c, e3), whereas "the bodily" (*to sômatoeides*, 273b4) is the "cause" (*aition*) of its potential or actual disarrangements (273b–d, esp. 273b4). And this opposition between two kinds of cause reminds us of the parallel distinction between divine and necessary causes that we analysed in the *Timaeus* (46c–e, 68e–69a).[18]

Now, if we focus more closely on the nature of god, we shall find that he is mythically presented as a Demiurge (*dêmiourgos*, 270a5, 273b1, as in the imagery of the *Timaeus*). Certainly, Plato resorts to tradition when making him (as we saw in the previous chapter) bear in different cosmic cycles the respective names of Cronus and Zeus. But in reality this distinction is not sharp: Cronus is called "Demiurge and Father" (*dêmiourgos kai patêr*) at 273b1–2 and Zeus "the god that ordered" (*theos ho kosmêsas*) the cosmos at 273d4, so that these expressions appear to refer to the same entity. Let us also bear in mind that god appears not only as one, but as one-and-many (since he is accompanied by lesser gods, cf. *Pol.* 271d–e, 272e). It would then seem that god does not have a distinct personality, despite his mythical disguises. Nonetheless, the main feature that prevails in him even when deprived of these is his function of being a "divine cause", something that also characterises god in the *Timaeus* (29a, 46c–e, 68e), *Philebus* (where he is also traditionally called Zeus, 30c–d), and *Laws* (X 899b).

According to the mythical picture, we have seen god performing two functions: First, he is the creator of the world as an ordered whole;[19] though this creation of order seems to occur not only once but in a sense periodically, since god is also the restorer of order under threat of chaos (cf. *Pol.* 273d–e, esp. *kosmei* at 273e3). Second, and above all, god is also a ruler or leader who takes care of the universe during its orderly periods (cf. 269c5, 270a3, 271d–e, 272e4, 273c3).[20] But if, as I have argued, it makes more sense to think of no periodic creation or restoration of cosmic order in time, but of a continuously fair and orderly universe, it would seem that, by being the cause of that order, god should be creating and sustaining the world, by his care of it, always and not just periodically (since, as the *Politicus* myth shows, his merely periodical presence does not suffice to guarantee constant order). These two features, namely being a principle of order and ruling, would be characteristic of the "divine cause" represented by god in the *Politicus*, just as they reappear as distinctive of god or the cause not only in the *Timaeus*, but also in the *Philebus* (27a–b) and the *Laws* (e.g. X 896a–c).

Furthermore, there seems to be good reason to suppose that in the *Politicus* myth god is a *nous*. The text in fact attributes intellectual activities to god (such as "being aware" – *gnontes* – at 272e8, and imparting teaching – *didachê* – at 274c6), and practical functions of ruling, like the tending of flocks, which had already been treated previously in the dialogue as a kind of knowledge or *epistêmê* (cf. 267a–b). In addition, there are several hints that support this notion in the light of other dialogues since, first, god is called a "pilot" (*kubernêtês*, *Pol.* 272e4), and this is the very term Plato uses in the *Phaedrus* to speak of intellect as the pilot of soul (247c7). Second, in the *Politicus* god has the essential feature of "turning itself always" (*auto heauto strephein aei*, 269e5) and this feature is twofold, since it involves (1.) circular motion and (2.) self-motion. On the one hand, we know from the *Timaeus* (34a) and *Laws* (X 897c, 898a) that circular motion is the property of *nous*. On the other hand, we learn from the *Phaedrus* (245c–e) and *Laws* (895e–896a) that self-motion is the definition of soul. This suggests that the god or Demiurge of the *Politicus* is a kind of *noetic soul*; a point independent of whether we take this *nous* as separate or not from the universe,[21] though, to be utterly consistent, we should rule out the former interpretation. For the text makes it clear that there cannot be constant order in the universe if it is separated (*chôrizomenos*) from god (*Pol.* 273c–d); so that when there is divine guidance (as I have argued to be always the case) god is not separated.

Now, god's very feature of motion prevents us also from taking him as a symbol of the Forms, which, on the contrary, are immutable and superior even to god's *nous*. The Forms' immutability is suggested at 269d5–6, where being always in the same state is said to belong only to the most divine of all beings,[22] by contrast with change (*metabolê*, 269e1) pertaining to the universe by virtue of its participation in body.[23]

At any rate, we are able to say that god, as *nous*, is a mediator in the ontological structure of the *Politicus*: He is both inferior to the immutable Forms, "the most divine of all things" (*Pol.* 269d6), with which he would nevertheless share invisibility and intelligibility;[24] and superior to the material realm he organises, with which he shares the property of motion (269d–e). And this mediating function may have a teleological aspect if we take this *nous* to bear a cognitive relation to the Forms (as in the *Timaeus*) and, as a self-mover, to be in turn an efficient cause or principle of motion (as suggested at *Pol.* 269e5–6)[25] and thus act upon the sensible realm according to the order of Forms. In this way we could explain how he is responsible for bringing beauty to the sensible universe (273b6–7).[26]

3. The Cosmological Meaning of Opposite Cycles

So we see that there are elements of cosmological importance in the myth of the *Politicus* that relate it to other late dialogues dealing with cosmology, even if, as I have argued earlier, the imagery itself of opposite cosmic cycles or cosmic drama seems unfeasible. Let us recall, however, that in denying the existence of cosmic drama in the *Politicus* I am not denying the existence of all sorts of disturbance in Plato's universe. I am just questioning that disorder might affect *the whole heaven* or universe. However, it is a matter of fact that confusion exists in human and political life (as we shall see later on) and there may also be disarrangements in the natural domain, even within the framework of an orderly universe. The very myth of the *Politicus* tells us that *there are* "small evils" (*smikra phlaura*) – due to the influence of the primeval condition of the universe, in turn related to its corporeal element – coexisting with "great goods" (*megala agatha*) even under the guidance of god (273b–c, esp. 273c2–4).

So, rather than having a successive opposition between good and evil, or their respective causes, we could think, with some interpreters,[27] that the *Politicus* mythically represents in a separate and abstract way the predominance of two factors (namely, *nous* and the corporeal) which in fact *coexist* in the cosmos as a mixture (*sunkrasis*) of them (*Pol.* 273b4; cf. *Tim.* 48a2); a mixture in which mind prevails over the cussed corporeal element. The coexistence of these two factors is made explicit, for example, at 273b6–c2: "From its constructor [the universe] has acquired all fine things; but from its previous state it retains in itself . . . whatever miseries and injustices arise in the universe" (cf. also 269d8–e1: the universe has received many blessed things from its begetter, but it also participates in body). In addition, I can also here agree with the suggestion[28] that the disorderly cycles of the *Politicus*, as much as the precosmic chaos in the *Timaeus*, are just hypothetical postulations, showing how the world would be *if* god were not present in it *at all times*, or – in the terminology of the *Timaeus* – if necessity (*anankê*) were left to itself without the direction of *nous*.

What has been said in the previous paragraph can then be taken as the *prima facie* cosmological meaning of the myth of opposite cosmic cycles, which can count as a first possible interpretation of that kind of imagery. However, I think that this interpretation, though correct as far as it goes, does not exhaust the purpose of the myth.[29] For, just by itself, the interpretation does not show that this story is not a cosmological digression in the dialogue, and so it is most important to exhibit its relation with Plato's anthropology and political thought. I now wish to show that the disorderly cycles can be regarded not only as a symbol of *hypothetical* states of the world as a whole, but also as a cosmic projection of *actual* human and social disorder. So I pass on to examine the ethical and political importance of the myth and its relation both to cosmology and to the political context of the dialogue. It goes without saying that these different levels of analysis, far from being exclusive, are complementary to one another.

II. THE ETHICAL AND POLITICAL MEANING OF THE MYTH

1. The Exaggeration of the Macro-Microcosm Parallelism

One of the most pervasive notions throughout the myth is that of a close parallelism between macro- and microcosm. Thus, we have seen that all changes in the universe involve changes in us who dwell in it. For example, both the "development" and "reverse process" of human age follow the forward or backward motion of the universe respectively (cf. e.g. *Pol.* 270d–e, 271b7–8, 273e–274a).[30] On the other hand, during the age of Cronus god takes personal charge of the universe as well as of humans; whereas in the era of Zeus, when the world becomes more independent (*autokratôr*), so do humans, with the subsequent need for political organisation, which was absent under Cronus's herdsmanship (cf. *Pol.* 271d–e, 273e–274d).[31] In sum, all of this shows how we "imitate and follow" the whole universe for all time (274a1, d6–7).

I daresay that this emphasis on the intimate relation between the human being and the cosmos makes Plato exaggerate the details of this parallelism, in a manner that contrasts with the differences he stresses in other late works (such as the *Philebus* and the *Timaeus*). This would explain why the world is so anthropomorphically described in the *Politicus*. Yet the exaggeration is not insignificant when we come to regard the cosmos not only as the stage but also as a symbol of human and political behaviour. To this I wish to turn, after reviewing first the political function attributed to the myth in the text. We shall then see how the role of god in the myth can, at the same time, be taken as a model for the politician to follow, in a way that will show the cosmos itself to be a projection of the *polis* or even individual human life.

2. God as a Model for Politicians. The Universe as a Projection of the *Polis*

As we saw in our previous chapter, the political purpose of the myth is the most evident one. We are told that its aim is to correct the first definition of politics given in the dialogue, as the collective rearing or breeding of humans. The main flaw of this definition, as revealed by the myth, is to have mistaken the shepherd of the age of Cronus, who was a god, with the politician of the present age, who is a human being. We should therefore think of politics not in terms of rearing, but in terms of *human concern* for its subjects (cf. *Pol.* 274e–275a, 276c–d).[32] In other words, the function of nurturing humans (spoken of in the first definition) would at the very most belong to god as depicted in the ideal era of Cronus (when no political organisation was needed but we were under the close care of regional gods) but not to a human being in the less ideal age of Zeus in which we live. In this way, the fictitious contraposition between two eras, those of Cronus and Zeus, becomes relevant to illustrate why we need politics in a more hostile universe where humans are left more to themselves.[33] We live in a universe where *nous* does not have complete force but coexists with *anankê*, and the need for political organisation would result from those constraints (cf. *anankazein* at 274c4).

However, the fact that politics cannot be *defined* in terms of a godlike close tending of human beings (like that depicted in the age of Cronus), does not mean that the latter cannot be taken, ideal as it is, as a paradigmatic *example* that human rulers should attempt to follow.[34] It is perhaps in this sense that the Stranger speaks of having introduced the myth in order to provide a *paradigm* for the king (277b3–5). In this way the ideal image of the age of Cronus would not be altogether deprived of political importance. This in turn accords, in its basic point, with a parallel passage in *Laws* IV (713c–714a), which also stresses the political moral of the myth of Cronus: During that age, in fact, we were governed not by humans but by god or *daimones*, that is, more divine and superior beings who provided peace, good order, and justice. God did what we now do with tame flocks: we do not have oxen ruling over oxen but we, who are a better race, ourselves take charge of them (cf. *Pol.* 271e7 for the same thought that the human being is "more divine" – *theioteron* – than the other animals). In like manner, now *we ought to imitate* (*mimeisthai dein*, *Laws* 713e6) the life of Cronus and order both our homes and our states in obedience not to the mortal but to the immortal element within us, namely *nous* (713e6–714a2; for an immortal part of the soul in the *Pol.* cf. 309c). Coming back to the *Politicus*, we can thus see how god would represent a kind of ideal model for human leaders to imitate. Now, even if it is true that the age of Cronus seems to be – usefully – fictitious in its ideal conditions for human life and in the notion that the kings and rulers of human congregations were gods so that there was no need for human rulers, it is certainly not fictitious in stating the guidance that god exerts on the overall universe. This, as we have seen, can be taken as a characteristic of god as such at any time (however he is mythologically described) and the same applies to other functions that he performs in the myth and which will strikingly also belong to the true politician in the third and final definition of the statesman in the dialogue.

So, for example, both god and the scientific ruler have "intelligence" (*nous*) and "concern" (*epimeleia*) devoted to keeping order and to seeing to justice and to the happiness of the whole; both try to save the world or the *polis* from corruption, physical and moral. Thus god, as we have seen in the myth, takes intelligent care of the universe (271d4), exerts kingly power (*basileia*, 269a7) and is responsible for the universe's blessed qualities (269d7–9), by contrast with the "hardships and injustices" (*chalepa kai adika*) that it increasingly undergoes without his guidance (273c–d); god preserves the universe from "risk of corruption" (*diaphthoras kindunon*, 273d3). Similarly, politics, in its normative definition, is said to be superior to other arts in its care (*epimeleia*) of the human community (276b7–c1, cf. 305e3). It is an art (*technê*) belonging to the intelligent king (*phronimos basileus*, 292d6, cf. 294a8), a "wise and good man" (*sophos kai agathos anêr*, 296e3), with unerring *nous*, who, by always administering justice, is able to preserve (*sôizein*) the *polis* and make it better (297a5–b3, cf. 293d8–9); in other words, someone who, by possessing these qualities, can through his rule secure happiness in the city (301d1–5, cf. 311c5–6). This ideal is set in contrast with the evils (*kaka*) that "occur and will occur" in cities that, by having no intelligent rule, are thus liable to destruction through ignorance (301e6–302b3); a situation that can in turn be compared with the cyclical risk of the universe being destroyed at 273d6.[35] Furthermore, in the *Politicus* Plato recurrently makes use of the similes of the pilot and his ship in portraying the ruler and his *polis*;[36] and these are the very same images he employs with regard to god and to the world in the myth (cf. 272e4–5, 273c2–e1).

In addition, the political *technê* tries to keep due measure and thus realise good and beautiful works (284a–b), as much as god in the myth, in his guiding function, realises order and beauty in the universe (273b6–7, e1–4). Even both god and the true politician bring opposites into harmony:[37] whereas god imposes limit upon the limitless, or opposite bodily properties that, left unchecked, would plunge the universe into utter destruction (cf. 273d–e), the scientific ruler has to weave the opposite characters of his collaborators within the society (309a8–b7). Both try to prevent or cure the "illnesses" that result from opposition (273e2–3, 307d ff.). And, just as god endows the world with intelligence (*phronêsis*) and provides instruction (269d1, 273b2, 274c6), so does the scientific ruler ensure that his citizens receive the right education (*paideia*) and share in virtue, by providing them with the divine bond of stable true opinion, which is akin to the immortal element in them, namely reason (308d1–309e13). The latter constitutes in turn an important difference

from the *Republic*, if now education is extended to all citizens (*Pol.* 308d1–
3, 309a8–b7) and if these stable true beliefs about what is good and just –
which are said to be common to all (309c–e, 310e6–11) – are accompanied by reasoned understanding.[38]

We must remember that the characteristics we have mentioned as belonging to the ruler are set as *normative* for him, and that the dialogue
stresses that this kind of human *technê* is by far the most difficult to acquire (*chalepôtatê*, 292d4), much as it constitutes the only true form of
government – of which, furthermore, all the other ones are better or
worse imitations (293e). In this way we can see further how god serves
as a paradigm for any true politician (a paradigm which can therefore
guide our political enquiry), as is already suggested by the assertion that
the ideal kind of human rule must be distinguished from all the other
inferior ones "as a god from humans" (303b4).

In addition, all the comparisons we have established serve to suggest
that god's *nous* in the *Politicus* myth may – at a deeper level that does
not dismiss the cosmological one – be a superhuman symbol, or a cosmic
projection, of the ideal ruler, as much as the world may stand for the *polis*
itself, which is prone to forget its leader's teachings and fall into total
confusion *if or when* an intellect does not govern it (cf. 301c6–302b3).
It is worthwhile insisting that in this case complete disorder is not just a
hypothetical state of affairs (as we took it to be with regard to the cosmos) but an *actual* risk or situation lived through by societies (ibid.).
The same stands if we analyse the myth from an individual point of view,
apart from the political one. In fact, the *polis* embodies on a larger scale
the same tendencies as human individual conduct (recall the correspondence between human personality and society in *Rep.* IV 434d–e, and
cf. *Pol.* 307e–308a).

3. The Universe as a Symbol of Human Drama. God as a Model for Human Beings

From this perspective we can understand why the world's behaviour and
structure in the *Politicus* myth look so unusually anthropomorphic. In
fact, when we read of "the corporeal element" in the universe's constitution (*to sômatoeides*, 273b4) which causes it confusion and disorder
(*thorubos kai tarachê*, 273a5) and even forgetfulness in the *Politicus* (*lêthê*,
273c6), what comes to mind is the exactly similar way in which Plato
speaks of the *human* body (*sôma*) in the *Phaedo* as a source of "confusion
and disorder" (*thorubos kai tarachê*) that prevents us from contemplating

the Forms (66d6–7).[39] On the other hand, the bodily in the *Politicus* is inherent in the world's "ancient nature" (*tês palai pote phuseôs*, 273b5); an expression that finds echo in a kindred passage in *Laws* III about the "ancient Titanic nature" (*palaian Titanikên phusin*, 701c2) displayed by people who lack self-control. Again, in the *Politicus* the universe has an innate *epithumia* responsible for the reversal of revolution ending up on the brink of chaos (cf. 272e6 ff.; *hormê* 273a2); and, even though in this case *epithumia* may be interpreted just as "tendency",[40] we cannot help thinking of an "inborn desire" of the world that reminds us of human baser instincts, referred either to the body or to the lower parts of the soul in Platonic writings (cf. e.g. *Phaedo* 66c, *Rep.* IV 439d, *Tim.* 70d–e, 88a8–b2). In any case, "the bodily", "ancient nature" and *epithumia* are opposed to *nous*, symbolised by the Demiurge or the world-soul on a macrocosmic scale. In this guise, the universe's behaviour in the *Politicus* would represent a conflict between reason and unreason, intelligence and bodily desire, and even remembrance and forgetfulness that in effect characterises human nature.

In addition, the behaviour of the world as depicted in the reverse cycles shows striking similarities with the behaviour of the human infant soul in the *Timaeus*. In the *Politicus* (273a–e), the reverse cycle starts with initial cosmic convulsion (*seismos*, 273a3), and temporary restoration of order thanks to the world's intelligence (cf. *phronêsis*, 269d1). Soon afterwards, however, everything starts going increasingly badly and the world becomes full of diseases (*nosêsanta*, 273e2) as memory of the teachings of the Demiurge grows dim (273b2–3, c6). Likewise, in the *Timaeus* (43a–44c), the infant soul starts having strong convulsions (cf. *seiousai*, 43d1) when it is implanted in a mortal body, after which its revolutions settle down and the individual becomes rational (*emphrôn*). But, if an adequate upbringing is missing, the individual's rationality will deteriorate and he will return to Hades without intelligence (*anoêtos*), suffering "the greatest disease (*tên megistên noson*)" (44b–c).

In this way we can also see that the relation between the world and god in the *Politicus* is analogous to that between humans and god in other dialogues. Thus, we find that the cosmos in the *Politicus* has the capacity to remember and to forget god's teachings (273b, c): in the light of the *Timaeus*, one could think that these consist in how the world ought to behave (i.e. its own celestial motions) according to the pattern of the Forms.[41] Now, in the *Politicus*, it is suggested that god has a perfect rotatory motion (cf. 269e5) to be imitated by the universe.[42] And this is especially noteworthy seeing that in other dialogues it is conversely *humans* that are liable to forget or to recollect the Forms (cf. e.g. *Phaedo* 72e ff., 76a–77a; *Phaedrus* 249b–c); or, even more, it is humans that are liable to forget or recollect, and even imitate, god: such is the situation in the *Phaedrus* (252d–253c), and also in the *Timaeus* (41e1–2 with 47a, 47b–c) where the god in question is the universe itself,[43] and can in turn constitute an intermediate stage towards one's knowledge of Forms.[44] From this standpoint, the relation of the world to the deity in the *Politicus* may be depicting humans' attitude towards god and the importance of their remembering god's instructions.

All these comparisons between macro- and microcosm in the *Politicus* and in the light of other dialogues serve to illustrate the anthropomorphic guise of the world in the myth, even though we have been led to acknowledge that the picture could hardly be taken literally as far as the whole universe is concerned. In point of fact, the *cosmic drama* referred to in that story stands for *human drama*, that is, an *ethical conflict* that is in general absent from the world but common in humans, considered either individually or collectively. If this is so, then we are right in saying that, in spite of the literary details, the universe (especially the heavens) is a pattern of order that human beings *ought* to imitate (cf. *Phil.* 28c–30c; *Tim.* 47b–c, 90d). And in this – ethical – sense the "imitating and following" of the universe by humans (*Pol.* 274d6–7) would be normative rather than descriptive. So, whereas in the universe absolute chaos is just a hypothetical state, since *nous* continuously governs *anankê* for the most part, complete disorder does exist in *human* life and may pervade the whole of it, and it depends on human beings to make *nous* rule or else be subdued by *anankê*. In other words, the universe is what humans and the *polis* ought to be. This too is the main difference between us and god: whereas *nous* defines god invariably and essentially, human rationality on the contrary is not something "given" but a task that remains to be achieved.

Nothing could be more telling on this point than that passage in the *Politicus* where, after describing the advantages that people in the carefree age of Cronus delighted in, the Stranger queries whether they were happier than those of the present era of Zeus or not. Surprisingly, there is no categorical answer to this question, and by means of this Plato rejects the most salient feature of the Hesiodic Golden Age, namely happiness as something unquestionably enjoyed by the human race (cf. *Op.* 106 ff., esp. 115 ff.).[45] By contrast, the Stranger's answer in the *Politicus* is conditional: *If* the nurslings of Cronus made use of their leisure time and their ability to have dialogue for the sake of philosophy and to the improvement of wisdom (*phronêsis*), then they were immensely happier than those of our age; otherwise they were not (cf. *Pol.* 272b–d). This is the same as to say that intelligence, philosophical life, and the happiness they entail, are not a mere gift but a task or ethical challenge for humans to undertake; a challenge that they cannot avoid even in the most idealised era of humanity.[46] Or, in other words, that "Golden Age" onto which so many human beings project our happiness is not something lost but an inner capacity of ours, and it depends on our choice to fulfil it. This conclusion, I would like to argue further, can also apply at least partly to its ideal environmental conditions.

4. The Age of Cronus, Politics, and our Environment

In the age of Cronus, people are portrayed as having the Earth as their mother who would cater for their needs (272a1–b1).[47] We are told that humans had the ability to converse not just among themselves but also with other animals, learning from each other (*Pol.* 272b8–c5), in a way that points at the notion of a kinship and fellowship (*homilia*, cf. 272c2) between humans that extends even to other beings in the scale of nature.

Can we draw any morals from this mythical description? We certainly do live in an age when we need politics, and human distinctions are created by our belonging to different families or nations. But we should not forget in this respect the Stranger's complaint that it is unnatural to divide humans into Greeks and Barbarians, as much as it is unnatural to create a division between human and nonhuman animals (262a–e).[48] So, without ignoring the constraints imposed by necessity in our present era, the myth can, when put in context, still suggest, through the age of Cronus, an ideal dimension that should again act as our paradigm. It is thus imaginable that, if our political rulers were themselves capable of using god as their model (a motif which we saw lies at the back of the third definition of the statesman), then the human and even natural world would exhibit conditions more similar to that ideal age where each region of the Earth was under intelligent care and all care-takers were in cooperation with each other so that it was possible for us to have a more harmonious relation with our environment.

If this suggestion is correct, then war (as violence among animals in general, *Pol.* 271e) would be absent from the ideal condition – even though Plato later allows that war might be necessary in some cases (cf. 304e–305a). So too in the *Laws* (I 625c–628e), war is compared to treatment needed on a sick body, the first best always being health or peaceful harmonious interaction. Similarly, in the *Republic* the need for war was introduced as a falling off from the simplicity of the first *polis* (II 372a–373e), and civil war was in any case condemned as threatening the unity of a state. If the universe in the *Politicus* is now a projection at large of the human world, we can understand how it would be important to avoid war and division to preserve its unity (273d–e).

But isn't it the case that in the *Politicus* this idyllic situation is described not as the ideal *polis*, but as the absence of politics? Maybe so, but what we are told is that under Cronus there were no constitutions or *politeiai*, in the plural (271e8). Thus, while Plato is still preoccupied with the best form of *human* constitution, the myth of Cronus may at the same time leave room for the notion of all humans as citizens of the universe, as we saw was the case in the *Philebus*.[49] Now, since reason by nature grasps the overall good – and the *Politicus* insists on the importance of having common views about moral values, no matter how different people are, cf. 309c–e, 310e – one could even argue that to have all nations ruled intelligently would facilitate a state of global cooperation after the model of the universe itself, just as in the age of Cronus all provincial deities are said to interact with the major god (271d3–6).

By contrast, we have seen that a world without intelligent rule and driven by desire is likely to accumulate many injustices (*adika*, 273c1) that threaten to separate it and destroy it (273d3–e1). If Plato after all does choose this imagery with some conscious use of emotional effect, then we can take the mythical possibility that the world might follow that course as a warning; and in god's mythical return to the helm we should perhaps discern an invitation for humans to act like god in taking responsibility for the spheres that are under their influence.[50] This, as I shall show in the next chapter, has further large-scale implications that should not escape our attention. In this regard, we can see how depicting human situations at a macro-level may help Plato present them to the observer with sufficient distance and clarity[51] – and, we could add in this case, a dreadful clarity: it exhibits how the whole cosmos would be if the same principles that can lead human life into chaos were operating without restraint in the universe.

III. CONCLUSION

In sum, even though my analysis of the cosmological bases of the myth has tended to deny any predominance of irrationality in the world as a whole and therefore the existence of alternating cosmic cycles (very far from what a literal interpretation would suggest), we can in any event understand the anthropomorphic picture of the world in the *Politicus* in the light of the ethical and political purpose of the myth. The world has appeared as the stage onto which Plato has projected human disarrangements; though, strictly speaking, the astronomical universe cannot but be a pattern for human behaviour to follow. So, in the same way as *nous* reigns over the universe, it must also govern the microcosm if order is ever to exist in humans and in politics (and harmony be promoted even with regard to our natural environment). In this way, we can see how the myth provides the macrocosmic background for ethics and a touchstone to seek the true definition of the statesman.

8

Laws X: First Causes and the Origin of Evil

The *Laws* presents Plato's last and vast attempt at laying the platform for a political project, where all the citizens will have an understanding of the reasons why they should abide by certain norms.[1] In this respect, the dialogue sustains the effort of other late dialogues to extend education to the many, and thus avail them of more solid foundations for the attainment of happiness. The *Laws* also lays down the groundwork for a system where political law is to be based on natural law; but establishing this point requires proving that there are norms of nature. To this effect, Plato finds it of importance to establish that there is *nous* – intelligence – pervading the cosmos, and that our own intelligence is akin to it. In particular, if it is the role of intelligence to grasp objective goodness, the hope is that by having all citizens acquire and use critical understanding, they will reach agreement about common values and this will in turn secure the rule of law in a way that is grounded in nature. Thus, book IV relates the etymology of *nomos*, law, to *nous*, intelligence (714a; cf. XII 957c), and presents the divine *nous* that ruled during the golden age of Cronus as paradigmatic for a political search.[2] In this way, in opposition to the view that laws are merely the arbitrary rule of the stronger, the *Laws* presents a normative concept of law; one which should, in a desirable political system, promote the individual flourishing of virtue.[3] To what extent cosmology is relevant for the achievement of this large ethical project in the *Laws* remains, however, underexplored. It is book X that contains the most significant evidence, and for that reason the chapter will be especially focused on this portion of text.

Book X of the *Laws* begins precisely as an attempt to refute theories of nature whereby it is not only deprived of, but even opposed to, normativity. The big divide between norm and nature, or *nomos* and *phusis*, that had been defended by several sophists is now given scientific support, Plato believes, by theories according to which the universe operates through chance and not *nous*, so that law, or any result of intelligence, is merely a human phantom or mortal creation, one which does not have anything to do with the way things are (889b–e). To establish that nature operates on the basis of intelligent design is then crucial if Plato is to show us that normative principles are not just a matter of relativistic conventions;[4] but this project becomes tantamount, in his eyes, to proving the existence of the gods and their providence. It is in this regard essential that all citizens should have a grasp of this issue not only by way of myth, but also by way of argument, if reasoned understanding is needed to dispel the ignorance that is so often at the root of vice.[5] And thus book X sets out to demonstrate three propositions as a preamble for the laws against impiety: (1.) that the gods exist (887c–899d); (2.) that they take care of human affairs (899d–905d); and (3.) that they cannot be bribed by sacrifice or prayer (905d–907b).[6]

Now, if this is the objective of Plato's enterprise in book X of the *Laws*, we would expect him to be particularly careful not to mislead the reader into believing that anything other than goodness may be at the basis of nature. Scholars have often pointed to the apologetic and exoteric character of book X,[7] which would even appear to present the gods as rather more powerful than in the *Timaeus*. But this attempt might seem to reveal a self-defeating character by the sudden introduction, in the middle of the argument devoted to proving the existence of god, of an "evil soul" possibly ruling the cosmos. What are we to make of this feature?

I intend to show that Plato's postulation of an evil soul, however disconcerting it may seem, is central to his argument for teleology, and that this postulation bears directly on his attempt to eradicate vice from the universe. So it is particularly relevant that this discourse should be addressed to the immoralist and revive concerns about the nature of the good life (887b–888b). For Plato feels that the flourishing of virtue needs not only the support given by a universe that (as he hopes to show again) is intelligent and organic; it also requires the contribution of humans towards fighting that evil soul which occupies such an important place in his argument.

In what follows, I shall present Plato's argument for the existence of god and show how the problem of evil arises within it. The discussion of evil will then take us further into an elucidation of its status and cause

within a finalistic arrangement of the universe, and I shall argue that in
Laws X it turns out that it is human beings (as opposed to some larger
cosmic force) who are responsible for every sort of evil. This may appear
a simple-minded answer on Plato's part, one that is insensitive to the
complexity of the issue. How can humans, for example, be responsible
for pestilence or disease? I will show that his reply is more profound than
would seem at first blush. By emphasising the large-scale effect of human
actions, it encourages us to take responsibility for our seemingly external
circumstances and our surrounding environment. Thus it reinforces the
picture of humans as autonomous beings who have the capacity, by their
undertakings, either to enhance or diminish the amount of goodness in
the universe.

I. THE PRIORITY OF SOUL OVER BODY

To prove the existence of god, Plato has the Athenian engage in a discussion of the nature of the first cause. What is the primary explanatory principle of the universe? According to his materialist opponents, it is chance
(*tuchê*, 889a5, b2) or chance by necessity (*tuchê ex anankês*, 889c1–2)
governing the motion, collision, and admixture of opposite corporeal
forces that gave rise to the heavenly bodies and the universe in general
(889a–c). Within this picture, body takes precedence over soul and any
mental properties, which are said to emerge "afterwards" (891c). Insofar
as those principles are devoid of intelligence and planning, their postulation provides, in Plato's eyes, the scientific support for atheism. The
Athenian purports to attack such theories by conversely establishing the
priority of soul over body "by nature". How are we to understand nature
(*phusis*)? Here the concern is less with nature as the result of a process
of growth than with nature as the *source* of that process.[8] Thus, to nature understood as chance and necessity the Athenian opposes his own
principles, namely god and design (*technê*) and intellect (*nous*) as things
akin to soul (889b–c, 892a–c). The latter, he intends to argue, should be
prior as the first cause of generation and corruption of everything and, if
by "nature" the materialists mean "the productive source associated with
the first elements" (*genesin tên peri ta prôta*, 892c2–3), it should be soul
(*psuchê*) and not fire or air that deserves to be first "by nature" (892c3–7),
since soul is the first source (*prôtê genesis*) of all things (896a6–8).[9]

   In this regard, we can see how it is vital for Plato to establish a connection between god and soul, understood as purposive intelligence
(cf. *technê* and *nous* at 889c and 892b). The struggle between theism

and atheism becomes then a struggle between teleology and chance (or random mechanism) as the key factor in explaining the universe. And proving the existence of god turns out to be equivalent to proving, first, the priority of soul to body, and, secondly, that soul in charge of the universe is intelligent and therefore good. This is the *Laws'* next task.

At 893b the Athenian starts his argument for the priority of soul over body with the following steps:

1. Of all things (*panta*), some are in motion, some are at rest (893b8–c1).
2. It is in a place (*en chôrai tini*) that the static things rest and the moving things move (893c1–2).
3. Among the things that move, we can distinguish ten kinds of motion, the last two being the two kinds of motion under which every other kind falls:[10]
   - "That motion which can move other things, but is unable to move itself" (894b8–9). This is to be understood not as another kind at the same level as the preceding eight, but as the way in which every kind of bodily change takes place, that is as a mechanical series,[11] in which each member is "constantly moving one thing and being moved by something else" (894c3–4).
   - "That motion which can always move itself and other things" by means of corporeal changes (894b9–c1).

The next step in the argument is to establish the priority of self-motion over mechanical motion. This is asserted on the grounds that every chain of motion should stop at a first mover. It cannot, by definition, be the kind of motion that has in turn been moved by something else (cf. 894e4–7). And if we imagine that everything were at rest, it would have to be self-motion that would appear first (895a6–b1). Thus, self-motion (895b1) turns out to be the principle of all motions (*archê kinêseôn pasôn*, 895b3) and the *condition of possibility* of all the corporeal changes. It is therefore the first (*prôtê*, 895b4) not only in the causal order but also in dignity (*presbutatê*, 895b5, 896b3) and efficacy (894d2, 895b6), whereas the motion that is moved by something else and in turn moves other things is secondary (*deutera*, 895b7).

This argument lends itself to several objections. For example, why accept, even if we need to stop the regress in the explanation of motion at a first mover, that such a first mover must itself be in motion, rather than unmoved (as Aristotle will claim)? We have seen in previous chapters why Plato may have in his late dialogues a preference for endowing his first cause with motion, particularly when it is efficient (rather than final, or formal) causation that he is concerned with.[12] But, even assuming that the first mover is in motion, or indeed a self-mover, why call it "soul" at all, as the Athenian will try to conclude?

Certainly, the Athenian thinks that the link will be just to define soul as that first kind of motion. Isn't this simply a question-begging manoeuvre? Perhaps not, if we take his argument as an appeal to his opponent's intuitions. It is indeed a vexed question (one that still haunts contemporary enquiry) what the features are that define "life"; but the Athenian puts his cards on the table. Assuming commonsensical agreement from his interlocutor, he proposes that it is motion initiated in a being from within, rather than having its source outside itself (895c). And in then switching from "life" to "soul" little more than a change of terms is involved.

We must remember, in this respect, that while the term "soul" often suggests something mystical or esoteric to us, it did not necessarily do so for the ancient Greeks. Talk of *soul* (*psuchê*) might be as humdrum as talk of *life*, and one term was often used for the other (in a way acceptable even to a materialist). Thus, the Athenian proceeds to point out that we call "living" those corporeal objects that move themselves, or that have a soul (i.e. are animate) interchangeably (895c). He shows how this can be explained by developing a distinction between a thing's reality or essence (*ousia*), its name (*onoma*), and its definition (*logos*). Thus, we may take "self-motion"[13] as the definition of that same reality to which we refer by the name of "soul" (896a1–4). Secondary motions, for their part, are referred to "the motion of an inanimate body" (896b7–8). In this way soul, being self-motion, is the cause (*aitia*) or principle of motion (*archê kinêseôs*) of everything, having priority over body and thereby ruling (*archousês*) over it according to nature (896b–c, cf. 892a). Here Plato seems to be exploiting the semantic richness of the word "*archê*", which suggests that the notion of being a *principle* is inseparable from that of having *rule*.

Soul is, in the first place, the cause of its own psychic motions, such as "tempers, habits, wishes, reasonings, true opinions, concerns and memories" (896c9–d1). Consequently, it is the cause of every kind of secondary motion of the corporeal (894e–895a), which in turn gives rise to the sensible qualities of things (cf. 897a7–b1).[14] If soul is prior to body, then things pertaining to the psychic realm (*ta psuchês*) must be prior to things pertaining to the corporeal realm (*ta tou sômatos*), such as length, width, depth, and strength of bodies (896c–d). Therefore, we might infer, intellect (*nous*), design (*technê*), and law (*nomos*), which at 892a–b had been settled as akin to soul, should also be prior by nature (*phusei*).

Now, what exactly does Plato mean by the "priority of soul"? Delving into this issue will be important if we are to grasp what is ultimately the view of nature and god presented in the dialogue. But that question is inserted into what seems to be a larger concern about the mind-body relation in general, given that the argument to this point concerns the genus soul as such, of which, as we shall see, both human and divine souls are kinds.

It might be tempting to think that, in principle, Plato wishes to establish a robust dualism in giving priority to soul or mind over body; this would be the kind of priority that makes soul or mind altogether independent from the body, just as one might think of god as a mind in principle independent of the universe under its care. But this is not, I shall argue, the picture we get in the *Laws*; and establishing some brief comparisons with other dialogues may shed some light on the issue.

The account in the *Laws* so far shows many points of contact with the *Timaeus*. The distinction between primary and secondary motion, referred to soul and body respectively, is parallel to that between primary and secondary causes in the *Timaeus* (46c–e; 68e–69a), and the rule of soul over body is affirmed in both (cf. *Tim.* 34b–c). Primary motion, in fact, is said in the *Laws* to operate by *making use* of secondary motions (cf. *kata* at 894b10 and *chrômenê* at 897b1), just as primary causes use the assistance of secondary causes in the *Timaeus* (68e, esp. *chrômenos* at e4). Even though the *Timaeus* does not explicitly say that the first kind of causes (i.e. souls) are self-movers, it seems to be implied by the context: secondary causes are those "which occur by other things being moved and in turn moving other things by necessity" (46e1–2), so that we can infer that primary causes are those which move themselves.

The account of soul as self-motion and first cause of motion is also parallel to that in the *Phaedrus* (245c–246a). As we have seen, this notion of soul was in the *Phaedrus* established in close connection to the body that is moved by soul. "All body (*sôma*) . . . which itself from itself has motion from within is animate, since this is precisely the nature of soul" (245e4–6); this in turn matches the further assertion that "all soul takes care of all the inanimate" (246b6), suggesting that soul and body go hand in hand.[15]

From here it would seem that, much as body depends on soul as its principle of motion, soul depends on body for the fulfilment of its activity, and thus the issue of the soul's priority turns out to be a little more complex than it seemed on the surface. The following objections, however, might be raised against comparing the *Laws* with the *Phaedrus* as proposed:

(I.) In the *Phaedrus*, the soul was clearly called ungenerated (*agenêton*, 245d3). In this *Laws* passage, by contrast, Plato often resorts to the language of generation for the soul itself. Thus, the soul is said to be "born first among all things" (*emprosthen pantôn genomenê*, 892a5) or "born among the first" (*en prôtois gegenêmenê*, 892c4). And this temporal language might suggest that soul was born first, and body second, which means that there was a time when the soul existed by itself. If this is so, then the soul can exist independently of the body, and Plato has *not* in the *Laws* moved away from a robust kind of dualism (or substance dualism, where the soul is represented as capable of autonomous existence independent of material conditions). This view is implied by T. M. Robinson.[16] Further, the objection assumes that, even though soul is a substance capable of generating motion in a body, it need not do so, but in any case it does not generate the bodily aspect of body itself; only its motion. On this picture, soul and body seem to be two disjoint entities that come to be associated by some mysterious kind of interaction.

(II.) An alternative to the last difficulty mentioned would make soul an independently existing substance, but the only one, which gives rise not only to the motions of body, but to the whole of reality. In such a case, Plato might be endorsing some form of mentalism,[17] which seems to be at the other extreme from the view that we have seen in the *Phaedrus*, where the soul tends to appear as a feature intrinsic to the body. And this might seem to find support in passages suggesting that the soul is the "cause of all things" (*ta panta*, 896d8, cf. 896a7–8).

Yet there are other passages in the *Laws* where the soul, as self-motion, is described as a "property" (*pathos*) of a body (895c), or said to be suitable for all actions and passions (894c), with the capacity (*dunamis*) to move itself and other things (cf. e.g. 892a, 894b, 896a). Such language again recalls the *Phaedrus*,[18] and may in turn bring to mind the *Sophist* (246c–247e), where the reformed materialist (with whom Plato seems willing to make friends) is the one who accepts the existence of invisible incorporeal properties, such as justice and intelligence, and agrees with a definition of "being" as the capacity to act and be acted upon, which could thus apply to the soul (after all, even in the *Laws* he prefaces this argument as targeted to persuading the materialists gently, 888a–b). So the *Laws* seems to have opened too much logical (or illogical?) space, ranging from what we could label as (I.) substance dualism to (II.) mentalism, without even excluding (III.) qualified materialism. Is such openness deliberate, or a sign of fatal confusion? A later passage in the *Laws* expresses Plato's awareness, and conceivably openness, about various ways in which the soul may relate to the body (898e–899a).[19] Yet I think a closer analysis of the text will help us better delineate his view. What kind of priority, then, does Plato have in mind for the soul?

First, (I.) does not commit Plato to substance dualism. For the talk of the soul as "born" need not be temporal. The soul may be "born" in a logical order, and born from itself, if soul *is* self-generated motion. Thus, even if the *Phaedrus* stresses that soul is *temporally* ungenerated, in the sense of having had no beginning in the past,[20] the *Laws* would be allowing that it can still be called "generated" insofar as it is constantly self-creating: The soul's definition consists in *self-motion* (so that if soul creates its own motion it creates itself) and it is the cause of motion of all things that "exist, have come to be, and will exist" (*tôn te ontôn kai gegonotôn kai esomenôn*, 896a7–8) among which we should then count not only bodies, but soul itself (cf. 894b9–10: soul can move "itself always and other things"). Otherwise it would be unintelligible to find soul described both as generated and at the same time as the "first cause of generation of all things" (*prôton geneseôs . . . aition hapantôn*), as we do at 891e5–7.

The mention of its being "of highest rank" or "oldest" (*presbutatê*, 895b5, 896b3) may play with the same kind of ambiguity without committing Plato to the temporal precedence of soul (and the ambiguity may in any case be usefully suggestive in opposing those crudely materialist cosmogonies that had postulated soul as born after bodies).[21] Thus, the soul is first born in the sense that it originates from itself and its identity conditions cannot be reduced to the identity conditions of matter considered in abstraction from it. But in any case, soul is clearly portrayed as pertaining to the realm of becoming (*genesis*) and as subject to time (in the mode of past, present, and future), like everything else in that realm (896a7–8).

Further, neither can the text imply some kind of mentalism whereby "soul" is a self-sufficing entity that does not inhere in anything else but rather originates everything else. For it is from the very start of the argument established in universal terms (cf. premise 2) that "whatever moves . . . moves in a place" (893c1–2); this will apply to every kind of motion, including the tenth, which is *psychic* motion. This means that the motion of soul takes place in space (*chôra*, cf. *Tim.* 52a8, d3).[22] So space is an antecedent "given", and a *necessary condition* for the existence of soul. Even if, as in the *Timaeus*, space is conceived as full of bodily properties or "traces" (53b), soul could still be the cause of "all things" not only insofar as becoming, or motion, can be seen as constitutive of the nature of soul and the sensible realm itself (cf. *Tim.* 35a) but also insofar as soul is the principle of all bodies *qua* organised bodies.[23] In this regard, soul is prior as a ruler of those bodies, who must be second to it by nature (*Laws* 896c1–3). Thus, we read that the soul's function is to "lead all things" (*agein panta*, 896e8), to "take control" of bodily motions (*paralambanein*, 897a5; cf. *Tim.* 30a4) and to "administer" (*dioikein*) and "dwell in" (*enoikein*) all things that move everywhere (896d10–e2). This view suggests again that there need not be a contradiction between the view of soul that we have seen in the *Phaedrus* and that of the *Laws*. Body and soul may imply one another and thus constitute a single inseparable whole:[24] If so, then the priority of soul over body would be logical, in the order of explanation (*kata logon*, 894d10), it still remaining true that, ontologically, soul cannot exist without space, nor can it exert its function of primary causation without "using" the body as a vehicle (897b1; cf. 894b). Soul, though "hopefully"[25] invisible (898d9–e2, cf. *Tim.* 36e6, 46d6), makes itself manifest in the body it moves; that is why Plato feels comfortable enough to have the Athenian say that "when we *see* a soul" in self-moving – corporeal – objects, we say that they live (895c11–12).

II. WHAT IS THE EVIL SOUL? SOME QUESTIONS

We have seen that the argument has so far (893b–896d) presented the priority of soul over body as a priority of primary motions over secondary motions, the former being the principle of the latter. In this context, it has been important to spell out what Plato means by the "priority" of the soul over the body and what kind of relation he envisages in *Laws* X between the two. However, just proving the priority of soul might not seem sufficient to establish the existence of god, which requires a further step in the argument. For soul in itself is morally ambivalent, that is, it can be good or bad, rational or irrational, whereas the notion of god at stake in the *Laws* requires that god's soul be purely rational and good.[26] Plato must show, then, that *this* is the kind of soul in charge of the universe; and the need for a proof becomes all the more pressing given that our intuitions may pull us strongly in the opposite direction. It is in this context that the postulation of an "evil soul", however surprising, may do some work.

It is still conceivable, for example, that the universe might be organised in the way it is for the sake of evil; or it may be that, despite its appearance of organisation, soul is not sufficient to sustain it because at bottom such a soul is leading the universe to disconnectedness and chaos due to its own lack of purpose and irrationality. How do we know that our universe is not after all under the rule of an "evil demon", or at least an extremely clumsy, forgetful and ignorant kind of soul?

It might even be that this soul is good, but only contingently good and caring (at certain points of our lives or the world's history), while at other points it might "abandon" us, by becoming bad or simply detached. After all, even the *Politicus* myth, on a literal reading, had suggested a picture of cosmic cycles of order and disorder, the latter being those when god becomes "absent" or withdrawn from the universe; it had also suggested that the universe's soul, left to itself, could be filled with increasing forgetfulness and eventually lead everything to ruin, just like a human being who ages and loses control of himself.

This kind of thought is not likely to have escaped atheists and believers alike, as it is not likely to have escaped those who draw conclusions from the apparent "good fortune" (*tuchas*) that the worst kind of people enjoy on this planet: if the universe is in the hands of some controlling power, so they think, either that power is responsible for evil or else it can't be of the kind that cares (cf. 899e–900b). Plato's introduction of an "evil soul" in the *Laws* is therefore of the utmost importance in confronting people's intuitions and dissatisfactions with regard to the moral compass of the world. To what extent he wants to challenge them, and to what extent he wants to agree with them, is as yet unclear. So we must follow the argument where it takes us.

The ethical ambivalence of soul is remarked upon in the next step of the argument, where it is presented as the "cause of the good and evil things, fair and foul, just and unjust and all the contraries, if we are to posit it as the cause of all" (896d5–8). At the same time, whereas the argument seems so far to have been speaking of soul in general, *qua* soul, a hint is subsequently made of the cosmic import of soul by the suggestion that "soul, which administers and inhabits all things which are moved everywhere, also administers the heaven (*ouranos*)" (896d10–e2).

Now, it is at this stage that we have to face a difficulty arising from the previous arguments, for:

(1.) on the one hand, soul is the principle of all contraries (including good and bad); but,

(2.) on the other hand, an incautious application of (1.) could lead us to violate a principle which Plato had established in the *Republic*

(IV 436b8–9), famously known as his "Principle of Opposites": "It is evident that the same thing will not admit to produce or undergo contrary effects in the same sense, with respect to the same thing and at the same time".

How, then, can one thing such as soul be the cause of all the contraries at *Laws* 896d? The passage of the *Republic* already mentioned concluded that if we find that happens, "we shall know that it was not the same one thing but more than one" (436b9–c1); and on this basis it proceeded to distinguish different parts, faculties or "kinds" (*eidê, genê*) within the individual soul (436c ff.). The principle settled in the *Republic* seems to be implicit in this discussion in the *Laws*; and an attempt to keep to it would justify the conclusion that it cannot be just one soul (or kind of soul) that is cause of all contraries, but it should be "more than one" (*pleious*, 896e4): "Let us postulate not less than two: the beneficent soul (*tês euergetidos*) and that which is capable of producing the opposite results (*tês tanantia dunamenês exergazesthai*)" (896e5–6), afterwards called "the evil soul" (*tên kakên*, 897d1).

Now, the cosmic import of soul seems again emphasised in the following passage, crucial for our discussion, which runs as follows:

Soul leads all things in heaven and earth and sea by its own motions, the names of which are: wish, reflection, concern, counsel, opinion true or false, joy, grief, boldness, fear, hate, love, and whatever motions akin to these, or primary motions, take over the secondary motions of body and lead everything to increase and decrease and separation and combination, and to the things derived from these: heat and cold, heaviness and lightness, hardness and softness, whiteness and blackness, bitterness and sweetness, and all those things which soul makes use of, both when, having acquired *nous* which is always rightly god in the case of gods,[27] it leads all things rightly and happily, and when conversely, associated with unreason (*anoiai sungenomenê*) it produces all the effects contrary to those (896e8–897b4).

Several problems result from different interpretations that might be given of this text. In particular, what is the scope of "soul" at the opening of the passage? Is, for example, the Athenian making a claim about a cosmic soul, or should we reject that possibility?

III. THE SCOPE OF "SOUL" AT *LAWS* 896E–897B

We may indeed be tempted to think that this passage concerns soul at a cosmic level. The first few lines, specifically, stating that "soul leads all things in heaven and earth and sea", are bound to recall the world-soul for any reader of the *Timaeus*. But if so, we cannot help being struck by the way Plato presents it. As to the psychic motions here referred to, we find that soul can not only have right opinions but also false ones, and not only intellect or reason (*nous*) but also unreason or folly (*anoia*) causing unwelcome results. These features are not just uncharacteristic of the world-soul in previous dialogues (cf. *Tim.* 36e, 37b–c, *Phil.* 28d–e, 30a–d); in addition, they seem to conflict with the goodness and rationality of god, which is an important part of what Plato is trying to establish in *Laws* X (cf. 899b5–7, 900d2, 902e7–8).[28]

In the face of this difficulty, one may feel inclined to surmise that in fact it is no cosmic soul at all that is referred to in this passage of the *Laws*; instead, the passage must simply concern human individual souls.[29] After all, affections such as fear-boldness, pleasure-pain (mentioned at 897a2–3) are associated in the *Timaeus* with the mortal part of the human soul (69c–d; cf. 42a–b); and false opinions are there said to result, like those affections, from the implantation of the immortal part of the soul in a mortal body (44a with 43a ff.). In particular, *anoia* is there analysed as a disease of *human* soul, due to physiological disturbances (86b). Further, the possibilities of *nous* or *anoia* are presented as belonging to the individual soul, and determining the different transformations of *human being* into animal or vice versa (92c). The main problem with this interpretation, however, is that, if it were *just* human souls that Plato means in this passage of the *Laws*, it is hard to understand how he says of them that only they lead "all things in heaven and earth and sea" (896e8–9) – or, as the Athenian will say afterwards (897b7–8), are "in charge of heaven and earth and the whole revolution".

But, I contend, these are not the only possible ways of resolving the problem, as "soul" at *Laws* 896e–897b need not refer exclusively either to cosmic soul or human soul. Instead, Plato may also be keeping the more general sense of *psuchê* as soul *qua* soul,[30] in which he had been speaking before, in the passage concerning the priority of soul over body, 894b–896d. This sense would *a fortiori* include *any* kind of *psychical* motion, like false opinion, *nous* or *anoia*. At the same time, however, he seems to be introducing "*psuchê*" as concretely referring to soul or the "kind of soul" (cf. *psuchês genos*, 897b7) ruling over the universe – the latter, as the text will later on suggest (898d), can include not only the world-soul but also the heavenly bodies.[31] In this regard, then, Plato seems to have *fused* two senses in which he speaks of soul in this passage. And the fusion is marked by the immediately preceding passage where the Athenian proposes that soul should be considered not only as administering all things that are moved anywhere (which I take to be soul *qua* soul) but also the heaven (*ouranos*, 896d10–e2), thus drawing our attention to a new dimension in the argument.

So, if we interpret the passage at 896e8–897b4 as transitional, and as speaking both of soul in general and of soul at a cosmic level here, we need not incur either of the difficulties involved in the two partial views mentioned earlier, the one being that if the passage refers exclusively to the world-soul, it would be awkward to think of it as associated with *anoia* or having false opinion, the other being that, if only human souls were meant, they could not be said to rule everything in the universe. The point rather seems to be that, when Plato speaks of false opinion or *anoia*, he is mentioning states of soul as such, and the question from here onwards will be to decide which state of soul, *nous* or *anoia*, prevails in the universe as a whole. In this way he will pass on to delimit the scope of soul to soul in charge of the universe, as we shall now see.

IV. THE STATUS OF AN EVIL SOUL AT A COSMIC LEVEL

In the next step of the argument (at 897b7–c1) the Athenian wonders:

Which of the two kinds of soul (*poteron psuchês genos*) shall we say is in charge of heaven and earth and the whole revolution? The one which is wise and full of virtue (*to phronimon kai aretês plêres*) or the one which lacks both things?

He does not give a direct answer, but poses a conditional alternative that appeals to the study of heavenly motions: *If* the whole route and motion of heaven and all things in it is akin to the motion, revolution, and calculations of reason – that is, if it is regular (*kata tauta, hôsautôs*), in the same place, around the same point and in the same direction (*pros ta auta*), according to a single proportion and order (*logon kai taxin*) 898a8–b1 – then it is the best soul that leads and cares for the whole cosmos.[32] *If, conversely, the universe's motion is mad and disorderly* (*manikôs kai ataktôs*), *it is the evil soul* (897c4–d1). To this alternative the interlocutors agree that it would not be pious to say anything but that it is the soul that is full of all virtue that drives the whole revolution of the universe (898c6–9).

This conclusion in fact presupposes a second premise, namely that the motion of the universe is orderly. Although this premise is only implicit here, it is explicitly posed as the basis of a similar kind of "physico-theological proof" both in the *Philebus* (28e–29a) and in *Laws* XII 966d–e, where the existence of a governing intellect is inferred from the good order of the cosmos.[33] In the *Laws* it is astronomy in the light of its recent discoveries – which show for example that planets do not "wander" but follow a single regular track, cf. VII 821a–822c, esp. 822a4–8 – rather than superficial and commonsense arguments, that supports the belief in gods ordering the universe (cf. also XII 966d–967e).[34] This is how *Laws* X can then reassert that it is one or several souls[35] that are good in respect of every excellence and therefore gods, which conduct all the stars and cause years, months, and seasons (899b). With this the Athenian concludes his demonstration of proposition (1.) concerning the existence of the gods after having shown, first, the priority of soul over body, and secondly, that the kind of soul in charge of the universe is absolutely good.

From this perspective, what has the status of the "evil soul" proved to be so far? It is clear from the argument at 896d–898c that an evil kind of soul in charge of the cosmos was a mere *hypothesis*, which Plato posed as an alternative to the good soul at the beginning but just in order to reject it. However, we should not think, as some have done,[36] that this is all we can say about the evil soul at 896e–897b, for the argument does not dismiss the existence of "evil soul" as such. What the conclusion clearly shows is that it is not an evil soul (but an excellent kind of soul) that rules over the universe, taken as the whole *astronomical system* (or "heavenly circuit", *ouranou periphora*, 898c3). Thus, the crazy and disorderly motions under the effect of an evil soul described in the text (897d1, cf. 898b5–8) could only be applied to the universe counterfactually: they show how the universe would be *if* it were not god, or a good kind of soul, that guides it.[37]

How much, however, does all this prove? Not that an evil soul could *never* be in charge of the universe, some might say. For it could still be argued that the conclusion just reached is consistent with a view of the universe in which the ruling soul could *successively* exhibit *nous* or *anoia* in different cosmic cycles.[38] But then, the proof for the existence of god would just be valid during the orderly cycle in which we live, without discarding the idea that in a different (disorderly) cycle the universe could be ruled by an evil soul. (The *Politicus* myth, after all, had flirted with the idea of different cosmic cycles, albeit not remitting each to opposite psychic forces.) Yet it is unlikely that this is what Plato has in mind. For the whole thrust of his argument seems to be that the good soul in charge of the universe can be called "god", and he would like further to contend that "god" is essentially good, powerful, and provident, so that there is no reason why he should at any time fail to take proper care of the universe or its parts (901c–903a). In *Laws* VII, in addition, the Athenian had asserted that the heavenly bodies follow *always* the same circular track (822a).[39]

The question, in any case, is not so much whether good and evil rule in different cycles of our universe, for "reifying" evil in this way does little work in answering the crucial question, which is how we explain evil in the *actual* universe in which we live. That evil is a given seems as clear to the Athenian as to us, and that is why he recurrently goes on speaking of the existence of evil in the universe even after he has argued for the existence of the gods (903d–906c). But then, if we keep to the principle according to which an evil kind of soul is the cause of the bad effects in the universe (cf. 896d5–e6), we should admit that *there is an evil kind of soul.* This kind of soul will not rule over the whole astronomical system, as the argument has just shown; that is why in that respect soul's association with *anoia* was just hypothetical. But we could say that both false opinion and irrationality as mentioned at 897a–b become *actual* states of soul[40] when we come to explain the existence of evil that is still present, especially at the sublunary level, within an orderly universe ruled by god. What, then, is the status of this actual evil kind of soul?

The issue can be explored further by distinguishing between moral evil, which, I shall argue, Plato thinks is caused by morally evil – human – souls, and natural evil, such as floods or droughts. It is the latter which is more difficult to explain, and not so intuitively ascribable to the agency of human beings. And perhaps for this reason some interpreters have remitted the cause of natural evil to some sort of soul at a cosmic – nonhuman – level, even though that cosmic cause, as we have seen, will not rule over the universe as a whole. I think, however, that this view cannot be sustained in the context of the *Laws*; I shall present it and show its difficulties before offering my own interpretation concerning the problem of evil here.

The view could take at least two different forms, each of them answering to ambiguities in the text. And we could also here present them as different ways to solve the contradiction that, as we saw, would emerge if only one soul, at the same time and in the same respect, were the cause of all the contraries. We have seen that it cannot be the same soul producing good and evil at different times, but we could still think, instead, that we are dealing with *two distinct* – and coexisting – souls, the one good and the other bad – as might be suggested by *Laws* 896e4, postulating "more than one" soul (*pleious*). Alternatively, it is imaginable that it is *the same soul* that can be associated both with *nous* and with *anoia* (as the singular *psuchê* at 896e8 might suggest), but *in different respects*: thus, the world-soul could have different faculties or parts producing contrary effects.[41]

Both of the positions just delineated have historical precedents: the former was held in its strongest form by Plutarch in antiquity and more moderately by some recent interpreters. The strongest version, as Plutarch put it, postulates two coexisting gods, the one good and the other bad, competing for the governance of the universe and even sometimes alternating in its rule.[42] We have, however, already seen that Plato believes the universe to be continuously (and not just cyclically) orderly, and god to be essentially (and not just contingently) good. So we should not accept the part of Plutarch's account that has two gods alternating their rule of the universe.[43] But we are still left with a more moderate view of the evil soul, according to which it cannot be said to be god or have equal power to the good soul, but rather act as a (mostly) subordinate "principle of matter", which could yet sometimes bring about undesirable effects.[44] Why, then, not attribute the source of natural evil to it?

The problem with this interpretation is that it would be endowing the universe with an internal principle of motion capable of producing evil effects, so that the universe would be the cause of good and bad in different respects. Yet Plato says that the universe itself is a god (*Laws* VII 821a)[45] and that god is only the cause of good, in an unqualified way (see again *Laws* X 899b5–7, 900d2). If this is so, it would seem that the universe cannot contain two principles at a cosmic level causing good and bad respectively but must only be the cause of good.

The same concern would apply if we view the evil soul as an irrational faculty of the world-soul, liable to unreasonable behaviour by which it brings about unwanted results.[46] For if it is the world-soul (and likewise the heavenly bodies) that has different faculties and therefore is said to be the cause of good and bad but in different respects, then, again, Plato could not say of the whole of the world and the heavenly bodies, but only of their *nous*, that they are gods, given that the gods are the cause of good alone. Yet he does say that the universe (including its whole soul) is a god,[47] and that the heavenly bodies' souls, taken either individually or collectively, are gods (X 899a–b). So, given that the goodness of the gods lies in their rationality (cf. e.g. X 900d),[48] the world-soul and that of the heavenly bodies must be essentially and exclusively rational, without any irrational faculty. Indeed, we read at 900d5–9 that being temperate or sound-minded (*to sôphronein*) is an essential part of virtue as belonging to the gods, while its opposite is part of evil; if this is so, such lack of self-control (as would occur if an inferior faculty of soul were sometimes to become insubordinate) could never befit a godly nature. This concept is in turn confirmed by 902a6–b3, where it is denied that gods, while knowing what is best, could yield to pleasure and pain, as people say is the case with the least worthy of humans.

It appears, then, that none of these attempts to give evil a cosmic source can find a place in the cosmology of the *Laws*. This being so, what are we to make of evil, and of the evil soul? In what follows, I shall argue that, in the context of *Laws* X, it is – only – human beings that are presented as responsible for evil, even for the natural evil that Platonic scholarship has tended to attribute to a cosmic source beyond humans. Why should Plato advance this contention, and how plausible is it? These questions will occupy us next.

V. HUMANS, EVIL, AND TELEOLOGY

1. Human Beings as Rulers in the Universe

We should now turn our attention to the section that follows the Athenian's argument for the existence of the gods, where he purports to prove that they care for human affairs and cannot be bribed (899d–907b). There we find that the kind of concrete evil souls spoken about are *human* souls (903d, 904a–e, 905d ff.; cf. 899d–e, 900e with 902b4–5). In addition, whereas moderation, *nous*, and courage are said to belong to excellence, their opposites, which would *a fortiori* include folly and unreason, are referred to evil (900d5–e2). In this context, the Athenian goes on to add that "whatever is bad (*phlaura*), *belongs to us* (*prosêkei hêmin*), if to anyone" (900e6). This is an important remark, and should retrospectively make us think that the *anoia* mentioned at 897b3 as associated with soul, if it is present in the universe at all, belongs to human soul.[49] But that was a passage, if we recall, where "soul" was presented as ruling or administering everything in the universe through its various psychic states (896d10–897b4). Is Plato really saying that human irrationality, or *anoia*, has cosmic reach?

In fact, the Athenian seems ready to allow that human souls have a share in the government of the universe (as is claimed for "soul" at 896e8–9), albeit to a lesser degree than that of god. For we read further on at 903b–c that god "has arranged all things towards the preservation and excellence of the whole", the parts of which also have *rulers* (*archontes*) of every action and passion even on the smallest scale (903b4–9). What are the "rulers" this passage talks about? Amongst them we can certainly read an allusion to lesser gods accompanying the main divinity (cf. *Pol.* 271d, 272e, *Tim.* 41a–d, 42d–e, *Phil.* 30d; and which in Plato's own cosmic religion could be the heavenly bodies ruled in turn by the world-soul). But the text clearly adds that "one of these portions [which have rulers] is also yours, and, however small, tends towards the whole and always looks to it" (903c1–2). Thus it would seem that human beings too are "rulers" of the portions (*moria*) that are allotted to them in the universe, since they have causal responsibility (*aitia*) for the changes, whether good or evil, that they provoke (904b8–c2, c6–7 with 904b2–3).[50]

If this is so, then human souls, as independent principles of motion, could be implicitly included in the scope of "soul" conducting the universe at 896e8, and in this way the government of their portions (for example whole cities, families or their own lives) could turn out to be bad.[51] But how do we get from here to the level of the cosmos? It will be important in this sense to see how the effects of one's actions are not limited to isolated spheres of influence, but have repercussions on a larger scale. In what follows, I shall focus first on the issue of human responsibility as far as moral evil is concerned, and later show how Plato thinks natural evil can be explained within a similar framework, on the basis of some organicist assumptions about the nature of the universe.

2. Cosmic Justice and Human Responsibility

This emphasis on human responsibility is worth noting. In the preceding section (893b–899d) the Athenian had spoken of soul as the cause (*aitia*) of everything, both good and bad, and argued that it is the gods that are the cause of the goodness or order exhibited in the revolution of the universe. This we may call an argument for *natural* teleology, based on the regularity of the astronomical system, which is a given fact. Now, in the section beginning at 899d, when dealing with evil, the notion of *aitia* is again remitted to soul, specifically in the sense of *moral responsibility* (cf. 904b–d). What concerns us now, then, is the issue of *ethical* teleology: how can we become moral agents that work together with god in the administration of the universe? And what happens if we don't?

We have so far seen that human souls must be included, together with the world-soul, under "soul" governing the universe in the difficult passage presenting the possibility of soul being associated either with *nous* or *anoia*. So, even when we have proved that such a possibility is merely hypothetical in the case of the universe, Plato may be deliberately keeping the ambiguity of the Greek to suggest that it can also become an actual possibility in certain cases, particularly as soon as *we* enter the picture.[52]

The very notion of soul as self-mover applied to human souls suggests, above all, that we have *self-determination*. That is, we initiate our own actions or chains of effects instead of these being a mere result of antecedent causes and effects; and this is what it means for our self-moving souls to have responsibility (*aitia*). But, unlike the soul of god, which is also a self-mover, we are not exclusively rational, and so we become a potential source of disorder and ugliness in the universe, and therefore of evil. Freedom, in particular human freedom, enters the scene here not just as the capacity or power to do good things (as the *Gorgias* had contended[53] – the kind of "positive freedom" we would imagine god to enjoy), but as what we may call "freedom of indifference": the capacity to opt for good or evil based on knowledge or ignorance respectively. That is why the "evil soul" is also called the "one lacking wisdom" (897b8–c1). But how does this kind of freedom fit into a teleological universe where, we are told, god has arranged everything "so that goodness might prevail and evil be defeated in the whole" (*nikôsan aretên, hêttômenên de kakian*, 904b4–5)?

The question is a serious one, since we would like to understand how it is possible for god to be providential if after all evil flourishes in our world like a weed. Further, how can god control everything without our being reduced to mere puppets in his hands?[54] And why should we even fight to make this a better universe if after all it is already made good by god? Here again it is important to see how the threads of divine law and human responsibility are interwoven, since in principle they may seem to conflict.

First of all, god is a legislator. But as such, god does not initiate our actions for us; rather, what god does is to lay down laws according to which certain consequences will follow inevitably from certain actions: reward if those actions are good, punishment if they are bad. These laws we can call "cosmic justice" (cf. *dikê*, 904e4). Unlike human courts of justice, which are fallible, cosmic justice, or justice established by god, determines *unfailingly* what effects will follow from the changes that we cause. Thus, we are told in the context of human affairs (*anthrôpina pragmata*, 902b4), how, depending on whether souls are better or worse, they will achieve a better or worse destiny (903d3–e1). In other words, it is *we* who have the *responsibility* (*aitia*, 904c6–7) for good or bad behaviour, according to our will (*boulêsis*, b8–c2), but the *consequences* of this behaviour obtain "according to the order and law of destiny" (*kata tên tês heimarmenês taxin kai nomon*, c8–9), these laws having in turn been settled by the gods (904e–905a, cf. *Tim.* 41e, 42d).

How do the laws of cosmic justice operate? In principle, one may find something a little off-putting in the seeming obscurantism of these

remarks. Is Plato trying to scare us with a vision of hell? On closer examination, we can see that there is no need to assume any of this. First, god
need not be a transcendent being intervening in our lives from above;
second, hell or heaven, punishment or reward, can be seen as a law operating in human life, and in *this* (rather than another) world, as relentlessly
as the natural law that a flame burns.

We must come to realise that the effects of any of our actions, like
throwing a stone into water, may go much further than their intended
target. Thus, the *Laws* is notable for the fact that its divine scheme of prizes
and punishments operates as a natural law of attraction of like to like. In
the *Timaeus*, the attraction of like to like obeyed the force of *ananke*, a
property inherent in the corporeal that fills in space.[55] In the *Laws*, the
principle of like to like becomes a necessary law of spiritual attraction
within the spatial universe. This system of cosmic justice guarantees that,
"*if* you become worse, you go towards worse souls, and, *if* you become
better, you go towards better souls" (904e5–7). The laws work conditionally, and thereby do not determine us to act in a specific way. What they
do determine is that certain consequences will follow given certain actions – just as *if* we ignite the flame, it will burn, although it is up to us to
ignite it. Do we need to suppose that these inevitable consequences take
place only after death? It seems not. For we are told that "both *in life* and
in every death you do and suffer what it is appropriate that like should
do towards like" (904e7–905a1). Thus we can see that the ethical theory
presented here does not necessarily depend on eschatology – though in
principle it doesn't exclude it either.[56]

After all, any reader of the *Republic* will remember how the tyrant has
to pay the most painful price of inner turmoil and a friendless existence,
being surrounded by the worst of people (IX 578e–580a); and already in
the *Apology* Socrates had expressed his awareness that, if he harmed any
of his associates, he would run the risk of being harmed in return (25e).
Similarly, here it is implied that it is punishment for the wicked to have to
live with the wicked (cf. *Laws* V 728b), and that wrongdoing causes harm
to the soul and brings its own punishment (V 727a–728c, cf. X 899d–e,
905b–c). But if so, then the *Laws* would be giving a cosmic framework
to those moral intuitions, in a way that does not necessitate an afterlife
for the implementation of this law, and suggests that hell may be other
people or a state of mind.[57]

But, if the way cosmic justice operates in the world is so to speak
"automatic",[58] there is not even a need to hypothesise a god over and
above the interconnected and organic universe to explain the way its
parts operate. No mysterious *deus ex machina*, no miracles that turn aside

the necessary course of things, are needed to explain why the virtuous
are happy and the wicked are miserable. Thus, despite the mythical description of god as "our king" (904a), a "checkers player" (903d) or (in
the plural) "the gods that dwell in Olympus" (904e), it is clear that in
actual practice this god is none other than the one whose existence has
been argued for previously, that is, the cosmic god or, more concretely,
the organic universe itself as a self-regulating system.[59] If so, one can understand why the way cosmic justice gets to be implemented in the world
is said to be "most easy" (903e, 904a).

These suggestions comport with our findings above about the mind-
body relation, and reveal that Plato does not need to postulate spiritual
laws operating in ways different from the physical ones.[60] Soul itself is
a self-mover, but since motion takes place in space, soul is some kind
of spatial and thus physical entity; the way it must be distinguished from
body is by initiating causal chains instead of being a mere effect of them –
an effect that would have the first source of its motion in something else;
and yet the laws of attraction and repulsion, as well as the capacity to
"adapt oneself to all actions and all passions" (894c) apply to souls no
less than bodies. In this manner, law is grounded in nature in the most
literal way possible; and even the most materialistically inclined person
must come to see that his actions cannot escape the necessary workings
of the universe.[61]

Even eschatology is in *Laws* X treated as a relocation of souls within
the spatial world. We read of the places (*tinas topous*, 904b8) that souls of
different sorts must occupy: the more wicked they are, the lower they will
fall until they reach the profundities of the places below the surface of the
Earth (904c–d), whereas good souls go in the opposite direction to some
other better place (904d–e). Even though this description is inserted
in the context of a "myth" (903b1), we can see there is no allusion to
"another world"; rather, as Saunders remarks,[62] the next world is here
identified with the physical world itself, which confirms our hypothesis
about soul not being able to exist independently of body and space in
Plato's late work.

But if things are arranged in such a way that the evil get their deserts,
why should the good fight against evil in this world? Isn't god (or the
universe) taking care of that already? This has in fact been one of the
most common arguments, from an ethical perspective, against teleological conceptions of the universe in general: What prevents us from falling
into inertia, if after all the universe is already arranged towards a good
outcome? Why should *our* contribution matter?[63]

Plato, in fact, believes that our contribution matters a great deal, but to understand whether he can consistently think this we need to introduce a distinction between first bests and second bests, and what we may call a system of "closed" teleology versus one of "open" teleology. A universe of closed teleology would be one where all or most things occur for the best independently of humans, the results of whose actions are indifferent with regard to, and have no impact on, the overall state of natural teleology. By contrast, a system of open teleology, as the one proposed by Plato, still grants that things in the universe are arranged for the best, but crucially distinguishes between first bests and second bests. A first best would be a universe in which *nous* prevails at all levels, including human. By contrast, a system of cosmic justice, according to which the wicked are inevitably victims of their own wrongdoing, is only a second best, for it shows that, even though some degree of rationality ends up prevailing, human *nous* does not always do so, and therefore the overall cosmic result is not as good as it would be if it could count on the active cooperation of humans in maintaining the universal order.

The treatment of punishment in *Laws* IX provides important clues in this respect. First, we are told that punishment is a second best from the very point of view of the individual, whose wrongdoing is intrinsically bad as a disease, even if – in the best of cases – punishment makes him better. Second, punishment is a second best from the point of view of the community, since a society of virtuous people is better than one that has to impose punishment on the wicked (cf. IX 854b–e with 853b–c). There is no question, then, that for Plato a world in which we use our reason to improve the degree to which everything participates in goodness is to be preferred. And the universe's teleological arrangement, rather than being an impediment to our intervention in the world, should act as an inspiration for it. For knowledge of cosmic justice – as an aspect of cosmic teleology – could not but make us act virtuously and therefore fight for the good (cf. X 885b). In fact, by doing so, we shall be acting as allies of god, with the invigorating conviction that the universe is on our side.

How dramatic an enterprise this is, though, is clearly portrayed later in *Laws* X, in a passage that is most important for illuminating the problem of evil and its cosmic implications in *Laws* X:

Since we have agreed among ourselves that the universe (*ouranos*) is full of many good things, but also of their opposites, and that *there are more of those which are not good (pleionôn de tôn mê)*, such a battle, we say, is immortal (*machê... athanatos*) and requires an extraordinary vigilance; and the gods and daemons are our allies (*summachoî*), and we in turn the possession of gods and daemons. And what corrupts us (*phtheirei hêmas*) is injustice (*adikia*) and arrogance (*hubris*) together with folly (*aphrosunê*); and what preserves us is justice (*dikaiosunê*) and moderation (*sôphrosunê*) together with wisdom (*phronêsis*), these residing in the ensouled powers of the gods, though one can see clearly a small portion also dwelling here in us (906a2–b3).

What does Plato mean by an immortal battle between good and evil? Is he perchance contemplating an alternative that we found implausible earlier, namely a dualistic fight between two cosmic principles, so that there is, after all, an evil cosmic soul? The "cosmic" aspect of this battle is clear from the text, as the battle is said to take place in the whole universe (*ouranos*). However, the possibility of an evil cosmic soul is immediately dismissed as we realise that *we* are the protagonists of this struggle, the gods and daemons being just our cooperators and only on the side of the good. From this perspective an extraordinary vigilance (*phulakê*) is a task that is now also remitted to us despite other passages stressing that the gods are guardians or *phulakes* (e.g. 907a): it is clear that we and the gods must share this responsibility. Folly, injustice, and arrogance are again left on our side. The pessimism of Plato's claim that there are more evils than goods in the universe is certainly astonishing, particularly within a discourse devoted to emphasising the existence and triumph of teleology.[64] But we can notice here how Plato has come to view the universe more and more as the stage of *human* life, and it can only be as regards the latter that he says that there are more evils than goods – as he had explicitly affirmed at *Rep.* II 379c.[65] In this way, Plato ends up presenting in the *Laws* a view of the universe that is coloured by ethical and political preoccupations, just as we saw him do in the myth of the *Politicus*.[66]

In fact, I would like to argue further that the text goes on to suggest that human greed is actually responsible not only for moral evils such as political injustice, but for natural evils such as pestilence and disease. Thus, after associating the gods only with good (906a–b), the Athenian mentions greed or "overgaining" (*pleonektein*) as a vice of unjust souls, in an attempt to eradicate the notion that humans can "overgain" without suffering hardship (906b3–c2). In this context, he passes on to affirm that "the vice just mentioned, namely greed (*pleonexia*), is what is called disease in bodies of flesh, pestilence in seasons and years, and . . . injustice in cities and states" (906c3–6), which could thus be taken as examples of those *human* overgainings.[67] But *must* we take it that way? Cannot Plato find a better explanation for natural evil?

3. Humans and Natural Evil

We previously saw the failure of several attempts to attribute natural evil to a cosmic source (such as an evil cosmic soul, or an irrational part of the world-soul). However, some room might in principle seem to be left for an explanation of this phenomenon that does not necessitate either the *prima facie* implausible conclusion that humans are responsible for every sort of evil, or the inconsistent claim that god (the universe in this case) is unqualifiedly good and yet in some respect morally responsible for its evils. Instead, the question about natural disorder could be answered by saying that it is an incidental, *unintended*, result of corporeal motions imparted by the purposive action of the world-soul. This explanation could arguably be given in the context of the *Timaeus*: Soul purposively moves one body, and this another body, until the purposive effect of soul starts waning and the corporeal begins to manifest random motion, which is no longer within the scope of soul's initial purpose (cf. 58a–c, 46d–e).[68] In that case, soul (even the good, divine soul) would still be the *cause* of all motion, including disorderly motion as an incidental result, which is not *meant* by it and for which it is therefore not *responsible*, in a way that would not affect god's goodness but, at the very most, stress the limitations with which he has to cope due to the nature of the corporeal.

Now, can this picture be applied to the *Laws*? Plato had in fact in book IX (863a ff.) contemplated a distinction between causation of evil and moral responsibility for it: if, when an action is performed, the opinion for the best prevails in the soul, then even if some harm is done the action thus performed must be said to be just (864a).[69] According to this passage there should, strictly speaking, be a distinction between a soul that is just but "capable of producing contrary effects" to the good ones and an "evil soul" as such. However, *Laws* X does not leave any room for such a distinction, since the two are plainly identified (cf. 896e6 and 897d1); and it is suggested that whatever is bad is due to a *bad kind of soul* (896d5–e6 with 897d1). So, if there are natural disorders or evils in the terrestrial realm, and if their ultimate source of motion is soul, then that soul should be evil at least in that respect (for it is the ultimate "cause" and hence "responsible"). Therefore the argument in *Laws* X seems to demand that the ultimate cause of evil be other than god or a completely good soul.

But why should Plato lead us to such a conclusion in the *Laws*? He does not focus on any cosmic source of disorder in *Laws* X, probably because he wants conversely to emphasise the pervasive presence and concern of the gods against atheism. So, we can start to explain Plato's silence about any cause of natural evil other than human by the kind of exoteric and protreptic discourse we are dealing with here,[70] which is meant to exalt the existence and providence of the gods (and even their power),[71] and to make people aware that the goodness of the gods is such that only humans seem to be responsible for evil.

In this respect, Cherniss may be right in noting that evil seems to have not one, but several sources in the dialogues – and so he distinguishes between negative evil (due purely to the inevitable imperfection of the sensible world as a mere reflection of the Forms), incidental evil (as the indirect result of the purposive action of soul), and positive evil, produced directly by morally responsible evil souls.[72] However, we should again note here that, at least as far as *Laws* X is concerned, the only explicit source of evil given is the last one. For we have seen that no room is left in the text for incidental evil and, on the other hand, in this discourse addressing the crowd no mention is made at all of Forms of which the universe as a reflection could be an imperfect copy and in that respect convey negative evil.

Conversely, it has already been asserted that whatever is bad belongs to us (900e6). According to this it appears that *we* should also have moral responsibility for what seems to be natural evil, and this would accord with the allusions to illness and pestilence as examples of *hamartêma* (vice) or *pleonexia* (overgaining) at 906c3–5, both words having a strong anthropological and moral connotation, which is in addition given here a cosmic import in the context of a battle between good and evil taking place in the universe (906a–b). If this is so, Plato would then be stressing in the *Laws*, with overt ecological resonances,[73] the cosmic implications of human behaviour. Human disorder is thus seen to be a *pleonexia*, an overgaining or cosmic disturbance insofar as it trespasses the limits of the portion (*meros, merismon, morion,* 903b–c) established for each thing.[74] Can this view find any purchase for us?

On the one hand, the modern reader may be tempted to relate Plato's suggestion to dramatic historical examples that would seem to support his point, such as famine caused by war, radiation in Chernobyl causing cancer, or global warming causing changes in the climate. We have also become increasingly aware of the large-scale effects of actions apparently narrow in scope, such as DDT spread in North America appearing as far as the bodies of fish in Antarctica. On the other hand, one could in all justice complain that Plato did not live in an age when such large-scale effects of human actions were so visible. Yet it appears that, nonetheless, he built a metaphysics that might explain them, and that he was indeed empirically aware of the undesirable consequences that – to a greater or lesser extent – the misuse of power could bring about.

To make sense of Plato's suggestion, we may here contrast the organicist view of the universe that we have seen him develop in the *Laws* with the view of the universe as an aggregate that seems presupposed by his materialist opponents. In an aggregate, the parts come first and relations between the parts are extrinsic to them. Thus, in a view of the universe as composed of atoms that come together in random bundles, these atoms as parts do not lose their nature when disaggregated, nor does their nature depend on their specific relations, both mutual and with the whole.[75] In an organism, by contrast, the whole comes first, and relations between the parts within that whole are not extrinsic, but intrinsic to them: thus, a heart would cease to be a proper heart if detached from the whole organic body. Indeed, the heart could not even be defined without reference to the function that it performs within that whole. Similarly, in an organism, any change in a part has repercussions for all the other parts and for the whole; so, as Plato would explain, if my finger hurts, it is my whole sentient body that suffers, not just my finger: that is why we say that *I* feel pain in my finger (*Rep.* V 462c–d).

Now, it is precisely because the universe is an organism for Plato, that we should not be surprised to find him assuming that any movement of a part should affect the whole and have consequences that reach well beyond its own initial sphere. In this light, it becomes clearer why the *Laws* should emphasise *both* the importance of our taking responsibility (*aitia*) as rulers (*archontes*) over the parts (*moria*) that have been allotted to us in this complex universe (903b–c, 904c7), *and* that we too share with the cosmic mind the administration of not just our part, but also the entire system (896e–897b). Further, it is also because we are parts in a larger interconnected system that we can understand why Plato should try to bridge the gap between concern for the common good and self-interest in his attack on greed (*pleonexia*): His claim is not simply that one should do what benefits the whole, at the expense of one's personal self-interest, but that it is in one's best interest to serve the interests of that whole, since "what is best for the whole is also best for you, by virtue of your common origin" (903d2–3). This is still consistent with the claim – which we can take as the cornerstone of his holism – that "the part [exists] for the sake of the whole, not vice versa" (903c7–d1) and that "the happiness of the life of the All" is the end of every change (903c3–5). In the same way as a heart cannot function or even be defined except by reference to the task that it fulfils within the whole, neither can we be defined or understood – or indeed flourish – without reference to the function that we are supposed to perform in the larger universe, and which, as we have seen, is to bring about beauty and order in imitation of the latter. This is also how knowledge of cosmology culminates in self-knowledge, and how the happy life coincides with a life in harmony with nature.[76]

How human life turns out to be a crucial part of Plato's description of the universe as an organism becomes particularly notable as the argument unfolds. It has been proposed that, in contrast with the *Timaeus,* *Laws* X fails to present the idea of an organised whole (*holon*), for it deals only with "all things" (*ta panta*, 895a, cf. 896d–e).[77] This provocative suggestion, though, could apply at the very most to the first section of *Laws* X,[78] which deals with the universe in general terms before introducing the role played by human beings in it (as happens from 899d onwards). However, it is noteworthy that we do get the desired notion of the universe as a unified whole as soon as we are introduced into the description. Thus, we are said to be the possession of the gods, to whom also the whole universe (*ton ouranon holon*) belongs (902b8–9). In an eschatological context we read that the one who cares for the All (*tou pantos*) has arranged everything towards the preservation and excellence of the whole (*tou holou*, 903b4–6).[79] The happiness of the life (*bios*) of the universe as "the All" (*to pan*) is the aim (cf. *heneka*) of every part and generation (903c–d); this indicating more than ever an organic whole. And we have earlier seen the universe (*ouranos*) as the battlefield of human good and evil (906a). All this suggests that Plato does not seem to think of such a universe as a complete whole unless we include human affairs as an essential part of it.[80]

In the light of this, now it is not so surprising that Plato should say that there are more evils than goods in the universe, or that we are "rulers" (*archontes*) in it. Neither should we be surprised at the importance of our cooperation with god for the fulfilment of teleology. For his conception of the universe or *kosmos* has proved to go hand in hand with anthropological concerns; and what Plato is stressing in *Laws* X is that, in the end, cosmology gains full significance when seen in its interaction with human life. So, whatever we do is reflected in the cosmos and affects it, and in turn triggers its allotted cosmic consequences, which also affect us. From this standpoint, ethics becomes inseparable from cosmology, and inquiry into the universe results in an enhanced understanding of ourselves.

9

Conclusion

In this book I have argued that Plato's cosmology is an indispensable framework for understanding his concerns about the happy life in the late dialogues. While the *Timaeus* and the *Philebus* emphasise the role of the universe as a model for human behaviour, the *Politicus* and the *Laws*, without dismissing the latter dimension, seem to open a new one: the universe as the stage of human actions, whose description can be tinged by anthropological concerns. This can reach the point of depicting on a cosmic scale an ethical drama that seems inherently human, as in the *Politicus*, or portraying the cosmos as the battlefield of human good and evil in the *Laws*, with a consequent warning, we might infer, about the cosmic dimension of human behaviour, since whatever we do is reflected in the cosmos and contributes to its being good or not.

The late dialogues, in addition, present the universe as a "common origin" for all souls (*Laws* X 903d2–3; cf. *Tim.* 41d, *Phil.* 30a), which therefore have a kinship not only among themselves but with their source. Hand in hand with this, we see Plato's tendency to extend more widely the possibility of an autonomous kind of happiness, a tendency that seems to rescue him, as it were, from the limitations of his elitist approach in the *Republic*. While it still remains true that only a few are cut out to be expert philosophers, for whom a distinctive form of happiness may be retained, it is now possible for the majority of people to attain happiness by receiving education in disciplines targeted to promoting an understanding of, and a love for, rational consistency. In this context, the study of astronomy and related mathematical sciences is recommended in the *Timaeus*, *Philebus*, and the *Laws* as a fundamental piece of public education.

Establishing the universe as our model, in addition, offers people a possibility for self-realisation even in the absence of a good political system. For now god (the universe) is the ultimate philosopher-king, unfailingly acting according to rational principles and providing a shelter for those seeking an adequate home. Undoubtedly Plato still continues to be preoccupied with the implementation of the right political system, as is evident in the *Politicus* and the *Laws*; and to this extent the late dialogues resume his middle-period interest in politics, accompanied by an awareness that the ideal or second ideal conditions for the realisation of this program were far from being within easy reach. But now the program is complemented by the presentation of the universe as a context for human flourishing, one that is available to all even in the absence of a good constitution.

Thus, the *Philebus* offers a self-contained treatment of human happiness, detached from any political concerns, and the *Timaeus* suggests that by one's own studies (particularly of the universe) we can counteract bad forms of government. We are invited, in this way, to regard ourselves as citizens of the universe, so that distinctions created by one's belonging to particular races or nations (such as the one between "Greek" and "Barbarian", *Pol.* 262c–d) become irrelevant or indeed "unnatural"; likewise, the *Laws* shows an explicit concern about the right education for everyone, "*whether Greek or Barbarian*" (II 654e). Even the *Politicus* myth, whose age of Cronus has been regarded as a projection of the authoritarian rule of the philosopher-king in the *Republic*, advances instead, I have argued, the challenge of dialogue and philosophy as the key to people's happiness in a way that affirms rather than overrides individual autonomy. To some extent, then, the late dialogues may be seen to resume a Socratic outlook, if one keeps in mind the emphasis laid in the early period on *everyone* pursuing the examined life, regardless of their social class or national affiliation (cf. *Ap.* 22c–e, 23b, 30a).

It is difficult to overstate the magnitude of this project. Plato has been grappling with many issues, perhaps too many for the modern reader who is accustomed to treat cosmology, ethics, and metaphysics as independent compartments. Plato has instead furnished us with a cosmic vision in which these various strands are closely intertwined. Of course we are still likely to find his teleological conception of the universe implausible, not to speak of its reliance on an identification of god with the universe itself. But, as I have suggested, it is intriguing to see how these views may offer answers to larger questions. For example, I have shown how we can refer Plato's notion of the universe as an organism to a broader concern about the mind-body relation in his late period, a concern that may be motivated by the problem of explaining how a mind can interact with the body (or god with the material universe). This prompts a reexamination of the nature of the mind and the conditions for its activity. We have seen Plato present a view of the mind in general (including both human mind and the mind of god) as a teleological agent that depends for its existence on material conditions. The mind needs body and space as much as body necessitates soul as the principle of its motion and organisation. One could say, then, that he is suggesting a form of panpsychism,[1] insofar as he attributes mental properties to the basic constituents of the universe. We are thereby invited to explore logical space and see what would follow from its traversal. At the very least, we can understand Plato's reasons for rejecting some of the alternatives, such as the robust dualism which, ironically enough, many still attribute to "Plato" today.

His teleological commitments, in addition, can be seen as an attempt to provide an adequate explanation of the *intelligibility* of the universe, and here again late Plato may be contrasted with the view that some have of middle Plato, who is usually perceived (rightly or not) as downgrading or belittling the natural world and the sensible universe in general. By contrast, our study of his late dialogues has revealed an elevated account of the phenomenal world, due partly to the fact that it has its active principle of organisation *from within*. Whether or not this represents a radical departure from the middle dialogues,[2] it is clear at any rate that Plato is availing himself of new tools and providing us with a detailed *explanation* of the sort that Socrates in the *Phaedo* was looking for but failed to find in Anaxagoras (97b–99d). This is a world that ought to be respected and exalted rather than ignored or fled. In fact, it is this same world that supplies us with the means to understand the contours of our own happiness. Thus the *Philebus*, for example, shows us how its fourfold classification, and its treatment of being and becoming, can be applied not only to an analysis of the universe but also to an analysis of pleasure, and its consequent role in a good or happy life. In this way ethics, or the life that we ought to pursue, is directly grounded in nature, which presents itself as a normative model for humans.

Is Plato, though, committing the naturalistic fallacy, the supposed fallacy of inferring values from facts? Why should our search for the happy life, or the way we *ought* to live, be grounded on an understanding of the way things *are* on the large scale? Plato need not be seen as offending even many of those who do find this move fallacious, if he can show, as he tries to do, that nature itself is intrinsically valuable (an attempt which a good part of Chapter 4 was devoted to exploring). Goodness, then, is a constitutive aspect of the sensible world itself, and thus it is no wonder that we should look up to it in our search for the good, particularly if our intellect is kindred to the rationality that pervades the universe, and thus well suited to discovering it. In this sense, Plato (rather than the Stoics, as has often been thought) can be seen as the father of one kind of ethical naturalism,[3] which posits "norms of nature" that can be discerned through the exercise of reason by humans who are citizens of a universe governed by laws exhibiting rationality, and which can thereby offer us a standard by which any positive law established by humans can be evaluated. To this extent, as we read in the *Laws*, it is god, and not humans, that should be "for us the measure of all things" (IV 716c).[4]

Plato has also been wrestling with the question of how it is possible to reconcile human responsibility, and the sense that our contribution matters, with a teleological outlook such that the universe already seems structured in accordance with goodness. We are fascinated these days by the Stoic attempt to accommodate human freedom within a universe operating according to necessary laws,[5] an issue that presents itself at least programmatically to the reader of *Laws* X. We have seen, in this regard, how Plato treats individual souls as independent principles of motion having self-determination side by side with the universe itself; but how, once they initiate a certain action, its consequences unfold as part of the established scheme of things. Thus, the law of "cosmic justice" works as a natural law of attraction of like to like, ensuring that goodness will harvest more goodness, while evil brings its own punishment.

In this respect, Plato has seen a logic to the way the human world works that goes much deeper than the common view that the wrongdoer is happy and the just person is wretched. We have a mechanism which, now against a cosmic backdrop, continues and crowns the manifesto of the *Republic* that justice provides its own reward and injustice its own misfortune. But even though the universe is organised intelligently so as to guarantee that certain consequences will follow from the choice of certain forms of behaviour, it can never determine that behaviour. It can never annihilate our freedom, though our freedom ought to serve the cause of the good.

In this context, we have seen how *Laws* X stresses the importance of our watchfully fighting on the side of the good where the whole universe is the theatre of war; a recommendation that would lose all meaning unless it is believed that what we do is not irrelevant to cosmic teleology but matters to it. To make sense of this suggestion, I have elaborated a distinction between open and closed systems of teleology, and first versus second bests, and proposed that Plato is encouraging us to fight for a first best kind of teleology on the assumption that it is a task for us to *improve* the degree to which the universe participates in goodness.

To this extent, it has been crucial to emphasise how far Plato is from believing that our universe is the best possible universe; instead, as the *Timaeus* shows, the very presence of rationality in it has to face restraints imposed by recalcitrant necessity. Our irrationality can be seen as part of (or in *Laws* X as virtually identical to) the cussed element with which cosmic intelligence has to cope; however, we are to help by harnessing this cussed element in ourselves and others. In this respect, humans, through the use of their own rational minds, must endeavour to act intelligently and virtuously and thus fulfil teleology as best they can. And the universe's teleological arrangement, rather than being an impediment to our taking action in the world, should conversely act as an inspiration for it, insofar as it is a model that can guide our behaviour. In this way we can give full application to the notion of our living in harmony with nature or according to nature (*Laws* X 890a, d); a notion that will subsequently enjoy a long career.[6] The importance of our contribution is conveyed particularly dramatically in *Laws* X, where we are presented as responsible even for natural evil, in a way that lays stress on how much work there is still to do to complete, so to speak, the work of god. In this regard the symbiotic relation between us and the universe is of an order that requires us not only to imitate but also to sustain the universe's harmonious structure.

Thus, we see Plato now extend to the universe the holistic premises that he had applied to the state in the *Republic*: it is the goodness of the whole system that matters, and it is the whole that provides an indispensable background for understanding and defining each part. That, then, is the goal that should inspire our actions, once we are made to realise that it is by promoting the interests of the whole that we shall also be promoting our self-interest, as we have seen in the *Laws*. This again is a provocative suggestion, when the contrast between egoism and altruism has become so deep rooted. Plato challenges us to reflect on what the boundaries are that demarcate our sphere of interests: Ourselves? Our families? Our institutions or states? Through an emphasis on the apparently unforeseeable large-scale effects of human actions, and the workings of an interconnected universe, we are invited to regard the boundaries of our interests as those of the universe itself. Even if self-interest is our only concern, we ought to make this a better world if after all we have to live in it and are directly affected by it: it is stupidity to think otherwise

(903c1). Some environmental philosophers may, indeed, find Plato a predecessor rather than an enemy in this regard.[7] At the very least, we can see how he has presented a model of nature that, by being endowed with intrinsic value, urges our respect, and at the same time highlights our responsibility for it.

In doing so, Plato has, as an artist and as a philosopher, resorted to a variety of literary strategies. Thus, for example, his appeal to myth in the *Timaeus* has helped him portray more vividly the ways in which humans can deal with "luck", including the recalcitrant circumstances that they do not cause, after the model provided by the cunning manner in which the Demiurge "persuades" necessity, and uses putative obstacles as instruments for his plans. In this regard, Plato intends to show us that it is ultimately god that can provide the best proximate model for human virtue, a model that will become increasingly abstract as we ascend from imaginative representations to a more rigorous understanding of science. And so the image of the personal Demiurge in the *Timaeus* still proves useful from an ethical perspective, even though Plato thinks we need to supplement it with a rational comprehension of the workings of the universe. Reviving the dramatic character of Socrates in the *Philebus*, on the other hand, has helped us remember how much there is still to think about (67b), and how provisional these findings may be.[8] In this way, Plato encourages us to take our own positions on the many questions posed by his dialogues, as was done by those philosophers who came after him.

Aristotle will try to offer a view of the relation of the mind to the body which, in its denial of robust dualism (at least as far as living organisms are concerned), seems concordant with Plato's late writings. Aristotle and the Stoics will disagree on whether the soul itself is material or not (an issue on which Plato himself seems to display more of an open mind than his successors),[9] and on whether teleology is to be understood in a global sense, or is just limited (as Aristotle seems to believe) to individual natures or species.[10] In any case, all of these philosophers will present god as some kind of ideal for humans, treading the path followed by Plato in his attempt to offer appropriate role models for human virtue.

In a sense, Plato's god, directly engaged in making this a better world, and coping with difficult materials, will be more humanitarian, so to speak, than the aseptic, nonprovidential god of Aristotle who is involved in purely theoretical activity. From this point of view, Plato's god is an exemplar available to the many, by contrast with the Aristotelian god which embodies the ideal of philosophical contemplation only suitable for a few and detached from any practical results.[11] This contrast is worth noting given how common it is these days, in discussions of virtue ethics, to go back to Aristotle and his own concern for role models. But even those who do so usually have a hard time accommodating his remarks on god and the contemplative life in book X of the *Nichomachean Ethics*, partly because they sound elitist, partly because they seem just peculiar.[12] Plato's notion of god, conversely, does not conflict with a relatively populist conception of happiness and, as we have seen, has its place in the quest, characteristic of the ancient Greek tradition, for the right kind of role model that may serve to shape the human personality and its virtues. To this extent, Plato may strike a chord with those who take the main concern of ethics to be the cultivation of our moral character in such a way that we aim at becoming not just mediocre good citizens, but as close to an ideal as we can be. If this ideal is what it is to be god, then there may be much of value, even (and perhaps especially) from a practical perspective, in Plato's suggestion that we should endeavour to "be like god insofar as it is possible".[13]

Notes

Chapter 1

1. Cf. Irwin (1995); Bobonich (2002: 504–5, nn. 4, 6, and 17).
2. Cf. Annas (1999: 12, 52 ff., 108).
3. Cf. also Sedley (1997) and (2000). I explain my main disagreements with Annas and Sedley in Chapter 3.
4. Johansen (2004) – which was made available to me in manuscript form after this book was completed – notes at the beginning and end of his study that there is an ethical side to the *Timaeus*' cosmological speculations, and has a chapter on how the Atlantis story may fit in the context of the *Timaeus/Critias*. But most of the work focuses on issues of cosmology proper and psychology in the *Timaeus*.
5. See McCabe (2000: 142 n. 7). Cf. also Rowe (1996: 160 n. 17).
6. See here e.g. Annas (1993: 142 ff.) and Cooper (1996).
7. See here e.g. Annas (1993: 159 ff.), (1999: 108), who, however, fails to find in Plato a concrete and articulate account of the connection between cosmic reason and human virtue; and Long (1996: 136, 188), who takes the Stoic idea of the connection between a divine government of the world and human rationality as historically "new", while still recognising that more study may be needed on the possible Platonic roots of this thought (185–6 n. 8).
8. See here 22B114; also 22B101 and 22B116 with 22B112 DK; Kahn (1960: 110), (1979: 21–2); Kirk et al. (1983: 211); Vernant (1985: 205 ff.) and my (2001a) on the relation between universe and human life in early Greek thinkers. Unless otherwise indicated, translations in this book are my own.
9. We shall see how Plato's last work, the *Laws*, presents the fullest response to the sophistic divorce; but compare the attempt already at *Gorg.* 488b–489b.
10. Moore (1903). This kind of concern goes back to Hume, *A Treatise of Human Nature*, III.1.1.
11. See here e.g. Prior (1960), Foot (1978: 110–31), Simpson (1987); for a critique of Moore on the Stoics see e.g. Long (1996: 137–8). For a discussion

of this question in the ancients see also Schofield and Striker (1986), Cooper (1996).

12. See e.g. Hudson (1986: 42–3); Sherman (1999: 36–7); Hursthouse (1997), (1999: 77–83).

13. See my (1998a) and (2001a).

14. For a review of an outlook of this kind see Burnyeat in Nussbaum and Rorty (1992: 15–26 at 16), a volume chiefly devoted to discussion of the relevance of Aristotle's views on the mind. The association of Plato with "robust dualism" owes largely to some of his remarks in the *Phaedo*, where the body is presented as a prison of the soul and the latter is said to work at its best without the former (66b–c, 67d, 82d–e). For the relation between the Greek "soul" (*psuchê*) and the English "mind" see below, n. 33; for a comparison between Plato in the *Phaedo* and Descartes on the mind-body relation see Broadie (2001b).

15. For an exposition of different interpretations of this *nous*, see e.g. Brentano in Nussbaum and Rorty (1992: 313–42).

16. See e.g. Armstrong (1968: 76–7); Boyd (1980: 68, 85); Lewis (1983: 362); Post (1987: 187).

17. As Wright points out, "it is the central logical property of teleological characterisations that they explain what they characterise. When we say 'A in order that B' or 'A for the sake of B' we ipso facto answer a question of the form 'why A'" (1976: 24).

18. Cf. *Ap.* 22c–e, 23b, 30a, 38a.

19. On *kosmos* see below, n. 32.

20. But see Sedley (1989) for the view that we can already find a sketch of a teleological account in the final myth of the *Phaedo*.

21. The reader should bear in mind that the Greek *eudaimonia* is difficult to translate, since it refers to a much richer concept than that which we tend to attach to the English "happiness" (even though this is the most common translation). It connotes not primarily a situation of perhaps temporary contentment or good feeling, but a state of fulfilment or well-being which by its very nature has an enduring quality.

22. Cf. *Rep.* VII 519e2–3; IV 420b.

23. Cf. *Rep.* VII 540a–c; IX 580b–583b.

24. Cf. *Rep.* VII 519e with IV 429b–c and 431d–e.

25. Cf. *Rep.* IV 432a–b, 433a–b.

26. Cf. Irwin (1995: 229–31).

27. Cf. Nussbaum (1986: 11); Irwin (1995: 235–6); and Bobonich (1996: 257), (2002: 203–4). On the lowest class's heteronomous reliance on reason cf. *Rep.* IX 590c–d.

28. Cf. *Meno* 97e–98a. This same thought might be expressed at the very end of the *Republic*, which would then contain the germ of its own self-criticism. Thus, in the myth of Er, we are given the example of a person who, when put in front of various options, goes on to choose the greatest tyranny: this was someone who had lived in a well-governed system, but "by habit and without philosophy" (X 619c–d).

29. Other than their technical training, and maybe some conditioning through e.g. the effect of music and myths on both children and adults alike (see

e.g. 389d–e, 380b–c). But it seems clear that even the preliminary educational programme of books II–III is designed with the guardians in mind: see e.g. 376c, 378b–c, 383c, 387e–388a, 395b–c, 398b, e, 401b–c, 402b–c, 403e, 413e–414a. For discussion of this issue see Reeve (1988: 186–91).

30. Cf. *Rep.* V 472c–473b; VII 540d.

31. Cf. *Pol.* 293c–d, 294a–b, 296d–297b, 301d–e; *Laws* IX 875c–d.

32. The Greek "*kosmos*" is particularly rich, since it can mean, among other things (such as adornment, cf. *Rep.* II 373c1, *Tim.* 40a6), both universe and order, or, in one go, the universe as order (cf. *Gorg.* 508a). Even though my use of the word will focus on the latter meaning, as "macrocosm" (which is most prominent in Plato's late writing), there is also an order both of the individual soul (cf. e.g. *Gorg.* 504b5, c2) and of the *polis* (cf. *Prot.* 322c3). To these I shall refer as "microcosm".

33. "Mind" serves as a convenient though only approximate translation. In practice, Plato will refer to the cosmos as having either intellect (*nous*) or soul (*psuchê*). The English "mind" is broader than the former and narrower than the latter, which includes in the Greek conception the notion of a principle of life. For a comparison of ancient and modern views on the mind see e.g. Ostenfeld (1987).

34. Compare here the complaint of certain environmentalists such as Attfield (1994: 81).

35. See here e.g. Brisson (1982).

36. For various discussions of Platonic myth cf. Frutiger (1930), Stewart (1960), Zaslavsky (1981), Brisson (1982), Annas (1982), Gaiser (1984), Mattéi (1988), and the bibliographies in Gaiser and Brisson, including other works referred to below. For a more recent study emphasising the interpenetration of myth and philosophy see Morgan (2000).

37. Gallop (1975: 224), quoted by Annas (1982: 122).

38. Cf. e.g. Nussbaum (1986); Kahn (1996); Gill and McCabe (1996). For a study that approaches this issue from the rather different perspective of Plato's use of character see Blondell (2002). On the *Timaeus* see Osborne (1996), Morgan (2000: 261 ff.), Gill (2002: 151–2).

39. As a matter of fact, the Platonic use of myth could in some cases be compared to the method used by analytic philosophers themselves when they resort to unverifiable "thought-experiments" as an attempt to illustrate or even enrich their arguments. See, for example, the myth of Gyges in *Rep.* II.

40. Cf. *Rep.* III 411a–b, X 605a–606d.

41. Cf. *Rep.* II 377d–378c.

42. For example, the ancient myths fail to depict god as unchangingly good, a feature for which Plato argues separately at *Rep.* II 379a–383c and which he will try to maintain throughout all the variety of his own myths.

43. Cf. *Rep.* III 401c–402a. Along the same lines, Plato's overt suggestiveness in framing his own myths can be seen as an invitation to his readers to participate in the dialogue, and as a means both to spur our emotions and to bring us to further rational awareness. For the general use of emotional effect in Plato's dialogues cf. Blank (1993), and with regard to myths Brisson (1982: 100–5 with 151). Myths also challenge the critical powers of the reader, insofar as they stimulate the discovery of the philosophical message of the

myth in relation to the discursive context in which it appears. Cf. McCabe (1992).

44. See also *Gorg.* 523a for the claim of truth, and 527a, where Socrates opposes any view of his story as "myth" in the pejorative sense of "old-wives' tale". In the *Timaeus* too Timaeus is not unwilling to use the word "true" in connection with his cosmological myth (cf. 30b8, 38a1), nor is Critias with regard to the Atlantis story (26e4–5). Johansen (2004: ch. 9) finds a contrast between the *Gorgias* final myth and Critias' story, because of Critias' claim that it is a true *logos*. Yet even in the *Gorgias* (523a2–3) Socrates calls his story a true *logos* (against the thought that it is a myth), which shows that passages having what we may call mythical structure still invite us to seek a deeper and "true" meaning: see here Morgan (2000: 262–3). On the truth content of Platonic myths cf. Frutiger (1930: 34), Brisson (1982: 144–51, 171), Gaiser (1984: 127), Morgan (2000: 157–9).

45. One might ask how any view expressed by a character in a Platonic dialogue (such as Socrates in the *Republic*) can be taken to be a view held by Plato himself. I discuss this question further in Section III.2.

46. See *Rep.* 378b ff. Cf. Annas (1982: 121); Brisson (1982: esp. 110).

47. Cf. e.g. *Pol.* 275b, *Gorg.* 522e.

48. Cf. Sedley (1989: 383).

49. Annas (1982: 119–22); compare with Gaiser (1984: 187). For Plato's dismissiveness of interpretation of popular myth cf. *Phaedrus* 229b–230a, whose lack of overt edifying message is also criticised at *Rep.* II 378d–e. See also Gadamer (1980: 43, 67) and Morgan (2000: 6–7).

50. Cf. Frutiger (1930: 103).

51. To adopt Brisson's (1982: 111 ff., 162–3) way of distinguishing properly argumentative discourse from mythical discourse – even though it remains true that *muthos* is one form of discourse or *logos* in a wider sense (on which see e.g. Morgan [2000: 275]). For passages that look more like *logos* in a narrow sense see e.g. the twofold ontological distinction at 27d–28a, the argument for the existence of Forms at 51b–52a, or the deduction that all bodies should be made out of triangles at 53c ff. The latter has been taken to belong rather to the domain of *dianoia* or mathematical knowledge (Ashbaugh [1988: 14–15]). Cf. also Frutiger (1930: 38), who excludes 27d–29c and 51b–52d from what he regards as mythical.

52. Cf. e.g. Gadamer (1975: 261).

53. Cf. Frede (1992). Similar worries are expressed in Annas (1993: 18–19), even though Annas has moved to a more unitarian perspective, at least on ethical issues, in her (1999).

54. Thus, Frede claims for example that it is not clear whether Plato fully identifies himself with the main character of a dialogue, such as Socrates, since Plato adopted a critical distance towards many standardly Socratic positions, such as lack of interest in metaphysics and disapproval of natural philosophy (204–5). But with this claim Frede is granting precisely what he wants to deny, for speaking of Plato's "critical distance" towards Socrates' aversions presupposes that there is something like Plato's views that we *can* pick up from the dialogues. In trying to detach Plato from the voice of his main character

in the dialogues, Frede also contends that the question-and-answer format makes the argument belong more to the respondent than to the questioner, since it is the former who says yes or no (205–6). However, the questioner often supports the answer if it is right, something indispensable for the argument to proceed or to finish (cf. e.g. *Soph.* 265d5, *Phil.* 29d1, 6, *Laws* X 896b–c). And the main speaker sometimes even speaks to or criticises the interlocutor from a position of authority (cf. *Pol.* 263d–e). At other times, it is the main speaker who advances a thesis and the respondent who supports it (cf. *Phil.* 29a–b, 67a–b), and at further times it is the minor interlocutor who asks questions that the main speaker can answer (cf. e.g. *Pol.* 274e, 294a–b). Frede does distinguish between aporetic and nonaporetic dialogues, but then seems to concentrate exclusively on the aporetic dialogues in drawing conclusions about the dialogue form as a whole. In these ways, it seems that Frede's radical scepticism is insufficiently warranted both by the evidence of the dialogues and from the standpoint of its own internal coherence. For views arguing that the main interlocutor in many late dialogues is presented with the authority of an expert teacher see e.g. Miller (1980: xii–xx), Gaiser (1984: 43), Sayre (1992: 221 ff.).

55. Cf. Irwin (1988), Kraut (1988). This interpretation is called "doctrinal" by interpreters such as Irwin, a word however that I prefer to avoid if readers might misleadingly take it to suggest dogmatism. See further below.

56. On this issue see the illuminatory treatment of Tigerstedt (1977: 101–3).

57. Cf. e.g. Rowe (1992b: 65–7), Kraut (1984: 12).

58. Cf. Craig (1994: xxxvi–xxxvii).

59. For organic unity as desirable in a text cf. *Phaedrus* 264c; compare Blondell (2002: 4).

60. Compare e.g. 28c, 30b with 48e–49a; and see e.g. McCabe (1992: 61 ff.).

61. Annas and Waterfield (1995: xvi).

62. For the complaint about the *Laws* see Stalley (1983: 173–4); for the *Philebus* see Waterfield (1982: 48).

63. Cf. Diogenes Laertius 7. 143 LS 53X; Seneca *On Leisure* 4.1 LS 67K; Arius Didymus (Eusebius, *Evangelical Preparation* 15.15.3–5) LS 67L; Diogenes Laertius 7. 87–9 LS 63(C)2–4.

64. Posidonius Fr. 186 Edelstein/Kidd. *Pace* those interpreters of Posidonius who have seen this conception as un-Platonic precisely insofar as "Posidonius puts our contemplation of the universe's structure to the service of a collaboration in this design" rather than as a mere imitation of it targeted to self-improvement (Reydams-Schils 1999: 114).

65. The *Phaedrus* being usually regarded as more or less transitional between the middle and late period: cf. e.g. Eggers Lan (1992: esp. 46); White (1993: 3–7); Nehamas and Woodruff (1995: xlv–xlvi); Nicholson (1999: 7–8). Certainly, I shall also be making some references to the early – or so-called "Socratic" – dialogues (normally thought to include *Apology, Euthyphro, Laches, Charmides, Protagoras, Gorgias,* and *Meno* among others, the latter two already containing some elements of transition towards the middle dialogues): for a discussion of the relation between Plato and Socrates in these dialogues see e.g. Irwin (1995: 13–15); Kahn (1992) and (1996). For

a volume that critically discusses the traditional distinction between early, middle, and late dialogues see Annas and Rowe (2002).

66. Cf. e.g. [Olympiodorus], *Prol.* 24 10–15 Westerink.

67. Cf. Owen (1953); Cherniss (1957). For further criticism of Owen's thesis based partly on his own later views cf. Fine (1988a: 373–90); and for an overall discussion of the chronological issue see Zeyl (2000: xvi–xx).

68. The main defender having been Robinson, though he has recently changed his mind (1995: xiv–xv); cf. his (2000: 47).

69. The only exception perhaps being Waterfield (1980), though his method has been criticised (cf. Benitez [1989: 2–3]; Hampton [1990: 8]) and has not gained support in the scholarly literature.

Chapter 2

1. See e.g. Schofield (1997: 213–14). We are told about the division of the city into craftsmen and guardians, whose soul should be at once spirited and philosophical, having been brought up through gymnastics, music, and all the studies appropriate to such people (*Tim.* 17c–18a; cf. *Rep.* II and III). Other features of the *polis* of the *Republic* are recalled, such as the lack of private property for the guardians, their having children and wives in common, and women having similar nature and occupations to men (*Tim.* 18b–c; cf. *Rep.* V).

2. Cf. Brisson (1982: 111 ff., 162–3).

3. Cf. Chapter 1, Section III with n. 51 of that chapter.

4. Thus, in a context in which he criticises Plato for the use of metaphors that he calls mere "empty words" (*kenologein*), he asks "what" (note: not "who") "is it that works looking to the Forms?" (*ti gar esti to ergazomenon pros tas ideas apoblepon*, *Metaph.* I 9, 991a21–23). The whole passage (a19–23) reads as follows: "Nor are the other things from Forms in any of the usual ways of speaking. And to say that the Forms are paradigms and that the other things participate in them is to use empty words and utter poetic metaphors. For what is that thing which works looking to the Forms?" This vocabulary is quite similar to that in the *Timaeus* (cf. *apergazesthai* and *blepein* of the Demiurge at 28a and 28c–29a), so that Aristotle's reference must be to the Demiurge, which he, however, evidently fails to take seriously, and surrounds with a tone of complaint as doing no explanatory work. Cf. Guthrie (1978: 255–6, n. 3); (1981: 246–7).

5. Cf. Sorabji (1983: 268 ff.).

6. For discussion of Socrates' religious commitments and their relation to his practice of philosophy cf. McPherran (1996).

7. As might be suggested by Lennox (1985: 212).

8. The ancient Greek for "cause" is *aition*, or *aitia* – which can also mean "explanation" or "reason why". In this creational context, "cause" shares much with our contemporary understanding of causes mainly as "efficient", i.e. as agents productive of change. Let us note, however, that in Greek this notion has a wider meaning (as will become apparent in Section II.3.2 and Chapter 4, Section II.2.); cf. Frede (1980: 217–18). For discussion of how explanation and causation go hand in hand in Plato see e.g. Vlastos (1981b);

in a different line cf. Sedley (1998). For a summary of the contemporary debate about causation see Sosa and Tooley (1993: 1–31), and for contemporary attempts to take "cause" in a wider sense than efficient cause see e.g. Sosa (1980).

9. This "reflection" upon the best way to achieve the end that guides the demiurgic task is restated in several passages: cf. e.g. *logisamenos* 30b1; *logismon* 33a6; *logismos theou* 34a8; *logou kai dianoias theou* 38c3–4; *dianoêtheis* 32c8; *nomisas* 33b7; *hêgêsato* 33d1.

10. Cf. e.g. *pronoia*, 30c1; *dianoia*, 38c3; *epinoia*, 37c8.

11. This conforms to the twofold meaning of the term *dêmiourgos*, which not only stands for "craftsman", but can also mean "magistrate", as pointed out by Brisson (1974: 50, 86–8); cf. LSJ *ad loc.* See also López (1963: 76–84), and *Laws* X 902d–e as an example where *dêmiourgos* seems to have the meaning of "governor" as well as that of "craftsman".

12. This kind of efficient or "creative" causality is also suggested by the use of terms such as *poiêtês* (28c3), *gennêsas* (41a5), *sunistas* (30b5, 32c7), *apergazesthai* (30b6), and *diakosmein* (69c1).

13. For the connection between goodness and order see further 29e–30a, where god, wanting all things to be good as far as possible, makes them pass from disorder to order; 46e, where good and fair effects are contrasted with disorderly ones. For this order understood in terms of mathematical proportion causing unity see also 41b1, where "what is in a good state" (*to echon eu*) is connected with "what has been finely harmonised" (*to kalôs harmosthen*); at 53b to shape (*diaschêmatizein*) the precosmic traces "with forms and numbers" (*eidesi te kai arithmois*) is to constitute them in the best and fairest way (from things which did not have that character); finally, at 92c, the beauty and excellence of the universe (cf. *aristos, kallistos*) is connected with the fact that it is one (*heis, monogenês*). Cf. Lennox (1985: 214, 216); Brisson (1991: 33 ff.). For the relation between unity and completeness see Patterson (1981: 114 ff.). For an analysis of the good in terms of unity also in the *Republic* cf. Burnyeat (1987: 238–40); Hitchcock (1985: 73–90). For how the goodness at stake in the *Timaeus* is an immanent goodness rather than a transcendent Form of the Good see n. 48.

14. For my treatment of necessity cf. Section II.3.

15. For other examples of how biological descriptions at the microcosmic level in the *Timaeus* seem to serve a moral or overall teleological end, see Steel (2001).

16. For how human souls can contribute to cosmic teleology cf. Chapter 3 on *Timaeus* (Section II.2) and Chapter 8 on *Laws* (Section 1). For how the stress laid on reason in the *Timaeus* should, however, not be mistaken for anthropocentrism see my (1998a). An important holistic principle seems to be at stake here, as the goodness and completeness of the universe takes precedence over any of its parts. Even the creation of the mortal parts of the world seems to be demanded by the goal of making it complete (*teleos*, 41c1). Goodness, then, is related to completeness, and we could here see an application of what Lovejoy (1936) was to call the "principle of plenitude", according to which a universe in which all the potentialities of being are realised, and which contains as many different kinds of being as possible, is

better than a universe containing only the best kinds. But, as noted by Broadie (2001a: 10–16), the application of this principle is restricted by reference to the model (which, itself being complete, contains the ideal counterparts of the mortal beings to be created, 41b–c), as it is not every kind of possible being that the Demiurge wants (e.g. he does not want the precosmic chaos).

17. This is noted by Cornford (1937: 280); Cherniss (1944: 608); Tarán (1971: 381); Grube (1980: 169). See e.g. 47b2, 90d6, where *'the gods'* (*hoi theoi*) are said to be responsible for the donation of philosophy, which has to do with the *immortal* part of the soul. In addition, in several places we find the singular and the plural used indifferently in the same passage to describe the divine activity (see *Tim.* 44e–45a; 46e8–47c5; 71a; 75b–d; and 80e1 with 77a3), while in other passages we find *theos* or the more impersonal *to theion*, instead of *theoi*, involved in the creation of mortal parts of the universe (see e.g. 80e1, also 71a7, 71e3, 74d6, 78b2, 92a3). It can certainly be argued that in all these cases *theos* can have a more collective and indeterminate meaning, as alluding to "the deity" in general rather than to a specific god – thus becoming closer to some uses of *'to theion'* in similar cases, cf. *Tim.* 76b2, 90a8. However, even this would be another indication that, with regard to the figure of the Demiurge, Plato is no longer concerned with the dramatic initial anthropomorphic distinction between a singular god on the one hand and several lesser gods on the other.

18. As we shall see, "polytheism" and "monotheism" are the wrong labels to use if taken to be mutually exclusive. From this perspective, the fact that we find allusions to god both in the singular and in the plural would go against the "monotheistic" interpretations of the *Timaeus*, such as that of Ritter (1933: 380); Hackforth (1936: 443). Cf. also the criticism of Taylor (1928: *ad* 29d7–30c1 and 69c3) by Cornford (1937: xi) and the response by Taylor (1938: 182–4), with a further reply by Cornford (1938: 324) in which he basically comes to an agreement with Taylor that Plato's monotheism does not exclude polytheism but subordinates it in that he has a leading god that rules lesser gods. It is significant that not only in the *Timaeus*, but in other dialogues too, when a principal god is mentioned, we also find allusion to other several gods (cf. *Phil.* 30d, *Pol.* 271d, 272e, *Laws* VII 821a–b). In the *Timaeus* cosmological structure this one-and-many character of god will turn out to be reflected in the relation between the one god of the universe and the several heavenly bodies as gods. Cf. Chapter 3, Section I.

19. For a literal interpretation cf. Vlastos (1939: 379–99), (1964: 402 ff.); Hackforth (1959: 17 ff.); Robinson (1970: 64–5), (1979: 105–8), (1993: 99 ff.); Guthrie (1978: 302–5); Mohr (1989: 293 ff.); Berti (1997: 119–32); Vallejo (1997: 141–48); Reale (1997: 149–64); Hankinson (1998: 111). Against, cf. Taylor (1928: 66–9, 79–80); Mondolfo (1934: 70 ff.); Cornford (1937: 37 ff., 176, 203 ff.); Cherniss (1944: 421–31); Tarán (1971: 372 ff.); Brisson (1974: 104–5), (1991: 38, 49 n. 21), (1992a: 36–7); Grube (1980: 162–3); Ostenfeld (1982: 240–2); Baltes (1996); Wright (2000: 15); Silverman (2002: 267). In antiquity we can count Aristotle (*De Caelo* I 10, 280a 28 ff.; *Metaph.* XII 6, 1071b37–1072a2), Plutarch (*De an. proc.* 1014a–b), and Atticus (*apud* Proclus *In Tim.* I 283, 27 ff. Diehl) in the first line,

and Xenocrates (fr. 54 Heinze), Crantor (*apud* Plutarch *De an. proc.* 1012f–1013b), and Proclus (*In Tim.* I 285, 26–28; I 287, 28–288, 1 Diehl) in the second.

20. Hackforth (1959: 19); Robinson (1995: 64–5). Cf. Vlastos (1964: 403–4).

21. Cf. Hackforth (1959: 17 ff.), Vlastos (1964: 402–3), Robinson (1979: 105 ff.), Prior (1985: 95), and Berti (1997: 119–32). Against, cf. Cornford (1937: 37 ff.), Tarán (1971: 382 ff.). For studies on the nature of the proemium and the *eikos logos* in the *Timaeus* cf. Runia (1997: 101–18); Donini (1988: 5–52).

22. Cornford (1937: 24–6); see also Cherniss (1944: 422), Tarán (1971: 384). On whether the controversial "always" (*aei*) at 27d6 should be kept in a reading of the text, cf. Cornford (1937: 25–6); Hackforth (1959: 18–19); Whittaker (1969), (1973); Robinson (1979: 105); Dillon (1989: 60–63).

23. Frede (1988) has challenged the idea that "becoming" in the *Timaeus* should be understood as change at least in some sense, by contending that, if there is some respect in which something is becoming, there is another one in which it isn't becoming, i.e. is, but objects of experience do not have any kind of being whatsoever, since this would go against "the clear and straightforward contrast between being and becoming" established by Plato at *Tim.* 27d6–28a1 (40). His argument, though, is unconvincing, since Plato immediately qualifies the contrast at 28a3–4 by saying that "what becomes... never *really* is" (*gignomenon... ontôs oudepote on*). As a matter of fact, Frede concedes this point on p. 39: "Plato may be ready to admit that ordinary objects of experience... can have 'being' in an ordinary sense of the verb 'to be', but he here would be denying that they could be said to be in some philosophical sense of 'to be'"; though he then overlooks his own provision in the process of his argument. Plato is not denying being or existence to the sensible, since he does indeed attribute "existence" (*ousia*) or "being" (*einai*) to it in the *Timaeus*: specifically, he speaks of "generated existence" (*ousia gignomenê*) at 35a1–3 and "scattered existence" (*ousia skedastê*) at 37a5; see also 52d3 for attribution of *einai* to *genesis*. What sensibles certainly don't have is real being in the sense of the constantly unchanging being of the Forms (cf. 29b6, 37e–38a), and these terms seem sufficient to account for the contrast between *genesis* and *ousia* in this context. For further discussion on being and becoming cf. Code (1988), Bolton (1975), Nehamas (1975), Irwin (1977), Jordan (1983: 48–66), Prior (1985: 89–93); on the philosophical meaning of being cf. Vlastos (1965), Kahn (1981). Cf. also Chapter 4, Section II.3.2. For the contrast in Plato being one that includes also the predicative and veridical meanings of "to be", see my (1998a: 117–18) with further references there. I think this point can be maintained as a general understanding of "becoming" in the *Timaeus*, which is independent of the further question whether *gegone* should, *pace* Cornford, be read in the specific sense of "has come into being" rather than as merely standing for a process of becoming as such.

24. Cf. Vlastos (1964: 403) quoting Hackforth (1959: 19).

25. See here e.g. Robinson (1995: 65).

26. This view was suggested by Proclus (*In Tim.* I 282, 27–30; 288, 14–17; 290, 23–291, 1; III 51, 7–10 Diehl) and I believe the text supports it. Cf. my (1991: 51 ff.), where I argue along similar lines.

27. For further arguments see my (2004c). For a review of classical arguments for and against see Zeyl (2000: xx–xxii).
28. Cf. Vlastos (1964: 410–11). For a "precosmic time" understood as duration cf. also Skemp (1942: 111), followed by Hackforth (1959: 22). For more recent defences of the same view, cf. Mohr (1985: 65) and Vallejo (1997: 147). In antiquity, Proclus reports and criticises a theory of a "twofold time" in support of a literal view of the precosmic chaos (*In Tim.* I 286, 20 ff. Diehl).
29. Cf. Vlastos (1964: 410–12).
30. Sorabji (1983: 249–52) records the history of the argument. Cf. Cherniss (1944: 425); Tarán (1971: 380–81). Dialogues before and after the *Timaeus* seem to support this suggestion. In the *Republic* (II 380d–381c) we read that, being perfect, god cannot change except for the worse. We must note that this is said in a context where general claims are being made about the *nature* of god as such (cf. 379a–b on the need to represent god "as he really is"), and that, *a fortiori*, these claims would apply not only to the Olympians – whose traditional accounts are being criticised in that dialogue – but to any kind of god represented in the form of myth. At *Laws* X (900c ff.), for its part, it is suggested that god cannot be inactive or lazy since his concern for the world is definitory of his goodness. Vallejo's (1997: 147) claim that "the immutability of god is compatible with any action that is coherent with his nature" (such as creation) is simply question-begging, for it could be argued (and the *Laws* does argue: see X 900c8–901c6) that it is not coherent with god's goodness not to care for the world when he could do so (as would be the case if one postulates a precosmic state).
31. Cf. Cornford (1937: 31), with particular reference to the Atomists. See also Chapter 7, Section I.3, for classical ways of reading the opposition between precosmos and cosmos within a nonliteralist framework.
32. Cf. my (1991: 52–6). In this respect, it is interesting and almost ironic that Aristotle, while taking creation literally and thus criticising Plato in favour of the view that the universe is eternal (*De Caelo* I 10, 279b12–280a11, 280a28 ff.), more than once, however, resorts to the artisanal metaphor (which he seemed to have criticised as "empty talk" at *Metaph.* I 9, 991a19–23; cf. n. 4) to emphasise the teleological arrangement in the cosmos (cf. e.g. *De Caelo* I 4, 271a33, *G.C.* II 10, 336b27–32, *P.A.* IV 10, 687a6 ff). For discussion of these and like passages see e.g. Mansion (1946: 261 ff.); Preus (1975: 246–7); Guthrie (1981: 106–9); Kahn (1985); Balme (1972: 93–6), (1987: 276–9); Lennox (1997: 171–3). Johansen (2004: ch. 4) moves in my view too quickly to identify the Demiurge in the *Timaeus* with something "not unlike Aristotle's master craftsman, nature" – this despite the fact that he wishes to maintain that the Demiurge is a principle external to the cosmos, which already obscures the comparison with Aristotle's conception of nature as an internal principle. Even though Aristotle does talk of nature working demiurgically at points, Johansen (rightly, I believe) refuses to take such assertions literally, but in that case there seems to be little room left for reading teleology in Plato and in Aristotle along similar lines. For one thing, even if one depersonalises Plato's god (an attempt to which I am in principle sympathetic), such a god still works as a unifying teleological principle for

the whole cosmos, while no such analogous function can be attributed to Aristotle's "nature". And after all, Johansen does not deny that "Timaeus' final causes . . . operate . . . via god's intelligence" (2004: ch. 5), while no such intelligence is to be found as part of Aristotle's conception of nature. On Aristotle see also my (2004c: 222–3).

33. Compare Osborne (1996: 200–1) and Morgan (2000: 273–4).

34. On the paradigmatic nature of the universe from an ethical point of view cf. Chapter 3. Johansen (2004: ch. 9) thinks that Timaeus' speech is pervaded by teleological ordering "similarly" to the universe, on the grounds that even the Demiurge has a difficult task to face with his materials. But such a claim seems to underplay the fact that Timaeus' complaint about his haphazard way of speaking at 34c refers to such a shortcoming as distinctively human, since it relates it to the fact that *we* participate to a great degree in the random (cf. 29d1, with its reference to our "human nature").

35. Since it is subsequently said that [he] gave shape to (*dieschêmatisato*) the precosmic traces with forms and numbers (b4–5).

36. See "intellect ordering everything" (*nous diakosmôn panta*) at *Phaedo* 97c1–2; cf. *Crat.* 400a8–10, *Phil.* 28e3, *Laws* XII 967b5–6; for god in the same role (as *kosmôn* or *diakosmôn*) cf. *Phaedrus* 246e4–5, *Pol.* 273d4, e3, *Laws* X 899b7–8. For *nous* as king (*basileus*) or ruler (*archôn*) cf. *Phil.* 28c7, 30d8; for god in the same role, cf. *Pol.* 271d5, *Laws* X 903b7, 904a6, 905e2.

37. Cf. 38c3–4, 39e7–9, and those passages mentioned in n. 9.

38. Note, however, that these materials cannot themselves yet be called "body" proper (*sôma*). What we have at most in a precosmic state is scattered "traces" (*ichnê*) of those four kinds (water, air, etc.), which will only be called "bodies" insofar as they receive intelligent organisation and are proportionally combined in the one "body" of the universe (53b ff., 32a–c). (Similarly, according to the *Philebus*, the universe couldn't be regarded as a "mixture" unless it has the right proportion by virtue of *nous*: in the absence of the latter we at most get an "uncompounded jumble" or "disjoint misfortune" – *akratos sumpephorêmenê*, 64d9–e3: see Chapter 4, Section II.3.1.) These original materials would in turn correspond with "the bodily" (*to sômatoeides*) at *Pol.* 273b4–6, which is said to be congenital (*suntrophon*) with the nature of the universe (cf. *emphuton* at 269d3) and to belong to the ancient nature that prevailed before the present cosmic order, related to an "unlimited sea of dissimilarity" (273d6–e1). For a connection with "the unlimited" (*to apeiron*) in the *Philebus* see Chapter 4, Section II.1.

39. The metaphor of the charioteer and the horses is employed by Plato himself in the *Phaedrus* (246a ff.), to symbolise the relation between individual reason and the lower parts of the soul, which, in the *Timaeus*, are said to arise "by necessity" (42a, cf. 69c–d).

40. The example of a dam is given in *Laws* VI 761a–b.

41. See the relation between things occurring by necessity (*ex anankês*) and random effects (*to tuchon*) corresponding to a type of cause at *Tim.* 46e; and compare "chance by necessity" (*tuchê ex anankês*) at *Laws* X 889c1–2 also in a causal context. In this latter case, chance as a cause (cf. 888e) is contrasted with art, *nous*, god and soul as kindred concepts, in the debate Plato holds with his materialist opponents as to the primary principle of everything

(889c, 892b–c). We find a similar opposition in the *Sophist* (265c, e), where chance seems to be put in terms of a "spontaneous cause" (*aitia automatê*) without purpose (*aneu dianoias*) in contrast with a divine productive art (*theia poiêtikê technê*) or a demiurgic cause operating with *logos* and *epistêmê*, and in the *Philebus* (28d), where the force of the irrational and random and mere chance (*tên tou alogou kai eikêi dunamin kai to hopêi etuchen*) competes with wisdom (*phronêsis*) or *nous* for the governance of the universe. These passages in turn parallel the opposition of causes at *Tim.* 46e, which we shall analyse shortly.

42. *[aitiai] hosai monôtheisai phronêseôs to tuchon atakton hekastote exergazontai.*

43. Cf. its relation with *anankê* in the same passage, and particularly *di'anankês* at 47e4–5.

44. *sunaition*, 46c7, cf. its connection with *ex anankês* at 46e1–2, and *summetaition* at 46e6.

45. *aitia hupêretousa* (68e4–5), cf. *ex anankês* at e1.

46. Cf. Cornford (1937: 174); Moreau (1939: 39 ff.); Strange (2000: 415) and its connection with the concept of "hypothetical necessity" in Aristotle, *P.A.* I 1; cf. *Physics* II 9, *Metaph.* V 5 (on which see also Cooper [1987]). In particular, see the relation between necessary causes (*anankaiai aitiai*) and things without which (cf. *aneu toutôn*) at *Tim.* 69a. At *Pol.* 281d–e Plato distinguishes two kinds of arts (*technai*), "co-cause" (*sunaition*) and "cause" (*aitia*), and describes the former as providing the instruments without which (*hôn mê paragenomenôn*) the demiurgic *technê* cannot do its work. Also in the *Phaedo* (99b3–4), we find a distinction between "the real cause" or "agent" (*to aition tôi onti*) and "that without which the cause would not be a cause" (*ekeino aneu hou to aition ouk an pot'eiê aition*), though here Plato refuses to call the latter causes in any sense and their importance is downgraded, by contrast with his attempt in the *Timaeus* to give detailed mechanical descriptions: cf. Easterling (1967: 34–5); Guthrie (1978: 273).

47. In this regard, the attitude of the *Timaeus* towards its materialist predecessors would be one not of exclusion but of subordination within its own teleological outlook. For Plato's debt to Presocratic accounts in the *Timaeus*, such as those of Empedocles and the Atomists, and his in turn original contribution to the mechanical description of phenomena, cf. Lloyd (1968: 84–90).

48. Cf. *to ariston* 46c8 and *to eu* 68e5. This "good" does not need to be the Form in the transcendent way Forms are described in the *Timaeus*, but can just be a character immanent to the world, which the Demiurge tries to "complete" (or "fulfil", *apotelôn*, 46d1) or "frame" (*tektainomenos*, 68e5). Neither of these two verbs would suit the Forms. First, the main Form that Plato mentions as guiding the demiurgic activity is that of Living Being (*ho esti zôion*, 39e8), which is already complete (*teleon*, cf. 30d2, 39e1) and whose completeness he tries to imitate in the world he produces. The word "framing", in addition, is used elsewhere to describe the Demiurge's generation of its product (*tektainomenos*, 28c6), by contrast to the paradigm to which he looks. Thus, the use of the word *idea* at 46c8 can be associated with an immanent (rather than transcendent) character of goodness, in the same way as in *Tim.* 28a6–8 *ho dêmiourgos* is said to "realise" (*apergazêtai*) the form (*idea*) of something

by looking at a paradigm, something that unequivocally suggests that *idea* does not have to be applied to the transcendent Form. *Pace* Robinson (1993: 104–5).

49. Terms denoting production and dynamic agency in fact abound in the description: cf. *apergazomena* at 46d3, *exergazontai* at 46e6, and *kinountôn* at 46e2 predicated of necessary causes, and *dêmiourgoi* of primary causes at 46e4.

50. To adopt Fine's terminology (1987: 93).

51. Cf. Fine (1987: 91).

52. This, together with the association of primary causes with soul at 46d6, would lead us to postulate, as present also in the *Timaeus*, the theory of soul as self-mover and principle of motion expounded in *Phaedrus* 245c ff. and *Laws* X 896a–b. I shall argue below that it is soul, and particularly the world-soul at the macrocosmic level, that should in fact be taken as principle of motion in that dialogue. Cf. nn. 61 and 90.

53. For the debate about Forms as causes in the *Phaedo* and, particularly, about whether Forms are final causes there or relevant at all for the positing of teleological causes cf., in favour, Fine (1987: 111–12), Byrne (1989: 8), Sedley (1998: 125–7); *contra*, Vlastos (1981b: 87–8). For Forms taken as formal causes in the *Phaedo* cf. Fine (1987: 97–101), Hitchcock (1985: 71), Sedley (1998: 127–32). For the Good interpreted as formal cause in the *Republic* see Hitchcock (ibid.); as final cause, see e.g. Dye (1978: 54–6).

54. Note, however, that a veiled allusion to the Form of the Good in its causal aspect seems to be made at 37a1–2, where we are told that the world-soul was generated "by (*hupo*) the best (*aristou*) of ever-existing intelligible things". But for different readings of this passage see Cornford (1937: 94 n. 2).

55. Cf. López (1963: 146) and Ross (1951: 239) as to the need of both kinds of causation for a teleological explanation. Cf. also n. 88 for a possible allusion to Forms as final causes in the *Timaeus*.

56. Cf. Fine (1987: 90–1, 110–11).

57. Cf. De Lacy (1939: 111–12); nor do we need to postulate "teleological overkill" in the *Timaeus*, as if either Forms or *nous* were redundant, as proposed by McCabe (1992).

58. In this respect I can agree with Lennox that "participation . . . understood as a relation between copy and paradigm in virtue of which the copy may bear the name of the paradigm, is not something which occurs independently of an intelligent agent aiming to achieve some good" (1985: 213); cf. also Fine (1987: 111) for the need of an agent for paradigms to be teleological causes. That the image of the Demiurge can provide a way to account for how participation between two heterogeneous ontological domains such as the Forms and sensibles is at all possible – a question so critically posed in the *Parmenides*, 133c–134e – has been suggested by several scholars such as Taylor (1928: 646); Cherniss (1932: 237); Solmsen (1942: 103); cf. also Prior (1985: 96) and Eggers Lan (1987: 56); and we shall take up this question again in section III.1.2. *Pace* Strange (2000: 413–14), who believes that the Demiurge's task is merely to improve the participation of sensibles in Forms

rather than inaugurate it (as precosmic sensibles could participate in the Form of Fire for example): the text clearly describes the precosmos as filled with bodily traces (53b) but these *did not deserve at all the names* of fire, water, and the like that nowadays we give to them (69b). *Tim.* 53b, on which Strange (413) bases his interpretation, does not talk (as Strange claims) of "the receptacle containing traces or *ichnê* of the Forms (Fire, Air, Earth and Water)" before the Demiurge's activity: in fact, there is no reference to Forms at all in that passage, so Strange's use of evidence becomes here rather question-begging.

59. Lennox (1985: 210); my italics. That the triumph of *nous* over *anankê* is complete was the thesis put forward by Taylor (1928: 293 *ad* 46e5–6), and afterwards opposed by Cornford (1937: 209), a line of thought shared, among others, by those mentioned in nn. 61 and 62. In this regard Lennox (1985: 209–12) has revived the old position.

60. It is striking that Lennox (1985: 210), when arguing for the opposite view that there is no residue of recalcitrant necessity left in a world demiurgically framed, quotes precisely the passage *Tim.* 48a2–3 above translated, which would rather count as counterevidence for his view, as it implies that there is a minority of things that would not be the subject of such cosmic ordering. In addition, Lennox supposes that there is no compromise in the *Timaeus* between the Demiurge and his materials, though this view, as we shall see, seems challenged by various passages such as *Tim.* 75a–c, which clearly suggests a compromise, as we are told that the head would have had a great deal of flesh and acute perception "*if these had admitted to coexist*" (75b4). Cf. my (unpublished).

61. These random effects could still be explained within a theory of soul as principle of all motion, as has been attempted by Cherniss (1944: 444–5) and Brisson (1974: 503–4); cf. Chapter 8, Section V.3.

62. See also Cornford (1937: 175–6); and Festugière (1949: 111–13) on the random motions of the infant at 43a–b as manifesting *anankê* without the rule of *nous.*

63. Note that the universe is described as a mixture arising from the combination of *anankê* and *nous* (*memeigmenê . . . ex anankês te kai nou sustaseôs,* 47e5–48a2), a description that would go against the view that the distinction between necessary and primary causes concerns merely our explanation and understanding of the world and is "not an account of distinct aspects of the world's makeup", as contended by Lennox (1985: 212).

64. This would rule out that the primary causes could correspond to the Forms, if intellect and Forms are distinct (see n. 84 and Chapter 3, Section I.2).

65. In the definition of primary cause at 46e4 we can note again two essential features of god: his rationality and (therefore) his goodness, which is known by its effects: the order in the cosmos, which is recurrently due, as we have seen, to a *nous diakosmôn.* For these features of rationality and goodness as characterising god in general cf., for god's goodness, *Tim.* 29e1–2, 30a6–7, 42e2–4, *Rep.* II 379a7 ff., *Phaedrus* 247a7, *Theaet.* 176a5–c1, *Laws* X 899b5–7, 900d2, 901e ff.; for god's rationality, *Tim.* 51e5, *Symp.* 204a1–2, *Phaedrus* 247c–d, *Theaet.* 176b1–3, *Laws* X 900d5–7, 902e7–8.

66. The idea that the Demiurge symbolises the primary causes at 46e4 is briefly suggested by Cherniss (1944: 607), (1950: 207), (1954: 25); cf. Tarán (1971: 381) after Cherniss, and I developed it in my (1990) and (1991: ch. 2).

67. As we can see from the plural, it is the demiurgic intelligent action in general (both that of the Demiurge Father and of the lesser gods, including the heavenly bodies) that corresponds to this kind of causation. Cf. Chapter 3, Section I.

68. See e.g. Priest (1991: 8–15, 57, 162), Putnam (1999: 97). Note that this kind of dualism – also called substance dualism – takes it that the mind "does not require any place or depend on any material thing" (Descartes, *Discourse on Method*, Part IV, 33; cf. *Meditation* VI, 78). Can one relate this to the view of the *Phaedo* that the mind works at its best separate from a body (76c, 79b–c)? For discussion see Broadie (2001b: 295–308). Cf. Chapter 1, n. 14. Ostenfeld, for his part, argues that Plato moves from a robust kind of dualism, though comparable only in some respects to Cartesian dualism, in the *Phaedo*, to a dualism of attributes in his later dialogues (1987: 4–5): thus, in the *Timaeus* mind is an attribute of matter (as its principle of order), and the material traces depicted in the precosmos are an attribute of space (240–58, esp. 252). Even though my view will share some points of contact with Ostenfeld's, one main reservation I have for comparing Plato with an attribute dualist in the modern debate is the following: For an attribute dualist, two entities could be physically identical without having the same mental properties (one of them could indeed have no mental properties), whereas the kind of body we get in Plato depends on whether that body has soul and of what kind. For example, a body that crawls on earth shows the dominion of an irrational kind of soul; an elongated head shows deficient use of reason, etc. (91e–92b). Later on, in the *Laws*, it is suggested that the brave person differs from the cowardly one even judging from the colour of her complexion (II 654e–655a). More generally, "body" as such seems to require some intelligent, organisational principle, without which we would only get scattered traces of the four elements: cf. *Tim.* 53b ff. and Section III.1. *in fine.*

69. Cf. Hackforth (1936: 439 ff.) (criticised by Cherniss [1944: 606–8]); after him Solmsen (1942: 113, 115); Brisson (1974: 81–4); Guthrie (1978: 215, 275 n. 1); Mohr (1985: 183); Menn (1992: 556, 558); Strange (2000: 409 n. 21).

70. For the former view cf. Taylor (1928: 64, 77, 82); Skemp (1942: 114); López (1963: 177–8); Demos (1968: 145); Robinson (1969: 251 ff.), (1970: 103), (1986: 145 n. 1). The latter view has tended to identify the Demiurge with the world-soul or with part of the world-soul. For total identification see Theiler (1925: 69–73, esp. 72), Bury (1929: 10), Festugière (1947: 20–1), (1949: 104–5), Claghorn (1954: 119), Grube (1980: 170); for partial identification (insofar as the Demiurge is seen to stand for the Circle of the Same in the world-soul) see Cornford (1937: 205, 208), Morrow (1950: 437), and Ostenfeld (1982: 246).

71. Hackforth (1936: 444).

72. *Phaedrus* 245c ff., *Laws* X 896a–b, something certainly suggested at *Tim.* 46c7–e2, cf. 37b5.

73. Cf. Hackforth (1936: 446), Brisson (1974: 333 ff.), and Strange (2000: 409–10). For more on soul as principle of motion see n. 90.

74. Cf. Bury (1929: 9). I speak of A as "ontologically prior" to B in the sense of A being able to exist independently from B, but not vice versa (cf. Aristotle, *Metaph.* V 11, 1019a2–4, who interestingly refers to Plato in this context).

75. And this seems to invalidate Mohr's (1985: 182–3) endorsement of the view that *nous* can exist independently of soul and does not have to do with becoming or change, as much as his suggestion that at *Laws* 897–898 it is rational soul (as different from *nous*) that has motion: see the explicit mention of the "motion and revolution of intellect" (*nou kinêsis kai periphora*, *Laws* 897c5–6; cf. *nou periodos* at 898a5). For criticism of Mohr see also Robinson (1995: xx–xxi).

76. *Pace* Hackforth's attempt to circumscribe it not to *nous* but to what has *nous*: the world (1936: 445); followed by Brisson (1974: 83).

77. See e.g. Mohr (1985).

78. See Chapter 8, Section I.

79. Or "the one which is especially concerned with *nous*" (*peri noun kai phronêsin malista ousan*, 34a2–3), and not just a mere model or analogy for the motion of *nous* (as contended by Lee [1976: 73] and Strange [2000: 410 n. 26] after him).

80. Again, this movement is no mere image of *nous* but indeed proper to *nous*: see n. 79.

81. Motion is also a feature characteristic of any soul, both cosmic and individual (37a6–7, 89e). Cf. Sedley (2000: 800) for the view that the rotation of human reason should be taken literally; also Sorabji (2000: 116–17), (2003: 154). See my (1991: 90–3) and (1994: 279–80) on the need of psychic or noetic motion for body and space.

82. A possibility perhaps contemplated at *Laws* X 898e–899a.

83. This is what Brisson has called "ontological generation", as an alternative to the interpretation of *genesis* as mere generation in the past: cf. Brisson (1974: 336–8). A similar suggestion is found in Hackforth (1936: 442); Cherniss (1944: 424); Osborne (1988: 107).

84. *Pace* Diès (1927: 550–1, 553–5); Mugnier (1930: 131 ff.); Robin (1938: 180); Moreau (1939: 35–6, 43–5); Verdenius (1954: 248); Hampton (1990: 90, 116 n. 66). The clear distinction between Forms and *nous* should make such an assimilation implausible if the Demiurge is a *nous*, as I have been arguing. As we shall see, it is an essential feature of the Forms to be immutable (*Tim.* 38a3), while *nous* is in motion. Further, when in several passages of the *Timaeus* we read that the world has been made in the image of the "perfect" or "intelligible living being" (cf. *zôion* 30c, *to panteles zôion* 31b1, *noêton zôion* 39e1, etc.) we should interpret Plato to be alluding not so much to the Forms as living (*pace* de Vogel [1970: 229], Perl [1998: 86–7], Masi [2001: 53]) as to the Form of Living Being. Cf. Cornford (1937: 40–1); Cherniss (1944: 576–7); Brisson (1974: 81–2); Patterson (1981: 112). Similarly, when one reads at *Soph.* 248e6–249b6 that "complete being" (*to pantelôs on*) must include intellect and wisdom, and therefore life, soul and motion, one should not take this as a suggestion that intelligible forms must move – *pace* de Vogel

(1970: 228–9) – but rather as saying that complete being or the all (*to pan*) must include not only immutable entities but also mutable ones (cf. esp. 249c10–d5): see Dorter (1994: 147–8); De Rijk (1986: 17–18, 106). Perl, following De Vogel, seems to fall into a contradiction when bringing the *Timaeus* together with the *Sophist* and thus asserting, on the one hand, that the Forms in the *Timaeus* are living and so necessitate motion (1998: 87–8), while previously conceding, on the other, the explicit statement of the *Timaeus* that the Forms are immutable (83; cf. *Tim.* 38a). See Chapter 3, Section I.2.

85. Among those who query that the notion of a "world-soul" should have any serious philosophical meaning at all for Plato cf. McCabe (1994: 184–5), who refers to the world-soul as "metaphysical glue", and wonders whether entities such as this are necessary at all.

86. Cf. nn. 38 and 68 and Chapter 4, Section II.4; also my (forthcoming).

87. On this see the analysis by Ross (1951: 228–32); from a different perspective, the same point is maintained by Teloh (1981: 210, 217–18). Let us recall that the *Timaeus* speaks of the relation between Forms and sensibles in terms of "paradigms", "copies", and "imitation" (cf. e.g. 28c–29a, 29c, 37c–d, 48e–49a), something that tends to stress, in principle, the ontological distance rather than the "communication" or "participation" between both domains. See also *Tim.* 51e6–52d1 and Devereux (2000: 196). Further, the *Timaeus* portrays vividly the Forms' separate existence from sensibles by having the Demiurge look at the model *before* he creates the sensible world (30c–d, 39e), which suggests that the Forms can exist independently of the latter. *Pace* Fine (2000: 16), who claims that Plato never refers to the Forms as separate, in the sense that "the form of F could exist whether or not any F sensible things exist."

88. At *Tim.* 50c7–d4, the Receptacle is compared to a mother, the sensible world to a son and the Forms to a father, which looks striking given that the Demiurge was called a father at 28c3. This, however, seems rather to be settling the latter comparison in terms of the resemblance between the product and its original, with which, again, Plato would be stressing the character of the Forms as paradigms rather than efficient causes. Cf. Brisson (1974: 129).

89. Cf. *archê kinêseôs* at *Phaedrus* 245c9, *Laws* X 895b3, and *aitia kinêseôs* at *Laws* X 896b1.

90. These are in fact passages that remind us of the theory of the soul as self-mover and principle of motion developed in *Phaedrus* 245c ff. and *Laws* X (e.g. 896a–b). In the first place, 46d–e draws a contrast between secondary causes, "which occur by other things being moved and in turn moving other things by necessity" (46e1–2) and "the first causes of the intelligent nature" (46d8), in a way that suggests that the latter are the principle of the former (cf. n. 52), something that is reinforced in the light of the analogous contra-position in *Phaedrus* 245c and *Laws* X 896a–b. The allusion to self-motion at *Tim.* 37b, for its part, may refer either to the world-soul or to the universe animated by it. But that Timaeus should on occasion attribute self-motion to organisms (rather than to the soul as such) should be no surprise if, as I

argue, soul is inseparable from body. See also 36e, where the world-soul is said to have "started for itself (*êrxato*) a divine beginning (*archê*) of unceasing and intelligent life for the whole of time"; the middle voice suggesting that the soul is its own principle. For other scholars in favour of the theory of soul as self-mover and *archê kinêseôs* as being present in the *Timaeus*, cf. Robin (1938: 165–6), Cherniss (1944: 428 ff., 455), (1954: 26 n. 24), Brisson (1974: 335–6), Morrow (1950: 437), Easterling (1967: 30 ff.), Strange (2000: 410); against, Vlastos (1939: 390–9), Herter (1957: 330), Demos (1968: 143 ff.), Robinson (1969: 249), Mohr (1985: 174).

91. For this function of *diakosmein* or *poiein* see e.g. *Phil.* 26e–27b, 28e, 30c5–7; cf. *Tim.* 47e4.

92. *Pace* Johansen (2004: ch. 4), who takes the cosmic soul as falling on the "becoming side" *simpliciter* of the *Timaeus'* ontological distinction. More precisely, *Tim.* 35a1–b1 describes the world-soul as composed of a mixture of three elements: existence (*ousia*), identity (*tauton*) and difference (*thateron*), each of which is intermediate between the indivisible (*ameriston*) and the divisible (*meriston*). For this interpretation (and the reading of the passage, which varies from Burnet's at 35a4) see Grube (1932; also 1980: 142), followed by Cornford (1937: 59–61) and now generally accepted. For how the soul's being composed of these elements puts it in a privileged position to make judgements about both the intelligible and the sensible, in a way that promises to do away with the problems of a "two-world" theory, see Frede (1996b).

93. Here we read that soul turns upon itself (in a circular fashion that implies orderly motion): *autê te anakukloumenê pros hautên*, 37a5; it grasps what has scattered or indivisible existence when "in motion through all of itself", *kinoumenê dia pasês heautês*, 37a6–7; it is "what is moved by itself", *to kinoumenon huph' hautou*, 37b5.

94. Cf. Festugière (1947: 21), (1949: 103).

95. As I shall argue also to be the case as regards *Laws* X 896e–897b in Chapter 8. I say "particularly" the world-soul since, as I shall show in the next chapter, I don't rule out that the heavenly bodies and even human souls can be primary causes.

96. *Pace* Morrow (1950: 437), who thinks that the disorderly motion in the *Timaeus* derives from the irrational part of the world-soul, and Cornford (1935: 205, 208) who supposes that the source of that irrational motion is the Circle of the Other, considered in abstraction from the Circle of the Same (cf. also Robin [1935: 166]). Apart from the evidence we are considering, we must remember that only after its constitution is the "mixture" of the world-soul divided into two Circles, which have therefore the same nature; cf. Cherniss (1944: 410 n. 339), (1954: 26 n. 28); Ostenfeld (1982: 328 n. 171). So I cannot agree with Cornford in his suggestion that the Demiurge symbolises *just* "Reason in the World-Soul" as a distinct part of it identical with the Circle of the Same (1937: 39, 208, 361).

97. Cf. *Tim.* 37a–c, where each function is remitted to the Circles of the Same and the Other respectively. It is through this role of knowing the Forms that the Circle of the Same is called the "most intelligent" (*phronimôtatês*) revolution, 39c2.

98. *Tim.* 43d ff. (esp. 44a–b) suggests that any true judgements about the sensible (which make the holder of the judgement rational, *emphrôn*) must be guaranteed by the ruling role of the Circle of the Same. And yet Timaeus can still say that mere correct opinion or *orthê doxa* is ungrounded (and in that sense irrational, *alogos*), as he claims for the majority of men at 51e (cf. 27d5–28a4). But precisely because the world-soul opines not only "truly" but "stably" at 37b8 (stability being a feature that was initially reserved for the Forms at 29b6) we have reason to believe that its *doxa* is not *alogos*: the world-soul would have *logos* insofar as, by knowing the Forms, it can, when apprehending the sensible, give an account of it in the light of the knowledge of that after which the sensible is copied. Compare *Laws* X 901d, where, in a context devoted to showing the providence of the gods, we are told that the gods know everything, and nothing which can be the object of *aisthêsis* or *epistêmê* escapes them.

99. *Pace* Ostenfeld (1982: 246), who sees no reason for identifying the Demiurge with the whole of the world-soul, and privileges its identification with the Circle of the Same.

100. Compare here the suggestion by Archer-Hind (1888: 38–9).

101. See n. 68 and Chapter 1, n. 14.

102. Cf. also *Laws* X 898d–e on the imperceptibility of soul. In particular, at *Tim.* 46d we are told that "the soul is invisible, whereas fire, water, earth and air as bodies have all become visible". Note, however, that the myth seems to treat the world-soul as having extension, as it is said to be "interwoven" (*diaplakeisa*) everywhere from the middle to the periphery of the heavens (36e2), much as it is immediately added that "the body of the universe is visible, and the soul is invisible" (36e5–6). And yet in the *Timaeus* Plato uses "invisible" (*aoraton*) not only for the soul in opposition to the body (see too *Tim.* 46d6), but also for corporeal entities which are "invisible due to their smallness" (83d3; cf. 43a, 91d) or to their transparency (67d5). Indeed Aristotle took Plato in the *Timaeus* to be a materialist about the soul, when criticising him for attributing extension (*megethos*) to his world-soul (*De Anima* 407a2–3). According to Sedley (2000: 800; cf. Burnyeat [2000: 58]), in the *Timaeus* the incorporeal differs from the corporeal "not by being altogether non-spatial, but by lacking essential characteristics of body, such as visibility and tangibility (cf. 28b, 31b)". But neither of the two passages to which he refers imply his view; rather, they simply state that corporeality, visibility, and tangibility are necessary and sufficient for something having *genesis* or generation, which leaves open the possibility that there could be invisible corporeal entities, as at 83d3–4 and 67d5. Nor does the text necessitate the adoption of Johansen's similar suggestion that "it is the perceptibility of body that distinguishes it from soul" on the basis of "36e5–6: 'the body of the heaven has been created visible; but the soul is invisible'" (2000: 91). For the claim at 36e5–6 concerns the (eminently visible) body of the world rather than any body as such. Thus, we have reason to doubt the consequent contention that the Stoic "corporeality" of god finds no "comparable views" in "fourth century thought" (Sedley 2002: 41), as the text seems to be a little more open than modern interpreters have taken it. I have analysed the way in which the

Timaeus can be seen as a precursor of Aristotelian and Stoic views in my (forthcoming).

103. In fact, some scholars have been tempted to see the world-soul as a feature inherent to the world-body such as its mathematical structure (cf. 31c–32a with 35b–c), or at least the source of that structure: cf. Ostenfeld (1982: 247).

104. Note that at 245e2–3 self-motion (as pertains to an immortal principle) is said to be the "essence and definition" (*ousian te kai logon*) of soul, immediately before it is suggested that this is so because (*gar*) the "nature" (*phusis*) of soul is (*ousês*) to animate a body from within. This makes us think that being the principle of motion of an organism is treated in the *Phaedrus* as constitutive of what it is to be "soul". Along similar lines, we are told that "all soul takes care of all the inanimate" (246b6), and that, while some souls take an earthly body (246c3–6), even god we imagine as a composite of body and soul naturally united through the whole of time (246c7–d2). Cf. Ostenfeld (1987: 21–2, 33), (1990). The conclusion might seem to clash with a further passage speaking of the body as tomb (cf. 250c). This, however, is most probably an allusion not to body as such, but to one's earthly body in a context which refers to the latter as a way of life (see esp. 250b8–c4; 250e–251a, where it is suggested that, by contrast, earthly bodily beauty can be revered as a semblance of true beauty; and 257b, where the conclusion of Socrates' second speech is that one ought to direct one's love and one's life – *ton bion* – towards philosophy).

105. The contrast with the *Phaedo* is still noteworthy whether one posits a difference of view or just of stress between the two outlooks on the body outlined above. It is certainly true that the body could also act as a hindrance to human fulfilment in the *Timaeus* (cf. 88a–b in relation with 90b), and that it had the status of a necessary condition in the *Phaedo* (99a–b). However, even when the *Phaedo* does mention the bodily as a necessary condition for intelligent activity, it is not clear that it takes the body to be a necessary condition for mental activity in any state (such as prenatal); and mechanistic explanations of nature are there downgraded, by contrast with the attempt of the *Timaeus* to integrate them into its teleological account of the world.

106. Cf. e.g. *Tim.* 68e with 46c–e, *Laws* X 897a–b.

107. As Cherniss (1950: 207 n. 1) seems to believe when, in his review of Festugière (1949), he criticises the latter for holding that the Demiurge stands for the world-soul *instead of* the notion of primary causation. Cf. also Tarán (1971: 407 n. 164).

Chapter 3

1. Naddaf (1997: 34).

2. See Sedley (1997), later incorporated in his (2000); Annas (1999: 57–8). My own thoughts on this point were originally expressed in my (1997). For criticisms of Sedley and Annas see nn. 47 and 49.

3. See my (1991).

4. Cf. Reverdin (1945: 47); Moreau (1939: 81). Cf. also *ton megiston theon kai holon ton kosmon, Laws* VII 821a2; for my reading of this phrase cf. Chapter 8, n. 45. For other passages treating the universe as god in the *Timaeus* cf. e.g. 34b1, 8, 68e4.
5. As is evident from the fact that, in the myth, their souls haven't given rise to a new mixture over and above the mixture out of which the world-soul is made (35a–36d). The celestial bodies are in turn called "visible gods" at 40d4.
6. As Cornford (1937: 79) has observed, "the motion of the Same is both a proper self-motion of the World-Soul, manifested physically as the axial rotation of the whole body of the world, and also an imparted motion", which affects the heavenly bodies. The Circle of the Same is called "the external motion" (*hê exô phora*) at 36c4, and the world-soul is said to pervade and envelop the world-body from the centre and even from the outside (*exôthen*) at 34b and 36e; so we should think that the outer motion of the circumference of the universe (i.e. that of the Same) coincides with the whole rotation of the sphere on its own axis.
7. Astronomically, this seems to imply that the world-soul imparts to the heavenly bodies a motion of forward rotation along the outer orbit of the Same (in the case of the fixed stars, 40b1–2), which, by coinciding with the axial rotation of the whole celestial sphere (alluded to at 34a), also carries round, and in that sense prevails over (39a1–2), all the inner planetary circles contained in the sphere, which can, however, still have the motion of the Other in the opposite direction to that of the Same (36c). (This latter phenomenon results in the spiral twist of the planets because they have two different motions in opposite directions, 39a4–b2.) Cf. Cornford – after Proclus – (1937: 76, 78–9); Heath (1913: 160).
8. Note also that in both cases there is imitation of the major god by the lesser gods: the young gods try to *imitate* their father in their task of creation (41c5, 42e8, 69c5); the shape of the heavenly bodies was made round by *imitation* of the universe (40a4).
9. The latter, we might suppose, include not only their own motions but also the Forms, insofar as the stars are said to be inserted in the Circle of the Same by which the Forms are known by the soul (cf. 36c, 37c).
10. See e.g. 36d; 38c7–8; and 39c–d where *planas* at 39d1 seems to be used ironically in a context that would conversely stress the regularity of the courses of the planets as measures of time. Cf. Vlastos (1975: 99–100, 101–2), (1980: 24–5 n. 26).
11. That the Demiurge is in some way responsible for the creation of all of them, including the traditional gods, is suggested by his advising them to perform their demiurgic function by imitating the power that he used in creating them, 41c5–6.
12. Compare 34b5–8, 40b8–c3 with 40e5; and Taylor (1938: 184). Even though the passage that introduces the gods of the traditional religion (40d6–e3) has often been taken to be ironical (cf. Taylor [1928: *ad loc.*]; Cornford [1937: 139]; Vlastos [1939: 381]; Reverdin [1945: 53]), we must note that Plato's irony seems to be directed at the poets rather than at the gods themselves.

13. Though let us note that Plato is not innovating in presenting the celestial bodies as gods (which seemed to be a common Greek and Barbarian belief, cf. *Ap.* 26d, *Crat.* 397c–d, *Laws* X 887e), but in the philosophical foundations that he gives to this view.

14. Cf. *auto eph' heautou*, 51b8, *auta kath' hauta*, 51c1; cf. 51d4–5.

15. Cf. 29a. At 37c *nous* itself is described as arising in soul when the latter is in contact with the Forms (cf. also *Rep.* VI 508d), so that intelligence as such seems to depend on the existence of its object (cf. *Tim.* 51d; rather than vice versa, as would be the case if Forms were concepts in god's mind, a view found e.g. in Ashbaugh [1988: 60–1] and countenanced by Gerson [1990: 80–1]; cf. *Parm.* 132b–c with Burnyeat [1982: 20–2]). In the *Phaedrus*, we read that the Forms are those things "by being in relation to which god is divine" (*pros hoisper theos ôn theios estin*, 249c6), and the traditional image of the gods' being nurtured on nectar and ambrosia – a key to their immortality – is replaced by the metaphor of the gods' being nurtured on the Forms (247c–e). This suggests that the Forms are the ultimate foundation of the gods' divinity and immortality.

16. One possible counterexample is *Tim.* 37c6–7, where the world is called *tôn aidiôn theôn gegonos agalma*, which could be read as "a generated image of the eternal gods", meaning that the world is an image of gods that are the Forms (*agalma* as a synonym of *eikôn* and opposed to *paradeigma* in the light of 37c7–8, 37d1, 37d5–7). However Cornford (1937: 99–102) has argued that an *agalma* is not an image but a place intended for occupation by a god or gods, thus a kind of "shrine". So he translates 37c6–7 as "a shrine brought into being for the everlasting gods", a shrine where, in the mythical description, these gods – the heavenly bodies or celestial gods of 39e10, called "everlasting" at 40b5 – still have to take their place.

17. *noêta*, cf. e.g. 30c7, 48e6, 51c5; *nooumena* 51d5. See also Chapter 2, n. 84.

18. See Grube (1980: 151–2).

19. Cf. *Tim.* 90c1, a passage to which I shall return. The concept of the "divine" (*theion*) seems to be applied more broadly to immortal entities, with positive axiological connotations. Cf. Mugnier (1930: 116–17). Thus, it is predicated not only of the Forms, but also of god in its different aspects or referents, 36e4, 40a2, b5, 68d4, e7, 76b2; and of human reason, 69d6, 72d4, 73a7, c7, 88b2, 90c4, 8. Derivatively, the term is applied to that which contains human reason, and so our head is called divine (44d5), since it is "the abode of what is most divine and sacred" (*tên tou theiotatou kai hierôtatou oikêsin*, 45a1). Cf. my (1991: 119–34).

20. Cf. n. 19 and *Tim.* 41d1, 42e7, 90a3–4, c5.

21. *Pace* Strange (2000: 411). For a similar way of tackling the reappearance of this Socratic paradox in the *Laws* (IX 860d–862c) cf. Stalley (1983: 151 ff.). For discussion of *Tim.* 87b see also Gill (2000).

22. Against the view that there should be any irrational parts in the world-soul (as defended e.g. by Cornford) see Chapter 2, Section III.3.

23. The lower parts of the soul can still however be called irrational insofar as they lack, unlike reason, the capacity to deliberate about what is good for the overall person (70e–71a, cf. *Rep.* IV 442c). At the same time, they can be said

to have a "rational" place in the universe insofar as they are part of a wider teleological plan, to which the virtuous person must make them conform.

24. Note that completeness or perfection and self-sufficiency in turn figure in the *Philebus* as marks of the happy life (20d). For more on psychosomatic interaction, and on how humans themselves should seek self-sufficiency in a way that promotes immunity to disease, see Section II.2.

25. See *Rep.* VI 509d–510a, 511a. Cf. Reverdin (1945: 243–6).

26. Cf. Ashbaugh (1988: 10), who points out in turn how the soul, at the level of *dianoia*, uses sensible objects themselves (which are the models of the objects of *eikasia*) as images of higher realities, in such a way that would explain the allusion to the sensible universe itself as an *eikôn* (and the corresponding discourse as *eikos*) at *Tim.* 29b–c. Note also that, interestingly, the rational part of the soul in the *Timaeus* is at times denominated *dianoia*, often (though not exclusively, cf. 71b3, c4) in contexts where this would be a suitable term to use if Plato were trying to stress a capacity for mathematical studies as he had done in the *Republic* (cf. VI 511d): see e.g. 88a8, c2, highlighting the balance that must exist between exercising *dianoia* (e.g. through mathematics) and the body through gymnastics; and 47b, where it is to correct the "thoughts" (*dianoêseis*) in us that we should imitate the revolutions of *nous* in heaven (described in turn as *dianoêseis* e.g. at 90c8).

27. Some degree of similarity must indeed be presupposed for any kind of imitation to take place: see *Critias* 107c–d. To this extent, we can say that an image contains "some truth" (as is predicated of Platonic myths at *Rep.* II 377a5–6).

28. Cf. Chapter 1, Section III.1. The *Timaeus* emphasises that it is in particular the irrational part of the soul that is fond of images and appearances (*eidôlôn kai phantasmatôn*, 71a5–6).

29. Compare here the remarks by a leading virtue ethicist such as MacIntyre (1981), who advocates "that moral tradition from heroic society to its medieval heirs according to which the telling of stories has a key part in educating us into the virtues" (201) – much as one may still raise the question whether "moral discourse while it may use fables and parables as aids to the halting moral imagination ought in its serious adult moments to abandon the narrative mode for a more discursive style and genre" (122). For a study of role models in Plato against the Homeric background see Hobbs (2000); also Gill (1996: 307–20). None of these studies, however, notes the importance of god as role model in the *Timaeus*.

30. See *N.E.* VII 13 1153b19–21 (Kraut's transl.); and Kraut (1979: 171) after him. This is probably an attack on Socratic views, as expressed e.g. at *Ap.* 30c6–d5, 41c–d.

31. Similarly, at *Laws* IV 709a ff. we get powerful suggestions about the importance of using skill (*technê*) and seizing the opportune moment (*kairos*) for humans to deal with luck in an artful way: the example is given of the pilot during a storm, who will try to "profit" from circumstances he did not cause (c1–3). For this issue in the *Laws* cf. my (2002) and (unpublished).

32. Note, however, that Plato's emphasis on beauty is not on superficial bodily beauty, but presupposes the correct relation between the mind and the body,

and that is why he takes pains to emphasise that, when soul and body have characteristics opposite to each other (e.g. the body is strong but the soul is weak, or vice versa) the whole is not beautiful (*kalon*); but the living being who is in the opposite condition is the most beautiful (*kalliston*) of all sights "for the one who can see" (87d). Cf. *Rep.* III 402d.

33. We read in the *Laws*: "...in order to live a happy life it is necessary, first, neither to do wrong oneself nor to be wronged by others: of these, the former is not very difficult, but it is very difficult to acquire the power (*dunamis*) not to be wronged, and impossible to possess such power perfectly in any other way than by becoming perfectly good (*teleôs agathon*)." To this point, the claim might simply appear to be that perfect virtue is *necessary* for preventing one from being wronged, but the lines to follow suggest that it is meant to be also *sufficient*: thus, in a context where the Athenian compares the state to an individual, we are told that if a state is [perfectly] good it will not suffer wrongs from others and will live at peace (VIII 829a–b). See my (2002).

34. Compare here how the *Republic* moves from stories for children to mathematical studies as part of the educational program of the guardians (e.g. VII 521d–522c).

35. Cf. Kucharski (1966: 319, 326). Frede (1996b), for her part, goes as far as suggesting that philosophy and dialectic, both for humans and for the world-soul, may be understood in a revisionist way, as dealing with concepts rather than with transcendent Forms, so that "no gazing at the Forms at the top end of an ontological ladder seems to be envisaged, as we find in the *katoptein* of the beautiful itself, in the *Symposium* (cf. 210e, 211d)" (p. 40 n. 19). For resonances of the *Symposium* in the *Timaeus* discussion see Section III.2.

36. On the subject see e.g. Vlastos (1980: 6–8).

37. Thus, the text speaks of apprehending the harmonies and revolutions of the All (*tas tou pantos harmonias te kai periphoras*, 90d3–4), after we are told that the world-soul itself is said to participate in calculation (*logismos*) and *harmonia* (36e6–37a1), being composed of mathematical intervals (35b–36a).

38. At *Tim.* 36d2–3 we read that "the inner circle [of the Other] was divided into seven unequal circles, according to each interval of the double and triple [proportions]", in a way that remits to the double and triple intervals into which the world-soul is divided at 35b–c, on the basis of the numbers 1, 2, 3, 4, 8, 9, 27, which form two geometrical (square and cubic) progressions. In the light of this, *Tim.* 36d2–3 would then suggest that the distances between the planetary orbits correspond to the six intervals between the seven terms of the series, 1, 2, 3, 4, 8, 9, 27; though the way that happens, as Cornford (1937: 79) has remarked, is subject to different interpretations. The simplest view seems to be that these figures measure the radii of successive orbits, so that the radius of the Moon's orbit equals one, that of the Sun's 2, and so on up to Saturn whose radius or distance from the Earth would equal 27. In this line of interpretation see e.g. Brisson (1974: 40–1). For different interpretations in antiquity see Heath (1913: 164).

39. It is certainly clear that the function of astronomy, as much as that of all the propaedeutic sciences, is to be conducive to being (*ousia*) and the Good in

the *Republic* (see e.g. VII 523a, 527b, d–e, 532c); though not much is explicitly said about the ethical immediate advantages that such a study could convey independently of its function as a prelude to dialectic. For an attempt to draw out the ethical implications of mathematics in the *Republic* cf. Burnyeat (1987: 238–40, esp. 240) and (2000: 43–6), though here again the emphasis is placed only on the training of the politician, and not people in general as I shall be claiming for the *Timaeus*.

40. Cf. esp. 44b8–c2.
41. As briefly noted by Brisson (1992a: 62, 246–7 n. 321 and 325) and suggested by Sedley (1989: 376–7).
42. Cf. e.g. *Phaedo* 79d3, e1, 84b2, *Rep.* VI 487a5, 490b4, X 611e2 for *sungeneia*, *Phaedo* 79b16, e1, 80b3, *Rep.* VI 500c5 for *homoiôsis*.
43. Cf. Des Places (1964: 88); Kucharski (1966: 327).
44. Plato stresses "similarity with god" as an aim to be striven for by humans in several dialogues. Cf. *Theaet.* 176b1–2: *homoiôsis theôi kata to dunaton*; also *Rep.* X 613b1, *Phaedrus* 253b–c, and *Laws* IV 716c–d.
45. Cf. Festugière (1949: 138–9), followed by López (1963: 196). For the fore-shadowing of Hellenistic conceptions see Solmsen (1983: 365). I don't see any basis for claiming that this resemblance with god is a process that cannot be achieved during our earthly existence – as Lovibond (1991: 55) seems to suggest; the text at 90d5–7 rather speaks of "the best life put forward by gods to humans *both for the present and for the future time*".
46. The language of "remaining" and identity or regularity used for the stars (see *menei* and *kata tauta* at 40b5–6, cf. 40a8–b1) does in fact recall similar language applied most properly to the Forms: see *menontos* used of the eternity of the Forms at 37d6 and *kata tauta* of the Forms at 38a3, 52a1.
47. Sedley (1997: 331–4), (2000: 798–806) rightly notes and emphasises this theoretical aspect of becoming like god (and that it foreshadows similar Aristotelian remarks in the *Nichomachean Ethics*), but appears to exclude the relevance of the practical aspect in the *Timaeus*, which I here purport to highlight. Instead, Sedley recognises that god has both practical and theoretical functions in the *Timaeus*, but takes this to be a "tension" in Plato's theory, which putatively advises us to imitate god only in the theoretical aspect (2000: 807); my reading, conversely, suggests that it is unnecessary to commit Plato to such a tension, and the text itself gives sufficient indication that Plato sees the two aspects as integrated. Similarly Annas (1999: 57–8) takes the passage to deal only with contemplative fulfilment, but in a way that neglects the ordinary business of life. Note that the text only condemns the *spending of intense effort* on the daily business of life – as would result from cultivating the lower parts of the soul at the expense of the highest (90b). It does, however, recommend their *proportionate* interaction (90a1–2), and leaves open a practical application of this recommendation to become like god, as I shall show below.
48. This mediating function can also be seen in the *Phaedrus*, where it was the traditional gods (though with a special emphasis on their noetic aspect, 247c–d) who lead the procession of souls to contemplate the Forms (cf. 247a, 248a, 250b). On this compare Ferrari (1987: 127–32).

49. Note that *peri ten genesin* at *Tim.* 90d1–2 can be read (and has standardly been read) as "around the time of our birth". Sedley, while not excluding this reading, favours instead a reading of 90d1–3 as summoning us to "correct the corrupted revolutions in our head concerned with becoming (*peri ten genesin*)", which he in turn takes to mean that our intellect's circular motion has become distorted by being concerned with becoming, rather than with being. In this way, astronomy would keep in the *Timaeus* the same function as in the *Republic*, namely that of driving the soul from becoming to being: see Sedley (2000: 805). As the context indicates, this reading is not necessitated by the *Timaeus* (which, as Sedley recognises, nowhere else uses *genesis* with the definite article for becoming in general as he contends is the case in this passage, and does use *genesis* in that construction more than once for "birth"). But even if one goes with Sedley's reading, the text needn't imply that the distorting of the revolutions of our intellect occurred by our being concerned with becoming; rather, it can simply be read as saying that we should correct "those revolutions of our head concerned with becoming which were corrupted" (in situations such as those described at the moment of birth and after, 43a ff.). Becoming as such could hardly be bad for the soul when the intellections of the world-soul themselves that we are recommended to imitate in this passage are described as motions (90c8–d1), and to that extent pertain to the realm of becoming (35a). Rather than downgrading becoming, I take Plato in the *Timaeus* to be elevating it in a way that matches rather than jeopardises his view of the whole material universe (and not just its noetic soul) as a god. For more on this see Chapter 4, Section II.3.2.

50. Similarly, speaking in general terms about the care and health of every living being (*zôion*), Timaeus states that in order to avoid disproportion between body and soul the only solution is neither to move (*kinein*) soul without body, nor body without soul, 87d, 88b (and then, e.g., practice gymnastics together with mathematics, 88c); but we know in the light of 90c–d that, as far as our rational soul is concerned, the motion recommended to it is the learning of the kindred motions of the universe.

51. For further discussion of this issue in the *Republic* cf. Cooper (1977b: 152–3); Vlastos (1981c: 136–9); Annas (1981: 136 ff., 306 ff.); Irwin (1995: 229 ff.); and Bobonich (2002: 51 ff.), with a reply by Kahn (2004: 349–53).

52. Cf. here my (1997: 346 n. 22).

53. Similarly dialectic, in one sense, will also keep its privileged position of access to the Forms. Cf. *Phil.* 57e6 ff., 58d4 ff. and Chapter 4, Section I.

54. In particular, at 61d10–e3 we are told of two kinds of *epistêmê*: one dealing with the eternal and another one dealing with the mutable. At 58e–59b, *epistêmê* is treated as including belief (*doxa*). For more on this see Chapter 5, Section II.

55. These terms are in the most proper sense used to refer to knowledge of the Forms (58d6–7, 59d1), but they are also used in a broader sense at other places. For this wide sense as regards *nous* see 59b7; and as regards *phronêsis* see 19b (which speaks of kinds of *phronêsis* that need to be divided, like *epistêmai* at 13e–14a), and 61d (where the question is posed whether all

kinds of pleasure or all kinds of *phronêsis* should be included in the mixture, and immediately passes on to distinguish different kinds of *epistêmê*, as if this and *phronêsis* were synonyms).

56. This must include some study of mathematics, particularly given that the overall thrust of the passage is to emphasise a balance between mental and physical activity, the mathematician being chosen as the exemplar of the former kind.

57. These include the fact that mathematics quickens the mind and improves one's own nature (*para tên hautou phusin epididonta, Laws* V 747b5–6; cf. *Rep.* VII 526b), and that a basic but sufficient knowledge of astronomy facilitates comprehension of the workings of the calendar as far as it is necessary for the administration of the city (VII 809c–d). Cf. Dicks (1970: 137–8).

58. After stating that every free person should learn arithmetic, measurement, and astronomy (VII 817e), the Athenian Stranger recognises explicitly that it is not necessary that "the many" (*hoi polloi*) should do that "with exactness" (*di'akribeias*), for that "is not easy nor at all possible for everybody" (818a). In other words, Plato is still aware of the limitations of the majority of people (as much as he was in the *Republic* when stating that "it is impossible that the crowd be philosophic", VI 494a4), though now positively willing to maximise their capacities.

59. This difference is one between more basic or simple pieces of knowledge and more complex or detailed ones, not between what is more or less true. For we are told that even the less accurate kind comprises what is necessary (*anankaion*) in mathematical studies, a necessity that binds even the gods (818a–b) and must be known as the right basis for further study (cf. *tauta estin ha dei labonta orthôs prôta epi talla ionta toutôn hêgoumenôn tôn mathêmatôn manthanein*, 818d6–8), even by the one who is going to take care of humans (818c2). The Stranger in addition complains in the subsequent lines that it is worse to learn something in the wrong way than to be absolutely inexperienced about these things (819a3–6).

60. As far as I am aware, this particular aspect of the *Timaeus* has not received due attention from other scholars. Kung (1989), while noting the importance of mathematical studies for human virtue (309), does not, however, draw any distinction between the philosopher and ordinary people in this regard, nor does she point out any difference between the ethical treatment of astronomy in the *Republic* on the one hand, and the *Timaeus* and the *Laws* on the other, which she takes as exhibiting the same line of thought (cf. ibid.). The same applies to Sedley (1997: 337), (2000: 801, 805), who, apart from focusing on the purely theoretical aspect of *homoiôsis theôi* in the *Timaeus* (in a way that includes only the philosopher), sees complete correspondence between the treatment of astronomy in the *Republic* and in the *Timaeus*.

61. Annas (1999: 57, 59).

62. See e.g. *Rep.* IX 573b ff.

63. Hence the vocabulary of "assimilation" with the object of thought (*exomoiôsai*) at 90d4.

64. Cf. e.g. *Gorg.* 510b, *Phaedrus* 255b, *Tim.* 88e, *Laws* IV 716c–d.

65. Cf. e.g. *Phaedo* 66b ff.; *Symp.* 210e; *Rep.* VI 504d–505b, VII 540a–b.

66. In this regard, again, we have good reason to treat such a god as "nonmythical", to go with the criteria demarcating myth from argumentative discourse discussed in Chapter 1. For Plato's detailed argument for the existence of god, which, as Craig (1980: 15) rightly notes, goes no further than the world-soul and the heavenly bodies, see Chapter 4, Section II.4 and Chapter 8, Sections I–IV. It is interesting to note that no separate *nous* (such as one could think the Demiurge to be) above the cosmic god plays any role in the cognitive ascent of the soul towards the Forms, so that one could wonder, if one wanted to posit the Demiurge as a separate *nous* apart from the world, whether there would be any point in building a metaphysics that has no epistemological correlate for every level.

Chapter 4

1. "*Apeiron*" admits of many translations, ranging from "indeterminate" or "indefinite" to "unlimited" or "infinite". In general, it connotes lack of determination (or limit, *peras*), which can be either qualitative, quantitative, or both.
2. I have argued for this point in my (2000: 257–83).
3. On the vexed question of whether we get two or three *aporiai* in this passage of the *Philebus* (an issue whose resolution either way does not affect our main argument here) see Frede (1993: xxi–xxii), Dancy (1984), Hahn (1978), Gosling (1975: 143–53).
4. The vocabulary here is similar to that used in the *Phaedrus* (266b) with regard to dialectic or the proper method of collection and division.
5. For Prometheus as probably a veiled reference to Pythagoras, and for the likely influence of Philolaus on this passage of the *Philebus* cf. Burkert (1972: 415 n.8, 64, 86 ff.); Huffman (1993: 106).
6. On the sophistic use of one and many see e.g. Benitez (1989: 34–8) and Frede (1993: xxiii–xxiv), which contains some interesting illustrations.
7. Cf. Bury (1897: xxxv–xxxix); Taylor (1926: 412); Cornford (1935: 186); Robin (1935: 68–70); Hackforth (1945: 21); Cherniss (1945: 18), (1947: 234); Ross (1951: 131 ff.); Robinson (1953: 70, 162, 231–2); Friedlaender (1969: 319–21); Grube (1980: 44–5); Davidson (1990: 33 ff., 174–5); Hampton (1990: 23–8); D. Frede (1992: 427); (1993: xxix–xxx); De Chiara-Quenzer (1993: 41–2). For a different line, cf. e.g. Gosling (1975: 196 ff.).
8. Forms can also be seen to contain *apeiria* in other senses: for example, insofar as there is an indeterminate number of things that each Form is not (cf. *Soph.* 257a, and 256e on each Form containing "an infinite amount of not-being"); and, conceivably, also as the relative indeterminacy of a genus, if considered by contrast with the higher determination in content of lower species (see on this Aristotle, *Metaph.* V 28, 1024a36–b4 and XIII 10, esp. 1087a16–18, for the notions of intelligible matter and indeterminacy applying to the genus insofar as it is the substrate of the differences, and his report on Plato – probably alluding to his unwritten doctrines – as positing two principles for the Forms: the One, acting as form, and the Indefinite Dyad, acting as matter, at *Metaph.* I 6). That the Forms may contain

"indeterminacy" in this sense remains possible but rather speculative, unless one takes the discussion of *peras* and *apeiron* at 23c ff. to apply also to Forms, as is done by Sayre (1983). See my discussion in Section II, esp. nn. 16–17. For a full discussion of the problem of Plato's unwritten doctrines see *Méthexis* 6 (1993), which is devoted to the subject. I am here assuming that one need not, and that it may be prudent not to, go beyond the dialogues to understand Plato's thought. For an extreme line that minimises the importance of the written dialogues, cf. e.g. Kraemer (1982) and Gaiser (1963). Sayre, on the other hand, relies on Aristotle but claims that what he refers to as the unwritten doctrines can in fact be found in the dialogues (cf. 1983: 11–3); whereas Kolb (1983: 310) maintains that the unwritten doctrines stand behind Plato's *Philebus* not as a necessary presupposition but as a helpful guide for the discussion of many of the problems there. For a note of caution cf. Frede (1997: 403–17).

9. Cf. Waterfield (1980: 282).
10. These "aspects" will constitute an intermediate layer between raw phenomena and the Forms, as will become clear through our analysis of the cosmic import of *peras* at 23c ff. See also n. 23.
11. See here Frede (1993: xvi).
12. For "art" and "knowledge" being used interchangeably cf. 57a ff.
13. If so, then the expression "the things that are always said to exist" at 16c9 can be taken to refer to reality in general in a way that includes both Forms and phenomena, and this conclusion is confirmed by the fact that Plato will go on to apply the notions of *peras* and *apeiron* to an analysis of phenomena (23c ff.). Gosling (1975: 83–4) believes that the expression "the things that are always said to exist" is unlikely to include the Forms, as Plato remits it to a previous tradition where such a concept was not coined; the "always" (*aei*) thus refers to the way we talk (and so he translates "the things that are from time to time said to exist"). Conversely, Striker takes the *aei* to refer to eternal realities and therefore to Forms (1970: 18–22). These interpretations, however, need not be exhaustive. Even when Plato acknowledges his predecessors in the handing down of the principle he is going to apply, he is perfectly entitled to apply it to his own conception of reality (*pace* Gosling); though it remains true that the grammatical position of "always" (*aei*) at 16c9 is ambiguous, and thus may qualify either our ways of talking about reality or reality itself. In some cases, it does seem that Plato is simply concerned with the relation determinable-determinate among given phenomena rather than with relations between Forms. In the "dialectical" passage, this appears to be the case in the illustrations of the method, namely vocal and musical sound (17a–18d). There is, however, much discussion of this passage. See Gosling (1975: 164 ff.); also Striker (1970: 26–30); Frede (1993: xxv–xxviii); Irwin (1995: 321–3).
14. Cf. Section II.2.1. For this twofold use of dialectic cf. Frede (1993: 71 n.1).
15. In this way we can explain the passage at 23c9–12 (where Socrates refers back to the god having revealed *apeiron* and *peras* at the start of the cosmological discussion), which does not, *pace* Meinwald (1998: 168), necessitate an exact correspondence of usage between these two notions in the dialectical and the

cosmological passages. Instead, the shift is marked by Socrates' assertion, at 23b–c, that he needs "other weapons" than those of the previous discussion, and that we should make a new beginning (*archê*).

16. For possible uses of *to pan* in that sense, see e.g. *Soph.* 249d4; on which cf. Chapter 2, n. 84 and this chapter, n. 54. Among scholars who take the scope of *to pan* at *Phil.* 23c in this way, see e.g. Jackson (1882: 283 ff.), Rodier (1926: 87), Migliori (1993: 161), and, from a different perspective, Sayre (1983: 161 ff.), who think of the Forms as a kind of mixed reality according to that classification.

17. When we are told, for example, about fire "in the All" (*en tôi panti*) at 29b–c, or that the body of the All (*to pan*) has a soul, at 30a, it is obvious that "the All" here must be the sensible universe. The governance of *nous* is said to be exerted on "the All" at 30d8, or on heaven and earth (*ouranou kai gês*) at 28c7–8, so that "the All" in the first case must again refer to the sensible universe as in the second case (as must "the whole" – *to holon* – at 28d5–6, whose context is a discussion of whether *nous* governs "the totality of things and this which is called the whole", *ta sumpanta kai tode to kaloumenon holon*). On several occasions "the All" is contrasted with our sphere, or "[things] among us" (*par' hêmin*, 29b9–10, c1–2, c6, d2, 30a3–6), just as the universe (*kosmos*) is at 29e1–6. In addition, when Plato recapitulates the discussion of the four genera at 30a–c, he considers them in the context of "the whole universe" (*ouranos*, b5), which echoes his consideration of the four genera as constituents of "the All" at 30c4 and 23c4.

18. See in this respect the *Timaeus*, which establishes a distinction between time and eternity and speaks of the word "now" (*nun*, 38a5) as a determination that applies exclusively to the temporal realm of becoming and is alien to the eternity of the Forms. Cf. Tarán (1979: 43–5); also Eggers Lan (1984: 179). This is then talk one would normally not expect about the Forms, which in the *Philebus* are in fact said to "exist always" (*onta aei*, 61e3). Cf. Waterfield (1980: 303 n. 61). *Pace* Striker (1970: 72), Moravcsik (1979: 94), Benitez (1989: 68), Hampton (1990: 40).

19. In this line cf. also e.g. Hackforth (1945: 37), Ross (1951: 136–8), Teloh (1981: 186).

20. See e.g. Davis (1979: 132–3), Teloh (1981: 188).

21. Cf. e.g. Teloh (1981: 188) and McCabe (1994: 250–1 and 255 n. 73).

22. Cf. Hackforth (1945: 37). I use the qualification "more" because, as we have seen, Timaeus' speech is not exempt from discursive or argumentative sections (e.g. 51b–52a, 53c ff.).

23. Before we consider them separately, the question might arise whether these kinds themselves are Forms, as, for example, Diès (1941: XCII–XCIV), Striker (1970: 49–50, 77–81), and Frede (1993: xxxviii, xxxix) have taken them to be. This might be suggested not only because of the use of the words *eidos* or *genos* (cf. e.g. 23c–d) but also because there is classification of a unity into different species involving collection and division (cf. *sunagein* at 23e5 and 25a3, where Socrates speaks of collecting the varieties of the unlimited together in order to discern their common nature; for allusions to the process of division, see e.g. 23d). As to the latter point, it has already been shown that not every kind of division needs to be concerned with

Forms (cf. e.g. Trevaskis 1967: 124–8). As to the former, it seems quite clear that the terms *eidos* and *genos* need not refer to the Forms in any metaphysically loaded sense, but can simply have the logical sense of "class" or "kind" into which something can be divided. With an analogous meaning Plato speaks e.g. in the *Timaeus* of model, copy, and the receptacle as three "kinds" (*eidê, genê*) of things (cf. *Tim.* 48e–49a, 50c7–d2, 52a) and in the *Phaedo* (79a6–7) of the visible and the invisible as "two kinds of things" (*duo eidê tôn ontôn*).

24. Cf. Benitez (1989: 71–2).

25. See e.g. Nehamas (1975: 116). For other discussions of compresence see e.g. Irwin (1977); Patterson (1985: 83 ff.); McCabe (1994: 37 ff.).

26. Cf. Chapter 2, Section II.3. In fact, we can take this *anankê* (47e5, 48a1) as related to the properties (*pathê*) of fire, water, air, and earth (48b5) that fill the receptacle before or in abstraction from their arrangement as bodies, i.e. those powers that are said to be "neither similar nor equally balanced" (*mêth' homoiôn dunameôn mête isorropôn*, 52e2). Cf. Cornford (1937: 173–6; 181 ff., esp. 181, 184; 202–3). "From these" (*ek toutôn*), in turn, other things are said to come (50a3–4). Among these properties we must count opposites such as hot and cold (cf. 32c–33a and 50a2–3; cf. *Phil.* 25c5–6), dense and rare, heavy and light (53a).

27. As far as I am aware, this connection between the concepts of *apeiron* and *anankê* has remained pretty much unargued for in the literature. Instead, most interpreters seeking cosmological correspondences between the *Philebus* and the *Timaeus* have identified *apeiron* with space (see n. 31 and Hankinson [1998: 119]); while others, failing to see this correspondence, have doubted that the *Philebus* passage has anything to do with the *Timaeus*: cf. Teloh (1981: 188); McCabe (1994: 250–1 and 255 n. 73). It is interesting that both *apeiron* and *anankê* are described as existing "in space" (*chôra, Phil.* 24d2, *Tim.* 52a–53a). In the *Timaeus*, however, *chôra* is a concept distinct from *anankê*, as the spatial medium is from the material contents that fill it. Space is that "in which" phenomena occur, not that "out of which" things are made (as both *anankê* – or the precosmic traces – and *apeiron* are said to be, cf. *Tim.* 48a1, 53a7, b6, *Phil.* 23d1, 27a11). (Although the comparison of *chôra* with gold at 50a–b and perfume at 50e may be thought to suggest that *chôra* is a material of some kind, the point of the analogies seems to be, in the one case, the changelessness of *chôra*, 49e–50a, 50b5–c2 (cf. Gill [1987: 45–7]), and, in the other case, its lack of form, 50e–51a; on which see e.g. Keyt [1961: 299–300].) In fact, at *Tim.* 51a6 *chôra* is explicitly said *not* to be "that out of which these things [= fire, water, air, and earth] have come into being" (*ex hôn tauta gegone*). Pace Algra (1994: 118). Note also that *chôra* is distinguished from becoming (*genesis*) even in a precosmic state at 52d3–4. Space in the *Timaeus* is described as a "this" (*touto, tode*, 50a1–2), suggesting something stable (49e3), and is intrinsically deprived of every quality (50d–51a) – unlike *apeiron*.

28. Compare the connection between the excess (*lian*, 26a7) conveyed by *apeiron* and the measure that removes the excess in the *Philebus*, with the importance of "the mean" (*to metrion*) as that which guarantees beauty and goodness (in this case, in the products of art or *technê*) in the *Politicus*, by

contrast with excess and deficiency in relation to one another (283c–284e, esp. 284a–b).

29. The text refers to the second group opposed to *apeiron* as *peras* (27b8) or *peras echonta* (24a2, 26b2) indifferently.

30. For the status of the Forms in the *Timaeus* cf. Chapter 2, n. 87; also Chapter 3, Section I.2.

31. In this tradition of interpretation see e.g. Grube (1980: 301–4); and similarly Brochard (1926: 199–202); MacClintock (1961: 49 n. 4); Friedlaender (1969: 324–5); Brisson (1974: 102–3); Benitez (1989: 74–80), who in turn think that there is an exact correspondence with the *Timaeus* insofar as the other consitutive element, *apeiron*, stands for the notion of space (*chôra*) in that dialogue; for this latter view see also Bury (1897: xlvii). I have argued that *apeiron*, for its part, is better understood as a correlate of the notion of *anankê* in the *Timaeus*. See n. 27.

32. See e.g. Owen (1953: 321 n. 3, 338), Teloh (1981: 179–80, 186, 188) and, from a different perspective, Sayre (1983: 10–13, 160–63). In an agnostic position cf. Shiner (1974: esp. 67–8). Defenders of revisionism typically claim that we do not tend to find transcendent Forms after the *Parmenides*.

33. Cf. 26a3, following Fowler's and Frede's reading of the text – after the MSS – instead of Burnet's. Cf. Fowler (1925: *ad loc.*), Frede (1993: 22).

34. Some other passages speak of *peras* not as being produced or realised (*apeirgasmenon*) but as itself exercising the function of *apergazesthai* or having a more active relation to the unlimited. For example, at 25e1–2 *peras* "makes the opposites proportionate and harmonious (*summetra kai sumphôna apergazetai*) by introducing number"; and at 27d9 *to apeiron* is said to be bound by the agency of limit (*hupo tou peratos*). What is the agent then, *peras* or *nous*? We could follow Hackforth in thinking that whether we say that it is reason or limit that modifies the nature of the unlimited matters little, "when we remember that all the *metra* that characterise good *meikta* are *meta tou peratos apeirgasmena* by the causality of *nous*" ([1945: 134], cf. *Phil.* 26d9). So, strictly speaking, it should be *nous* as cause that has an active power over the unlimited *with the help of* the limit it introduces. The seemingly active vocabulary that Plato uses of *peras* before the introduction of the cause can also be seen as influenced by Philolaus, who speaks of *perainonta* (rather than *peras*) with an active role *vis-à-vis apeira* (cf. 44B1 and 44B2 DK), and who does not include the cause in his scheme, as Plato is about to do.

35. Cf. Chapter 2, n. 87.

36. Cf. Fahrnkopf (1977: 202–5), against Shiner's (1974) defence of revisionism. It seems irrelevant to decide whether the "divine Circle" in the passage of the *Philebus* is an intermediate mathematical entity, or a Form, for under either interpretation the passage would rule out the basic claim of the revisionist, namely that there is no entity that is not an aspect of the sensible domain in the *Philebus*. It is suggestive, though, that in the same passage other items such as "Justice Itself" are mentioned (62a3). Other opponents of the revisionist view include Bolton (1975: 84–94), Mohr (1983), Benitez (1989: 4, 129–32), Hampton (1990: 9–11).

37. Cf. e.g. Hackforth (1945: 41).

38. *Phil.* 65a presents an ambiguity in this regard. There Socrates, after having associated measure with beauty and excellence (64e5–7), states "if we cannot capture the good through one idea, let us grasp it with three: beauty (*kallos*), proportion (*summetria*) and truth (*alêtheia*)" (65a1–2). The subsequent lines (*legômen hôs touto hoion hen orthotat'an aitiasaimeth'an tôn en têi summeixei*, 3–4) can be read as saying either: (1.) "and let us say that this, considered as one, we would most rightly give as cause of the things in the mixture"; or (2.) "and let us say that, among the things in the mixture, we would most rightly give this, considered as one, as cause". The first translation could encourage an interpretation of the good as being something other than the elements of the mixture (the latter including measure, proportion, and truth) and so over and above the goodness inherent in the mixture. The second, conversely, would be considering the good just as a property inherent in the mixture. For the former interpretation cf. e.g. Benitez (1989: 62), Hampton (1990: 83–4); for the latter, Gosling (1975: 65). Thus, we can say that this passage of the *Philebus* is at least consistent with the postulation of a Form of the Good, even though it does not necessitate it (but remember that the Good is mentioned in an aporetic context at 15a, as one of those monads escaping generation and corruption).

39. Cf. *meixomen alêtheian* at 64b2. For how "truth" may here connote "being" or "reality", and this in turn stability of the sort brought about by *peras*, see section 3.2. For the relation between goodness, beauty, and measure compare *Tim.* 87c.

40. Compare with the allusions to an immanent goodness of the world in the *Timaeus* (*to ariston, to eu*, 46c8, 68e2, 5); and see Chapter 2, n. 48.

41. We might certainly be struck by the fact that Socrates starts his search for the cause of the mixture in the *Philebus* by positing *nous* as cause (28c ff.), and towards the end offers instead measure and proportion as the cause of the mixture. However, even at the beginning Socrates seemed to be paving the way for his suggestions at the end, by saying not only that *nous* could be claimed to be the "cause" of the mixture in which the happy life consists (22d2), but also that *nous* is "more akin and similar" (*sungenesteron kai homoioteron*) to that through which the mixed life becomes good (22d4–8), something that will at the end of the *Philebus* include measure and proportion (which is an aspect or mark of the good), as the cause that makes the mixture good (64c, d). To this, the text reiterates, *nous* will be "more akin" and "most similar" (65b1, c3, d3). So the answer to the question whether *nous* is the cause or akin to the cause would be that it is akin to the cause in a formal sense, though it is itself the cause in an efficient sense.

42. We read that the cosmos was generated as a "mixture arising from the combination of necessity and *nous*" (*Tim.* 47e5–48a2: *memeigmenê… ex anankês te kai nou sustaseôs*; cf. *Phil.* 23d1: *ex amphoin* [sc. *peras* and *apeiron*] … *summisgomenon*). We have seen a correspondence between necessity in the *Timaeus* and *apeiron* in the *Philebus*, but does the correspondence not seem broken by the fact that the *Timaeus* talks of *nous*, rather than of *peras*, being mixed? We must remember however that the *Philebus* too speaks

of *nous* (as well as *peras*) as being mixed with *apeiron*; a prominent example of this is Plato's reference to the good life as a mixture of intelligence and pleasure (27d, 59d–e). As we have seen, this ambivalence may be explained if we consider that the presence of *nous* in the mixture implies the presence of *peras*, and vice versa: see n. 34.

43. On this problem see Gosling (1975: xvi–xvii).

44. Cf. Hackforth (1936: 38). For discussion cf. also Silverman (2002: 233) and Harte (2002: 210–12).

45. By "things" here we do not need to think in terms of Aristotelian substances. Plato rather picks up as examples of the third kind items such as health, physical strength, etc. which seem to refer more to states or conditions than to individual objects. But there is good reason why he should prefer these examples, since after all the purpose of this cosmological background is to provide him with the tools to analyse the mixture of *nous* and pleasure in which happiness consists (and this particular case he might well have in mind at *Phil.* 26b–c); but happiness, we are told at 11d4, is to be understood in terms of a condition (cf. *hexis kai diathesis*) of the soul.

46. Cf. Philolaus, 44B1 and 44B2 DK. The influence of the Philolaic concepts of "limitings" (*perainonta*) and "unlimiteds" (*apeira*) on those of *peras* and *apeiron* in the *Philebus* seems to be well established, as much as the "third kind" (*to triton*, 23c12) of the mixture in the *Philebus*, which includes harmony among its instances (31c), reminds us of *harmonia* as a third factor in addition to *perainonta* and *apeira* in Philolaus (B5 and B6 DK). Cf. Burkert (1972: 64, 86 ff., 254 ff).

47. Owen (1953: 322–4).

48. Teloh (1981: 184–5).

49. Thus *Tim.* 35a speaks both of the sensible and the intelligible *ousia*; at 52d3 we are told of "there being (*einai*) genesis... before the generation of the universe"; and at *Laws* X 895d–896a *ousia* is used of soul as an example of the reality that corresponds to any name or definition. This is not a late period innovation, since we can find a similar use of "being" at least as early as *Phaedo* 79a6, where we are told that the visible and the invisible constitute "two kinds of *beings*" (*duo eidê tôn ontôn*). According to this, the expression *genesis eis ousian* at *Phil.* 26d8 could be simply interpreted – as other scholars have done – as meaning that what is generated comes into existence, and *gegenêmenê ousia* (27b8–9) as meaning that the mixture is a kind of generated reality. Therefore in these passages *genesis* need not be opposed to *ousia* but may be related to it as in ancient Greek the verb for "coming to be" (*gignesthai*) may be related to "being" (*einai*), despite the fact that, in other metaphysical contexts, Plato contrasts *genesis* with *ousia*. Cf. Diès (1941: XXVIII–XXIX); Hackforth (1945: 49, n.2); Cherniss (1957: 353); Bolton (1975: 87–9). But see Frede (1988) for possible nuances in the ancient Greek usage that Plato may be incorporating in his metaphysical contrast.

50. Cf. Waterfield (1980: 284–5), Benitez (1989: 102–8). The contrast between *genesis* and *ousia* is kept also at 53c–54d, in a context that seems fundamentally ethical, and that betrays what I shall show is Plato's extended notion of "being".

51. To that extent, Teloh (1981: 184–5) may be right that in the *Philebus* "Plato . . . upgrades the status of the phenomenal world"; even though this, as I show, does not entail abandonment of transcendent Forms and, in addition, need not represent a "radical" change from Plato's middle-period dialogues (as contended by Teloh). See e.g. Turnbull (1988) and n. 54.

52. Cf. pleasure called *apeiron* at 27e and *genesis* at 54c–55a, and Chapter 5, Section I.1.2.

53. For this distinction between two kinds of *gignomena* in the *Philebus* see also Frede (1993: lvii); from another perspective, see Turnbull's view (1988: 1–14, esp. 13–14 on *Phil.*) on the "two worlds of becoming" in *Philebus* and *Timaeus* with Fine's response, which basically agrees with the distinction (1988b: 15–16). For another view that endorses the "respectable view of becoming" in Plato's late dialogues – including *Philebus* and *Timaeus* – though still within the coordinates of the *genesis-ousia* contrast, cf. Bolton (1975: 84–5). On becoming in the *Timaeus* see also Chapter 2, Section II.2. "Becoming" is usually understood as "change", and change in terms of compresence or succession of opposite properties. A universe of sheer opposition with nothing stable to underpin that opposition might well depict the reign of *apeiron* at its rawest (which, as we saw, is characterised precisely in terms of opposites); and for that reason it may be related, as we shall see next (cf. 43a), to a hypothetical picture of radical flux, which allows for no sense in which things retain their identity or "are" stably something at least in some respect – by contrast with proper mixtures, whose element of *peras* enables us to identify precise mathematical ratios grounding their natures.

54. With this I do not mean, as e.g. Shiner (1974: 64) appears to take it, that the *Philebus* and the *Timaeus* introduce a different metaphysics of the world of phenomena by contrast with the middle dialogues, which would instead be committed to radical flux; for how the middle dialogues need not imply such a commitment see e.g. Irwin (1977) and McCabe (1994: 30 ff.). What the late dialogues do seem to be introducing in any case, however, is an *account* of how the world of phenomena is not a world of unintelligible flux, thanks to nature possessing a mathematical structure that is intelligently designed; and it is the articulating of such an account that may lead Plato to adopt distinctive vocabulary in its description, as when calling mixtures "generated realities". This elevated view of becoming is also apparent at *Laws* XII 966e, where soul (as the agent of teleology) is described as "taking over becoming" (*genesin paralabousa*) and thus providing "ever-flowing being" (*aenaon ousian*). Similarly, at *Soph.* 248e6–249b6 we get the suggestion that "complete being" (*to pantelôs on*) must comprise not only immutable entities but also mutable ones, by virtue of including intellect (*nous*) and wisdom (*phronêsis*) which imply life, soul, and motion. For further discussion of *Soph.* 245e–249d cf. e.g. Cornford (1935: 242–8); Runciman (1962: 76–82); Seligman (1974: 30–40); Bluck (1975: 89–102); Teloh (1981: 190–1, 194–5); Malcolm (1983); Prior (1985: 129–39); De Rijk (1986: 13–17, 106); Dorter (1994: 142–50); Notomi (1999: 216–23).

55. The example given by Protarchus, and which Socrates endorses, is that "ship-building exists for the sake of ships" (54b). The fact that the Forms do

not seem to be alluded to in this passage does not damage the point made in the previous paragraph, since, as I shall show in the next chapter (Section I.1.2), the scope of the passage is limited by its immediate ethical purpose of offering some clarification of the status of pleasure in the phenomenal world.

56. See 64b2 and e.g. Hampton (1990: 83) after Hackforth (1945: 133) on "truth" here being closely tied up with being or reality; cf. also Frede (1993: 78 n. 3). For a different interpretation see Gosling (1975: 134–5). I do not rule out, however, that the meaning of "truth" here may be overdetermined, so that "truth" may also be understood in a propositional sense (as opposed to falsity). This seems plausible if mathematical proportion grounds intelligibility, and if knowledge and intelligibility are also related to truth in that sense.

57. See e.g. Mohr (1983: 169) against Shiner (1974: 64); but see also above, n. 54. Shiner (1983: 177), for his part, denies the metaphysical relevance of this passage. Further, Mohr seems wrong to compare the *Philebus* to the *Theaetetus* as if the latter were suggesting Plato's own views on flux (182c ff.): for philosophical reasons why Plato would not endorse such a picture see Burnyeat (1982: 527) and Frede (1988: 42–3).

58. Mohr (1983: 169) also invokes the passage at *Philebus* 59a–b, where a complaint is levelled against those who, even if they think they research nature, spend their lives investigating how things in this world "came into being, are acted upon and act" on other things (*gegonen kai paschei kai poiei*); though these things lack stability (*bebaiotêta*). Is Plato *really* having Socrates here deny that stability can be found at all in the sensible universe? I believe not. Instead, the emphasis of this passage is rather epistemological, as we are told that most practical crafts deal with beliefs (*doxais*, 59a1) in a way that doesn't show a particular concern with truth (58c–e), and, *because of that*, they cannot get to the more stable aspects of becoming. That is, it is sensible things on the (false) *description* under which these arts deal with them that have no stability whatsoever. That is why the arts referred to in this passage are said only to "*think* they investigate nature" (59a2), as the *Philebus* has shown there is more to nature than mere change. Indeed, it is 59b–d that gives the clue, by passing on to attribute stability (*bebaiotêta*) to *nous*: If the cosmos itself has intellect (as has been argued at 28c–30d) then it should at least to that extent have stability, much as *nous* is only second (reading *deuterôs* at 59c4) in stability to the Forms (cf. 52c2–5).

59. *Phil.* 26e–27b, 28d–e, 30a–b, c.

60. Cf. *Tim.* 28a–29a, 29e–30a, 34b10–35a1, 42e1–3.

61. Cf. *Phil.* 27b1, 26e6–8, 27a5.

62. Cf. *Tim.* 28c3, 29a3.

63. See e.g. Gosling (1975: 206).

64. That the universe itself is divine (or to be called "Zeus" if one resorts to tradition) may be suggested by the parallel allusions both to it and to Zeus as having a kingly *nous* (28c7, 30d1–2).

65. See e.g. *Tim.* 46c–d, *Laws* X 889c, and esp. Chapter 8, Section I.

66. In this regard, the lower parts of the soul that are distinctive of humans may be viewed as capacities simply resulting from the fact that both our soul and

our body are second grade by comparison with the purity of their source (cf. *Tim.* 41d). While the *Philebus* does not make any explicit reference to tripartition, it does talk of subrational psychic tendencies such as anger and *erôs* at 47e, 50b–d.

67. See esp. Chapter 2, Section III.4 and n. 104. In this way, Plato's view on the soul has some affinity with hylomorphism (for discussion of Aristotle's views see e.g. Nussbaum and Rorty [1992], Heinaman [1990], Shields [1993], and Burnyeat [2002]). Wherever Aristotle's philosophy of mind is taken to stand in relation to the modern debate, it seems that Plato's late views may well represent an important antecedent to Aristotle's conception of the soul as the principle of organisation of a body and ontologically inseparable from it (*De An.* I 3, 407b15–19; I 5, 411b7–8; II 1, 413a4; II 2, 414a19–20, 415b8; II 4, 416a6–8), notwithstanding Aristotle's rejection of souls as self-movers and of a cosmic soul. Indeed, it has puzzled scholars who still tend to classify Plato as a dualist in the modern debate that Aristotle, even when distancing himself from Plato, should not so classify him himself. Thus, Witt notices with surprise, commenting on *De Anima* 403b31–404b6, that "Aristotle here attributes a materialist account of soul to both the Pythagoreans and Plato, whom we would tend to identify as early dualists" (1992: 172 n. 8). The tendency to commit even late Plato to robust dualism may be due to passages that still talk of the human soul's immortality and reincarnation, as it is hard to see how the soul would retain its identity in those cases unless it has an existence in principle independent of the body (see on this Priest [1991: 9]). It has also been emphasised, though, that "someone who believes in immortality is not thereby committed, logically, to dualism and the possibility of disembodied existence" (Shoemaker [1984: 139]), for the mind could be conceived as being always in some kind of material embodiment (as I argue is the case even on a literal reading of immortality in late Plato: see e.g. Chapter 2, Section III.4. *in fine*). In any event, note that neither of those two concepts (individual immortality and reincarnation) occurs in the *Philebus*; and, as I have argued elsewhere (see my [1989] and [forthcoming]), there is still a question as to what their significance is when they occur in the other late dialogues that we are considering. For example, little or nothing is said of reincarnation outside mythical contexts (cf. *Tim.* 42b–d, 90e–92c, *Pol.* 272e, *Laws* IX 870d–e, 872d–e). As for immortality, more than once we find it treated as a possibility that humans can realise even on earth through communing with the cosmic god and the Forms (see esp. *Tim.* 90b–d), or through reproduction (*Laws* IV 721b–c, cf. *Symp.* 207d) rather than as endless duration of individual existence.

68. In favour of the latter view of the cause in the *Philebus* see Robinson (1995: 144); Mohr (1985: 174). Against, see e.g. Teloh (1981: 187–8); Ostenfeld (1982: 238).

69. I.e. in addition to limit, unlimited, and the mixture.

70. The construction of this passage is difficult but intelligible. That the *toutôn* at b4 must refer to fire, water, earth, and air becomes clear from the reference to "those things" as "beautiful and pure" at b6, which refers back to 29b6–c3 on fire etc. existing in the universe in a "pure" and "beautiful" manner. Cf. Gadamer (1991: 147–8 n. 15).

71. Cf. e.g. Hackforth (1936: 439), who [mis]translates b7 as "that which is fairest and most precious". Frede, while disagreeing with the idea of a separate *nous*, still takes b7 to refer to the world-soul: see her (1993: 29 n. 1) and (1997: 38, 216–18).

72. This line however is followed by Hackforth (1936) – see also Mohr (1985: 178, n. 3) – and was already in antiquity defended by Proclus (*In Tim.* I 402, 15 ff. Diehl).

73. As e.g. Robinson (1995: 142–4) suggests.

74. Cf. Ostenfeld (1982: 237–8).

75. Cf. *Tim.* 36c–d, 38c, 40a.

76. The verb for "arising" is *gignesthai*. This, in turn, may be taken simply to emphasise the ontological dependence of *nous* on soul (precisely insofar as *nous* cannot exist without soul), without that implying a commitment to the view that the *nous* in this passage should be generated by a higher *nous*. As we shall see, soul can be the cause of its own generation. *Pace* Mohr (1985: 178–83).

77. Likewise in the *Timaeus*, we have seen in Chapter 2, necessity without *nous* is equivalent to chance (cf. 46e5–6). Now, if *apeiron* in the *Philebus* corresponds to brute necessity (as we saw in Section II.1.) and this to chance in the *Timaeus*, then we have further reason to think that in the *Philebus apeiron* is related to chance.

78. Cf. Chapter 2, Section II.3.1.

79. Note that in the *Timaeus* pleasure and pain are themselves said to be *anankaiai* (or to arise by necessity, 42a5–6, 69c8–d2), thus constituting an element upon which human *nous* must work, as the Demiurge does on the precosmic necessity.

Chapter 5

1. See e.g. D. Frede (1992: 440, 443, 448), (1993: xliii); Irwin (1995: 329); also Nussbaum (1986: 462); Gosling (1975: 103, 125); Hampton (1990: 65). For other examples of the widespread view that god's life is pleasureless in the *Philebus* see Annas (1999: 152); Carpenter (2003: 93–4); Russell (2004: 249).

2. Cf. 27e–28a and n. 13.

3. The words "mixed" or "mixture" will be employed in the subsequent discussion in several senses, which it might be helpful to delineate. In the present context, "mixed pleasures" means pleasures mixed with pain ("pure" pleasures connoting pleasures unmixed with pain), as opposed to the meaning of "mixture" (between *peras* and *apeiron*) that we saw in the fourfold classification. In this latter sense, intelligence might bring to our pleasures limit or determination, giving us a desirably "mixed" life, as we shall see.

4. On this see e.g. Frede (1993: xlv) and Gosling (1975: 212–13).

5. For a discussion of false pleasures cf. Williams (1959); Dybikowski (1970); Penner (1970); Frede (1985); Delcomminette (2003); in a different line cf. Hampton (1987).

6. E.g. Frede (1993: xlv–xlvi) and Irwin (1995: 328–9).

7. As opposed to the moderate ones, which are included in the good life (63e). In a second sense, however, all mixed pleasures could be regarded as false insofar as they can all be seen as having a propensity to mislead a person (particularly when she hasn't experienced pure pleasure) in various directions, such as making her overestimate their size, or think that they constitute unqualified instances of pleasure when they don't. In this second, strong sense Socrates privileges pure, unmixed pleasures as true (51b, 62e). On this ambiguity see Cooper (1977a: 723–4).

8. Cf. Waterfield (1980: 278–9). Connectedly, Socrates uses the expression "by themselves" (*kath' hauta*), in opposition to "relative to something" (*pros ti*) at *Phil.* 51c6–d1 when talking of the objects of pure pleasures by contrast with pleasures such as scratching.

9. For *apeiron* as a source of unintelligibility and randomness cf. Chapter 4, Section II.1.

10. See e.g. Frede (1993: xliii), (1996a: 236–7); Hampton (1990: 75). A similar line is followed by Silverman (2002: 241).

11. See my (2000: 264–70).

12. As shown by my translation, at 51b3–7 I take the succession of *kai... kai... kai* as a simple enumeration of examples, in turn displayed by the passage that follows. Thus, at 51c1–d3 we are told more about the pleasures of beauty of form and colour; at 51d6–9, about those of fine sounds; at 51e1–4, about those of smell; and at 51e7–52b8 the pleasures of learning are given as an example of pure pleasures as long as they do not originate in painful hunger for learning. (For an interpretation along these lines, see Hackforth [1945: 98–9].) By contrast, D. Frede (1993: 60) translates 51b3–7 as follows: pure pleasures are "those that are related to so-called pure colors and to shapes and to most smells and sounds and *in general* all those that are based on imperceptible and painless lacks, while their fulfillments are perceptible and pleasant" (my italics). From this, she infers that: (1.) since all pure pleasures are fillings of a lack, then the gods could not feel them (1992: 440), (1996a: 235–6); and (2.) for the same reason, all pure pleasures too must be processes of filling, or *geneseis* (1993: 60 n. 2). Against (1.), let us note that no "in general" is mandated by the Greek, so one needn't commit to the thesis that *all* pure pleasures are fillings of a lack. In any case, and against (2.), we should add that *plêrôsis* at 51b6 need not mean a mere "process" of filling, but can also mean a result, or a "state", of fulfilment (as conveyed by the ambiguity of the suffix -*sis*, which in ancient Greek can refer both to a process and to a result). This interpretation, as I shall presently show, proves to be more congenial to the rest of the *Philebus* suggestions about the nature of pure pleasures. For another view against the treatment of all pleasures as replenishments of lacks in the *Philebus* see Gosling (1975: 122–3 *ad* 51e7–52b8), Gosling and Taylor (1982: 138–9). For others who take all pleasures in the *Philebus* as fillings of a lack see Annas (1999: 156); Van Riel (1999).

13. This is congenial with Socrates' initial resistance in the dialogue to treating pleasure as an undiscriminated unity, and his insistence on the need to apply the method of division to it (12c–13d). This method will take him beyond his initial treatment of pleasure as *apeiron* at 27e, which seemed very

much introduced as a concession to Protarchus (28a3–4), after he had anyway made it clear that he was referring to pleasures unmixed with limit
(*ameiktos* 27e1).

14. Nussbaum (1986: 148–50) comments that the criterion of *emmetria* captures
"the absence of internal ebb and flow" and so is related to stability which,
at 59c, "is explicitly listed, along with purity (unmixedness) and truth, as
a mark of value". Stability, she proposes, can be understood in two different ways: first, as the feature intrinsic to the activity; second, as a feature
proper to the object of the activity. So pure pleasures are stable in either
of these two ways, or in both. "On the first account, smelling a rose will
be stable in spite of the transience of roses, whereas on the second it will
not". The pleasure of intellectual activity, for its part, is stable in both senses
(148–9).

15. According to the being-becoming distinction of 53c–54d. While I don't rule
out that this passage may be leaving room for a more metaphysically loaded
distinction between being and becoming, I have argued that Plato is here,
as elsewhere in the *Philebus*, extending his notion of "being" to include not
just transcendent Forms, but also things in the phenomenal world having
peras, or even *peras* itself, as conveying some kind of stability (cf. e.g. *Phil.*
27b8–9, which treats the mixture as a generated *ousia*, and 24d5 for *peras*
being stable). In this latter sense, things like pure pleasures can belong to the
realm of *ousia*. For more discussion on being and becoming in the *Philebus*
see Chapter 4, Section II.3.2.

16. It seems conceivable, from Plato's example at 51e7–52b8, that experiences
having the same name (such as the pleasures of "discovering" or "knowing",
tas peri ta mathêmata hêdonas, 51e7–52a1) may constitute either a pure or a
mixed pleasure depending on context: for example, contemplating beauty
is likely to provide a pure pleasure to the person who has reached the top of
the ladder of love in the *Symposium*, but, presumably, it will still involve some
felt dissatisfaction (and in that sense pain) for anyone lower on the ladder.
Pure pleasures as a kind of undisturbed state must still be distinguished from
neutral conditions in that the former, unlike the latter, are accompanied, like
any pleasure, by the soul's awareness (*aisthêsis*, 43b–c, cf. 34a) of the positive
experience it is undergoing. While the simple absence of pain is insufficient to call something a pleasure (43d4–5), in the case of pure pleasures,
by contrast, the soul positively enjoys the state of fulfilment they represent
(51b) – *pace* D. Frede (1992: 448, 453–4), who seems to regard all undisturbed states as neutral conditions.

17. In this regard, Socrates seems to be attacking especially excessive or intense
mixed pleasures (cf. *Phil.* 65d8, 65e9), and thus alluding to pleasure as commonly conceived (65c5), when he presents his argument for the superiority
of *nous* over pleasure with regard to truth, measure, and beauty (65b–66a).
For it can easily be shown that pure pleasures participate in those three aspects of the good, by being *true* pleasures (51b1), proportionate (52d1), and
fine (53c2).

18. For the first claim, cf. e.g. D. Frede (1992: 440), (1993: xliii), (1996a: 236–
7); Hampton (1990: 65, 75, 120 n. 28); Gosling (1975: 103, 225). For the

second, see e.g. Irwin (1995: 329); compare also D. Frede (1992: 443 and 448). Along similar lines, Nussbaum (1986: 462 n. 58) takes Socrates in the *Philebus* to be claiming that pleasures cannot be ranked by a quantitative standard. I have raised objections to these claims at greater length in my (2000).

19. Cf. Hampton (1990: 7); and Chapter 4, Section II.3.2., for the right mixture of *peras* and *apeiron* as one kind of *ousia*. With Cooper, I don't even rule out that certain pleasures, such as eating, could be both "necessary" or derivatively good (insofar as their satisfaction is a means to the fulfilment of other goods, e.g. contemplation) and intrinsically good, for the moderate person who can enjoy them *qua* having a limit. Cf. Cooper (1977a: 717). For the possibility that something might be a good *both* derivatively *and* intrinsically in Plato, compare the examples of health and virtue in *Rep.* II 357b–358a, where, interestingly, "harmless pleasures" – which are included in the final good at *Phil.* 63a4 – are presented as good in themselves (357b6–8).

20. Particularly if having certain beliefs is constitutive of one's pleasures: on this issue see the first four authors mentioned in n. 5. In this regard, the "good" mixed pleasures of the moderate person can be contrasted with those of the immoderate or unhealthy one, who enjoys the very release of pain in her mixed pleasures, so that the existence of pain constitutes part of her choice and her enjoyment (*Phil.* 54e–55a). See also Cooper (1977a: 726–8).

21. Nussbaum (1986: 150).

22. The first point is proved in particular by book IV (justice is to be sought for itself, as mental heath, cf. 444a–445c), while book IX contributes to proving the second (in terms of pleasure, cf. 580d ff.). So, as Annas points out, in the *Republic* Plato is far from advocating virtue on purely intrinsic grounds: he also makes use of consequentialist arguments, as two distinct but still related aspects of a single project. See Annas (1981: 60–64, 294, 318). For Plato's attempt at reconciling a life of virtue with one enjoying the most pleasure cf. also *Laws* II 662d–663d and V 732e–734e with my (2003).

23. Unless they are in a relation of coimplication that would make the life of most pleasure and the life of knowledge necessarily coinstantiated. Plato will actually exploit this possibility in the *Laws*, in a way that will render the claim that the happy life is one of maximal pleasure consistent with the Sufficiency Thesis that virtue is sufficient for happiness (as we saw in the *Timaeus*). I have argued for this view in my (2003).

24. See Irwin (1995: 329).

25. This agreement is made between Socrates and Protarchus (who has taken over the argument on behalf of hedonism from Philebus), without Philebus' objecting. It is interesting, however, that a little later, at 12a7, Philebus explicitly rejects Socrates' proposal to subject both hedonism and intellectualism to a test, and instead dogmatically asserts: "it seems to me and it will continue to seem to me that pleasure wins, at all costs (*pantôs*)". After that, Philebus pretty much withdraws from the discussion. Philebus' early withdrawal has already attracted attention in the literature (cf. Frede [1996a: 218–20]; McCabe [2000: 268]): one must note that he withdraws without

Socrates making the slightest attempt at keeping him as an interlocutor. This must suggest, *inter alia*, that Socrates cannot take Philebus seriously, and that amenability to dialogue and readiness to argue for one's views, as shown instead by Protarchus, is a necessary prerequisite for this kind of *elenchos* and for hedonism to be a proper theory.

26. The question might be asked how Plato could establish a ranking even among pure pleasures themselves according to the quantitative criterion alone (cf. Gosling and Taylor [1982: 141]). One answer to this is that, if stability is a feature proper to pure pleasures and also one which is desirable in the happy life, the pleasures of knowledge and intellectual activity in general are likely to last longer (and thus render more pleasure) than those of the senses – apart from the fact that pure pleasures, when associated with knowledge, can be seen as having the ability to multiply pleasure: that is, insofar as these pleasures accompany the discovery of truth, they present the extra advantage of conducing to the gain of further genuine pleasures.

27. That Plato is in the *Philebus*, as he is not in the *Protagoras*, dissatisfied with a quantitative criterion for pleasure, and instead privileges quality, is a common interpretation: see e.g. Hackforth (1945: 102); Gosling and Taylor (1982: 141); Nussbaum (1986: 462 n. 58); Irwin (1995: 331).

28. Note that also in the *Republic* pure pleasures – including those of smell – are said to possess an unimaginable quantity (584b7), and a life experiencing them to be pleasantest (583a3), despite mixed pleasures being called "greatest" (*megistai*, 584c6).

29. Frede (1993: xliii), cf. (1992: 440); Gosling (1975: 103). See also Hampton (1990: 65).

30. Though note that even here the suggestion is pretty tentative. For Socrates says that "perhaps (*isôs*) there is nothing strange if it is the most divine of all lives", and Protarchus points out (and Socrates agrees) that "it is at any rate not likely (*oukoun eikos ge*) that the gods feel pleasure or the opposite" (33b6–9). One should take in a similarly tentative way the early passage at 22c5–6, where Socrates suggests that divine *nous* might be the good, even if his (human) *nous* isn't: the end of the dialogue will anyway make clear that *nous* – with no distinction between human and divine – is not the good, even though it is most akin to it (64e ff., see esp. 65a7–b2). The "third life" (with no pleasure or pain, but the purest possible thought) reappears at 55a5–8, but there too the discussion concerns mixed pleasures.

31. Passages from other dialogues support the thought that the gods do not experience mixed pleasures or pains, and that it would be unbecoming (*aschêmon*, *Phil.* 33b10) for them to do so. First, they do not undergo disintegrations or restorations caused by external agents. So, in the *Timaeus*, where the universe itself is called "god" (34b1, 92c7), we are told that such a god is complete (*teleon*, 32d1), and there is nothing outside the universe that might make it age or perish – or, for that matter, feel pain (32c–33d): the universe never gets thirsty or hungry as we do. Further, the gods will also be free from mixed pleasures of the soul, such as envy (*phthonos*) discussed at *Phil.* 48b ff.: cf. *Tim.* 29e1–2, *Phaedrus* 247a7. But they will still experience pure pleasures: cf. *Tim.* 37c6–d1.

32. For evidence in other dialogues, see, for example, *Laws* X 899b7–9 for gods being called "living beings" (*zôia*), and compare with *Tim.* 30d3, 32d1, 92c7, and 40a–d for the godly universe or the heavenly bodies as alive. Similarly, at *Phaedrus* 245c–e "soul" is said to be the self-moving principle of life in an organism, and at 246b6–c2 is said to "take care of all the inanimate", in a way that includes the "perfect" soul of the gods, which "rule the whole cosmos". Also, for *nous* implying life compare *Soph.* 249a4.

33. Cf. nn. 31 and 36.

34. Cf. e.g. *Rep.* IV 440a–b, 442b–c.

35. Cf. *Rep.* IX 586b–c, 572b ff.

36. Compare with *Tim.* 42a and 69c–d about the nonrational parts of the soul experiencing pleasure-and-pain. For how the movements experienced by the mortal body can affect the soul both in the *Timaeus* and *Philebus*, cf. *Tim.* 64a–65a, 43b–d with *Phil.* 33d–34a and Ostenfeld (1982: 239–40).

37. Vlastos (1988: 94).

38. I am not here considering the role of Socrates in other late dialogues such as the *Theaetetus*; for a discussion of its significance see e.g. Burnyeat (1977); Annas (1994: 337–40); Sedley (1996: 79 ff.), (2004); McCabe (2000: 25–59). For a study linking the dialectical nature of Socrates' method in the *Philebus* with other late dialogues see Rowe (1999b).

39. Cf. e.g. Frede (1993: lxiv–lxix). See also Davidson (1993) for an attempt to link Socrates' method in the *Philebus* with that of the early dialogues.

40. This seems to be an echo of – or an elaboration upon – the *Apology* (20d), where Socrates' second-order knowledge, or awareness of his own lack of knowledge (cf. 22c–23b), is called "human wisdom". First-order knowledge of all things, by contrast, would there presumably be deemed to be divine wisdom, or "wisdom more than human", in particular when it comes to finding an accurate definition of moral values (20d–e, cf. 20b). Compare with the *Charmides*' own reflections about sound-mindedness (*sôphrosunê*) at 167b, 173e ff. and my (1998b). As I pointed out there (282–5 and n. 24), Socrates' "wisdom more than human" in the *Apology* will actually be embodied in the knowledge of the guardians in the *Republic*, insofar as there is a divine element in them.

41. Cf. e.g. *Prot.* 358b–d. That the *Philebus* should affirm this Socratic tenet need not represent a change from Plato's middle dialogues. Contrary to what is commonly assumed, I have argued in my (2001b) that the *Republic* does not in fact depart from Socrates on this issue.

42. Cf. Chapter 4, Section I.

43. *Pace* Waterfield (1980: 286), who claims that in the *Philebus*, as in the middle dialogues, "it is still only the philosopher who can live the good life, since he is the only one who has access to true knowledge in addition to the other branches of knowledge." Waterfield uses in his support the passage at 62d1–3, which reads as follows: "I do not know, Socrates, what harm it could do to someone to take all the other pieces of knowledge if he has the first ones". This passage, however, does not imply that only the philosopher can lead the good life. At 62d2–3 Protarchus refers to the first kinds of knowledge, *in the plural*, which allows us to think that Plato must be alluding not only

to dialectic in the strict sense, but also to disciplines involving number and measurement, as described at 55c ff. This interpretation is confirmed when we see that in that passage those disciplines are precisely referred to as "first" (*prôtas*, 56c9–d1; cf. 55d10), just as at 62d1–3. And these, as I show here, form part of the educational curriculum for all.

44. Further, at X 888b, as we shall see in Chapter 8, we are told that it is crucial that everyone should adopt the correct views about the nature of god (in particular, the cosmic god) for answering the question whether humans "should live well or not".

45. Cf. the parallel listings at *Rep.* VII 528e ff. and *Laws* VII 818a ff., XII 967d–968a. For an allusion to the heavenly bodies and the existence of intelligence and *peras* governing them in the *Philebus*, see esp. 30a–c with the analysis in Chapter 4, Section II.4.

46. On how, even in the early dialogues, self-knowledge is understood in terms of inserting oneself in a wider (in that case, social) environment cf. Annas (1985). For how this represents an overall tendency in ancient Greek thought cf. my (2001a).

Chapter 6

1. Lane (1998: 10).
2. Cf. Owen (1953: 332–5).
3. Cf. e.g. Cornford (1937: 206–7); Skemp (1952: 114); Diès (1935: xxxiii); Crombie (1963: 155); Rosen (1979: 75–6); Gill (1979: 156); Miller (1980: 39); Scodel (1987: 77, 79); Dorter (1994: 192–3); Hirsch (1995). The idea is also suggested by Owen (1973: 352) and Guthrie (1978: 182). By "we" I mean both people at the time when this myth is narrated (272b) and presumably also we as readers of Plato, given that human conception and rearing are observable features of this age now as well as then: see *Pol.* 274a.
4. See e.g. *Phil.* 28c ff., *Tim.* 46c–e, 48a, *Laws* XII 966d–e, 967d–e for the claim that the world as a *kosmos* is orderly due to the presence of a designing *nous* that orders it, and *Tim.* 29a5 (cf. *Phaedo* 99c1–2) for the goodness of the world being treated as a given. This *nous* is generally described as god, and its governance over the universe is vigorously defended against materialistic opponents who conversely propose chance, spontaneity, necessity or, in general, principles devoid of purpose and intelligence in their cosmological accounts (*Soph.* 265b–266b, *Phil.* 28d, *Tim.* 46c–e, *Laws* X 888d ff.). A similar opposition between intelligent and mindless causes seems to be present in the *Politicus*, insofar as the age in which god is the "cause" of all good things (*aitia*, 270a3, cf. 273b6–7) is contrasted with a period in which the bodily (*to sômatoeides*) is presented as the cause (*aition*, 273b4) of the universe's reversals. This bodily element is said to participate in great disorder (*ataxia*) before the *kosmos* is established, and to be inherent in the universe's "ancient nature" (*to tês palai pote phuseôs suntrophon*, 273b4–5), which is also called "the state of ancient disharmony" (*to tês palaias anarmostias pathos*, 273c7–d1). On the *Laws* see also Chapter 8.
5. Cf. Brisson (1974: 478–96) and (1995).

6. Cf. e.g. Annas and Waterfield (1995: xiv, 21 n. 24); Wright (2000: 7); Ferrari (1995: 392); Rowe (1995: 13); Lane (1998: 103–4). The last three do take account of Brisson's suggestions, but to my mind fail to counter them adequately. For other adherents to the traditional view cf. Morgan (2000: 254 and n. 22), which contains a brief reference to Brisson but relies on Lane, and McCabe (2000: 148, 142 n. 8), who talks of the "Brisson/Rowe" interpretation as if they were the same (147 nn. 31 and 32), when in fact, as we shall see, they differ in fundamental ways.
7. Cf. 267c–268e; 274e–276d.
8. For expressions of this view, see Skemp (1952: 52) and Annas and Waterfield (1995: xvi); also Lane (1998: 9–10, 125–6), who believes that the length of the myth will become later a matter of criticism. But see Rowe (2000: 240), who notes that, despite the interlocutors' initial qualms about the length of the myth, "the Visitor's final view seems to be that it was not, after all, excessive": cf. *Pol.* 286b–287a.
9. See e.g. Gill (1979: 156); Lane (1998: 108, 113); McCabe (2000: 161–2, 240); Gregory (2000: 105). I shall return to this issue in Section IV.
10. Lane (1998: 103–4). Along similar lines cf. McCabe (2000: 142 ff.). Lane believes that the universe's self-rule would *not* be so impressive if it had "started moving rectilinearly when left to itself". Yet Lane's account, while relying on 269d5–270a8, misses the complete picture of reverse cycles given in the *Politicus*, where exact circular rotation (the effect of intelligence) takes place only at their very beginning and for the very briefest period after god's release of the universe, which is soon followed by increasing deterioration and accumulation of greater evils than goods (273a1–d4); and this, through the increasing rule of the corporeal, must result in disorderly motion (see n. 11; and for the relation between disorderly and rectilinear motion see n. 61 *in fine*). The passage Lane mentions (269d5–270a8) must therefore be read side by side with the further evidence provided by the myth, which suggests that the "extremely well-balanced" state of the universe at 270a8 is a mechanical explanation for why the universe continues rotating circularly after release from god, but cannot be its sustained state for a prolonged period of time. Thus, I read the *pollas periodôn muriadas* of 270a7 to qualify the *anapalin poreuesthai* (so that each reverse cycle takes place for tens of thousands of years), and the explanation that follows ("because the universe is most big and extremely well balanced on a very small base") to be an account of how rotation in reverse can occur in the first place. (This account, in addition, is not exhaustive, since later on further causes will be given for the rotation in reverse: see n. 11.)
11. This bodily element (*to sômatoeides*) appears as the main cause of those cosmic reversals (cf. *toutôn . . . aition*, 273b4). In this way, the bodily can be seen to determine the *direction* of the universe's motion (*to anapalin ienai*, 269d2), even though the reverse cycle starts by being *circular* (cf. *periagetai*, 269c7) due to the world's intelligence (269c7–d2). But the bodily is full of disorder (*ataxia*, 273b6), so its rule must result in the loss of that originally circular motion.
12. Cf. Lane (1998: 10–11, 146). For various authors who, to a greater or lesser extent, acknowledge the realisability of the ideal ruler of the third definition

as a human possibility see also Owen (1953: 332, 335); Gill (1979: 150); Rowe (2000: 240). All of these authors, however, believe that we live in one of those cycles that the text describes as leading to increasing destruction (273a–d; cf. nn. 3 and 6). Lane, for her part, later on concedes that, on her interpretation, the universe is "slowly descending into chaos" (110), but resorts to the notion of second-order imitation, by which humans need not imitate the cosmos in everything it does, but rather – only – in the fact that it is autonomous, which allows that humans may (contrary to the cosmos) "climb out of their helplessness" (ibid.). But this reading is neither the most natural nor the one literally suggested by the text, which presents us as "following" the universe in a more direct way: thus, for example, when the universe undergoes a reversal of its direction so does human life (270d–e). It must be noted also that the realisation of the ideal constitution would require the cooperation of arts dealing with the satisfaction of external needs (such as food and shelter, 288d–289b): but if, as Lane concedes, the universe itself is on the path of deterioration (so that astronomical disorder affecting the climate will ensue), in time it will inevitably cease providing us with the raw materials for the satisfaction of those needs. In that regard again, the realisation of Plato's political ideal seems to need the support of the universe (and this intuition recurs at *Laws* IV 704a–705c, 709a–c).

13. Cf. Skemp (1952: 114); Rowe (1995: 13); also Cornford (1937: 207).

14. Cf. *Pol.* 271e8.

15. The translation and commentary of the *Politicus* by Rowe (1995: 12–13) actually considers three cycles instead of the standard interpretation which has two, though Rowe, far from the view that I wish to defend, believes that our age of Zeus, though still following the same direction as that of Cronus, is one that is *not* under divine care at all; in this latter sense then he has not departed from the traditional view. See also his (1999a: 21) and (2000: 239–40).

16. For a literal interpretation cf. e.g. Robinson (1967); Mohr (1978) and (1985: 141–57). Against, cf. e.g. Cornford (1937: 207); Festugière (1949: 129–30); Cherniss (1954: 29 n. 44); Brisson (1974: 478–96); Ostenfeld (1982: 118); Naddaf (1993: 123); Rowe (1995: 13); Dillon (1995: 374); McCabe (2000: 142 n. 7).

17. Cf. Euripides, *Electra* 699–730 and *Orestes* 996–1012, cited by Vidal-Naquet (1978: 136 n. 31), for the reference to Zeus.

18. It cannot be held, as Dorter (1994: 193) implies, that it is "some more fundamental god" than Zeus or Cronus who both turns the universe in the age of Cronus and reverses its direction in the present age, given the text's denial that the same god could turn the universe in opposite directions (269e6–7, 269e9–270a1).

19. Rowe (1995: 187 *ad* 269a7).

20. Cf. Rowe (1995: 192–3 *ad* 271d3–4).

21. As is done by Scodel (1987: 80).

22. Thus, the universe "being turned" at 273e6, in the passive, suggests that it was turned by an external factor, not by itself; and that external factor must most likely be the god who was just given the function of "turning" (*strepsas*)

at 273e3. Cf. especially 269e8–270a2, where the possibility of the universe turning itself (*strephein heauton*) is contrasted with its being turned by god (in the passive, *hupo theou strephesthai*) or god turning it (*strephein auton*). For more details on *strephein* at 273e3–6 see Section III.6.

23. As contended by Scodel (1987: 80) and Rowe (1995: 193 *ad loc.*), and suggested by Ferrari (1995: 394 n. 17). The same interpretation could be given of "the gifts of the gods told of old" at 274c5–6: see e.g. McCabe (2000: 149 n. 40).

24. Even though the care he exerts now is different from the one in the age of Cronus: cf. Section III.6.

25. Let us notice that, as some scholars have suggested, it may be necessary to restore a connective here – and so read, e.g., *hôs nun {kai} kata* after Hermann, followed by Diès (1935: *ad loc.*); an omission that might be explained by a kind of haplography, given the similarity between *kai* and the first three letters of *kata*.

26. Cf. Vidal-Naquet (1978: 137); Gill (1979: 156); Dillon (1992: 29); Lane (1998: 106); McCabe (2000: 160).

27. As contended by Scodel (1987: 79).

28. Cf. *anêken*, 269c5; *anethêi*, 270a5; *aphethenta*, 270a6; *aphemenos*, 272e4; *aphesis*, 273c5.

29. Cf. n. 17.

30. Cf. Brisson (1995: 353, 358–9), who understands the reign of Cronus as starting at 271c3.

31. Either reading seems to be possible depending on whether one takes the *hepomenon* at 271b4 to mean logical dependence of events (which may take place within the same cycle) or a temporal transition between different cycles respectively.

32. Cf. 272a–b for the connection between *gêgeneis* and the age of Cronus.

33. As the *tês emprosthen* appears to suggest literally "the one temporally previous" to ours.

34. Brisson presents the interesting suggestion that "in those turnings" (*en ekeinais tropais*) at 271c5 may refer to a generic past, including more than one cycle. The same could apply to the "at that time" (*tote*) at 271a2 and 4. Cf. Brisson (1992b). However, I find his further claim that "the previous one" at 271c8–d3 refers not to the age of Cronus, but to the reverse cycle immediately previous to ours, where people were also born from the earth (1995: 354 n. 15), rather strained. For, when put in context, 271c8–d3 is given as an answer to Young Socrates' question about the age of Cronus (cf. 271c3–d1), and the text will continue narrating such an age (271d ff.).

35. We should take in like manner the allusion to the age of Cronus as "contrary" (*enantia*) to our present "revolution and generation" at 274e10–11, which is made in a context meant to emphasise and contrast the role of shepherding fulfilled by god at that time and the (more modest) political care given by human leaders in the present epoch.

36. Rowe (1995: 13) in fact suggests that the last two circumstances described (respectively the convulsion and the restoration of order) occur in two opposite

cycles: the first would depict the reversal following the golden rule of Cronus and the second would mark the start of *our new, present cycle*, the "age of Zeus". The latter would, according to Rowe, go in the same direction as the golden period (see also his [1999a: 21]); the difference is that, instead of being ruled by god, the universe would follow the rule of its own intelligence (*phronêsis*). This interpretation postulates then two successive periods when the universe marches by itself (without god) in opposite directions; something, however, that seems precluded by 269e7 ff., which precisely denies, amongst various possibilities, that the universe should turn itself in opposite directions. In addition, Rowe's justification for his postulating not only a reverse but also a forward cycle without god, namely, that if the universe "always went in the reverse direction when left to itself, its claim to rationality [*phronêsis*] would look weak", is unconvincing. For, while it is true that the bodily determines the *direction* of the motion of the universe in the reverse cycle (as he himself notes), i.e. its *anapalin ienai* (269d2 ff.), we must also note that the world's intelligence is mentioned there specifically in the context of the cycles which move opposite to those of god's guidance, and its relevance is to explain the *circularity* of its motion (*periagetai zôion on kai phronêsin eilêchos*, 269c7–d1) – at least as far as the beginning of the reverse cycle is concerned, when memory of god's teaching is still fresh (cf. nn. 10 and 11).

37. Thus, it would not be surprising to find this kind of earthborn (*gêgeneis*) immediately before the age of Zeus (273e) after we saw a similar kind in a similarly regressive cycle described in the myth previous to the age of Cronus (270d–e). Brisson (1995: 352), for his part, has proposed that this could equally well refer to the cycle preceding our age (so that there might be no reverse cycle preceding the age of Cronus), since in both cases the direction is the same. In this way, Brisson's picture only has three cycles: age of Cronus, reversal, age of Zeus (1995: 353, 358–360). While this idea is not implausible, the talk of "another" (*allên*) destruction of animals at 273a3 seems instead to suggest that the latter is different from the one mentioned at 270c11–12, thus making the two reverse cycles distinct. This interpretation is in turn reinforced if we take 271b4 as marking a temporal transition between the reversal of ageing and the age of Cronus that follows (see Section III.4.1.). Now, if the age of Cronus is preceded by a reverse cycle, the latter must in turn be preceded by a forward cycle, when god would impart the circular motion to the universe that it then preserves for some time (cf. n. 36), and when animals would be created that would then get destroyed in the reversal mentioned at 270c11. This would render a picture of at least five cosmic cycles: (1.) creation of the universe by god ordering it (cf. Section III.1.); (2.) reversal (cf. Section III.3.); (3.) age of Cronus (cf. Section III.4.); (4.) reversal (as analysed in this section); (5.) age of Zeus.

38. In the light of this, we can also give an explanation of the passage 271a7–b1, where we are told that the earthborn "were remembered by our first ancestors, who were neighbours to the end of the previous cycle during the succeeding time". The earthborn that are recalled here by our ancestors

need not be those of the age of Cronus but must most likely be those of our immediately previous – reverse – cycle. Cf. also n. 34.

39. See e.g. Skemp (1952: 114) and Cornford (1937: 207), who take the return of god to the helm as a description of an event that is still to come. On Rowe's interpretation, the return will mark the beginning of a new age of Cronus, which he takes as following directly our present period as one of god's absence, both these periods, however, having the same – forward – direction. (Cf. Rowe [1995: 13, 197 *ad* 274c1–2].) But this description does not sit well with the overall structure of cosmic cycles presented in the myth, according to which periods of god's guidance are always in the opposite direction to periods of god's absence (cf. Section III.2).

40. See n. 22. One possible objection deserves mentioning. After describing the god as turning the universe and making it immortal at 273e3–4, the Stranger remarks: "This has been said as the end of everything. And as regards the demonstration of the king, it is sufficient for us to grasp the account from before" (273e4–6). To this he adds: "For when, moreover, the universe was turned along the road towards its present generation, the age came again to a stop, and produced new things opposite to the ones before" (e6–8). The fact that at 273e4–6 the Stranger suggests going back in the description might be taken to hint that his further allusion to our present era at e6–8 means to insert it in a period previous to god's returning to the universe at 273e3–4 (in which case the universe could have been turned back simply by its own "fated and innate desire", cf. 272e6). Yet this conclusion needn't follow. Instead, I take the Stranger's invitation to start from before as simply alluding to the reversal of the ageing process in the cycle immediately previous to ours: this is indeed confirmed by the subsequent lines, which talk about bodies due to disappear, and born from the earth with grey hair, before the situation is reversed to the present one (cf. 273e6–11). And the motivation he may have for starting the account from that point is to establish a contrast between our cycle and the preceding cycles (both forward and reverse) in the history of the universe, where living beings sprang from the earth (as *gêgeneis*) so that there was no place for human conception and presumably rearing (cf. 274a).

41. Cf. Brisson (1995: 351–2 and 360).

42. Erler (1995: 377) presses this passage against Brisson.

43. After all even at 273c2–3, referring to a forward cycle, it is the universe *itself* which breeds the living beings, *with the assistance* of the pilot. Furthermore, one should note that the caring role of god in the overall description of the forward cycles is never overstated. For we literally read that god "co-guides and helps the universe revolve as it goes" (*sumpodêgei poreuomenon kai sunkuklei*, 269c4–5; cf. *hup' allês sumpodêgeisthai theias aitias*, 270a3), which suggests that god is the helper of the universe's motion rather than the sole agent of it.

44. Cf. Brisson (1995: 350).

45. Note, however, that these are just *terrestrial* shortcomings (in the same way as *anankê* manifests itself in the *Timaeus* mainly at a terrestrial level: cf. 73a–74b, 75a–b), which can be subsumed in the overall guidance or *agôgê* that I shall mention. There is here no suggestion of the astronomical disorder that

characterises the periods without guidance of god, and which would mean the *governance* of the bodily or of *anankê* over the whole universe (*Pol.* 273c–d). The latter – though not the former – seems incompatible with intelligent design, as we can see from the *Philebus* (28d–e), *Timaeus* (46c–e, 47e–48a), and *Laws* (X 888e ff. with 891c–892a, XII 966e–967a). Cf. Chapter 2, Section II and Chapter 7, Section I.1, Chapter 8, Section I.

46. Cf. Brisson (1974: 490–2).

47. Rowe (1995: 197 *ad* 274c6) admits that "it is surprising to find gods giving gifts to us human beings" in a period when according to him we are not under god. On my interpretation, that there *is* a divine presence in this period, the giving of such gifts is no longer surprising.

48. Note the plural "gods" (*theôn*) at 274d3 and the "daemon tending us" (*nemontos hêmas daimonos*) at 274b5–6, probably being a reference to each of the daemons (*daimones*) who tended (*enemen*) [us as] a particular kind of flock during the age of Cronus at 271d6–e1.

49. Cf. Brisson (1995: 361).

50. Cf. 267d, where politics was said to be an art of tendance or collective nurture (*nomeutikê, koinotrophikê*) concerned with the human flock (*agelê*).

51. Cf. particularly 271d6–e1, where the animals are divided by *flocks* among gods who tended them, and the allusion to people under Cronus as his nurslings (*trophimoi*) at 272b8.

52. The myth also invites methodological reflection on what the kind of measurement is that makes an art a proper art (284d ff., 286d–e). See on this Rowe (1995: 198–9); and especially Lane (1998: 118–19), with a clear enumeration of the various methodological flaws that the myth comes to denounce, thus paving the ground for further treatments in the dialogue.

53. On the exemplarity of the age of Cronus see especially Chapter 7, Section II. *Pace* Lane (1998: 120–2), who basically believes that the myth (and god in it) fails as an example.

54. And for how the support of the universe is needed in this regard cf. n. 12 *in fine.* Note that not only the satisfaction of external needs but even some leisure time through the existence of play will later on be presented as an indispensable means towards the happiest state (287b ff., 288c, 311c); and in this regard as well the age of Cronus can prove paradigmatic for a political search in our age (cf. 272b9).

55. Cf. 287b ff., 303e–311c.

56. On how collaboration is relevant to our age see McCabe (2000: 159). But this collaboration is reminiscent, in a more effortful manner, of the way in which all parts of the universe were under the charge of different divinities effortlessly following the one design of the major god in the Golden Age (271d–e).

57. *Pace* Owen (1953: 332–5), who sees in divine shepherding an echo of the kind of rule that characterises the philosopher-ruler in the *Republic*, when such rule, as has been generally recognised, seems to doom the larger part of the population to heteronomy.

58. See here Bobonich (1995: 322–3). Cf. also Chapter 7, Section II.2 and n. 50 of that chapter.

59. See Chapter 7, Section II.3. and my (1993).

60. *Pace* Gill, who claims that "divine shepherds do not only guide their flock, but control their whole life" (1979: 156); Nightingale (1996: 84), for whom "the 'nurslings of Cronus' were not autonomous agents", Cronus having "complete control over every aspect of the life of his herd"; Lane (1998: 10), who treats the latter as "a tame and unthinking population", and "the contrast between the age of Kronos and the age of Zeus" as one "between the life of heteronomy and the life of autonomy" (113); and similarly, McCabe (2000: 237). While McCabe acknowledges that "in both eras, philosophy is apparently possible" (160), she contends that "the nurslings of Cronus *would* be happy if they could pursue philosophy" (her italics), but they can't. Yet the text contains none of the counterfactual language in which McCabe puts her point. Rather, it says quite plainly (in the indicative) that if the nurslings of Cronus used their leisure and other external conditions for the sake of philosophy, "it is easy to decide (*eukriton*) that they *were* immensely happier than those of now" (272c4–5). Thus, it is not the *possibility* of philosophy but its *realisation* that is left open-ended; the possibility itself is taken for granted. See also note 61.

61. *Pace* McCabe (2000: 160), who however grants that "the process of ageing is seen, outside the myth, as a process of becoming wise" (ibid.). The fact that the text says at 272a1–2 that "all returned to life from the earth, not re-membering the previous [events]" need not be taken to suggest, as McCabe does (2000: 160), that in the age of Cronus there was no memory at all. The passage may simply be referring to people not remembering their past lives (something that may be true of any state of rebirth or reincarnation). And 270e6–7, suggesting that people become children in soul, refers, on my reading, not to the age of Cronus (as McCabe takes it) but to the cycle imme-diately opposite to Cronus: see Section III.3. Indeed, the growing younger of the old (as a microcosmic reflection of the universe at large) seems to fit much better in a universe that is moving towards the increasing rule of the corporeal, as we can see also from *Tim.* 43a–b, where the infant soul mani-fests erratic and disorderly motions which are identical to the six rectilinear motions of *anankê* without the rule of *nous*; compare this in turn with the original state of *ataxia* before the cosmic order is created at *Pol.* 273b6.

62. Note in this regard 297b7–c2, and especially 301c6–e2, where the Stranger remarks that the ideal statesman does not arise *now* among us (possibly be-cause there is not, unlike the case of a queen bee in a hive, a social matrix to support it), but does seem to allow for the possibility of its realisation (pre-sumably in a more distant time) by complaining about the disbelief of the many. See Section I, and especially Vlastos (1957: 235–7) for a lucid discus-sion of *Pol.* 301c ff. My point also applies if one takes it, as Rowe at one place suggests, that "the figure of the ideal statesman, someone completely knowl-edgeable and competent to exercise judgement in all important spheres, is to serve as a standard, to which we must approximate as nearly as we can" (2000: 237). For even this view presupposes the possibility of human politi-cal progress, which I have argued makes better sense if inscribed in a forward cosmic cycle.

63. See n. 61. Alternatively, it has made the people under Zeus go backwards in age, equally precluding the possibility of intellectual growth: see Section 1 and n. 27. But note that even Brisson (2000: 182), (1992b) reads the age of Cronus as one devoid of philosophy.
64. See n. 62.

Chapter 7

1. See e.g. Brisson (1974), Ostenfeld (1982), Mohr (1985), Robinson (1995).
2. See e.g. Rowe (1996: 160); McCabe (2000: 142 n. 7).
3. For the bodily as a cause of evil, in turn understood in terms of disorder, cf. 273b4–d4. Such disorder does not lie in design but in its absence, e.g. in illness or ignorance, as is the case when the world becomes "forgetful" of god's instructions and full of "diseases" (273c6, e2). For evil lying in absence of intention, ignorance, or illness, cf. *Prot.* 358c1–7; *Gorg.* 480b1, 488a2–4, 509e5–7; *Rep.* I 351a5; *Soph.* 228b8–9, c7–8, e1–5; *Tim.* 86b–e; *Phil.* 22b6–8; *Laws* V 731c2–5, IX 860d.
4. Cf. 273b4 for the bodily as the main cause of those cosmic reversals, which would then explain their tendency to disorder, given that the bodily itself is said to participate in great disorder (*ataxia*) before the *kosmos* is established (b4–5). Certainly, intelligence too seems to play some role in these periods. But it can hardly be said to prevail: cf. Chapter 6, Section I and nn. 11 and 36 of that chapter.
5. Note that, when at *Tim.* 59c7–d2 Timaeus refers to his own engagement with generated realities as a *paidia*, he stresses however that this *paidia* is "moderate" (*metrion*) and "sober" (*phronimon*). For the generally serious tone of the *Timaeus* cf. Lloyd (1968: 81–4). See also the claims of truth that Timaeus makes for his discourse at *Tim.* 30b8, 38a1, 56b4.
6. This fact becomes all the more suggestive when we note that, unlike the *Politicus*, invocation of the gods in support of the theories expounded is present not only in the *Timaeus* but also in *Philebus* (25b) and *Laws* X (893b), that is, in the three major pieces of cosmological theory that we find in the late dialogues apart from the *Politicus*.
7. Recall here our criteria for philosophical interpretation of myths in Chapter 1, Section III.1.
8. Neither in the *Republic* (X 616b–617d), nor in the *Timaeus* myth, nor in the *Laws* (VII 822a–b), even though all these passages deal with astronomy either discursively or mythically, and even though reverse (or at least opposite) direction is mentioned e.g. in the *Timaeus* as a characteristic of the planets moving in the Circle of the Other which, however, revolves simultaneously with and is embraced by the Circle of the Same (cf. 36c–d, 39a–b).
9. See Skemp (1952: 89): "The *Politicus* uses for didactic purposes the picture of a periodic cosmic reversal which no astronomer would accept". Cf. also n. 16.
10. Certainly, in the *Republic* there is some "variation" (*parallattein*) predicated of the heavenly bodies (i.e. *ta en autôi* [= *ouranôi*], 530a6–7, the referent of *tauta* at 530b2). However, this does not in itself suggest anything like the

picture of deterioration of the heavenly motion that we find at the end of the *Politicus* myth (*pace* Gregory 2000: 102–3), but must be taken in its context: it would be absurd to think that "these things turn out to be always in the same state (*aei hôsautôs*) and do not vary at all with respect to anything" (*oudamêi ouden parallattein*), 530b1–3. Note the qualifications here (*oudamêi ouden*): it is rather to be expected that sensible things as such should be subject to change at least in some respect, the whole point of the propaedeutic sciences being to elevate the soul from becoming to being. And after all even in the *Timaeus* the planets undergo certain variations (such as retrograde motion at 40c5; cf. its relation to *parallaxis* at *Pol.* 269e3–4; also *Tim.* 22d1) even within the same regular circular revolution. Cf. n. 8 and Knorr (1990: 315).

11. Cf. Mourelatos (1981: 29).

12. That disorder ends up affecting the whole heaven is suggested at *Pol.* 273a ff. At 273a1–3 the text mentions a convulsion (*seismos*) in the cosmos as an immediate result of god's release of the helm; after that calm and order briefly follow but at 273c we are told about the hardships and injustices (*chalepa kai adika*) ocurring in the heaven or universe (*en ouranôi*, c1) which "it itself has and communicates to the living beings [within it]" (c2). These disorders increase as time passes, so that in the end the *ouranos*, "mixing together small goods with a great mixture of the opposite things, reaches danger of destruction of itself and of the things within it" (273d1–4), so that we do not arrive at complete chaos but get very near to it at the time of god's intervention. All this, however, is incompatible with continuing astronomical order.

13. This would in turn be consistent with the astronomical picture in the *Timaeus*, which presents the circular routes of the Same and the Other as the only ones traversed by the heavenly bodies, however complex the movements of some of them may be. Remember also that the *Timaeus* myth starts and ends with an exaltation of the sensible universe as the most beautiful of sensible things (29a5, 92c6–9) as had already been done in the astronomical passage of the *Republic*.

14. *Pace* Gregory (2000: 4), who claims that the *Timaeus* "introduces" the idea of the heavenly bodies as "immortal deities, an idea which differs significantly from the *Republic*". See also *Ap.* 26d and the reference to the universe and heavenly bodies as gods in the *Timaeus* in Chapter 3, Section I.1. It is revealing, by contrast with these other dialogues, that the universe and the heavenly bodies are *not* called gods in the *Politicus*. Plato seems to be consistent in his reasons for not doing so, if on a literal picture the world can here exhibit behaviour that is other than intelligent and good.

15. This point I think can be maintained regardless of whatever difference in detail can be found in Plato's treatment of astronomy between the *Republic* and *Timaeus* and *Laws*. For discussion of this issue (particularly as far as the role of observation is concerned) see e.g. Heath (1913: 139–40); Shorey (1935: 186); Dicks (1970: 106); Vlastos (1980: 1–16); Mourelatos (1980: 33 ff.), (1981: 16–17, 24 ff.); Kung (1985: 23); Lloyd (1991: 333–4, 348).

16. Heath (1913) does not even mention the *Politicus* in his detailed consideration of Plato's astronomical views in the dialogues, whereas Dicks (1970: 115), in his very brief allusion to the *Politicus* myth, stresses that it "adds

little to our knowledge of Plato's astronomy" and is "highly fanciful". Nor do we find any consideration of the *Politicus* passage in the analytic studies on Plato's astronomy compiled in Anton (1980). I shall be suggesting, however, that, astronomical details aside, the cosmology of the *Politicus* reveals itself as more than sheer fancy.

17. Cf. Chapter 2, Section II.3.3.
18. "Necessity" is also mentioned at *Pol.* 269d3, 270c11. Cf. things occurring "by necessity" (*ex anankês*) as something innate (*emphuton*) to the universe at 269d2–3, which will afterwards be referred to the bodily (273b4–5; cf. 269d9–e1). In addition, "the bodily" in the *Politicus* is analogous to *anankê* in the *Timaeus* insofar as the latter is related to the opposite properties (or traces, *ichnê*) of the four primary bodies (*Tim.* 48a–b, cf. 52d–53b). Both of them, if uncontrolled by *nous* and not unified in a *kosmos*, are the cause of merely random effects, threatening to sink the world in "the limitless sea of dissimilarity" (*Pol.* 273d–e; cf. *Tim.* 46e). Note also the association between *apeiron*, division, and dissimilarity at *Pol.* 273d6 (and disharmony at 273c7), which brings to mind how *apeiron* conveys division and discord between opposites in the *Philebus* (25e1, 27d9).
19. *gennêsas*, 269d9; cf. *sunarmosas*, 269d1; *suntheis*, 273b7; *kosmêsas*, 273d4.
20. In other words, god in the mythical picture has not only a "cosmogonic" or generating role but also a "cosmonomic" or organising one – to put it in the terminology of Verdenius (1954: 251). In the *Politicus* the latter seems more emphasised than the former, which is in turn much more detailed in the *Timaeus*. Cf. Brisson (1974: 35–54).
21. In favour of an interpretation of god as nontranscendent in the *Politicus*, cf. Cornford (1937: 206 ff.); Festugière (1947: 20–1, 43–4), (1949: 104–5, 120 ff., 145); Ostenfeld (1982: 236). Against, cf. Robinson (1967: 61), (1970: 134); Brisson (1974: 83–4, 479 ff.); Mohr (1985: 42–3, 45–7).
22. *to kata tauta kai hôsautôs echein aei kai tauton einai tois pantôn theiotatois prosêkei monois.*
23. Cf. n. 42. For a characterisation of the Forms in similar terms to those of the *Politicus* see *Phaedo* 78c6, d2–3 (in contrast with *metabolê* at d4), *Tim.* 29a1, *Phil.* 59c4. For discussion about whether the Forms are present in passages of the *Politicus* other than the myth cf. e.g. Guthrie (1978: 176–80) and Mohr (1977: 232–4) versus Owen (1973); Rowe (1995: 4–8), (2000: 238–9) versus Skemp (1952: 72–7).
24. *Tim.* 46d6 and *Laws* X 898d9–e2 suggest that these are features of every soul as such.
25. We are there told of god that "to turn itself always is hardly possible except for the one who leads all things that are in turn moved" (*tôi tôn kinoumenôn au pantôn hêgoumenôi*). Cf. also *Phaedrus* 245c ff., *Laws* X 896a–b.
26. See also the relation between measure, beauty, and goodness at *Pol.* 284b1–2.
27. Cf. Cornford (1937: 207); Cherniss (1954: 29 n. 44); Brisson (1974: 490–92). This kind of interpretation had already been offered by Proclus (*In Tim.* III 273, 25 ff. Diehl), and is also usually applied by nonliteralists to the opposition between the precosmic chaos (under the rule of necessity) and the works of *nous* in the *Timaeus*.

28. Cf. Festugière (1949: 129–30); and those authors mentioned in n. 27.

29. Also, this interpretation by itself seems insufficient to explain why, if that were the only message Plato were trying to convey, he would need to postulate the complicated picture of different successive forward and reverse cycles, and not (more simply) just one moment of prevailing disorder followed by prevailing order, as in the *Timaeus*. Cf. Mohr (1978).

30. Likewise, the picture of opposite cosmic cycles serves Plato as a framework for palingenesis, recalling the argument of compensation of opposites to prove cyclical immortality in the *Phaedo* (cf. *anabiôskesthai* in *Phaedo* 71e13–72a2 and *Pol.* 271b6–7, 272a1). In fact, the *Politicus* would seem to portray dynamically the *Phaedo*'s suggestion about death coming from life and vice versa (71e–72b), by inscribing each of these situations in opposite cosmic periods accompanied by the mythical picture of opposite directions of ageing, as at 271b4–8.

31. To this effect, it is interesting to see how Plato has taken over and reconciled opposite views on the origins of civilisation within the synthetical unity of an original story, by inscribing them in different cosmic periods: on the one hand, the old religious legends about the "fall" of humans from an ideal state (age of Cronus) and, on the other, the modern theories of sophists and physicists about human "progress" from an initially defenceless condition (age of Zeus). Cf. Skemp (1952: 110).

32. Another mistake in the first definition was not to specify in what way the politician rules the whole *polis*, since many other people (such as peasants, grocers, doctors, and gym trainers, 267e–268c) could claim that it is to them, much more than to the politician, that the function of breeding or nurture belongs (275a–b, 276b). This mistake, again, we are now told, could have been avoided by speaking of concern instead of rearing. Cf. 275c–276c. For further corrections that the myth invites see Chapter 6, Section IV.

33. And it is in serving this political purpose that it becomes meaningful and necessary that Plato introduce the two different cycles of Cronus and Zeus. In this way we can provide an answer to the problem posed in n. 29.

34. Cf. Miller (1980: 51): "To be aware of what the god was in the age of Cronus is to know what man, within his limits as different from the god, must strive to be for himself in the age of Zeus". One may certainly wonder how something can function as a model or exemplar when it has been rejected as an adequate definition. But take for instance the case of virtue as defined in the *Republic*: on the one hand, it is internal psychic harmony (IV 443c ff.); on the other, the Forms are presented as models for it in their order and stability (VI 500b–d), much as it would be unreasonable to define virtue in terms of a state of immutability, which is a feature essential to the Forms.

35. Cf. especially *dialutheis* at 273d6 with *diolluntai kai diolôlasi kai eti diolountai* at 302a6–7. Similarly, we are told about the bad government that exists when ignorant people rule who follow their basest desires (*epithumiai*) (*Pol.* 301b10–c4 with 302a5–b3) – this leaving the *polis* with no means of salvation (*sôtêrias mêchanê*, *Laws* IV 714a). Compare with the brink of dissolution that the universe reaches due to the governance of innate desire or *sumphutos epithumia* (*Pol.* 272e6 with 273d3).

36. 296e4–297a5, 297e8–12, 302a5–b3; cf. *Rep.* VI 487è ff., VIII 551c. Likewise, recall that in the *Republic* the philosopher-king has been called precisely a "demiurge" (*dêmiourgos*) of justice and all kinds of virtue in his fellow-citizens (cf. VI 500d).

37. Cf. Miller (1980: 109), though his comparison is drawn in terms rather different from mine.

38. In support of this view see Bobonich (1995: 322–5); also Lane (1995: 282 n. 24), Cooper (1997: 93–4); and Chapter 6, Section IV. *Pace* Skemp (1952: 97 n. 49). Other differences between the *Politicus* and the *Republic* I take to include: (1.) the possibility that the true statesman need not be the ruler in charge of the society but could instead be his adviser (cf. *Pol.* 259a–b, 292e9–293a1); (2.) the insistence upon laws as a *deuteros plous* or "second best" in case we do not find in reality the ideal personality of the true statesman described in the third definition (cf. *Pol.* 293e ff., 300c ff.). This second feature being more adjusted to facts, the *Politicus* comes closer to the theory developed in the *Laws*, even though neither of these dialogues rules out the ideal notion of a gifted statesman whose superior skill would be capable of doing without legislation (cf. *Laws* IX 875c–d). For discussion, see e.g. Laks (2000: 267–75). The alliance between philosophy and politics in the *Politicus* is suggested by the assertions that true politicians are "in possession of true knowledge and not only belief" (*alêthôs epistêmonas kai ou dokountas monon*, 293c7), and that the political science (*epistêmê*) is *the highest* (*megistê*) *and most difficult* (*chalepôtatê*, 292d4) – dialectic in turn having as its aim *the highest objects* (*megista*), 285d4–286a7. For the association between philosophy and politics in the *Politicus* see also Diès (1935: LII–LVII, LIX), Saunders (1992: 485 n. 10). For discussion, see e.g. Gill (1979, 152), Schofield (1997).

39. See also *Phil.* 63d–e for the most intense pleasures (connected with the body, cf. 45a ff.) as provoking confusion (*tarachê*), carelessness (*ameleia*), and forgetfulness (*lêthê*) in human life.

40. Cf. Brisson (1974: 486–7 n. 9).

41. Cf. *Tim.* 36d4–7, 38e6 for the heavens learning their prescribed motion from the Demiurge. See also Chapter 3, Section I.1.

42. At *Pol.* 269d5–e6 the Stranger starts by suggesting, in a strongly axiological way, the immutability of the Forms, and it would seem that it is by having this pattern in mind that he then treats – with a tone of regret – the lack of changelessness of the world (due to its participation in body), though the best it can achieve is circular motion. This, however, is liable to reversal, in contrast, again, with the perfect and unidirectional circular motion of god, which would therefore seem to stand as directly paradigmatic for the universe's own motion.

43. Recollection of the cosmic god would be suggested in the *Timaeus* insofar as it it said at 41e2 that the Demiurge "showed the nature of the universe" (*tên tou pantos phusin edeixen*) to the human soul before its earthly existence, and at 47a7 it is again the nature of the universe (*tou pantos phusis*) that we can now investigate with the help of sight. Cf. Kucharschi (1966: 319 ff.).

44. See e.g. 90b–d and Chapter 3, Section III.2. On the intermediary role of the gods in the *Phaedrus* cf. Chapter 3, n. 48.

45. Cf. Solmsen (1962: 185 ff.). See also Chapter 6, Section IV.
46. The fact that Plato leaves the possibility of philosophy open during the era of Cronus goes against those who claim that philosophy could not exist during that cycle but only in ours, such as Scodel (1987: 79), Brisson (1992b), Howland (1993: 26), Nightingale (1996: 84), Blondell (2002: 342). See also Chapter 6, n. 60.
47. This recalls similar allusions to the Earth in other dialogues: see e.g. *Rep.* III 414d–e, *Tim.* 40b8, *Laws* V 740a5–7.
48. See on this Clark (1995: 236 ff.). For suggestions of animal intelligence in Plato see Sorabji (1993: 9–10) and my (1998a: 121–5). Certainly, in other senses there are differences among humans themselves (e.g. insofar as nature and training play an important role in the preselection of the ideal citizen body and political officers, cf. 308c ff.). But, as I have argued in my (1998a), Plato's main distinction is not so much between human and non-human animals, as between animals who exercise reason and animals who don't (the latter including a large number of humans). Likewise, the *Politicus* myth emphasises the value of learning from any being which has a particular capacity for the acquisition of wisdom that would distinguish it from the rest (272c2–4).
49. Cf. Chapter 5, Section II.3.
50. We may apply this suggestion not only to ideal political rulers but also to ideal citizens (as those ruled by the best constitution), if one agrees that in the *Politicus* it becomes possible for those citizens to understand securely and in unison, through education, what is best and act accordingly (309a–e, 310e). By doing so, they would be letting divine reason rule in them not only from without, but also from within. Thus, this very race of citizens is itself said to be daemonic (*daimonion*) and possess a divine (*theia*) quality (309c), in a way that seems to bring home the mythical picture of the *daimones* exerting close provincial care in the age of Cronus (271d).
51. Compare the similar strategy with regard to the *polis* and the individual in *Rep.* IV 434d.

Chapter 8

1. Compare Bobonich (1991) and (2002: esp. 97 ff.). Arguably, such a concern extends beyond the citizens themselves, given that strangers (to whom, for example, the performance of trade and craft is allotted, VIII 846d–847b, XI 920a) are, together with other noncitizens, subject to law and said to be the addressees of its preambles side by side with ordinary citizens (cf. e.g. IX 853c–854a with IV 722a–723b). Likewise, education seems to be extended to the multitude (*plêthos, hoi polloi*) of free people (VII 817e–818a, 819a–b).
2. 713e–714a; cf. 720e ff. Cf. Morrow (1960: 565); Cleary (2001: 125, 140). For a comparison between the Demiurge in the *Timaeus* and the legislator in the *Laws* see also Morrow (1954) and Laks (1990a), (1990b).
3. Cf. e.g. *Laws* II 652b–653c, III 693b–c, IV 714b–715b, X 889e–890a.

4. So that the Athenian can say that god, and not humans, is "for us the measure of all things", as he does in book IV (716c), clearly against Protagoras' measure doctrine (presented at *Crat.* 385e ff., *Theaet.* 152a ff.).

5. Cf. 885b, 886a–b.

6. The three propositions are summarised at 885b4–9 and 907b5–7. Cf. *Rep.* II 365d–e.

7. One may note that the proemium in book X is addressed even to the person "of little intelligence", 891a. Cf. *Laws* VII 811c–e, which gets to the point of suggesting that Plato's *Laws* is a model discourse for even children to learn.

8. The suffix *-sis* in Greek can in fact refer to both (*phusis* being related to *phuesthai*, the process of coming into being or growing). In the latter sense "nature" becomes a synonym of "principle" (*archê*); cf. *phusis* as a "from which" or *ex hês* at 891c and England (1921: 26) *ad loc.*; also Naddaf (1992: 492, 500).

9. Note the connection between soul as first origin (*prôtê genesis*) and soul as cause (*aitia*) of all change for all things at 896a–b.

10. For motion Plato uses *kinêsis* or *metabolê* (cf. e.g. 894c3–4, 7, 894e4–895a3, 896b1) meaning not only locomotion but every kind of motion. The first eight may be summarised as follows: rotation, locomotion, division, mixture, increase, decrease, corruption, and generation (893c–894a). For a detailed explanation of the different kinds of motion in the *Laws* and a comparison with the *Timaeus* see Skemp (1942: 100–7). Let us add that the account of the ten motions in the *Laws* should not be taken to contradict the six rectilinear motions that characterise necessity at *Tim.* 43b. For these could be included, in the scheme of the *Laws*, as different kinds of locomotion, according to their different directions.

11. Cf. Moreau (1939: 62).

12. And we can understand this concern especially after the problems raised in the *Parmenides* as to how the Forms by themselves could have any influence or *dunamis* on the sensible world (cf. e.g. 133c–134a). The first cause is evidently expected to have efficient power over the mutable (cf. its "efficacy" and "strength", *Laws* 894d1–2; its "power" or *dunamis* at 892a3); but how could this be so if it were itself immutable? Note that even Aristotle would seem to require the mediation of a first mover in motion between his first unmoved mover as final cause and other things: The unmoved mover "moves as the object of love, and moves the other things by means of what is moved" (*kinei de hôs erômenon, kinoumenôi de talla kinei, Metaph.* XII 7, 1072b3–4).

13. This is both characterised as "the motion itself capable of moving itself" (*tên dunamenên autên hautên kinein kinêsin*), or "the moving of itself" (*to heauto kinein*).

14. Compare here how the *Timaeus* explains, for example, the property of "hot" in the cosmos as resulting from the impact of the prickling geometrical corpuscular shape imparted by the Demiurge to the precosmic traces of fire (61d–62a).

15. On the *Phaedrus* see Chapter 2, n. 104. Compare Skemp (1942: 6).

16. Robinson (1969: 251 ff.); (1995: 147). Cf. also Vlastos (1964: 414); Stalley (1983: 174).

17. To adopt the terminology of Armstrong (1968: 5). Cf. here the suggestions by Benardete (2000: 302) and Moreau (1939: 63–5).

18. Cf. *Phaedrus* 246c4 for soul having the *dunamis* to move a body and 270c–d, with its reference to Hippocrates' theory of nature (*phusis*) as including the capacity to act and be acted upon. For soul as being *phusei* in the *Laws* cf. e.g. 892c5.

19. In this passage, Plato has the Athenian allow for three possibilities in relation to the soul of the sun, namely that soul conducts it (*agei*, 898e5) (1.) from inside the sun's body, as the human soul does with our body; (2.) from outside, by means of another body moving the sun's body by force; and (3.) without a body but with some marvellous powers. We can suppose that the reason for leaving this question open among others (such as the unity or multiplicity of souls ruling the cosmos, cf. 898c7–8, 899b5) is that to solve this problem is not crucial for his argument against atheism. However, Plato appears to reject (2.) in the *Critias* (109b–c) and would seem here to be very puzzled about (3.). This is suggested by his vocabulary, such as the allusion to powers exceedingly wondrous (*dunameis... huperballousas thaumati*) at 899a3, and the concessive tone of "in whatever manner" (*eith' hopôs eith' hopêi*) at 899a9, particularly after he has just been arguing that soul "leads" (*agei*) all things in heaven by making use (*chrômenê*) of the corporeal (896e8 with 897a4–b1). By contrast, (1.) is supported by the parallelism between macro- and microcosm established in the *Philebus* (29a–30a, esp. 30a3–7; cf. *Tim.* 30b4–5 for soul being in body, *psuchê en sômati*).

20. Cf. Brisson (1974: 336–7).

21. *Laws* X 891c–e. Cf. Vlastos (1939: 397). The merely hypothetical character of any temporal generation of soul as preceding that of body is highlighted at *Laws* 895a6–b1, in an argument where the postulation of an original state of rest without motion, as propounded by some, is considered audacity (*tolma*) by the Stranger. *Pace* Vlastos (1964: 414); Robinson (1969: 251 ff.); Stalley (1983: 174).

22. *Pace* Ostenfeld (1982: 267) who, in analysing the *Laws* and arguing for attribute dualism about the mind-body relation, remarks that we cannot infer "from Plato" that he took "the motion of the self-mover to be *spatial*" (his italics); and Parry (2002: 292–3), who believes spatial motion to apply only to the first eight kinds, and thus wonders how soul can transfer motion to things in space when it itself is not in space. Further suggestions about the soul being *always* in space and associated with body are found in a mythical context later in *Laws* X: thus, at 903d we are told that the soul is always (*aei*) associated with some kind of body; and how for the soul to receive reward or punishment means simply a change of "place" (*topos*, 903d7, cf. 904b8 and *hedra* at 904b7) in the physical universe. *Laws* VIII 828d4–5, for its part, asserting that "the association of body and soul is not better than their dissolution", should not be taken to challenge this point in any metaphysical sense (nor to advise us, accordingly, to "flee from worldly affairs", as suggested by Armstrong [2004: 182]). For there the Athenian is simply making an ethical point, meant to encourage the warriors not to fear death on the grounds that death is not intrinsically evil (and even passes on to recommend active engagement with worldly affairs by

emphasising the importance of fighting injustice for the sake of happiness, 828d5–829c1). Cf. *Laws* IV 707d stressing that what matters is the good life, not life at any cost. For another view on this see Ostenfeld (1982: 266). Cf. also Section V.2.

23. See Chapter 2, nn. 38 and 68.

24. This means that at least in one sense body and soul are coextensive, and so we have some form of "panpsychism" (that is, the view that even "the basic physical constituents of the universe have mental properties", as Nagel puts it [1979: 181]). To this extent, even fire or water participate in soul insofar as they are part of a wider ensouled cosmos (thus, "all things are full of gods", *Laws* 899b9), but can at the same time be called inanimate (cf. *Phaedrus* 245e5, *Laws* 896b8) from an individual point of view. For coimplication between mind and body see my (forthcoming).

25. We are told at 898d–e that we "hope" (cf. *elpis*, 898d11) that the soul is imperceptible by all bodily senses, and is instead intelligible. But Plato may not have ruled out some kind of materiality for the soul itself: see Chapter 2, n. 102.

26. As will be stated in *Laws* X 899b5–7, 900d2, 5–7, 901e1–902b3 and 902e8.

27. The first words of 897b2 present philological difficulties. We can read, amongst various possibilities, either "*theon orthôs theois*" (Burnet), or "*theion orthôs theos ousa*" (Diès [1956: *ad loc.*]), which would call soul rightly god when having acquired divine reason. My translation follows Burnet's reading, but I shall also be making reference to that of Diès.

28. Some of the other psychic states mentioned here can also seem striking but are perhaps less problematic. For example, Plato had not in the *Timaeus* spoken of hate and love, though this could be understandable as predicated of more humanised gods ruling over the cosmos (like the Olympians), who in the *Republic* (X 612e), according to Plato's purified version, are said to love the just and hate the unjust (cf. also here at 901a). Plato had already in the *Philebus* identified the world-soul with the soul of "Zeus" (30c–d), so there should be no wonder if he is now thinking of the power(s) ruling over the universe in similar terms. (Indeed Plato will further on call the latter "the gods who dwell on Olympus", *Laws* 904e4.) "Fear", "grief", and "joy" could be fitted into the same kind of anthropomorphic picture. The Demiurge feels joy in the *Timaeus* when perceiving the similarity of the copy with the model (37c7). In the *Politicus* we read that god becomes "worried" (*kêdomenos*) lest the world might fall into dissolution and destruction (273d5); at a further passage in *Laws* X Plato wonders whether we can compare god with peasants who await with "fear" the usual barren periods for the production of plants (906a2). There is on the other hand no need to explain states such as wish, reflection, concern, and counsel, which recurrently characterise the provident demiurgic activity (see e.g. *Tim.* 29e–30b, 34a8, 71a7, 75b8; cf. also *epimeleia* at *Pol.* 271d4).

29. Cf. e.g. Rist (1964: 107). This possibility is also considered by Grube (1980: 147).

30. For scholars who take a view of this passage as restricted to soul *qua* soul, see e.g. Moreau (1939: 69), Solmsen (1942: 141), Cherniss (1954: 26,

n. 29), also Robinson (1970: 148–51), who however tend to deny that there is any allusion to the world-soul in *Laws* X. I shall show that this view is only partially correct, since Plato is adding here a second sense (see also n. 31). On the other hand, I do not think there is any explicit reference to the world-soul before 896e, as is claimed by Gaudin (1990: 178, 183), nor any identification of soul with reason at 893c–896e, as Craig (1980: 8, 13) and Stalley (1983: 171) suppose.

31. In fact, when Plato has the Athenian ask which "kind" of soul rules the universe (897b7), and further concludes that it is good soul, "either one or many" (*mian ê pleious*, 898c7–8; cf. *psuchê ê psuchai*, 899b5), we could think at first sight that for him the question about the unity or multiplicity of souls ruling the universe is left open (as is claimed by the first four authors quoted in n. 30). The reason for this may be that to decide the problem is not crucial for the point Plato is making in this kind of exoteric discourse, namely that the masses should believe in god, be it one or many. However, a careful reading of the text suggests that in fact *both* levels of divinity – the singular and the plural – are maintained here, and that he is thinking of both the world-soul and the heavenly bodies, as in the *Timaeus* (without either excluding the Olympians as their traditional counterparts, cf. *Laws* 904e4). At 898d3–4 we read, with regard to the sun, moon, and other stars, that "soul turns round all and each" (*psuchê periagei panta . . . kai hen hekaston*): in other words, that soul conducts the whole astronomical system (as a world-soul) and each heavenly body individually, which should also have its own soul (cf. 898d9–10 on the soul of the sun). This would in turn be consistent with the question about what "kind of soul" rules over the universe, since both the world-soul and the soul of each heavenly body are shown in the *Timaeus* to be of the same "kind" or nature (cf. Chapter 3, n. 5). Thus, the "one or many" (*mian ê pleious*) of 898c7–8 turns out to be a "one and many". Cf. also Cornford (1937: 108); Festugière (1947: 21).

32. This movement corresponds to motion number (1.) in the original classification (893c–d; cf. n. 10), which is here said to be an image of *nous* in the sense that the orderly rotation of the physical universe *reflects* the fact that it is the result of wonderful calculations which are irreducible to bodily motions left to themselves (cf. XII 967a–d).

33. In the latter text it is said that two things lead us to believe in the existence of the gods, first, the priority of soul over body and second, "the order (*taxis*) of the motion of the stars and all other things under the control of *nous* which has ordered everything" (966e2–4). We see here again an example of the recurrent suggestion that order is due to *nous* or to god.

34. Cf. Moreau (1939: 72, 76). Contrast this with Protarchus' naïve appeal to the "look" or "aspect" (*opsis*) of the heavens in the *Philebus* (28e3; cf. *Laws* XII 967c2 ff. for the hint that the eyes can be insufficient in this regard); and Clinias' equally naïve appeal to the order of the universe at *Laws* 886a.

35. See n. 31.

36. Cf. e.g. Festugière (1949: 125, 129–30); Diès (1956: LXXVII); Montoneri (1968: 330–1).

37. Similarly, I have interpreted acosmic disorder as a *hypothesis* in the *Timaeus* and *Politicus*. Cf. Chapter 2, Section II.2; Chapter 7, Section I.3; and here, n. 38, for the possibility of a hypothetical reading.

38. This reading might be suggested by the phrase *noun proslabousa... anoiai sungenomenê* at 897b1–3, if we take the participles not only conditionally (that is, as "*if,* having acquired reason" and "*if,* associated with unreason") but temporally (= "*when,* having acquired reason" and "*when,* associated with unreason"). This "cyclical" view was suggested to me by Conrado Eggers Lan.

39. Further, if the ruling soul can pass from "acquiring" *nous* and being "god" (the latter feature being suggested by Diès's reading of 897b1–2, and confirmed in any event by the conclusion at 899b; cf. 898c) to being invaded by folly (which would imply not being god at that time), then "god" would be just an accidental property of soul which comes into being and perishes according to soul's association with *nous* or *anoia* respectively, something that contradicts the very notion of god as immortal (cf. XII 967d). Let us also notice that the "cyclical" hypothesis would be equally implausible on a view that attempted to posit *nous* not as a faculty immanent to soul, but as a separate entity as god. For if *nous* is separate and has no intervention in the universe during periods of disorder (as a literal reading of *Pol.* 272e ff. would suggest) then this would contradict proposition (2.) in the *Laws* about god's essentially, 900d2–3, and continuously (with Stobaeus) or completely (with the MSS), 905e2–3, taking care of the whole universe. Indeed, at *Laws* X 901c–903a it is denied that the gods could fail to take care of the universe through laziness, ignorance, or lack of power. Similar grounds were used by Proclus to deny that god could have started ordering the universe at one point in time and not earlier (cf. *In Tim.* I 288, 17–27 Diehl). The same evidence could be used against any postulation of cyclical states of the universe without divine care. Cf. also the arguments I shall present shortly against the postulation of an irrational faculty in the world-soul, which could apply also to this "cyclical" interpretation if we consider that the possibility that soul become associated with *nous* or *anoia* at different times could be explained by the fact that soul has an irrational faculty.

40. Here we can make use of the ambiguity of the participle in the phrase *anoiai sungenomenê* at 897b3, which can be read both conditionally and temporally: see n. 38.

41. This latter possibility might seem to find verbal support at 897b7, asking which "kind" or "part" (*genos*) of soul rules the astronomical universe, if we bear in mind that *genos* is one term used in the *Republic* for the different "parts" of the soul: see e.g. 441a1, c6 and compare *Tim.* 69d5.

42. Cf. *De Iside et Osiride* 370b–371a. There he compares the evil soul with Ahriman (bringing "pestilence", *loimon,* cf. *Laws* X 906c5) in Persian dualistic religion and with what the Greeks call "Hades". In *De an. proc.* 1014d–1015f he considers the evil soul as a soul of matter, though as the irrational precosmic principle from which god, by introducing intelligence, created the world-soul. On these inconsistencies see Cherniss (1976: 136–40). Dualistic interpretations have echoes even these days: thus, Annas and Waterfield hold that "*Laws* 896c [ff.] ... seems to assert a cosmic dualism of a good and an evil cosmic soul" (1995: 23 n. 25).

43. This seems in any case explicitly contradicted in the *Politicus* myth: "we should not say that . . . two different gods, with opposite designs, turn the universe" (269e8–270a2). Cf. Festugière (1947: 12 ff.). *Pace* Jaeger's (1948: 132) claim that the evil soul in *Laws* X is a tribute that Plato pays to Zoroaster.

44. Cf. e.g. Dodds (1965: 21), followed by Guthrie (1978: 97 n. 1). This possibility is also allowed by Grube (1980: 147 n. 1).

45. Cf. *ton megiston theon kai holon ton kosmon* at a2. I translate "the greatest god, namely, the whole universe", taking the *kai* as epexegetic, given that Plato is speaking here in an astronomical context and refers to the "sun and moon" as great gods (*megalôn theôn*) at 821b6, which suggests that the greatest god is the whole universe. For the universe as "greatest god" (*megistos theos*) cf. also *Tim.* 92c7.

46. As suggested by Hackforth (1952: 75–6); cf. also Robin (1908: 164). I myself defended this view as an explanation of natural disorders within the orderly cosmos in my (1988), though I now find it more problematic.

47. *Laws* VII 821a2, cf. also X 897b2 on Diès's reading.

48. For the connection between these two features cf. Chapter 2, n. 65.

49. Similarly, there is an allusion to folly (*aphrosunê*) as something that corrupts *us* at 906a7–8, as we shall see later.

50. Remember how the notion of being a principle (*archê*) was related before to the notion of ruling (896b–c).

51. Accordingly, it is human souls that would be subject to the false opinions attributed generically to soul leading the universe at 896e8–897a2.

52. See n. 38 for how the participles at 897b1–3 can be read both categorically and hypothetically.

53. The following argument could be given in support of this view: if freedom (or power, *dunamis*) is the capacity to do what one wants, and one only wants good things, then freedom is the capacity to do good things. Cf. *Gorg.* 466b ff. and my (2004b: 61–67) on this general issue.

54. The image of the "puppet" appears in book I, 644d–645b (cf. VII 803c). But see Stalley (1983: 60–61). God is in turn referred to as a checkers player at *Laws* X 903d.

55. Cf. *Tim.* 47e4–5 with 52d–53a, Cornford (1937: 202–3).

56. For the same suggestion cf. *Gorg.* 470e9–11, 478d7–8, 527b–e, *Rep.* X 621c–d. For other allusions to eschatology and reincarnation in the *Laws* cf. IX 870d–e, 872d–e, even though they are prefaced as "stories" (as here at *Laws* X 903a10–b2) and so it is hard to decide how seriously committed Plato was to such a view. That he was not might perhaps be suggested by *Laws* IV 721b–c, where we are told that procreation is *the* way – and not just a way – humans have of participating in immortality (as in the *Symposium*, 207d); cf. Chapter 4, n. 67.

57. Cf. Dodds (1951: 221 and 233–4 n. 77) for the suggestion that "hell" in the description of *Laws* X is a state of mind.

58. On this point cf. Saunders (1973: 234, 237) and (1991: 204, 206).

59. For those personal descriptions occurring in the context of a "myth" used to "enchant" the spirit, cf. 903a10–b2. But that this god who takes care of the universe cannot be other than the god, that is, the good soul (world-soul or the souls of the heavenly bodies), whose existence and governance has

been argued for previously, becomes clear given that the second proposition that Plato is trying to prove in *Laws* X (namely, that the gods take care of human affairs) is said to build on the first (concerning the existence of the gods): Thus, an explicit link is affirmed between the arguments (*logoi*) supporting them (cf. 900b1–3 with b6–c1). Further, at 900d1–3, in the context of proving proposition (2.), there is an allusion to the concern (*epimeleia*) of the gods for human affairs that explicitly remits to their *epimeleia* for the macrocosm mentioned within the argument for the existence of god at 898c.

60. Rather, we have seen that both body and soul share the capacity to act and be acted upon within the domain of *phusis*: cf. Section I. To this extent, Plato seems immune to the accusation, often levelled by the materialist against the dualist, that "the world studied by science contains nothing but physical things operating according to the laws of physics with the exception of the mind", as Armstrong puts it (1968: 49).

61. In this regard the argument about cosmic justice can be seen as a direct response to the Athenian's opponent, who had presented "the right life according to nature" as one of dominion over others as opposed to "serving others according to law" (890a).

62. Cf. Saunders (1973: 233–4).

63. See here e.g. the complaints of Attfield (1994: 81).

64. Certainly, one could also read Plato's statement about the existence of more evils than goods in the universe at *Laws* X 906a as just making a point about the *numerosity* of evils. Evil human souls or their effects may be much greater in number than the good souls – including those of the gods – in the universe (after all we find more multiplicity in the earthly domain than in heaven), but this need not dismiss the fact that the latter have *predominance*, since "more evils" does not imply "more evil". For the numerous individual evils may each be small compared with the much fewer but much greater goods. Still, it is interesting that Plato does not mention *here* the predominance of good. Rather he stresses that between the forces of good and evil there is an immortal battle in which humans play the leading role.

65. In fact, 906a3 ambiguously lends itself to be read also as: "...we have agreed that the universe is *for ourselves* (*hêmin autois*) full of many good things" while there are more of the opposite kind; if taken this way, the *hêmin autois* at 906a3 would be directly reminiscent of *Rep.* II 379c4–5, where we are told that goods are much fewer than evils *for us* (*hêmin*).

66. Recall the similar projection of human drama onto the cosmos that I argued for with respect to the *Politicus* myth in Chapter 7, Section II.

67. Cf. especially the "overgaining among people" (*pleonektousin... en anthrôpois*) at 906c1–2.

68. For this interpretation of the *Timaeus* see Cherniss (1944: 444–5), applied to the *Laws* in (1954: 28–9 and n. 44); followed by Brisson (1974: 503–4), who in turn applies this solution to the *Laws* in his (2000: 259). For different explanations concerning the *Timaeus*, cf. Vlastos (1939: 394–8) followed by Robinson (1970: 95–7); Easterling (1967: 31, 37–8); Mohr (1985: 159–70, 184–8).

69. For the implications of this distinction in Plato's moral and penal theory cf. Roberts (1987: 23 ff.); Mackenzie (1981: 174–5, 245–9).

70. On this feature of *Laws* X cf. Vlastos (1939: 392–3).

71. It is in fact noteworthy that, whereas the *Timaeus* pointed out that *nous* guides (only) the majority of things (*ta pleista*) towards the best (48a3), here the Athenian remarks that god has arranged everything (*panta*) for the excellence of the whole (903b5) and insists that it is easier for god, as for any demiurge, to care for the small parts than the large ones (902c–903a), thus suggesting that there is virtually nothing that is beyond his control. This has led scholars such as Mohr (1985: 185) to believe that, in contrast with the *Timaeus*, Plato's god in the *Laws* is omnipotent (cf. also Cleary [2001: 135]). One might find 901d7–8 especially suggestive ("the gods are capable of doing *everything* which is in the power of mortals and immortals"); though perhaps we are dealing here with a difference of stress rather than of thought. In fact, we must not forget that the phrase at 901d7–8 does not itself imply omnipotence, for the power of immortals might be limited in some ways (cf. *Laws* VII 818b, V 740e–741a).

72. See Cherniss (1954); after him Brisson (1974: 449–52).

73. Plato was, indeed, aware of environmental problems, such as the deforestation of Attica and the increasing nonabsorption by the soil of rainfall there, as he evinces in the *Critias* (111c–d; as noted by Hughes [1982: 7]). But, far from indifference, his attitude seems to have been a critical one towards his contemporary society. In the *Gorgias* Socrates had already complained of an Athens full of ships and material success but devoid of virtue (518e–519a) and it seems no accident that later in the *Critias* Plato contrasts the situation of his contemporary Athens with the ideal environmental conditions of a past Athens which was also excelling in virtue (*Crit.* 109c4–d2, 110e3–111a2, 111b–d, 112e2–6). In fact, Plato's critique of his contemporary society has been taken by recent studies to be the main message of the *Critias* story. Cf. Brisson (1992a: 324–5), with references to C. Gill and Vidal-Naquet on p. 319. For the land (*chôra*) as our home deserving our care and as a god see *Laws* V 740a5–7. Cf. my (1998a).

74. Cf. Friedlaender (1969: 439).

75. See Cornford (1937: 31) for the suggestion that Atomism figures at the forefront of Plato's attack in his discussion of teleology, even though it is likely that Plato's account of his materialist predecessors is not based on a particular theory, but rather presents a combined account of theories in vogue among enlightened Athenians in the fifth century. See on this e.g. Solmsen (1942: 133, 137).

76. Thus, we can see how Plato is very far from suggesting an anthropocentric kind of teleology. This is so even when great stress is laid on human beings' responsibility for nature, and even when, as I argue, Plato's description of the universe may end up being coloured by ethical concerns. The *Laws* suggestion that it is the goodness of the whole that matters, and that we are a part of the whole, the part existing for the sake of the whole, not vice versa (903b–d), finds a parallel in the *Timaeus* suggestion that living beings (humans implicitly included) must exist in order to preserve the

completeness of the universe, the whole being more perfect than the part (30c–d, 39e–40a with 41a–c). Could *Tim.* 39b–c (which describes how the sun was kindled "so that it would shine throughout the whole heaven and those creatures [*zôia*] for whom it was appropriate might share in number, learning from the revolution of the same and similar") be taken to suggest "partial anthropocentrism" (as suggested by Sedley 2002: 65)? Even here talk of *anthropo*centrism seems inadequate, as the text notably avoids specific mention of human beings in this context (remember that animals too have in the *Timaeus* the possibility of promoting themselves by exercising reason: 42c–d, 92b–c; cf. *Laws* X 904c–e), and emphasises once more, as I explained in Chapter 2, that it is reason (also shared by the cosmos, and precisely because of its capacity to apprehend and implement the common good), not human beings as such (who may in turn fail to exemplify reason), that has a privileged place in Plato's cosmology (cf. Chapter 2, Section I.1. and n. 16; Chapter 7, n. 48).

77. Cf. Moreau (1939: 67). Along similar lines, it has often been claimed that the argument in the *Laws* concerns soul *qua* soul rather than an all-encompassing world-soul: see n. 30.

78. In fact even here there are references to the universe or *ouranos* (e.g. 896e1, 899b8), though Moreau is right to say that *to holon* does not appear in this context.

79. This immanent goodness of the whole sets the goal for soul as the agent of teleology (cf. also 904b4–5, 903d1–3, XII 966e–967a); an aim that is not very different from the one to which the Demiurge tends in the *Timaeus*, namely "that everything should be good, and nothing bad as far as possible" (30a2–3). In the *Timaeus*, however, this was understood in terms of similarity with the model (cf. 39d–e); and the notion of a unified organic whole was given its Ideal counterpart by positing the "Living Being Itself" (*ho estin zôion*, 39e8) which is perfect (*teleon*, 30c–d) as the model that guides the demiurgic activity to produce just one visible world as a *zôion* (32d–33a). *Laws* X does not seem to make any explicit allusion to the Forms. Whether or not Plato still believes in them in the way they are presented in the *Timaeus*, it is clear that such metaphysically loaded claims are not needed for his point against atheism here, nor is knowledge of these entities required for the mass of citizens to live justly. However that may be, we can discover both in the *Timaeus* and in *Laws* X the same effort to assert teleology by virtue of an intelligent cause.

80. This does not mean that Plato does not conceive of the universe, *qua* astronomical system, as a unity (for he does at *Laws* VII 821a, for instance, as we have seen). But it does show that, having earlier in book X focused on the universe as an astronomical system (897b–899b), Plato is now emphasising that the human world must form part of any complete account of the *kosmos*.

Conclusion

1. Cf. Chapter 8, n. 24.
2. Cf. Chapter 4, Section II.3.2., nn. 51 and 54, and Chapter 7, Section I.1.

3. This is not to deny Presocratic influences, such as Heraclitus (e.g. B114 DK). But undoubtedly Plato provides the first extensive and articulate account of this trend of thought. A good specific example of the application of this theory is given in *Laws* IV, where the Athenian tries to base his laws about marriage and conception of children on humans' teleological desire for immortality (720e–721d; see esp. the relation between *nomon* and *kata phusin* at 720e). Cf. also *Laws* V, where some kind of normative hedonism is inferred from the fact that we all wish (*boulometha*) and choose (*hairoumetha*) the maximum pleasure and the least pain by nature (*phusei, kata phusin*) (733a–734d; cf. *nomon* at 733e1), an argument that considerably predates Epicurus', even though it differs from the latter, among other things, in being grounded on a teleological conception of nature. On Epicurus see Brunschwig (1986: 119–20). On normative hedonism in the *Laws* see my (2003).

4. It is noteworthy that this is said in the *Laws* precisely in the context of trying to establish the foundation for a legislative system: see esp. 713e–715b. Compare here the Stoic view as expressed in Cicero, *Republic* 3.33 LS 67S, Arius Didymus in Eusebius, *Evangelical Preparation* 15.15.3–5 LS 67L, Alexander, *On Fate* 207, 5–21 LS 62(J)1, Marcus Aurelius, *Meditations* 4.4. The thought was echoed in Christianity: see Paul, *Romans* 2.14–15 and later Thomas Aquinas, *Summa Theologica*, questions 90, 91, 94 and 95. Among contemporary defences of natural law see especially Finnis (1980), and discussion in Harris (1980: 6–23). *Pace* Striker, who regards the Stoics as innovators of the view that "happiness, or a good human life, will be achieved precisely by organizing one's life in accordance with the rational pattern provided by nature" (1996: 219); and Stalley (1983: 33), who recognises the importance of Plato as an antecedent of the natural law tradition, but fails to find in his work the notion of humans as citizens of the universe, claiming instead that it is the Stoics who are the founders of this version of ethical naturalism. For others who find the origin of the concept of the natural law in the Stoics see e.g. Harris (1980: 7), Schofield (1991: 2).

5. For recent discussion see Bobzien (1998), esp. ch. 6.

6. For the history of this concept in ancient Greek philosophy see my (2001a); in Aristotle, see e.g. Annas (1993) and among Hellenistic philosophers see e.g. Annas (1993), Schofield and Striker (1986) and Striker (1991). See also n. 4. The concept is these days widely used (albeit often axiomatically, and to that extent unexplained) by environmental philosophers: see e.g. Naess (1973), Goodpaster (1982), Devall and Sessions (1985), Fox (1984), Taylor (1986), Botkin (1990), Matthews (1991), Katz (2000).

7. Compare here the basic golden rule of contemporary holism: a thing is right if it tends to preserve the integrity, stability, and beauty of the whole; it is wrong otherwise: Leopold (1949), Callicot (1989: 84); also Devall (1988: 70). I have analysed other aspects in which Plato may be relevant to the modern environmental debate in my (1998a); (2001a).

8. This openness to argument and future findings is acknowledged even by the Athenian in the *Laws* (VI 769d–e, II 667a), in passages that help us counter the not uncommon view that Plato has fallen into some kind of dogmatism in

that work. Recall also the *Timaeus'* frequent remarks about the provisionality of its verisimilar account (29c–d, 68d, 72d).

9. Cf. Chapter 2 n. 102, Chapter 4 n. 67, Chapter 8 n. 25, and my (forthcoming). For this issue in the Stoics see especially Annas (1992), who however *contrasts* Stoic materialism with what she takes to be strong Platonic dualism (4, 6); in the same line cf. e.g. Betegh (2003: 295 n. 46).

10. For discussion of Aristotle see e.g. Sedley (1991); also Cooper (1982); Furley (1985) and the studies mentioned above, Chapter 2, n. 32.

11. Cf. Aristotle, *N.E.* X 7 1177b26–1178a2, X 8 1178a9–14, 1178b7–28.

12. See here e.g. Nussbaum (1986: 373–7); Simpson (1997: 245–7).

13. *Theaet.* 176b1–2; cf. above, Chapter 3, nn. 44 and 47. Compare here the insistence on ideal role models in virtue ethics as expounded e.g. by Mayo (1958), and discussion in Louden (1992: 49–54); Chapter 3, n. 29.

Bibliographical References

Algra, K. (1994): *Concepts of Space in Greek Thought*, Leiden
Allen, R. E. (ed.) (1965): *Studies in Plato's Metaphysics*, London
Annas, J. (1981): *An Introduction to Plato's Republic*, Oxford
—— (1982): "Plato's Myths of Judgement", *Phronesis* 27, 119–43
—— (1985): "Self-Knowledge in Early Plato", in O'Meara (ed.), 111–38
—— (1992): *Hellenistic Philosophy of Mind*, Berkeley
—— (1993): *The Morality of Happiness*, Oxford
—— (1994): "Plato the Skeptic", in P. A. Vander Waerdt (ed.), *The Socratic Movement*, Ithaca, 309–40
—— (1999): *Platonic Ethics, Old and New*, Ithaca
—— and Rowe, C. (eds.) (2002): *New Perspectives on Plato, Ancient and Modern*, Cambridge, Mass.
—— and Waterfield, R. (1995): *Plato: Statesman*, Cambridge
Anton, J. P. (ed.) (1980): *Science and the Sciences in Plato*, New York
—— and Preus, A. (eds.) (1989): *Essays in Ancient Greek Philosophy*, vol. 3: *Plato*, Albany
Archer-Hind, R. D. (1888): *The Timaeus of Plato*, London
Armstrong, D. (1968): *A Materialist Theory of the Mind*, London
Armstrong, J. (2004): "After the Ascent: Plato on Becoming Like God", *Oxford Studies in Ancient Philosophy* 26, 171–83
Ashbaugh, A. F. (1988): *Plato's Theory of Explanation: A Study of the Cosmological Account in the Timaeus*, New York
Attfield, R. (1994): *Environmental Philosophy: Principles and Prospects*, Aldershot
Balme, D. M. (1972): *Aristotle's De Partibus Animalium I and De Generatione Animalium I*, Oxford
—— (1987): "Teleology and Necessity", in Gotthelf and Lennox (eds.), 275–85
Baltes, M. (1996): "*Gegonen*. Ist die Welt real entstanden oder nicht?", in K. Algra et al. (eds.), *Polyhistor: Studies in the History and Historiography of Ancient Philosophy*, Leiden
Benardete, S. (2000): *Plato's Laws*, Chicago

Benitez, E. E. (1989): *Forms in Plato's Philebus*, Assen

Berti, E. (1997): "L'oggetto dell' *eikos muthos* nel *Timeo* di Platone", in Calvo and Brisson (eds.), 119–31

Betegh, G. (2003): "Cosmological Ethics in the *Timaeus* and Early Stoicism", *Oxford Studies in Ancient Philosophy* 24, 273–302

Blank, D. L. (1993): "The Arousal of Emotion in Plato's Dialogues", *Classical Quarterly* 43, 428–39

Blondell, R. (2002): *The Play of Character in Plato's Dialogues*, Cambridge

Bluck, R. S. (1975): *Plato's Sophist: A Commentary*, ed. G. C. Neal, Manchester

Bobonich, C. (1991): "Persuasion, Compulsion, and Freedom in Plato's *Laws*", *Classical Quarterly* 41, 365–87

——— (1995): "The Virtues of Ordinary People in Plato's *Statesman*", in Rowe (ed.), 313–29

——— (1996): "Reading the *Laws*", in Gill and McCabe (eds.), 246–82

——— (2002): *Plato's Utopia Recast*, Oxford

Bobzien, S. (1998): *Determinism and Freedom in Stoic Philosophy*, Oxford

Bolton, R. (1975): "Plato's Distinction between Being and Becoming", *Review of Metaphysics* 29, 66–95

Botkin, D. (1990): *Discordant Harmonies: A New Ecology for the Twenty-First Century*, Oxford

Boyd, R. (1980): "Materialism Without Reductionism: What Physicalism Does Not Entail", in N. Block (ed.), *Readings in Philosophy of Psychology*, vol. 1, Cambridge, Mass., 57–106

Brentano, F. (1992): "*Nous Poiêtikos*", in Nussbaum and Rorty (eds.), 314–42

Brisson, L. (1974): *Le Même et l'Autre dans la structure ontologique du Timée de Platon*, Paris

——— (1982): *Platon, les mots et les mythes*, Paris

———(with F. W. Meyerstein) (1991): *Inventer l'univers: le problème de la connaisance et les modèles cosmologiques*, Paris

——— (1992a): *Platon: Timée/Critias*, Paris

——— (1992b): "Interprétation du mythe du *Politique*", paper presented at the Third Symposium Platonicum, Bristol

——— (1995): "Interprétation du mythe du *Politique*", in Rowe (ed.), 349–63

——— (2000): *Lectures de Platon*, Paris

Broadie, S. (2001a): "Theodicy and Pseudo-History in the *Timaeus*", *Oxford Studies in Ancient Philosophy* 21, 1–28

——— (2001b): "Soul and Body in Plato and Descartes", *Proceedings of the Aristotelian Society* 101, 295–308

Brochard, V. (1926): *Études de Philosophie Ancienne et de Philosophie Moderne*, Paris

Brunschwig, J. (1986): "The Cradle Argument in Epicureanism and Stoicism", in Schofield and Striker (eds.), 113–44

Burkert, W. (1972): *Lore and Science in Ancient Pythagoreanism*, Engl. transl., Cambridge, Mass.

Burnet, J. (ed.) (1900–7): *Platonis Opera*, vols. 1–5, Oxford

Burnyeat, M. F. (1977): "Socratic Midwifery, Platonic Inspiration", *Bulletin of the Institute of Classical Studies* 24, 7–16

—— (1982): "Idealism and Greek Philosophy: What Descartes Saw and Berkeley Missed", *Philosophical Review* 91, 3–40

—— (1987): "Platonism and Mathematics: A Prelude to Discussion", in Graeser (ed.), 213–40

—— (1990): *The Theaetetus of Plato*, Indianapolis

—— (1992): "Is an Aristotelian Philosophy of Mind Still Credible? A Draft", in Nussbaum and Rorty (eds.), 15–26

—— (2000): "Plato on Why Mathematics is Good for the Soul", in T. Smiley (ed.), *Mathematics and Necessity, Proceedings of the British Academy* 103, Oxford, 1–81

—— (2002): "*De Anima* II 5", *Phronesis* 47, 28–90

Bury, R. G. (1897): *The Philebus of Plato*, Cambridge

—— (1929): *Plato: Timaeus*, London

Byrne, C. (1989): "Forms and Causes in Plato's *Phaedo*", *Dionysius* 13, 3–16

Callicot, J. B. (1989): *In Defense of the Land Ethic: Essays in Environmental Philosophy*, Albany

Calvo, T. and Brisson, L. (eds.) (1997): *Interpreting the Timaeus-Critias*, Sankt Augustin

Carone, G. R. (1988): "El problema del 'alma mala' en la última filosofía de Platón (*Leyes* X, 893d ss.)", *Revista de Filosofía* 3, 143–63

—— (1989): "La racionalidad humana como tarea en la filosofía de Platón", *Nova Tellus* 7, 59–79

—— (1990): "Sobre el significado y el *status* ontológico del demiurgo del *Timeo*", *Méthexis* 3, 33–49

—— (1991): *La noción de dios en el Timeo de Platón*, Buenos Aires

—— (1993): "Cosmic and Human Drama in Plato's *Statesman*", *Polis* 12, 99–121

—— (1994): "Teleology and Evil in *Laws* X", *Review of Metaphysics* 48, 275–98

—— (1997): "The Ethical Function of Astronomy in Plato's *Timaeus*", in Calvo and Brisson (eds.), 341–9

—— (1998a): "Plato and the Environment", *Environmental Ethics* 20, 115–33

—— (1998b): "Socrates' Human Wisdom and *Sophrosune* in *Charmides* 164c ff.", *Ancient Philosophy* 18, 267–86

—— (2000): "Hedonism and the Pleasureless Life in Plato's *Philebus*", *Phronesis* 45, 257–83

—— (2001a): "The Classical Greek Tradition", in D. Jamieson (ed.), *A Companion to Environmental Philosophy*, Oxford, 67–80

—— (2001b): "*Akrasia* in the *Republic*: Does Plato Change His Mind?", *Oxford Studies in Ancient Philosophy* 20, 107–48

—— (2002): "Pleasure, Virtue, Externals, and Happiness in Plato's *Laws*", *History of Philosophy Quarterly* 19, 327–44

—— (2003): "The Place of Hedonism in Plato's *Laws*", *Ancient Philosophy* 23, 283–300

—— (2004a): "Reversing the Myth of the *Politicus*", *Classical Quarterly* 54, 88–108

—— (2004b): "Calculating Machines or Leaky Jars? The Moral Psychology of Plato's *Gorgias*", *Oxford Studies in Ancient Philosophy* 26, 55–96

—— (2004c): "Creation in the *Timaeus*: The Middle Way", *Apeiron* 37, 211–26

——— (forthcoming): "Mind and Body in Late Plato", *Archiv für Geschichte der Philosophie*

——— (unpublished): "Luck and Human Excellence: A Platonic Perspective"

Carpenter, A. (2003): "Phileban Gods", *Ancient Philosophy* 23, 93–112

Cherniss, H. (1932): "On Plato's *Republic* X 597b", *American Journal of Philology* 53, 233–42

——— (1944): *Aristotle's Criticism of Plato and the Academy*, Baltimore

——— (1945): *The Riddle of the Early Academy*, Berkeley

——— (1947): "Some War-Time Publications concerning Plato", *American Journal of Philology* 68, 225–65

——— (1950): review of A. J. Festugière (1949), *Gnomon* 22, 204–16

——— (1954): "The Sources of Evil according to Plato", *Proceedings of the American Philosophical Society* 98, 23–30

——— (1957): "The Relation of the *Timaeus* to Plato's Later Dialogues", in Allen (ed.), 339–78

——— (1976): *Plutarch's Moralia* 13, Part I, London

Claghorn, G. S. (1954): *Aristotle's Criticism of Plato's Timaeus*, The Hague

Clark, S. (1995): "Herds of Free Bipeds", in Rowe (ed.), 236–52

Cleary, J. (2001): "The Role of Theology in Plato's *Laws*", in F. Lisi (ed.), *Plato's Laws and Its Historical Significance*, Sankt Augustin

Code, A. (1988): "Reply to Michael Frede's 'Being and Becoming in Plato'", *Oxford Studies in Ancient Philosophy* suppl., 53–60

Cooper, J. (1977a): "Plato's Theory of the Human Good in the *Philebus*", *Journal of Philosophy* 74, 714–30

——— (1977b): "The Psychology of Justice in Plato", *American Philosophical Quarterly* 14, 131–57

——— (1982): "Aristotle's Natural Teleology", in M. Schofield and M. Nussbaum (eds.), *Language and Logos*, Cambridge, 197–222

——— (1987): "Hypothetical Necessity and Natural Teleology", in Gotthelf and Lennox (eds.), 243–74

——— (1996): "Eudaimonism, the Appeal to Nature, and 'Moral Duty' in Stoicism", in S. Engstrom and J. Whiting (eds.), *Aristotle, Kant, and the Stoics*, Cambridge, 261–84

——— (1997): "Plato's *Statesman* and Politics", *Proceedings of the Boston Area Colloqium in Ancient Philosophy* 13, 71–104

Cornford, F. M. (1935): *Plato's Theory of Knowledge*, London

——— (1937): *Plato's Cosmology*, London

——— (1938): "The Polytheism of Plato: an Apology", *Mind* 47, 321–30

Craig, L. H. (1994): *The War Lover: A Study of Plato's Republic*, Toronto

Craig, W. C. (1980): *The Cosmological Argument from Plato to Leibniz*, London

Crombie, I. M. (1963): *An Examination of Plato's Doctrines*, vol. 2, London

Dancy, R. M. (1984): "The One, the Many, and the Forms", *Ancient Philosophy* 4, 160–93

Davidson, D. (1990): *Plato's Philebus*, New York

——— (1993): "Plato's Philosopher", in T. Irwin and M. Nussbaum (eds.), *Virtue, Love, and Form*, Apeiron 26, Edmonton, 179–94

Davis, P. J. (1979): "The Fourfold Classification in Plato's *Philebus*", *Apeiron* 13, 124–34

De Chiara-Quenzer, D. (1993): "A Method for Pleasure and Reason: Plato's *Philebus*", *Apeiron* 26, 37–55

De Lacy, P. (1939): "The Problem of Causation in Plato's Philosophy", *Classical Philology* 24, 97–115

Delcomminette, S. (2003): "False Pleasures, Appearance and Imagination in the *Philebus*", *Phronesis* 48, 215–37

Demos, R. (1968): "Plato's Doctrine of the Psyche as a Self-Moving Motion", *Journal of the History of Philosophy* 6, 133–45

De Rijk, L. M. (1986): *Plato's Sophist: A Philosophical Commentary*, Amsterdam

Descartes, R. (1984–5): *Discourse on Method* (1637) and *Meditations* (1641), in *The Philosophical Writings of Descartes*, vols. 1–2, ed. and transl. by J. Cottingham et al., Cambridge

Des Places, E. (1964): *Sungeneia: La parenté de l'homme avec Dieu d'Homère à la patristique*, Paris

Devall, B. (1988): *Simple in Means, Rich in Ends*, Salt Lake City

——— and Sessions, G. (1985): *Deep Ecology*, Salt Lake City

Devereux, D. (2000): "Separation and Immanence in Plato's Theory of Forms", in Fine (ed.), 194–216

De Vogel, C. (1970): *Philosophia* I: *Studies in Greek Philosophy*, Assen

Dicks, D. R. (1970): *Early Greek Astronomy to Aristotle*, Bristol

Diehl, E. (ed.) (1903–6): *Procli Diadochi In Platonis Timaeum Commentaria*, vols. 1–3, Leipzig

Diels, H. and Kranz, W. (eds.) (1951): *Die Fragmente der Vorsokratiker*, vol. 1, Berlin, 6th ed. (=DK)

Diès, A. (1927): *Autour de Platon*, vol. 2, Paris

——— (1935): *Platon: Le Politique*, Paris

——— (1941): *Platon: Philèbe*, Paris

——— (1956): *Platon: Les Lois* (VII–X), Paris

Dillon, J. (1989): "Tampering with the *Timaeus*: Ideological Emendations in Plato, with special reference to the *Timaeus*", *American Journal of Philology* 110, 50–72

——— (1992): "Plato and the Golden Age", *Hermathena* 153, 21–36

——— (1995): "The Neoplatonic Exegesis of the *Statesman* Myth", in Rowe (ed.), 364–74

Dixsaut, M. (ed.) (1999): *La fêlure du plaisir: Études sur le Philèbe de Platon*, Paris

Dodds, E. R. (1951): *The Greeks and the Irrational*, Berkeley

——— (1965): "Plato and the Irrational", *Journal of Hellenic Studies* 45, 16–25

Donini, P. L. (1988): "Il *Timeo*: unità del dialogo, verisimiglianza del discorso", *Elenchos* 9, 5–52

Dorter, K. (1994): *Form and Good in Plato's Eleatic Dialogues*, Berkeley

Dybikowski, J. (1970): "False Pleasures in the *Philebus*", *Phronesis* 15, 147–65

Dye, J. W. (1978): "Plato's Concept of Causal Explanation", *Tulane Studies in Philosophy* 27, 37–56

Easterling, H. J. (1967): "Causation in *Timaeus* and *Laws* X", *Eranos* 65, 25–38

Edelstein, L. and Kidd, I. (eds.) (1988): *Posidonius: The Fragments*, vol. 1, Cambridge, 2nd ed.

Eggers Lan, C. (1984): *Las nociones de tiempo y eternidad de Homero a Platón*, Mexico City

———— (1987): "Dios en la ontología del *Parménides*", in C. Eggers Lan (ed.), *Platón: Los diálogos tardíos*, Mexico City, 49–56

———— (1992): "Zeus e anima del mondo nel *Fedro* (246e–253c)", in Rossetti (ed.), 40–6

England, E. B. (1921): *The Laws of Plato*, vol. 2 (VII–XII), Manchester

Erler, M. (1995): "Kommentar zu Brisson und Dillon", in Rowe (ed.), 375–80

Fahrnkopf, R. (1977): "Forms in the *Philebus*", *Journal of the History of Philosophy* 15, 202–7

Ferrari, G. R. F. (1987): *Listening to the Cicadas: A Study of Plato's Phaedrus*, Cambridge

———— (1995): "Myth and Conservatism in Plato's *Statesman*", in Rowe (ed.), 389–97

Festugière, A. J. (1947): "Platon et l'Orient", *Revue de Philologie* 21, 5–45

———— (1949): *La révélation d'Hermès Trismégiste*, vol. 2: *Le dieu cosmique*, Paris

Fine, G. (1987): "Forms as Causes: Plato and Aristotle", in Graeser (ed.), 69–112

———— (1988a): "Owen's Progress", *Philosophical Review* 97, 373–99

———— (1988b): "Plato on Perception: A Reply to Professor Turnbull, 'Becoming and Intelligibility'", *Oxford Studies in Ancient Philosophy* suppl., 15–28

———— (ed.) (2000): *Plato*, Oxford

Finnis, J. (1980): *Natural Law and Natural Rights*, Oxford

Foot, P. (1978): *Virtues and Vices*, Berkeley

Fowler, H. (1925): *Plato: Philebus*, London

Fox, W. (1984): "Deep Ecology: A New Philosophy of Our Time?", *The Ecologist* 14, 194–200

Frede, D. (1985): "Rumpelstiltskin's Pleasures: True and False Pleasures in Plato's *Philebus*", *Phronesis* 30, 151–80

———— (1992): "Disintegration and Restoration: Pleasure and Pain in Plato's *Philebus*", in Kraut (ed.), 425–63

———— (1993): *Plato: Philebus*, Indianapolis

———— (1996a): "The Hedonist's Conversion: The Role of Socrates in the *Philebus*", in Gill and McCabe (eds.), 213–48

———— (1996b): "The Philosophical Economy of Plato's Psychology: Rationality and Common Concepts in the *Timaeus*", in M. Frede and G. Striker (eds.), *Rationality in Greek Thought*, Oxford, 29–58

———— (1997): *Platon: Philebos*, Göttingen

Frede, M. (1980): "The Original Notion of Cause", in M. Schofield et al. (eds.), *Doubt and Dogmatism. Studies in Hellenistic Epistemology*, Oxford, 217–49

———— (1988): "Being and Becoming in Plato", *Oxford Studies in Ancient Philosophy* suppl., 37–52

———— (1992): "Plato's Arguments and the Dialogue Form", in Klagge and Smith (eds.), 201–19

Friedlaender, P. (1969): *Plato*, vol. 3, English transl., London

Frutiger, P. (1930): *Les Mythes de Platon*, Paris

Furley, D. (1985): "The Rainfall Example in *Physics* ii.8", in Gotthelf (ed.), 177–82

Gadamer, H. G. (1975): *Truth and Method*, English transl., New York

—— (1980): *Dialogue and Dialectic: Eight Hermeneutical Studies on Plato*, English transl., New Haven

—— (1991): *Plato's Dialectical Ethics: Phenomenological Interpretations relating to the Philebus*, English transl., New Haven

Gaiser, K. (1963): *Platons Ungeschriebene Lehre*, Stuttgart

—— (1984): *Platone come scrittore filosofico*, Italian transl., Naples

Gallop, D. (1975): *Plato's Phaedo*, Oxford

Gaudin, C. (1990): "Automotricité et auto affection: un commentaire de Platon *Lois*, X 894d–895c", *Elenchos* 11, 169–85

Gerson, L. (1990): *God and Greek Philosophy*, London

Gill, C. (1979): "Plato and Politics: The *Critias* and the *Politicus*", *Phronesis* 24, 148–67

—— (1996): *Personality in Greek Epic, Tragedy, and Philosophy*, Oxford

—— (2000): "The Body's Fault? Plato's *Timaeus* on Psychic Illness", in Wright (ed.), 59–84

—— (2002): "Dialectic and the Dialogue Form", in Annas and Rowe (eds.), 145–71

—— and McCabe, M. M. (eds.) (1996): *Form and Argument in Late Plato*, Oxford

Gill, M. L. (1987): "Matter and Flux in Plato's *Timaeus*", *Phronesis* 32, 34–53

Goodpaster, K. E. (1982): "From Egoism to Environmentalism", in K. E. Goodpaster and K. M. Sayre (eds.), *Ethics and Problems of the 21st Century*, Notre Dame, 21–35

Gosling, J. (1975): *Plato: Philebus*, Oxford

—— and Taylor, C. (1982): *The Greeks on Pleasure*, Oxford

Gotthelf, A. (ed.) (1985): *Aristotle on Nature and Living Things*, Pittsburgh

—— and Lennox, J. G. (eds.) (1987): *Philosophical Issues in Aristotle's Biology*, Cambridge

Graeser, A. (ed.) (1987): *Mathematics and Metaphysics in Aristotle*, Berne

Gregory, A. (2000): *Plato's Philosophy of Science*, London

Griswold, C. L. Jr. (ed.) (1988): *Platonic Writings. Platonic Readings*, London

Grube, G. (1932): "The Composition of the World-Soul in *Tim.* 35a–b", *Classical Philology* 27, 80–2

—— (1980): *Plato's Thought*, with new introduction and bibliography by D. Zeyl, Indianapolis

Guthrie, W. K. C. (1978): *A History of Greek Philosophy*, vol. 5, Cambridge

—— (1981): *A History of Greek Philosophy*, vol. 6, Cambridge

Hackforth, R. (1936): "Plato's Theism", in Allen (ed.), 439–47

—— (1945): *Plato's Examination of Pleasure*, Cambridge

—— (1952): *Plato's Phaedrus*, Cambridge

—— (1959): "Plato's Cosmogony (*Tim.* 27d ff.)", *Classical Quarterly* 9, 17–22

Hahn, R. (1978): "On Plato's *Philebus* 15b1–8", *Phronesis* 23, 158–72

Hampton, C. (1987): "Pleasure, Truth and Being in Plato's *Philebus*: A Reply to Professor Frede", *Phronesis* 32, 253–62

—— (1990): *Pleasure, Knowledge and Being. An Analysis of Plato's Philebus*, Albany

Hankinson, R. J. (1998): *Cause and Explanation in Ancient Greek Thought*, Oxford
Harris, J. W. (1980): *Legal Philosophies*, London
Harte, V. (2002): *Plato on Parts and Wholes*, Oxford
Heath, T. (1913): *Aristarchus of Samos, the Ancient Copernicus: A History of Greek Astronomy to Aristarchus*, Oxford
Heinaman, R. (1990): "Aristotle and the Mind-Body Problem", *Phronesis* 35, 83–102
Heinze, R. (ed.) (1965): *Xenokrates: Fragmente*, Hildesheim
Herter, H. (1957): "Bewegung der Materie bei Platon", *Rheinisches Museum für Philologie* N. F. 100, 327–47
Hirsch, U. (1995): "*Mimeisthai* und verwandte Ausdrücke in Platons *Politikos*", in Rowe (ed.), 184–9
Hitchcock, D. (1985): "The Good in Plato's *Republic*", *Apeiron* 19, 65–92
Hobbs, A. (2000): *Plato and the Hero*, Cambridge
Howland, J. (1993): "The Eleatic Stranger's Condemnation of Socrates", *Polis* 12, 15–36
Hudson, S. (1986): *Human Character and Morality*, Boston
Huffman, C. A. (1993): *Philolaus of Croton: Pythagorean and Presocratic*, Cambridge
Hughes, J. D. (1982): "Gaia: Environmental Problems in Chthonic Perspective", *Environmental Review* 6, 92–104
Hume, D. (1739): *A Treatise of Human Nature*, ed. L. A. Selby-Bigge, Oxford, 1888
Hursthouse, R. (1997): "Virtue Ethics and the Emotions", in D. Statman (ed.), *Virtue Ethics*, Washington, D.C., 99–117
——— (1999): *On Virtue Ethics*, Oxford
Irwin, T. H. (1977): "Plato's Heracliteanism", *Philosophical Quarterly* 27, 1–13
——— (1988): "Reply to David L. Roochnik", in Griswold (ed.), 194–9
——— (1995): *Plato's Ethics*, New York
Jackson, H. (1882): "Plato's Later Theory of Ideas", *Journal of Philology* 10, 253–98
Jaeger, W. (1948): *Aristotle: Fundamentals of the History of His Development*, English transl. 2nd ed., Oxford
Johansen, T. (2000): "Body, Soul, and Tripartition in Plato's *Timaeus*", *Oxford Studies in Ancient Philosophy* 19, 87–111
——— (2004): *Plato's Natural Philosophy*, Cambridge
Jordan, R. W. (1983): *Plato's Arguments for Forms*, Cambridge
Kahn, C. (1960): *Anaximander and the Origins of Greek Cosmology*, New York
——— (1979): *The Art and Thought of Heraclitus*, Cambridge
——— (1981): "Some Philosophical Uses of 'To Be' in Plato", *Phronesis* 26, 105–34
——— (1985): "The Place of the Prime Mover in Aristotle's Teleology", in Gotthelf (ed.), 183–205
——— (1992): "Did Plato Write Socratic Dialogues?", in H. Benson (ed.), *Essays on the Philosophy of Socrates*, Oxford, 35–52
——— (1996): *Plato and the Socratic Dialogue*, Cambridge
——— (2004): "From *Republic* to *Laws*", *Oxford Studies in Ancient Philosophy* 26, 337–62

Katz, E. (2000): "Against the Inevitability of Anthropocentrism", in E. Katz et al. (eds.), *Beneath the Surface: Critical Essays in the Philosophy of Deep Ecology*, Cambridge, Mass., 17–42

Keyt, D. (1961): "Aristotle on Plato's Receptacle", *American Journal of Philology* 82, 291–300

Kirk, G. S., Raven, J. E., and Schofield, M. (1983): *The Presocratic Philosophers*, 2nd ed., Cambridge

Klagge, J. C. and Smith, D. (eds.) (1992): *Methods for Interpreting Plato and His Dialogues, Oxford Studies in Ancient Philosophy* suppl., Oxford

Knorr, W. R. (1990): "Plato and Eudoxus on the Planetary Motions", *Journal for the History of Astronomy* 21, 313–29

Kolb, D. A. (1983): "Pythagoras Bound: Limit and Unlimited in Plato's *Philebus*", *Journal of the History of Philosophy* 21, 497–511

Kraemer, H. (1982): *Platone e i fondamenti della metafisica*, Italian transl., Milan

Kraut, R. (1979): "Two Conceptions of Happiness", *Philosophical Review* 88, 167–97

———— (1984): *Socrates and the State*, Princeton

———— (1988): "Reply to Clifford Orwin", in Griswold (ed.), 177–82

———— (ed.) (1992): *The Cambridge Companion to Plato*, Cambridge

Kucharski, P. (1966): "Eschatologie et connaissance dans le *Timée*", in *La spéculation platonicienne*, Paris, 1971, 307–37

Kung, J. (1985): "Tetrahedra, Motion and Virtue", *Nous* 19, 17–27

———— (1989): "Mathematics and Virtue in Plato's *Timaeus*", in Anton and Preus (eds.), 309–39

Laks, A. (1990a): "Raison et plaisir: pour une caractérisation des *Lois* de Platon", in J. Mattéi (ed.), *Actes du Congrès de Nice*, Paris, 291–303

———— (1990b): "Legislation and Demiurgy: On the Relationship between Plato's *Republic* and *Laws*", *Classical Antiquity* 9, 209–29

———— (2000): "The *Laws*", in Rowe and Schofield (eds.), 258–92

Lane, M. (1995): "A New Angle on Utopia: The Political Theory of the *Statesman*", in Rowe (ed.), 276–91

———— (1998): *Method and Politics in Plato's Statesman*, Cambridge

Lee, E. N. (1976): "Reason and Rotation: Circular Movement as the Model of Mind (Nous) in Later Plato", in W. H. Werkmeister (ed.), *Facets of Plato's Philosophy, Phronesis* suppl. vol. 2, Assen, 70–102

Lennox, J. G. (1985): "Plato's Unnatural Teleology", in O'Meara (ed.), 195–218

———— (1997): "Material and Formal Natures in Aristotle's *De partibus animalium*", in W. Kullmann and S. Follinger (eds.), *Aristotelische Biologie, Intention, Methoden, Ergebnisse*, Stuttgart, 162–81

Leopold, A. (1949): "The Land Ethic", in *A Sand County Almanac*, New York, 201–26

Lewis, D. (1983): "New Work for a Theory of Universals", *Australasian Journal of Philosophy* 61, 343–77

Liddell, H., Scott, R. and Jones, H. (1968): *A Greek-English Lexicon*, repr. with suppl., Oxford (=LSJ)

Lloyd, G. E. R. (1968): "Plato as a Natural Scientist", *Journal of Hellenic Studies* 88, 78–92
———— (1991): "Plato on Mathematics and Nature, Myth and Science", in *Methods and Problems in Greek Science*, Cambridge, 333–51
Long, A. (1996): *Stoic Studies*, Cambridge
———— and Sedley, D. (1987): *The Hellenistic Philosophers*, vols. 1–2, Cambridge (=LS)
López, M. L. (1963): *El problema de Dios en Platón. La teología del Demiurgo*, Salamanca
Louden, R. (1992): *Morality and Moral Theory*, Oxford
Lovejoy, A. (1936): *The Great Chain of Being*, Cambridge, Mass.
Lovibond, S. (1991): "Plato's Theory of Mind", in S. Everson (ed.), *Companions to Ancient Thought* 2: *Psychology*, Cambridge, 35–55
MacClintock, S. (1961): "More on the Structure of the *Philebus*", *Phronesis* 6, 46–52
MacIntyre, A. (1981): *After Virtue*, Notre Dame
Mackenzie, M. M. (1981): *Plato on Punishment*, Berkeley
Malcolm, J. (1983): "Does Plato Revise his Ontology in *Sophist* 246c–249d?", *Archiv für Geschichte der Philosophie* 65, 115–27
Mansion, A. (1946): *Introduction a la Physique Aristotelicienne*, Louvain
Masi, G. (2001): *Platone: Il Timeo*, Bologna
Mattéi, J. F. (1988): "The Theater of Myth in Plato", in Griswold (ed.), 66–83
Matthews, F. (1991): *The Ecological Self*, London
Mayo, B. (1958): *Ethics and the Moral Life*, London
McCabe, M. M. (1992): "Myth, Allegory and Argument in Plato", in A. Barker and M. Warner (eds.), *The Language of the Cave*, Apeiron 25, Edmonton, 47–67
———— (1994): *Plato's Individuals*, Princeton
———— (2000): *Plato and His Predecessors*, Cambridge
McPherran, M. (1996): *The Religion of Socrates*, University Park
Meinwald, C. (1998): "Prometheus's Bounds: *Peras* and *Apeiron* in Plato's *Philebus*", in J. Gentzler (ed.), *Method in Ancient Philosophy*, Oxford, 164–80
Menn, S. (1992): "Aristotle and Plato on God as *Nous* and as the Good", *Review of Metaphysics* 45, 543–73
Migliori, M. (1993): *L'uomo fra piacere, intelligenza e Bene: Commentario storico-filosofico al "Filebo" di Platone*, Milan
Miller, M. H. Jr. (1980): *The Philosopher in Plato's Statesman*, The Hague
Mohr, R. (1977): "Plato, *Statesman* 284c-d: An 'Argument from the Sciences'", *Phronesis* 22, 232–4
———— (1978): "The Formation of the Cosmos in the *Statesman* Myth", *Phoenix* 32, 250–2
———— (1983): "*Philebus* 55c–62a and Revisionism", in Pelletier and King-Farlow (eds.), 165–70
———— (1985): *The Platonic Cosmology*, Leiden
———— (1989): "Plato's Theology Reconsidered: What the Demiurge Does", in Anton and Preus (eds.), 293–307
Mondolfo, R. (1934): *L'infinito nel pensiero dei Greci*, Florence
Montoneri, L. (1968): *Il problema del male nella filosofia di Platone*, Padova

Moore, G. E. (1903): *Principia Ethica*, Cambridge

Moravcsik, J. M. (1979): "Forms, Nature, and the Good in the *Philebus*", *Phronesis* 24, 81–104

Moreau, J. (1939): *L'Âme du Monde de Platon aux Stoïciens*, Hildesheim

Morgan, K. (2000): *Myth and Philosophy from the Presocratics to Plato*, Cambridge

Morrow, G. (1950): "Necessity and Persuasion in Plato's *Timaeus*", in Allen (ed.), 421–37

——— (1954): "The Demiurge in Politics: The *Timaeus* and the *Laws*", *Proceedings and Addresses of the American Philosophical Association* 27, 5–23

——— (1960): *Plato's Cretan City*, Princeton

Mourelatos, A. (1980): "Plato's 'Real Astronomy': *Republic* 527d–531d", in Anton (ed.), 33–73

——— (1981): "Astronomy and Kinematics in Plato's Project of Rationalistic Explanation", *Studies in History and Philosophy of Science* 12, 1–32

Mugnier, R. (1930): *Le sense du mot* THEIOS *chez Platon*, Paris

Naddaf, G. (1993): *L'origine et l'evolution du concept grec du phusis*, Lewiston

——— (1994): "Mind and Progress in Plato", *Polis* 12, 122–33

——— (1997): "Plato and the *Peri Phuseôs* Tradition", in Calvo and Brisson (eds.), 27–36

Naess, A. (1973): "The Shallow and the Deep, Long-Range Ecology Movement: A Summary", *Inquiry* 16, 95–100

Nagel, T. (1979): "Panpsychism", in *Mortal Questions*, New York, 181–95

Nehamas, A. (1975): "Plato on the Imperfection of the Sensible World", *American Philosophical Quarterly* 12, 105–17

Nehamas, A. and Woodruff, P. (1995): *Plato: Phaedrus*, Indianapolis

Nicholson, G. (1999): *Plato's Phaedrus*, Indiana

Nightingale, A. (1996): "Plato on the Origins of Evil: The *Statesman* Myth Reconsidered", *Ancient Philosophy* 16, 65–91

Notomi, N. (1999): *The Unity of Plato's Sophist*, Cambridge

Nussbaum, M. (1986): *The Fragility of Goodness. Luck and Ethics in Greek Tragedy and Philosophy*, Cambridge

——— and Rorty, A. (eds.) (1992): *Essays on Aristotle's De Anima*, Oxford

O'Meara, D. J. (ed.) (1985): *Platonic Investigations*, Washington, D.C.

Osborne, C. (1988): "Topography in the *Timaeus*: Plato and Augustine on Mankind's Place in the Natural World", *Proceedings of the Cambridge Philological Society* 214 (N.S. 34), 104–13

——— (1996): "Space, Time, Shape, and Direction: Creative Discourse in the *Timaeus*", in Gill and McCabe (eds.), 179–211

Ostenfeld, E. (1982): *Forms, Matter and Mind: Three Strands in Plato's Metaphysics*, The Hague

——— (1987): *Ancient Greek Psychology*, Aarhus

——— (1990): "Self Motion, Tripartition and Embodiment", *Classica et Mediaevalia* 41, 43–9

Owen, G. E. L. (1953): "The Place of the *Timaeus* in Plato's Dialogues", in Allen (ed.), 313–38

——— (1973): "Plato on the Undepictable", in E. Lee et al. (eds.), *Exegesis and Argument*, Assen, 349–61

Parry, R. (2002): "The Soul in *Laws* X and Disorderly Motion in *Timaeus*", *Ancient Philosophy* 22, 289–301

Patterson, R. (1981): "The Unique Worlds of the *Timaeus*", *Phoenix* 35, 105–19
———— (1985): *Image and Reality in Plato's Metaphysics*, Indianapolis

Pelletier, F. and King-Farlow, J. (eds.), *New Essays on Plato, Canadian Journal of Philosophy* suppl. vol. 9, Guelph

Penner, T. (1970): "False Anticipatory Pleasures", *Phronesis* 15, 166–78

Perl, E. (1998): "The Demiurge and the Forms: A Return to the Ancient Interpretation of Plato's *Timaeus*", *Ancient Philosophy* 18, 81–92

Post, J. (1987): *The Faces of Existence*, Ithaca

Preus, A. (1975): *Science and Philosophy in Aristotle's Biological Works*, New York

Priest, S. (1991): *Theories of the Mind*, New York

Prior, A. N. (1960): "The Autonomy of Ethics", *Australasian Journal of Philosophy* 38, 199–206

Prior, W. J. (1985): *Unity and Development in Plato's Metaphysics*, London

Putnam, H. (1999): *The Threefold Cord. Mind, Body, and World*, New York

Reale, G. (1997): "Plato's Doctrine of the Origin of the World, with special reference to the *Timaeus*", in Calvo and Brisson (eds.), 149–64

Reeve, C. D. C. (1988): *Philosopher-Kings*, Princeton

Reverdin, O. (1945): *La religion de la cité platonicienne*, Paris

Reydams-Schils, G. (1999): *Demiurge and Providence*, Turnhout

Rist, J. M. (1964): *Eros and Psyche*, Toronto

Ritter, C. (1933): *The Essence of Plato's Philosophy*, English transl., New York

Roberts, J. (1987): "Plato on the Causes of Wrongdoing in the *Laws*", *Ancient Philosophy* 7, 23–37

Robin, L. (1908): *La théorie platonicienne de l'amour*, Paris
———— (1935): *Platon*, Paris

Robinson, R. (1953): *Plato's Earlier Dialectic*, 2nd ed., Oxford

Robinson, T. M. (1967): "Demiurge and World-Soul in Plato's *Politicus*", *American Journal of Philology* 88, 57–66
———— (1969): "Deux problèmes de la psychologie cosmique platonicienne", *Revue Philosophique* 159, 247–53
———— (1970): *Plato's Psychology*, Toronto
———— (1979): "The Argument of *Timaeus* 27d ff.", *Phronesis* 24, 105–9
———— (1986): "The *Timaeus* on Types of Duration", *Illinois Classical Studies* 11, 143–51
———— (1993): "The World as Art-Object: Science and the Real in Plato's *Timaeus*", *Illinois Classical Studies* 18, 99–111
———— (1995): *Plato's Psychology*, 2nd ed., Toronto
———— (2000): "Mind-Body Dualism in Plato", in J. P. Wright and P. Potter (eds.), *Psyche and Soma*, Oxford, 37–55

Rodier, G. (1926): *Études de Philosophie Grecque*, Paris

Rosen, S. (1979): "Plato's Myth of the Reversed Cosmos", *Review of Metaphysics* 33, 59–85

Ross, W. D. (1951): *Plato's Theory of Ideas*, Oxford

Rossetti, L. (ed.) (1992): *Understanding the Phaedrus*, Sankt Augustin

Rowe, C. (1992a): "La data relativa del *Fedro*", in Rossetti (ed.), 31–9
———— (1992b): "On Reading Plato", *Méthexis* 5, 53–68

———— (1995): *Plato: Statesman*, Warminster
———— (ed.) (1995): *Reading the Statesman*, Sankt Augustin
———— (1996): "The *Politicus*: Structure and Form", in Gill and McCabe (eds.), 153–78
———— (1999a): *Plato: Statesman*, Indianapolis
———— (1999b): "La forme dramatique et la structure du *Philèbe*", in Dixsaut (ed.), 9–25
———— (2000): "The *Politicus* and Other Dialogues", in Rowe and Schofield (eds.), 233–57
———— and Schofield, M. (eds.) (2000): *The Cambridge History of Greek and Roman Political Thought*, Cambridge
Runciman, W. G. (1962): *Plato's Later Epistemology*, Cambridge
Runia, D. (1997): "The Literary and Philosophical Status of Timaeus' *Proemium*", in Calvo and Brisson (eds.), 101–18
Russell, D. C. (2004): "Virtue as "Likeness to God" in Plato and Seneca", *Journal of the History of Philosophy* 42, 241–60
Saunders, T. J. (1973): "Penology and Eschatology in Plato's *Timaeus* and *Laws*", *Classical Quarterly* 23, 232–44
———— (1991): *Plato's Penal Code*, Oxford
———— (1992): "Plato's Later Political Thought", in Kraut (ed.), 464–92
Sayre, K. (1983): *Plato's Late Ontology*, Princeton
———— (1992): "A Maieutic View of Five Late Dialogues", in Klagge and Smith (eds.), 221–43
Schofield, M. (1991): *The Stoic Idea of the City*, Cambridge
———— (1997): "The Disappearance of the Philosopher-King", *Proceedings of the Boston Area Collogium in Ancient Philosophy* 13, 213–41
———— and Striker, G. (eds.) (1986): *The Norms of Nature*, Cambridge
Scodel, H. R. (1987): *Diairesis and Myth in Plato's Statesman*, Göttingen
Sedley, D. (1989): "Teleology and Myth in the *Phaedo*", *Proceedings of the Boston Area Colloquium in Ancient Philosophy* 5, 359–83
———— (1991): "Is Aristotle's Teleology Anthropocentric?", *Phronesis* 36, 179–96
———— (1996): "Three Platonist Interpretations of the *Theaetetus*", in Gill and McCabe (eds.), 79–103
———— (1997): "Becoming Like God in the *Timaeus* and Aristotle", in Calvo and Brisson (eds.), 327–39
———— (1998): "Platonic Causes", *Phronesis* 43, 114–32
———— (2000): "The Ideal of Godlikeness", in Fine (ed.), 791–810
———— (2002): "The Origins of the Stoic God", in D. Frede and A. Laks (eds.), *Traditions of Theology*, Leiden
———— (2004): *The Midwife of Platonism*, Oxford
Seligman, P. (1974): *Being and Not-Being: An Introduction to Plato's Sophist*, The Hague
Sherman, N. (1999): "Character Development and Aristotelian Virtue", in D. Carr and J. Steutel (eds.), *Virtue Ethics and Moral Education*, London, 35–48
Shields, C. (1993): "Some Recent Approaches to Aristotle's *De Anima*", in *Aristotle: De Anima Books II and III (with passages from book I)*, transl. by D. W. Hamlyn and with a report by C. Shields, Oxford, 157–87

Shiner, R. (1974): *Knowledge and Reality in Plato's Philebus*, Assen
—— (1983): "Knowledge in *Philebus* 55c–62a: A Response", in Pelletier and King-Farlow (eds.), 171–83
Shoemaker, S. (1984): *Identity, Cause, and Mind*, Cambridge
Shorey, P. (1935): *Plato: The Republic*, vol. 2, London
Silverman, A. (2002): *The Dialectic of Essence: A Study of Plato's Metaphysics*, Princeton
Simpson, P. (1987): *Goodness and Nature: A Defence of Ethical Naturalism*, Dordrecht
—— (1997): "Contemporary Virtue Ethics and Aristotle", in Statman (ed.), 260–85
Skemp, J. B. (1942): *The Theory of Motion in Plato's Later Dialogues*, Cambridge
—— (1952): *Plato's Statesman*, London
Solmsen, F. (1942): *Plato's Theology*, Ithaca
—— (1962): "Hesiodic Motifs in Plato", *Entretiens* VII, Vandoeuvres-Genève, 173–211
—— (1983): "Plato and the Concept of the Soul (*Psuchê*): Some Historical Perspectives", *Journal of the History of Ideas* 44, 355–67
Sorabji, R. (1983): *Time, Creation and the Continuum*, London
—— (1993): *Animal Minds and Human Morals*, London
—— (2000): *Emotion and Peace of Mind*, Oxford
—— (2003): "The Mind-Body Relation in the Wake of Plato's *Timaeus*", in G. Reydams-Schils (ed.), *Plato's Timaeus as Cultural Icon*, Notre Dame
Sosa, E. (1980): "The Varieties of Causation", in Sosa and Tooley (eds.), 234–42
—— and Tooley, M. (eds.) (1993): *Causation*, Oxford
Stalley, R. F. (1983): *An Introduction to Plato's Laws*, Oxford
Statman, D. (ed.) (1997): *Virtue Ethics*, Edinburgh
Steel, C. (2001): "The Moral Purpose of the Human Body: A Reading of *Timaeus* 69–72", *Phronesis* 46, 105–28
Stewart, J. A. (1960): *The Myths of Plato*, 2nd ed., London
Strange, S. (2000): "The Double Explanation in the *Timaeus*", in Fine (ed.), 399–417
Striker, G. (1970): *Peras und Apeiron*, Hypomnemata 30, Göttingen
—— (1991): "Following Nature: A Study in Stoic Ethics", *Oxford Studies in Ancient Philosophy* 9, 1–73
—— (1996): "Origins of the Concept of Natural Law", in *Essays in Hellenistic Epistemology and Ethics*, Cambridge, 209–20
Tarán, L. (1971): "The Creation Myth in Plato's *Timaeus*", in J. P. Anton and G. Kustas (eds.), *Essays in Greek Philosophy*, New York, 372–407
—— (1979): "Perpetual Duration and Atemporal Eternity in Parmenides and Plato", *The Monist* 62, 43–53
Taylor, A. E. (1926): *Plato. The Man and His Work*, London
—— (1928): *A Commentary on Plato's Timaeus*, Oxford
—— (1938): "The Polytheism of Plato: An Apologia", *Mind* 47, 180–99
Taylor, P. (1986): *Respect for Nature*, Princeton
Teloh, H. (1981): *The Development of Plato's Metaphysics*, University Park
Theiler, W. (1925): *Zur Geschichte der teleologischen Naturbetrachtung bis auf Aristoteles*, Zurich
Tigerstedt, E. N. (1977): *Interpreting Plato*, Uppsala

Trevaskis, J. R. (1967): "Division and its Relation to Dialectic and Ontology", *Phronesis* 12, 118–29

Turnbull, R. (1988): "Becoming and Intelligibility", *Oxford Studies in Ancient Philosophy* suppl., 1–14

Vallejo, A. (1997): "No, It's Not a Fiction", in Calvo and Brisson (eds.), 141–8

Van Riel, G. (1999): "Le plaisir est-il la réplétion d'un manque? La définition du plaisir (32a–36c) et la physiologie des plaisirs faux (42c–44a)", in Dixsaut (ed.), 299–314

Verdenius, W. J. (1954): "Platons Gottesbegriff", *Entretiens* I, Vandoeuvres-Genève, 241–93

Vernant, J. P. (1985): *Mythe et pensée chez les Grecs*, nouvelle ed., Paris

Vidal-Naquet, P. (1978): "Plato's Myth of the *Statesman*: The Ambiguities of The Golden Age and of History", *Journal of Hellenic Studies* 98, 132–41

Vlastos, G. (1939): "The Disorderly Motion in the *Timaeus*", in Allen (ed.), 379–99

—— (1957): "Socratic Knowledge and Platonic "Pessimism"", *Philosophical Review* 66, 226–38

—— (1964): "Creation in the *Timaeus*: Is it a Fiction?", in Allen (ed.), 401–19

—— (1965): "Degrees of Reality in Plato", in R. Bambrough (ed.), *New Essays on Plato and Aristotle*, London, 1–19

—— (1975): *Plato's Universe*, Seattle

—— (1980): "The Role of Observation in Plato's Conception of Astronomy", in Anton (ed.), 1–31

—— (1981a): *Platonic Studies*, 2nd ed., Princeton

—— (1981b): "Reasons and Causes in the *Phaedo*", in Vlastos (1981a), 76–110

—— (1981c): "Justice and Happiness in the *Republic*", in Vlastos (1981a), 111–39

—— (1988): "Socrates", *Proceedings of the British Academy* 74, 89–111

Waterfield, R. A. H. (1980): "The Place of the *Philebus* in Plato's Dialogues", *Phronesis* 25, 270–305

—— (1982): *Plato: Philebus*, Harmondsworth

Westerink, L. G. (ed.) (1962): *Anonymous Prolegomena to Platonic Philosophy*, Amsterdam

White, D. (1993): *Rhetoric and Reality in Plato's Phaedrus*, Albany

Whittaker, J. (1969): "*Timaeus* 27d ff.", *Phoenix* 23, 181–5

—— (1973): "Textual comments on *Timaeus* 27c–d", *Phronesis* 27, 387–91

Williams, B. (1959): "Pleasure and Belief", *Proceedings of the Aristotelian Society* 33, 57–72

Witt, C. (1992): "Dialectic, Motion, and Perception: *De Anima*, Book I", in Nussbaum and Rorty (eds.), 169–183

Wright, L. (1976): *Teleological Explanations*, London

Wright, R. (ed.) (2000): *Reason and Necessity. Essays on Plato's Timaeus*, London

—— (2000): "Myth, Science and Reason in the *Timaeus*", in Wright (ed.), 1–22

Zaslavsky, R. (1981): *Platonic Myth and Platonic Writing*, Washington, D.C.

Zeyl, D. J. (2000): *Plato: Timaeus*, Indianapolis

Index Locorum

Plato

Apology
20b: 239n40
20d: 239n40
20d–e: 239n40
22c–e: 190
22c–23b: 239n40
23b: 190
25e: 181
26d: 218n13, 249n14
28e: 116
29d–30d: 117
30a: 190
30c6–d5: 219n30
38a: 117
41b–c: 143
41c–d: 219n30

Charmides
167b: 239n40
173e ff.: 239n40

Cratylus
385e ff.: 254n4
397c–d: 218n13
400a: 48
400a8–10: 207n36

Critias
107a–b: 63

107c–d: 219n27
107d–108a: 63
109b–c: 255n19
109c4–d2: 261n73
109d ff.: 149
110c–111d: 67
110e3–111a2: 261n73
111b–d: 261n73
111c–d: 261n73
112e: 25, 68
112e2–6: 261n73
120e5: 67
120e–121a: 67
120e ff.: 64
121b–c: 65, 68
121c: 68

Euthyphro
6a–c: 26

Gorgias
461c: 77
466b: 259n53
470e9–11: 259n56
478d7–8: 259n56
480b1: 248n3
482b–c: 17
488a2–4: 248n3
488b–489b: 197n9
490e9–11: 7

Gorgias (*cont.*)
491b5–8: 7
497d–499b: 111
503d–e: 87
503e–504a: 34
504b5: 199n32
504c2: 199n32
507e6–508a4: 8
508a: 199n32
509e5–7: 248n3
510a–e: 223n64
512d–513c: 223n64
518e–519a: 261n73
522e: 200n47
523a: 200n44
523a2–3: 200n44
527a: 200n44
527b–e: 259n56
527d: 77
527d7: 7

Laches
188d: 76

Laws
625c–628e: 159
644d–645b: 259n54
652b–653c: 253n3
654e: 190
654e–655a: 211n68
662d–663d: 237n22
667a: 263n8
677a ff.: 149
693b–c: 253n3
701c2: 157
704a–705c: 242n12
707d: 256n22
709a–c: 242n12
709a ff.: 219n31
709c1–3: 219n31
713c–714a: 154
713e6: 154
713e6–714a2: 154
713e–714a: 253n2
713e–715b: 263n4
714a: 162, 251n35
714b–715b: 253n3

716c: 192, 254n4
716c–d: 221n44
720e: 263n3
720e ff.: 253n2
720e–721d: 263n3
721b–c: 233n67, 259n56
721e ff.: 253n2
722a–723b: 253n1
727a–728c: 181
728b: 181
730d–e: 68
731b–d: 68
731c2–5: 248n3
732e–734e: 237n22
733a–734d: 263n3
733e1: 263n3
740a5–7: 253n47, 261n73
740e–741a: 261n71
747b5–6: 223n57
761a–b: 207n40
769d–e: 263n8
788c ff.: 67
789c–d: 67
797e–798a: 67
803c: 259n54
807d: 67
809c–d: 223n57
811c–e: 254n7
817e: 223n58
817e–818a: 120, 253n1
818a: 223n58
818a1–2: 12
818a ff.: 240n45
818a–b: 223n59
818b: 261n71
818c: 120
818c2: 223n59
818d6–8: 223n59
819a3–6: 223n59
819a–b: 253n1
821a: 177, 262n80
821a2: 217n4, 259nn45,47
821a–b: 204n18
821a–822c: 175
821b6: 148, 259n45
821c7: 148
821c–d: 148

821c–e: 76
822a: 56, 175
822a4–8: 175
822a6–8.: 56
822a7: 148
822a–b: 248n8
828d4–5: 255n22
828d5–829c1: 256n22
829a: 67
829a–b: 220n33
846d–847b: 253n1
853b–c: 183
853c–854a: 253n1
854b–e: 183
860d: 248n3
860d–862c: 218n21
863a ff.: 185
864a: 185
870d–e: 233n67, 259n56
872d–e: 233n67, 259n56
875c–d: 11, 252n38
885b: 183, 254n5
885b4–9: 254n6
886a: 257n34
886a–b: 254n5
887b–888b: 163
887c–899d: 163
887e: 218n13
888a–b: 168
888b: 240n44
888d ff.: 240n4
888e: 207n41
888e ff.: 246n45
889a5: 164
889a–c: 164
889b2: 164
889b–c: 164
889b–e: 163
889c: 100, 164, 208n41, 232n65
889c1–2: 164, 207n41
889e–890a: 253n3
890a: 193, 260n61
890b ff.: 76
890d: 193
891a: 254n7
891c: 164, 254n8
891c–e: 255n21

891c–892a: 246n45
891e5–7: 169
892a: 166, 168
892a3: 254n12
892a5: 168
892a–b: 167
892a–c: 164
892b: 164
892b–c: 207n41
892c2–3: 164
892c3–7: 164
892c4: 168
892c5: 255n18
893b: 165, 248n6
893b8–c1: 165
893b–896d: 170
893b–899d: 179
893c1–2: 45, 165, 169
893c–894a: 254n10
893c–896e: 257n30
893c–d: 257n32
894b: 168, 170
894b8–9: 165
894b9–10: 169
894b9–c1: 165
894b10: 167
894b–896d: 173
894b ff.: 51
894c: 168, 182
894c3–4: 165, 254n10
894c7: 254n10
894d1–2: 254n12
894d2: 165
894e4–7: 165
894e4–895a3: 254n10
894e–895a: 166
895a: 188
895a6–b1: 165, 255n21
895b: 41, 48
895b1: 165
895b3: 165, 213n89
895b4: 165
895b5: 165, 169
895b6: 165
895b7: 165
895c: 166, 168
895c11–12: 168, 170

Laws (cont.)
895d–896a: 230n49
895d–896b: 51
895e–896a: 151
896a: 168
896a1–4: 166
896a6–8: 164
896a7–8: 168, 169
896a–b: 209n52, 211n72, 213n90,
  250n25, 254n9
896a–c: 150
896b1: 213n89, 254n10
896b3: 165, 169
896b7–8: 166
896b8: 256n24
896b–c: 166, 201n54, 259n50
896c1–3: 170
896c9–d1: 166
896c–d: 166
896c ff.: 258n42
896d: 172
896d5–8: 171
896d5–e6: 176, 185
896d8: 168
896d10–e2: 170, 171, 174
896d10–897b4: 178
896d–898c: 175
896d–e: 188
896e: 257n30
896e1: 262n78
896e4: 172, 176
896e5–6: 172
896e6: 185
896e8: 170, 176, 179, 255n19
896e8–9: 173, 178
896e8–897a2: 259n51
896e8–897a4: 50
896e8–897b4: 172, 174
896e–897b: 48, 172, 173, 175, 187,
  214n95
897–898: 212n75
897a2–3: 173
897a4–b1: 255n19
897a7–b1: 166
897a–b: 176, 216n106
897b1: 167, 170
897b1–2: 258n39

897b1–3: 258n38, 259n52
897b2: 256n27, 259n47
897b3: 178, 258n40
897b7: 173, 257n31, 258n41
897b7–8: 173
897b7–c1: 174
897b8–c1: 180
897b–899b: 262n80
897c: 151
897c4–d1: 174
897c5–6: 44, 212n75
897c ff.: 43
897d1: 172, 175, 185
898a: 151
898a5: 212n75
898a8–b1: 174
898b5–8: 175
898c: 48, 258n39, 260n59
898c3: 175
898c6–9: 174
898c7–8: 255n19, 257n31
898d: 173
898d3–4: 257n31
898d9–10: 257n31
898d9–e2: 170, 250n24
898d11: 256n25
898d–e: 215n102, 256n25
898e5: 255n19
898e–899a: 169, 212n82
899a3: 255n19
899a9: 255n19
899a–b: 177
899b: 48, 150, 175, 258n39
899b5: 255n19, 257n31
899b5–7: 173, 177, 210n65, 256n26
899b7–8: 207n36
899b7–9: 239n32
899b8: 262n78
899b9: 256n24
899d: 179, 188
899d–905d: 163
899d–907b: 178
899d–e: 178, 181
899e–900b: 171
900b1–3: 260n59
900b6–c1: 260n59
900c8–901c6: 206n30

900c ff.: 206n30
900d: 177
900d1–3: 260n59
900d2: 173, 177, 210n65, 256n26
900d2–3: 258n39
900d5–7: 210n65, 256n26
900d5–9: 177
900d5–e2: 178
900e: 178
900e6: 178, 186
901a: 256n28
901c–903a: 175, 258n39
901d: 215n98
901d7–8: 261n71
901e1–902b3: 256n26
901e ff.: 210n65
902a6–b3: 177
902b4: 180
902b4–5: 178
902b8–9: 188
902c–903a: 261n71
902d–e: 203n11
902e7–8: 173, 210n65
902e8: 256n26
903a10–b2: 259nn56,59
903b: 149
903b1: 182
903b4–6: 188
903b4–9: 178
903b5: 261n71
903b7: 207n36
903b–c: 178, 186, 187
903b–d: 261n76
903c1–2: 179
903c3–5: 187
903c7–d1: 187
903c–d: 188
903d: 178, 182, 255n22, 259n54
903d1–3: 262n79
903d2–3: 187, 189
903d3–e1: 180
903d7: 255n22
903d–906c: 176
903e: 182
904a: 182
904a6: 207n36
904a–e: 178

904b: 149
904b2–3: 179
904b4–5: 180, 262n79
904b7: 255n22
904b8: 182, 255n22
904b8–c2: 179, 180
904b–d: 179
904c6–7: 179, 180
904c7: 187
904c8–9: 180
904c–d: 182
904c–e: 262n76
904d–e: 182
904e: 182
904e4: 180, 256n28, 257n31
904e5–7: 181
904e7–905a1: 181
904e–905a: 180
905b–c: 181
905d–907b: 163
905d ff.: 178
905e2: 207n36
905e2–3: 258n39
906a: 188, 260n64
906a2: 256n28
906a2–b3: 184
906a3: 260n65
906a7–8: 259n49
906a–b: 184, 186
906b3–c2: 184
906c1–2: 260n67
906c3–6: 184
906c3–5: 186
906c5: 258n42
907a: 184
907b5–7: 254n6
920a: 253n1
957c: 162
966c ff.: 76
966d–967a: 46
966d–967e: 175
966d–e: 174, 240n4
966e: 231n54
966e2–4: 257n33
966e–967a: 246n45, 262n79
966e–968a: 76
967a–d: 257n32

Laws (cont.)
967b5–6: 207n36
967c2 ff.: 257n34
967d: 48, 258n39
967d–968a: 240n45
967d4–968a4: 76
967d–e: 240n4
967e1: 46

Lysis
214a–215c: 223n64

Meno
97e–98a: 198n28

Parmenides
131a–e: 81
132b–c: 218n15
133c–134a: 69, 254n12
133c–134e: 46,
    209n58
133e5: 46
134b–c: 69

Phaedo
65a10: 50, 157
66b–c: 198n14
66b ff.: 223n65
66c: 157
66c1: 50
66d6–7: 157
67d: 198n14
71e13–72a2: 251n30
71e–72b: 251n30
72e ff.: 158
76a–77a: 158
76c: 211n68
78c6: 250n23
78d2–3: 250n23
78d4: 250n23
79a6: 230n49
79a6–7: 227n23
79b16: 221n42
79b–c: 211n68
79d3: 221n42
79d–80a: 71
79e1: 221n42

80b1: 71
80b3: 221n42
80e–81a: 74
81a5: 71
82d–e: 198n14
84b2: 221n42
97b–99d: 191
97c1–2: 207n36
98b–c: 8
98e–99a: 39
99a–b: 216n105
99b3–4: 208n46
99c1–2: 8, 240n4
100b ff.: 39

Phaedrus
229b–230a: 200n49
245c: 213n90
245c9: 50, 213n89
245c–e: 39, 239n32
245c–246a: 167
245c ff.: 50, 209n52, 211n72, 213n90,
    250n25
245d3: 168
245e: 98
245e2–3: 216n104
245e4–6: 50, 167
245e5: 256n24
246a ff.: 207n39
246b6: 167, 216n104
246b6–c2: 239n32
246c3–6: 216n104
246c4: 255n18
246c7–d2: 216n104
246e4–5: 207n36
247a: 221n48
247a7: 210n65, 238n31
247c7: 150
247c–d: 210n65, 221n48
247c–e: 218n15
248a: 221n48
249b–c: 158
249c6: 218n15
250b: 221n48
250b8–c4: 216n104
250c: 216n104
250e–251a: 216n104

252d–253c: 158
253b–c: 221n44
257b: 216n104
264c: 35, 201n59
266b: 224n4
270c–d: 255n18

Philebus
11b7–c1: 122
11c1–2: 112
11c2: 112
11d: 121
11d4: 230n45
11d4–6: 80, 111, 122
11d5: 75
11d–12a: 79
11d–e: 101, 108
11e2: 80, 111
12a7: 80, 237n25
12b–14b: 81
12c–13d: 235n13
13e–14a: 222n55
14–31: 79
14a: 119
14b: 17, 118
14c8: 81
14c ff.: 119
14c–15a: 94
14c–19b: 80, 82
14d ff.: 82
14e1: 82
15a: 81, 90, 229n38
15a7: 82
15a–b: 82
15b: 82, 83, 94
15b1–8: 81
16b5: 81, 82
16b6: 81
16b–17a: 119
16c2–3: 81, 83
16c7–10: 82
16c9: 225n13
16d: 82
17a: 81, 82
17a–18d: 225n13
17b ff.: 87
19b: 222n55

19b3: 84
19c2–3: 118
20d: 119, 219n24
20d4: 84, 122
20d8: 122
20e–21e: 84
21c: 121
21d–e: 110
22a5: 121
22b4–8: 121
22b5: 115
22b6: 119
22b6–8: 119, 248n3
22c5–6: 238n30
22d: 84
22d2: 229n41
22d4–8: 229n41
23a3: 226n23
23b–c: 226n15
23c: 226n16
23c12: 230n46
23c–d: 226n23
23c4: 86, 226n17
23c4–5: 85
23c9–12: 225n15
23c–30c: 121
23c–31a: 84, 85
23c–65a: 80
23c–d: 226n23
23c ff.: 108, 121, 225nn8,10,13
23d: 226n23
23d1: 227n27, 229n42
23d7: 92
23e5: 226n23
24a2: 228n29
24b8: 86, 107, 108
24c1–d7: 88
24c–d: 86, 88
24d: 113
24d2: 227n27
24d4: 80, 86, 88, 94, 108, 109
24d4–5: 90
24d5: 88, 108, 236n15
24e7: 87
24e7–8: 86, 94, 108
24e–25a: 86
25a3: 226n23

Philebus (cont.)
25a6–b2: 88, 108
25a6–b3: 108
25a–b: 107
25b: 248n6
25c5–6: 227n26
25c10–11: 86
25c–d: 86
25d11–e2: 88, 90, 91
25e: 92
25e1: 250n18
25e1–2: 228n34
25e7–8: 92
25e–26a: 91
26a: 86, 87, 89
26a2–4: 92
26a4: 107
26a7: 227n28
26a–b: 92
26b: 88, 92
26b1–2: 88, 89
26b2: 108, 228n29
26b5–6: 92
26b–c: 230n45
26d: 89, 93
26d8: 92, 93, 94, 230n49
26d8–9: 92, 93
26d9: 88, 91, 108, 228n34
26e3: 94
26e6–8: 232n61
26e–27b: 214n91, 232n59
27a1: 94
27a5: 232n61
27a8–9: 97
27a11: 227n27
27a–b: 150
27b: 93
27b1: 90, 99, 113, 122, 232n61
27b8: 228n29
27b8–9: 92, 93, 230n49, 236n15
27b9: 94
27d: 230n42
27d9: 88, 228n34, 250n18
27e: 86, 87, 231n52, 235n13
27e1: 236n13
27e7–9: 80
27e–28a: 234n2

28a3–4: 235n13
28c7: 207n36, 232n64
28c7–8: 226n17
28c–e: 80
28c–30c: 158
28c–30d: 232n58
28c ff.: 229n41, 240n4
28d: 208n41, 240n4
28d5–6: 226n17
28d5–9: 100, 101
28d7: 101
28d–29a: 100, 101
28d–e: 97, 173, 232n59, 246n45
28e: 46, 101, 214n91
28e3: 207n36, 257n34
28e–29a: 174
29a4: 101
29a–b: 201n54
29a–30a: 97, 255n19
29a–30b: 121
29a–30d: 115
29b6–c3: 233n70
29b9–10: 226n17
29b ff.: 121
29b–c: 226n17
29c1–2: 226n17
29c2–3: 92
29c6: 226n17
29d: 98
29d1: 201n54
29d2: 226n17
29d6: 201n54
29e1–6: 226n17
29e2–3: 98
29e–30a: 149
30a: 121, 189, 226n17
30a3–6: 226n17
30a3–7: 255n19
30a5–7: 100
30a6: 92
30a9–b7: 99
30a9–c7: 92
30a10: 92, 99
30a10–b2: 100
30a–b: 232n59
30a–c: 226n17, 240n45
30a–d: 80, 173

30b1: 99
30b4: 233n70
30b5: 99, 121, 226n17
30b6: 112, 233n70
30b7: 92, 99, 234n71
30c: 232n59
30c4: 99, 101, 226n17
30c5: 99, 116
30c5–7: 100, 214n91
30c9–10: 43, 99, 100
30c–d: 97, 150, 256n28
30d: 178, 204n18
30d1–2: 114, 115, 232n64
30d8: 97, 207n36, 226n17
30e1: 99
31a: 86, 107
31b–32b: 105
31b ff.: 84
31c: 230n46
31e–32a: 114
32a9–b1: 92
32b–40e: 105
32d9–e2: 114
33b6–9: 238n30
33b7: 115
33b8–c4: 114
33b10: 238n31
33c ff.: 114
33d–34a: 239n36
34a: 236n16
35a–d: 100
35d: 98
40c1–2: 112
41a–42c: 105, 107
41b–42c: 106
41d: 105
42b: 105
42b–c: 106
42c–44a: 105, 106
42d–e: 96
43a: 95, 231n53
43a3: 80
43a8: 96
43b–c: 236n16
43c–e: 96
43d4–5: 236n16
44a–50e: 105

44c–d: 109
45a1: 111
45a1–2: 111
45a4–5: 111
45a7: 111
45a7–b10: 111
45a ff.: 105, 252n39
45b8–9: 111
45c–e: 109
45d: 113
45d–e: 101, 105
45e: 106
45e9–10: 111
46a: 109
46d: 109
46d7–e3: 111
47d–e: 116, 233n66
48b ff.: 238n31
50b–c: 116
50b–d: 233n66
51a6–9: 111
51b: 235n7, 236n16
51b1: 236n17
51b3–7: 108, 235n12
51b6: 235n12
51b–52a: 226n22
51b–52b: 116
51b ff.: 114
51c1–d3: 235n12
51c6–d1: 235n8
51d6–9: 235n12
51e1–4: 235n12
51e7–52a1: 236n16
51e7–52b8: 235n12, 236n16
51e–52a: 116
52a2–3: 88
52a–b: 108
52b: 115, 118
52b7–8: 116
52c: 105
52c1–d1: 108, 115
52c2–5: 232n58
52d1: 236n17
52d7: 111
52e3: 110, 116
53b10–c2: 111, 112
53c: 107

Philebus (cont.)
53c1: 115
53c2: 236n17
53c–54d: 95, 230n50, 236n15
53c–55a: 107
53d–54c: 107
54b: 231n55
54c1–2: 97
54c9: 95
54c10: 95, 108
54c–55a: 231n52
54d: 107
54d1–2: 109
54e2: 107
54e–55a: 112, 237n20
55a5–6: 119
55a5–8: 238n30
55a7–8: 115
55b1–c1: 80, 111
55c ff.: 120, 240n43
55d10: 240n43
55e: 87, 107
55e ff.: 95, 120
56c9–d1: 240n43
56d: 120
56d5–6: 118
57a ff.: 225n12
57c–d: 120
57d: 121
57d6–7: 120
57e: 120
57e6 ff.: 222n53
57e–58a: 83, 119
57e–58c: 83
57e–58d: 118
58a: 90
58a2–3: 83
58c–e: 232n58
58d: 100
58d4 ff.: 222n53
58d5: 83
58d6–7: 222n55
58e–59a: 94
58e–59b: 222n54
59a1: 232n58
59a2: 232n58
59a7: 89

59a–b: 83, 232n58
59b7: 75, 222n55
59b–c: 90
59b–d: 232n58
59c: 90, 236n14
59c2–d2: 111
59c4: 89, 232n58, 250n23
59c–d: 83, 90, 113
59d1: 222n55
59d1–2: 110
59d10–e3: 113, 122
59d–e: 230n42
59e2: 101, 113
60c–61a: 110
60c11: 122
60c–e: 115
60d7–e1: 111
61b11–c2: 113, 122
61b–c: 113
61d: 222n55
61d1–5: 108, 109
61d10–e3: 75, 222n54
61d10–e4: 75
61d–e: 90, 94
61e3: 226n18
61e6–9: 115
61e7–8: 120
61e–62a: 83
61e–62b: 120
62a: 90
62a3: 228n36
62a8: 115
62b4: 115
62d1–3: 239n43, 240n43
62d2–3: 120, 239n43
62e: 109, 112, 235n7
62e9: 101
63a1–5: 109
63a4: 109, 237n19
63b–c: 75
63c: 118
63d3–e3: 112
63d–e: 113, 252n39
63e: 112, 113, 235n7
63e3–4: 115
63e4–6: 109
63e4–64a2: 109

63e6: 110
63e–64a: 113
64a1–2: 91, 101, 116
64a–65a: 107
64b: 35
64b2: 229n39, 232n56
64b7: 98
64b7–8: 119
64c: 229n41
64c5–6: 91
64c–65a: 92
64c–66a: 110
64d: 229n41
64d4: 91, 95, 109
64d9: 91
64d9–e3: 92, 207n38
64d11: 113
64d–e: 91
64d–65a: 91
64e1: 91
64e5–7: 229n38
64e6–7: 108
64e ff.: 238n30
65a: 91, 108, 229n38
65a1–2: 229n38
65a3–4: 229n38
65a7–b2: 238n30
65b1: 229n41
65b1–2: 91, 116
65b–66a: 236n17
65c3: 229n41
65c5: 236n17
65d3: 229n41
65d8: 236n17
65e9: 236n17
66c4–6: 108
67a7: 84
67a–b: 201n54
67b: 18, 121, 194

Politicus
259a–b: 252n38
262a–e: 159
262a ff.: 70
262c–d: 190
263d–e: 201n54
267a–b: 150

267c–268e: 241n7
267d: 246n50
267e–268c: 251n32
268d8: 147
268e5–6: 147
269a1–5: 129, 134
269a4–5: 130
269a7: 155, 242n19
269b5–c1: 130
269c4: 133
269c4–5: 133, 245n43
269c4–d2: 133
269c5: 133, 134, 141, 150, 243n28
269c5–7: 133
269c7: 241n11
269c7–d1: 243n36
269c7–d2: 241n11
269c–d: 133, 147
269c–273e: 139
269d1: 149, 155, 157, 250n19
269d2: 133, 241n11
269d2–3: 250n18
269d2 ff.: 244n36
269d3: 207n38, 250n18
269d5–6: 151
269d5–e6: 252n42
269d5–270a8: 241n10
269d6: 151
269d7–9: 155
269d8–e1: 152
269d9: 132, 250n19
269d9–e1: 250n18
269d–e: 129, 151
269e1: 151
269e3–4: 249n10
269e5: 151, 157
269e5–6: 151
269e5–270a5: 134
269e6–7: 242n18
269e7 ff.: 244n36
269e8–270a2: 133, 243n22, 259n43
269e9–270a1: 242n18
269e–270a: 129
270a: 129, 133
270a1–2: 130
270a3: 133, 149, 150, 240n4, 245n43
270a3–5: 35, 138

Politicus (*cont.*)

270a3–7: 133
270a5: 132, 133, 139, 149, 243n28
270a5–6: 141
270a5–7: 133
270a6: 243n28
270a7: 241n10
270a8: 241n10
270b: 134
270b7–8: 133
270b10–271b3: 134
270c11: 244n37, 250n18
270c11–12: 134, 137, 244n37
270d3–4: 131, 134
270d4: 135
270d–e: 131, 134, 153, 242n12,
    244n37
270e6–7: 247n61
270e8–9: 132
270e10–11: 132
271a2: 243n34
271a2–b3: 134
271a2–c2: 136
271a4: 243n34
271a4–c2: 135
271a7–b1: 244n38
271b2–3: 131
271b3: 135
271b4: 135, 243n31, 244n37
271b4–8: 135, 251n30
271b4–c2: 135
271b6–7: 135, 251n30
271b7–8: 131, 134, 135, 153
271b–c: 136
271c2: 135
271c3: 243n30
271c3–d1: 243n34
271c4: 135
271c4–5: 136
271c5: 243n34
271c8–d3: 243n34
271c9–d3: 136
271c ff.: 135
271d: 178, 204n18, 253n50
271d1: 136
271d2–3: 136
271d3: 136

271d3–4: 242n20
271d3–6: 160
271d4: 131, 155, 256n28
271d5: 207n36
271d6–e1: 140, 246nn48,51
271d–e: 142, 150, 153, 246n56
271d–272b: 136
271d ff.: 243n34
271e: 159
271e7: 154
271e8: 160, 242n14
272a1: 251n30
272a1–2: 247n61
272a1–b1: 159
272a–b: 243n32
272b: 240n3
272b1–4: 136
272b2–3: 130, 134, 139
272b8: 246n51
272b8–c5: 159
272b9: 246n54
272b–d: 159
272c: 143
272c1–4: 143
272c2: 159
272c2–4: 253n48
272c4: 144
272c4–5: 247n60
272d6–e6: 137
272d6–273d4: 137
272e: 141, 150, 178, 204n18, 233n67
272e3: 131, 134, 138
272e4: 150, 243n28
272e4–5: 155
272e4 ff.: 138
272e5: 133
272e6: 245n40, 251n35
272e6 ff.: 157
272e8: 150
272e ff.: 140, 147, 258n39
273a1–3: 249n12
273a1–d4: 241n10
273a2: 157
273a3: 157, 244n37
273a3–4: 134, 137
273a5: 156
273a5–7: 137

273a7: 139
273a–d: 242n12
273a–e: 157
273a ff.: 249n12
273b: 157
273b1: 149
273b1–2: 132, 150
273b2: 140, 155
273b2–3: 137, 157
273b4: 149, 152, 156, 240n4, 241n11,
    248n4
273b4–5: 240n4, 248n4, 250n18
273b4–6: 207n38
273b4–d4: 248n3
273b5: 157
273b6: 241n11, 247n61
273b6–7: 151, 155, 240n4
273b6–c2: 152
273b7: 250n19
273b–c: 133, 149, 152
273b–d: 149
273c: 157, 249n12
273c1: 160, 249n12
273c2: 249n12
273c2–3: 245n43
273c2–4: 152
273c2–e1: 155
273c3: 150
273c5: 243n28
273c5–6: 127, 137
273c6: 156, 157, 248n3
273c7: 250n18
273c7–d1: 127, 240n4
273c–d: 49, 151, 155, 246n45
273d1–4: 127, 249n12
273d3: 155, 251n35
273d3–4: 137
273d3–e1: 160
273d4: 150, 207n36, 250n19
273d4–e4: 138
273d5: 256n28
273d6: 155, 250n18, 251n35
273d6–e1: 207n38
273d–e: 150, 155, 160, 250n18
273e: 129, 137, 244n37
273e1: 141
273e1–4: 155

273e2: 157, 248n3
273e2–3: 155
273e3: 130, 139, 149, 150, 207n36,
    243n22
273e3–4: 138, 245n40
273e3–6: 242n22
273e4–6: 245n40
273e6: 130, 242n22
273e6–7: 139
273e6–8: 245n40
273e6–11: 245n40
273e6–274e1: 137
273e7–11: 138
273e8–9: 138
273e10–11: 132
273e11–274a1: 131
273e–274a: 153
273e–274d: 153
273e–274e: 139
274a: 131, 138, 240n3, 245n40
274a1: 134, 153
274a2–4: 138
274a4–b1: 140
274a5: 141
274a7: 141
274b1: 141
274b5: 140
274b5–6: 139, 142, 246n48
274b–c: 66, 141
274c: 66
274c1–2: 245n39
274c4: 142, 154
274c5: 142
274c5–6: 243n23
274c5–d2: 141
274c6: 150, 155, 246n47
274c6–7: 140, 141
274d2–7: 139, 140
274d3: 246n48
274d3–4: 142
274d6–7: 127, 131, 134, 153, 158
274e: 201n54
274e10–11: 243n35
274e–275a: 142, 153
274e–276d: 241n7
275a–b: 251n32
275b: 200n47

Politicus (*cont.*)
275c–276c: 251n32
276b: 251n32
276b7–c1: 155
276c–d: 142, 153
277b3–5: 142, 154
277b4–5: 148
281d–e: 41, 208n46
283c–284e: 228n28
283d–e: 106
284a–b: 155, 228n28
284b: 23
284b1–2: 250n26
284d ff.: 246n52
285d4–286a7: 143, 252n38
286b–287a: 241n8
286d–e: 246n52
287b ff.: 142, 246nn54,55
288c: 246n54
288d–289b: 242n12
292d4: 156, 252n38
292d6: 155
292d ff.: 126
292e9–293a1: 252n38
293c7: 252n38
293d8–9: 155
293e: 156
293e ff.: 252n38
294a8: 155
294a–b: 201n54
294c ff.: 11
296e3: 155
296e4–297a5: 252n36
297a5–b3: 155
297a–c: 144
297b7–c2: 247n62
297b ff.: 11
297c–301e: 11
297e8–12: 252n36
300c ff.: 252n38
300e–301a: 144
301b10–c4: 251n35
301c6–e2: 247n62
301c6–302b3: 156
301c–d: 144
301c ff.: 247n62
301d1–5: 155

301e6–302b3: 155
301e–302b: 11
302a5–b3: 251n35, 252n36
302a6–7: 251n35
303b4: 156
303e–311c: 246n55
304e–305a: 159
305e3: 155
307d ff.: 155
307e–308a: 156
308c ff.: 253n48
308d1–3: 156
308d1–309e13: 155
309a8–b7: 155, 156
309a–e: 253n50
309c: 154, 253n50
309c1–3: 143
309c5–e8: 143
309c–e: 156, 160
310e: 160, 253n50
310e6–11: 156
311c: 246n54
311c5–6: 155

Protagoras
322c3: 199n32
356a–e: 106
356c8–e2: 111
358b–d: 239n41
358c1–7: 248n3
361c–d: 18

Republic
II: 58, 202n1
III: 58, 202n1
V: 202n1
351a5: 248n3
354a: 9, 74
357b6–8: 237n19
357b–358a: 110, 237n19
365d–e: 254n6
372a–373e: 160
373c1: 199n32
376c: 199n29
376e–377a: 15
377a: 57
377a5–6: 219n27

377d–378c: 199n41
377d ff.: 57
378b: 27
378b–c: 199n29
378b ff.: 200n46
378d–e: 200n49
378e ff.: 26
379a: 15
379a7 ff.: 210n65
379a–b: 206n30
379a–383c: 199n42
379c: 27, 184
379c4–5: 260n65
380b–c: 199n29
380d–381c: 206n30
381b–c: 148
383c: 199n29
387e–388a: 199n29
389d–e: 199n29
395b–c: 199n29
397c: 184
398b: 199n29
398e: 199n29
401b–c: 199n29
401c–402a: 199n43
402b–c: 199n29
402d: 220n32
403e: 199n29
411a–b: 199n40
413e–414a: 199n29
414d–e: 253n47
420b: 74, 198n22
428e–429a: 75
429b–c: 10, 75, 198n24
431d–e: 198n24
432a–b: 198n25
433a–b: 198n25
434d: 253n51
434d–e: 156
436b8–9: 172
436b9–c1: 172
436b ff.: 42
436c ff.: 172
439d: 157
440a–b: 239n34
441a1: 258n41
441c6: 258n41

442b–c: 239n34
442c: 218n23
442c–d: 10, 77
443c–d: 74
443c–444a: 77
443c ff.: 251n34
443e: 10, 74
444a–445c: 237n22
462c–d: 187
466a: 74
472c–473b: 199n30
476a: 82
477c ff.: 93
487a5: 221n42
487e ff.: 252n36
490b4: 221n42
491a9–b1: 118
491b4: 118
494a4: 118, 223n58
494d: 42
500b–c: 58
500b–d: 251n34
500c5: 221n42
500d: 8, 52, 122, 252n36
503b7: 118
504d–505b: 223n65
507c: 8
508a4: 148
508d: 218n15
508d4–6: 43
509b2–4: 56
509d–510a: 219n25
511a: 219n25
511d: 219n26
516b9–c2: 56
519e: 122, 198n24
519e2–3: 198n22
520c: 49, 75
521a: 9, 74
521b ff.: 76
521c7: 118
521d–522c: 220n34
523a: 221n39
523b ff.: 87
526b: 223n57
527b: 221n39
527d–e: 221n39

Republic (*cont.*)
528e–530c: 70
528e ff.: 72, 240n45
529c8–d1: 148
529d7: 148
530a3–7: 148
530a5–7: 8
530a6–7: 248n10
530b1–3: 249n10
530b2: 248n10
532c: 221n39
534a: 93
540a8–b1: 8, 52
540a–b: 223n65
540a–c: 74, 198n23
540d: 199n30
551c: 252n36
572b ff.: 239n35
573b ff.: 223n62
578e–580a: 181
580b–583b: 198n23
580d ff.: 237n22
583a3: 238n28
584b7: 238n28
584c6: 238n28
586b–c: 239n35
590c–d: 198n27
605a–606d: 199n40
611e2: 221n42
611e2–3: 71
612e: 256n28
613b1: 221n44
616b–617d: 248n8
617e4–5: 60
619c–d: 198n28
621c–d: 259n56

Sophist
228b8–9: 248n3
228c7–8: 248n3
228e1–5: 248n3
245e–249d: 231n54
246c–247e: 168
248e6–249b6: 212n84, 231n54
249a: 43
249a4: 239n32
249c10–d5: 213n84

249d4: 226n16
256e: 224n8
257a: 224n8
265b–266b: 240n4
265c: 208n41
265d5: 201n54
265e: 208n41

Symposium
204a1–2: 210n61
207d: 233n67, 259n56
210e: 220n35, 223n65
211d: 220n35
211e1: 89
212a5: 71

Theaetetus
152a ff.: 254n4
176a5–8: 40
176a5–c1: 210n65
176b1–2: 221n44, 264n13
176b1–3: 210n65
182c ff.: 232n57

Timaeus
17c: 24
17c–18a: 202n1
18b–c: 202n1
19a–b: 24
19b–c: 25
20d–26e: 25
22c–d: 25
22c ff.: 149
22d: 25
22d1: 249n10
23a: 25
23b–c: 68
24d: 68
24e–25c: 25
25b–c: 68
26e4–5: 200n44
27a: 62
27a5–6: 25
27b–d: 147
27d5–28a4: 215n98
27d6–28a1: 32, 205n23
27d–28a: 93, 200n51

27d–29c: 200n51
28a: 202n4
28a3–4: 205n23
28a4–5: 29
28a6–8: 208n48
28a8: 90
28a–29a: 232n60
28a–b: 47
28b: 45, 215n102
28b4–c2: 32
28b7: 32, 33
28b7–c2: 31, 32
28c: 63, 147, 201n60
28c2: 35
28c2–3: 29
28c3: 34, 203n12, 213n88, 232n62
28c6: 208n48
28c–29a: 202n4, 213n87
29a: 29, 36, 46, 69, 73, 89, 150,
    218n15
29a1: 90, 250n23
29a3: 232n62
29a5: 35, 240n4, 249n13
29a5–6: 41
29a6: 29, 35
29b6: 205n23, 215n98
29b–c: 26, 219n26
29c: 63, 213n87
29c3: 32
29c–d: 264n8
29d1: 207n34
29d2: 16, 26, 32
29d7–e1: 32, 94
29d7–30c1: 204n18
29e: 58
29e1–2: 210n65, 238n31
29e4: 29, 32, 35, 47, 94
29e–30a: 34, 203n13, 232n60
29e–30b: 256n28
29e ff.: 46
30a: 29
30a2–3: 262n79
30a4: 170
30a4–5: 88
30a6–7: 210n65
30b: 29, 201n60
30b1: 203n9

30b3: 43, 44
30b4–5: 44, 54, 149, 255n19
30b5: 203n12
30b6: 90, 203n12
30b7: 16
30b8: 200n44, 248n5
30c: 36, 212n84
30c1: 203n10
30c7: 218n17
30c–d: 213n87, 262nn76,79
30d: 29, 35
30d2: 208n48
30d3: 239n32
31a: 45
31a8–b1: 29
31b: 215n102
31b1: 36, 212n84
31b–32c: 46, 94
31c: 88
31c–32a: 216n103
32a–c: 207n38
32c: 46
32c7: 203n12
32c8: 203n9
32c–33a: 88, 227n26
32c–33b: 29
32c–33d: 45, 238n31
32d: 35
32d1: 238n31, 239n32
32d–33a: 262n79
33a: 59, 62
33a6: 203n9
33a–d: 58
33b7: 203n9
33d: 62
33d1: 203n9
34a: 43, 44, 48, 151, 217n7
34a8: 203n9, 256n28
34b: 44, 45, 59, 62, 217n6
34b1: 217n4, 238n31
34b5–8: 217n12
34b7–8: 58
34b8: 58, 217n4
34b10–35a1: 55, 232n60
34b–c: 35, 58, 62, 167
34c: 47, 48, 207n34
34c2–4: 35

Timaeus (*cont.*)
34c4–5: 140
35a: 94, 170, 222n49, 230n49
35a1–3: 205n23
35a1–b1: 47, 70, 214n92
35a2–3: 70
35a–36d: 217n5
35b–c: 216n103, 220n38
35b–36a: 220n37
35b–36b: 54, 59
35b ff.: 70, 71, 94
36b–d: 54
36b ff.: 45
36c: 55, 217nn7,9
36c1: 55
36c4: 217n6
36c7: 55
36c–d: 234n75, 248n8
36d: 55, 217n10
36d2–3: 71, 220n38
36d4–5: 55
36d4–7: 140, 252n41
36e: 50, 58, 59, 173, 213n90, 217n6
36e2: 215n102
36e3–4: 45
36e4: 218n19
36e4–5: 48
36e5–6: 215n102
36e6: 170
36e6–37a1: 220n37
37a1–2: 209n54
37a2: 58
37a5: 205n23, 214n13
37a6: 43
37a6–7: 214n93
37a–b: 47
37a–c: 43, 47, 69, 214n97
37b: 213n90
37b3–c3: 72
37b5: 47, 211n72, 214n93
37b8: 48, 215n98
37b–c: 173
37c: 217n9
37c1–3: 43
37c3–5: 43, 44
37c6–7: 218n16
37c6–d1: 238n31

37c7: 256n28
37c7–8: 218n16
37c8: 203n10
37c8–d1: 90
37c–d: 30, 73, 213n87
37c–38b: 73
37d1: 218n16
37d5–7: 218n16
37d6: 33, 221n46
37e1–3: 33
37e3: 33
37e4: 34
37e4 ff.: 33
37e–38a: 205n23
38a: 213n84
38a1: 200n44, 248n5
38a3: 44, 46, 49, 212n84, 221n46
38a5: 226n18
38a7–8: 33, 34
38b6: 33
38b–c: 30
38c: 234n75
38c1–3: 33
38c3: 33, 203n10
38c3–4: 203n9, 207n37
38c7–8: 217n10
38c ff.: 54
38e: 56
38e5: 55
38e6: 55, 140, 252n41
39a1–2: 55, 217n7
39a4–b2: 217n7
39a–b: 248n8
39b4–c1: 72
39b–c: 262n76
39c: 100
39c2: 214n97
39c–d: 217n10
39d1: 73, 217n10
39d7–e2: 73
39d–e: 262n79
39e: 29, 69, 73, 90, 213n87
39e1: 36, 208n48, 212n84
39e7–9: 207n37
39e8: 208n48, 262n79
39e10: 54, 218n16
39e–40a: 70, 262n76

40a: 234n75
40a2: 218n19
40a2–b6: 54
40a3: 90
40a4: 217n8
40a6: 199n32
40a8–b1: 7, 55, 77, 221n46
40a–b: 56
40a–d: 239n32
40b: 59
40b1–2: 217n7
40b2: 55
40b5: 55, 71, 218nn16,19
40b5–6: 221n46
40b6: 55
40b6–8: 54
40b8: 253n47
40b8–c3: 217n12
40b–c: 56
40c2–3: 54
40c5: 249n10
40d4: 217n5
40d6–e3: 217n12
40e5: 217n12
41a3–6: 56
41a5: 203n12
41a–b: 45
41a–c: 262n76
41a–d: 178
41a–42e: 35
41a ff.: 55, 140
41b1: 203n13
41b–c: 204n16
41b–d: 29
41c1: 203n16
41c4–5: 56
41c5: 217n8
41c5–6: 217n11
41c6: 73
41d: 48, 50, 73, 121, 189, 233n66
41d1: 218n20
41d2: 56
41d3: 56
41d–e: 51
41e: 61, 180
41e1–2: 158
41e2: 50, 69, 252n43

41e–42d: 29
42a: 207n39, 239n36
42a3–b1: 59
42a5–6: 234n79
42a–b: 61, 65, 173
42b–d: 65
42b: 25, 66
42b2: 73
42b2–5: 51, 74
42b4: 73
42b–d: 68, 233n67
42c: 59
42c–d: 59, 262n76
42d: 55, 60, 180
42d–e: 140, 178
42e: 60
42e1–3: 232n60
42e2–4: 210n65
42e3: 56
42e3–4: 60, 65
42e7: 218n20
42e8: 217n8
42e–43a: 59
43a: 59, 215n102, 231n53
43a–b: 210n62, 247n61
43a–e: 72
43a–44c: 74, 157
43a ff.: 173, 222n49
43b: 254n10
43b4: 60
43b–d: 239n36
43d: 59
43d1: 157
43d–44c: 72
43d ff.: 215n98
43e–44a: 60
44a: 59, 173
44a4: 59
44a–b: 72, 215n98
44b8–c2: 74, 221n40
44b–c: 60, 157
44d5: 218n19
44d–e: 61
44e–45a: 204n17
45a1: 218n19
45b4–6: 38
45b–d: 38

Timaeus (cont.)

46c7: 208n44
46c7–d1: 40, 41
46c7–e2: 38, 39, 211n72
46c8: 29, 41, 208n48, 229n40
46c–d: 232n65
46c–e: 41, 149, 150, 167, 216n106, 240n4, 246n45
46d: 46, 50, 215n102
46d1: 30, 208n48
46d1–e6: 41
46d3: 209n49
46d4: 39
46d5–6: 47
46d6: 170, 209n52, 215n102, 250n24
46d8: 38, 41, 213n90
46d–e: 38, 47, 51, 185, 213n90
46e: 46, 61, 64, 65, 100, 203n13, 207n41, 250n18
46e1: 39
46e1–2: 167, 208n44, 213n90
46e2: 37, 209n49
46e4: 38, 41, 209n49, 210n65, 211n66
46e5–6: 37, 234n77
46e6: 208n44, 209n49
46e8: 38
46e8–47c5: 204n17
46e–47c: 30
47a: 70, 158
47a4–b2: 38, 71
47a7: 69, 252n43
47a–c: 50
47b: 219n26
47b2: 204n17
47b6–c3: 74
47b7: 48
47b8: 73
47b–c: 38, 46, 72, 158
47c: 71, 73
47c2: 73
47d: 56
47e4: 36, 214n91
47e4–5: 208n43, 259n55
47e5: 227n26
47e5–48a2: 210n63, 229n42
47e5–48a5: 36, 38

47e–48a: 141, 246n45
47e ff.: 38
48a: 35, 36, 37, 49, 65, 66, 141, 149, 240n4
48a1: 227nn26, 27
48a2: 29, 35, 36, 152
48a2–3: 40, 210n60
48a3: 60, 261n71
48a7: 37, 60
48a–b: 36, 37, 250n18
48b3–5: 37
48b5: 227n26
48d–e: 147
48e: 89
48e6: 218n17
48e–49a: 201n60, 213n87, 227n23
49e3: 227n27
49e–50a: 227n27
50a1–2: 227n27
50a2–3: 227n26
50a3–4: 227n26
50a–b: 227n27
50b5–c2: 227n27
50c7–d2: 227n23
50c7–d4: 213n88
50d–51a: 227n27
50e: 227n27
50e–51a: 227n27
51a6: 227n27
51b7–52a4: 70
51b8: 218n14
51b–52a: 200n51, 226n22
51b–52d: 200n51
51c1: 218n14
51c5: 218n17
51d: 218n15
51d3–5: 70
51d4–5: 218n14
51d5: 218n17
51e: 70
51e5: 210n65
51e6–52d1: 213n87
52a: 227n23
52a1: 221n46
52a1–2: 89
52a1–3: 46
52a2–3: 89

52a8: 169
52a–53a: 227n27
52d: 44
52d3: 169, 205n23, 230n49
52d3–4: 94, 227n27
52d–e: 37
52d–53a: 88, 259n55
52d–53b: 250n18
52e2: 227n26
53a: 227n26
53a7: 227n27
53a8–b4: 35
53a–b: 38, 46
53b: 37, 49, 169, 203n13, 210n58
53b4: 44
53b4–5: 207n35
53b6: 227n27
53b ff.: 37, 207n38, 211n68
53c ff.: 46, 200n51, 226n22
56b4: 248n5
58a: 45
58a–c: 185
59c7–d2: 248n5
61d–62a: 254n14
64a–65a: 239n36
67d5: 215n102
68d: 264n8
68d4: 218n19
68e: 91, 150, 167, 207n41,
    216n106
68e1: 208n45
68e1–2: 29
68e1–69a5: 38
68e2: 229n40
68e3: 41
68e4: 167, 217n4
68e4–5: 97, 208n45
68e4–6: 41
68e5: 29, 30, 208n48, 229n40
68e6–69a5: 41
68e7: 218n19
68e7–69a2: 72
68e7–69a5: 38
68e–69a: 36, 38, 41, 149, 167
68e–69b: 46
69a: 208n46
69b: 30, 91, 209n58

69b–c: 37, 38
69c: 61
69c1: 203n12
69c3: 204n18
69c5: 217n8
69c7: 50
69c8–d2: 234n79
69c–d: 61, 173, 207n39, 239n36
69c ff.: 59
69d5: 258n41
69d6: 218n19
70a: 30, 59
70a–d: 61
70d7–8: 61
70d–e: 157
70e–71a: 218n23
71a: 204n17
71a5–6: 219n28
71a7: 204n17, 256n28
71b3: 219n26
71c4: 219n26
71d: 35
71e3: 204n17
72d: 264n8
72d4: 218n19
73a: 30
73a7: 218n19
73a–74b: 40, 245n45
73c7: 218n19
74d6: 204n17
75a7: 65
75a7–b1: 40
75a–b: 245n45
75a–c: 65, 210n60
75b4: 210n60
75b8: 256n28
75b–c: 40
75b–d: 204n17
75c: 65
76b2: 204n17, 218n19
77a: 30
77a3: 204n17
77a–b: 121
78b2: 204n17
80e1: 204n17
83d3: 215n102
83d3–4: 215n102

Timaeus (cont.)
86b: 173
86b–e: 248n3
86b ff.: 60
86d–e: 60
86e1–2: 74
87a–b: 122
87b: 60, 74, 75, 218n21
87b6–8: 72
87c: 30, 95, 229n39
87c4–5: 35
87c5: 62
87c–d: 61, 67
87c–88e: 62
87d: 30, 220n32, 222n50
87d1–3: 61
87d7: 67
87d–88b: 67
87d–88c: 67
87e: 60
87e5–6: 67
88a8: 219n26
88a8–b2: 157, 216n105
88a–b: 60, 216n105
88b: 222n50
88b1–2: 61, 77
88b2: 218n19
88b–e: 67
88c: 67, 75, 222n50
88c2: 219n26
88d–89a: 62
88e: 223n64
89a1–3: 48
89d: 67
90a: 51, 73
90a1–2: 61, 221n47
90a3–4: 218n20
90a5: 73
90a8: 204n17
90b: 216n105, 221n47
90b6: 77
90b–c: 61, 71
90b–d: 72, 233n67, 252n44
90c: 65
90c1: 218n19
90c1–2: 71
90c4: 218n19

90c5: 218n20
90c5–6: 72, 73
90c6: 74
90c6–8: 223n64
90c8: 73, 218n19, 219n26
90c8–d1: 48, 71, 222n49
90c–d: 46, 71, 222n50
90d: 73, 158
90d1: 74
90d1–3: 222n49
90d3: 73
90d3–4: 71, 220n37
90d4: 71, 72, 223n63
90d5: 72, 73, 77
90d5–7: 221n45
90d6: 73, 204n17
90e–92c: 51, 233n67
91d: 215n102
91d6–e1: 71
91d–e: 74
91e–92b: 211n68
92a3: 204n17
92b–c: 262n76
92c: 35, 58, 62, 173, 203n13
92c6–9: 249n13
92c7: 238n31, 239n32, 259n45
92c7–8: 54
92c8: 58

Other Ancient Authors

Alexander

On Fate
207, 5–21 (LS 62J): 263n4

Aristotle

De Anima
III 5: 5
403b31–404b6: 233n67
407a2–3: 215n102
407b15–19: 233n67
411b7–8: 233n67
413a4: 233n67
414a19–20: 233n67
415b8: 233n67
416a6–8: 233n67

De Caelo
271a33: 206n32
279b12–280a11: 206n32
280a28 ff.: 204n19, 206n32

De Generatione et Corruptione (= *G.C.*)
336b27–32: 206n32

De Partibus Animalium (= *P.A.*)
I 1: 208n46
687a6 ff.: 206n32

Metaphysics
I 6: 224n8
V 5: 208n46
991a8–11: 46
991a19–23: 202n4, 206n32
991a21–23: 202n4
991b3–5: 46
1019a2–4: 212n74
1024a36–b4: 224n8
1071b37–1072a2: 204n19
1072b3–4: 254n12
1073a3–7: 5
1087a16–18: 224n8

Nicomachean Ethics (= *N.E.*)
II 6: 4
1153b19–21: 219n30
1177b26–1178a2: 264n11
1178a9–14: 264n11
1178b7–28: 264n11

Physics
II 9: 208n46

Politics
1264b24–9: 23

Cicero

Republic
3.33 (LS 67S): 263n4

Diogenes Laertius

7.87–9 (LS 63C): 201n63
7.143 (LS 53X): 201n63

Euripides

Electra 699–730: 242n17

Orestes 996–1012: 242n17

Eusebius

Evangelical Preparation
15.15.3–5 (LS 67L): 201n63,
    263n4

Heraclitus

Fragments (22B DK)
101: 197n8
112: 197n8
114: 197n8, 263n3
116: 197n8

Hesiod

Works and Days (= *Op.*)
106 ff.: 158
115 ff.: 158
181: 132

Marcus Aurelius

Meditations 4.4: 263n4

[Olympiodorus]

*Anonymous Prolegomena to
    Platonic Philosophy* (Westerink)
    (= *Prol.*)
24 10–15: 202n66

Paul

Epistle to Romans
2.14–15: 263n4

Philolaus

Fragments (44B DK)
1: 228n34, 230n46
2: 228n34, 230n46
4: 87
5: 230n46
6: 230n46

Plutarch

De Animae Procreatione in Timaeo
1012f–1013b: 205n19
1014a–b: 204n19
1014d–1015f: 258n42

De Iside et Osiride
370b–371a: 258n42

Posidonius

Fragments (Edelstein/Kidd)
186: 201n64

Proclus

Procli Diadochi In Platonis Timaeum
  Commentaria (Diehl) (= *In Tim.*)
I 282, 27–30: 205n26

I 283, 27 ff.: 204n19
I 285, 26–28: 205n19
I 286, 20 ff.: 206n28
I 287, 28–288, 1: 205n19
I 288, 14–17: 205n26
I 288, 17–27: 258n39
I 290, 23–291,1: 205n26
I 402, 15 ff.: 234n72
III 51, 7–10: 205n26
III 273, 25 ff.: 250n27

Seneca

On Leisure
4.1 (LS 67K): 201n63

Xenocrates

Fragments (Heinze)
54: 205n19

General Index

affinity. *See* kinship
afterlife, 14, 181, 182
altruism, 193
Anaxagoras, 8, 191
animals,
  classification of, 70, 159,
    253n48
  and happiness, 121–122
  kinship with humans, 159, 253n48,
    261n76
  transformation into, 74, 173, *see also*
    reincarnation
Annas, J., 1, 15, 76, 78, 197nn2,3,6,7,
    199nn36,37, 200nn46,49,53,
    201nn61,65, 216n2, 221n47,
    222n51, 223n61, 234n1, 235n12,
    237n22, 239n38, 240n46,
    241nn6,8, 258n42, 263n6, 264n9
apeiron,
  and becoming/flux, 80, 94–95,
    231n53
  and the bodily, 207n38
  and chance, 101, 234n77, 250n18
  and dialectic, 81–84, 86–87, 224n8,
    225nn13,15
  and disorder, 87–88, 101, 207n38,
    250n18
  and the fourfold classification,
    86–88, 225n15
  and imperfection, 87–88, 104

meaning/s of, 224n1
mixture with *peras, see* mixture
and necessity, *see* necessity
and pleasure, 84, 85, 101, 104–109,
    235n13
and space, 227n27, 228n31
Aquinas, T., 263n4
Aristotle,
  on creation/eternality of the
    universe, 204n19, 206n32
  critique of Platonic Forms, 46–47
  on the Demiurge, 26, 202n4
  on first movers, 165, 254n12
  on god, 194–195, 221n47
  on the *Laws,* 23
  on mind-body relation, 5–6, 194,
    198n14, 215n102, 233n67
  on nature, 4, 194, 206n32
  on ontological priority, 212n74
  on Plato's unwritten doctrines,
    224n8
  ridiculing Sufficiency Thesis, 66,
    67–68, 219n30
  on role models, 4, 195
  on teleology, 194, 206n32
art (*technê*). *See* craft
assimilation with god (*homoiôsis theôi*),
    1–2, 19–20, 72–73, 194–195,
    221nn44,45,47, 223nn60,63,
    233n67

astronomy,
  and consistency, 76–78, 189
  and the cosmic god, 54–57, 70–78,
    174–175, 257n33
  and education, 12, 46, 63, 68–69,
    75–76, 220n39, 222n50,
    223nn57,58,59
  and happiness, 19–20, 53, 57, 68,
    70–78, 119–121, 124, 189
  and *Politicus* myth, 148–149,
    245n45, 248nn8,9,10,
    249n16
  propaedeutic character of, 72–74,
    220n39
  and the senses, 70–71, 74, 77,
    249n15, 257n34
  as therapy, 74–76, 77
  two types of, 76, 120–121, 223n59
  See also heavenly bodies; planets;
    stars
atheism, 27, 76, 164–165, 171,
    185–186, 255n19, 262n79
Athens, old, 25, 67, 261n73
Atlantis, 24–25, 64, 66–67, 68, 197n4,
    200n44
Atomism, 206n31, 208n47, 261n75
authority,
  of main speaker, 117, 200n54
  political, 124, 190
autonomy, 10–12, 21, 68–69, 75,
    124–125, 126, 140–144, 164,
    189–190, 247n60, 253n50

beauty,
  Form of, 81, 216n104, 220n35,
    229n38
  and good, 67, 75–76, 91–92, 95,
    108, 116, 123, 229nn38,39
  of heavenly bodies, 99–100, 148
  and measure, 30, 91, 92, 108, 123,
    155, 227n28, 229nn38,39,
    250n26
  and pleasure, 108, 111, 116, 235n12,
    236nn16,17
  psychosomatic, 67, 75–76, 219n32
  of the universe, 30, 116, 148,
    149–151, 155

becoming *(genesis)*,
  vs. being, *see* being
  and Demiurge, 29, 44, 47
  elevated account of, 20, 94–95, 104,
    222n49, 231nn51,53,54
  and pleasure, *see* pleasure
  and the soul, 70, 169, 222n49
being,
  vs. becoming, 31–35, 83, 93–96,
    107–109, 119–120, 205n23,
    230nn49,50, 231nn53,54,55,
    236n15, 248n10
  broader notion of, 20, 93–95, 104,
    108, 168, 205n23, 212n84,
    225n13, 230nn49,50, 231n54,
    236n15
  and good, *see* good
  and pleasure, *see* pleasure
belief,
  false, 60, 61, 105, 110, 173–174,
    176, 232n58, 237n20,
    259n51
  stable, 48, 143, 155–156, 215n98
  true, 48, 59, 70, 74, 143, 155–156,
    215n98
  unstable, 10, 232n58
  well grounded, 18
  and pleasure, 104–105, 106–107,
    110, 237n20
bodies (heavenly). *See* heavenly
    bodies
bodies (primary, or so-called four
    elements),
  in macro-microcosm analogy, 97, 99
  and precosmos, 36–37, 209n58,
    227n26, 250n18, *see also* traces
bodily *(sômatoeides)*, 37, 147, 149, 152,
    156, 157, 207n38, 240n4,
    241n11, 243n36, 245n45,
    248nn3,4, 250n18
  See also cause; necessity
body,
  cosmic, 30, 31, 45, 46, 48, 50, 58,
    59–60, 62, 70, 97–98, 207n38,
    215nn102,103, 217n7
  mortal, 30, 59–60, 97–98, 157,
    173

as hindrance to soul or *nous*, 9, 50,
  59–61, 156–157, 198n14,
  216n105
as instrument or vehicle of soul or
  nous, 50–51, 60–61, 70, 167,
  216n105, 255n19
necessitated by soul or *nous*, 19, 21,
  28, 44–45, 67, 167, 170, 182, 191,
  216n105
organised by soul or *nous*, 46, 98,
  170, 191, 207n38, 211n68,
  216n103, 233n67
and secondary motion or causation,
  37–38, 47, 164–166, 167, 182, 185
See also mind-body balance;
  mind-body relation/problem;
  motion; soul
bravery, 10, 61, 178
Brentano, F., 198n15
Brisson, L., 2, 26, 126, 128, 135, 139,
  141, 199nn35,36,43,
  200nn44,46,51, 202n2,
  203nn11,13, 204n19, 210n61,
  211n69, 212nn73,76,83,84,
  213nn88,90, 220n38, 221n41,
  228n31, 240n5, 241n6, 242n16,
  243nn30,34, 244n37,
  245nn41,42,44, 246nn46,49,
  248n63, 248n1, 250nn20,21,27,
  252n40, 253n46, 255n20,
  260n68, 261nn72,73
Burnyeat, M., 198n14, 203n13,
  215n102, 218n15, 220n39,
  232n57, 233n67, 239n38

care, divine. *See* providence
cause/s,
  auxiliary or co-cause, 37, 38, 40, 41,
    88, 97, 208n46
  bodily as, 147, 149, 152, 156, 240n4,
    241n11, 248nn3,4, 250n18
  chance as, 37, 164, 207n41,
    240n4
  errant/wandering, 37, 39–40,
    60–61
  Forms as, 39, 46, 209nn53,54,
    213n88, 229n38

in fourfold classification, 85, 89–90,
  96–100, 112–113
god as, 19, 27, 28, 29, 35, 40, 41, 51,
  56, 129–130, 149–151, 152, 175,
  177, 179, *see also* Demiurge
humans as, 60–61, 64–66, 112–113,
  116, 176, 178–181, 184–188,
  214n95, *see also* responsibility
meaning/s of, 51, 179, 202n8
necessary, 36, 38–39, 41, 64, 149,
  208n46, 209n49, 210n63
necessity as, 36, 39, 40–41, 60,
  210n60, 240n4, 250n18, *see also*
  necessity
nous as, 35–42, 47–48, 84, 90, 91,
  96–100, 101, 102, 112–113, 147,
  149, 207n41, 228n34, 229n41,
  240n4, 262n79
peras as, 90–91, 92, 95, 96, 102, 109,
  228n34, 229n41
primary/divine, 19, 38–39, 40–42,
  46–48, 51, 56, 61, 65, 71–72, 149,
  150, 164, 166–167, 209nn49,52,
  210nn64,65, 211nn66,67,
  213n90, 214n95
productive or efficient, 37–39, 41,
  46–47, 56, 90, 91, 96, 102, 151,
  164–166, 202n8, 209n49,
  213n88, 228n34, 229n41, 254n12
secondary, 38–39, 41, 47–48, 167,
  213n90
soul as, 46, 164–170, 171–172, 175,
  176, 179–180, 185, 234n76,
  254n9, *see also* soul
chance, 35, 37, 64, 100–102, 163–164,
  207n41, 234n77, 240n4
change, 9, 32, 44, 48–49, 95, 148, 151,
  165, 187, 202n8, 205n23, 231n53,
  232n58, 248n10, 252n42
See also compresence; flux; motion
chaos, precosmic, 34–35, 37, 62, 85,
  87, 133, 152, 203n16,
  206nn28,31, 250n27
character,
  immanent, 90, 203n13, 208n48,
    262n79
  moral, 195

Circle/s of the soul (Same and
    Other), 54–55, 59, 99–100,
    214nn96,97, 215n98, 217nn6,7,9,
    220n38, 248n8, 249n13
citizens,
    and noncitizens, 116–117, 253n1
    and understanding, 8–10, 116–117,
        155–156, 162, 198n29, 253n50,
        253n1
    of the universe, 12–13, 22, 121–122,
        159–160, 189–190, 192, 263n4
    city (*polis*), 8, 9, 10, 13, 52, 74, 75, 122,
        153, 155, 156, 158, 160, 179, 184,
        199n32, 202n1, 223n57, 246n56,
        251nn32,35, 253nn50,51
completeness,
    of good life, 62, 84, 110, 219n24
    of universe, 62, 188, 203nn13,16,
        208n48, 238n31, 261n76,
        262n80
compresence, 87, 231n53
consistency, 8, 12, 13–14, 16–17,
    76–77, 124, 189
control. *See* rule
convention (*nomos*), 162–163
    See also law
Cooper, J., 197nn6,11, 208n46,
    222n51, 235n7, 237nn19,20,
    252n38, 264n10
Cornford, F. M., 32, 33, 126,
    204nn17,18,19, 205nn21,22,23,
    206n31, 208n46, 209n54,
    210nn59,62, 211n70, 212n84,
    214nn92,96, 217nn6,7,12,
    218nn16,22, 220n38, 224n7,
    227n26, 231n54, 240n3,
    242nn13,16, 245n39,
    250nn21,27, 257n31, 259n55,
    261n75
corruption,
    of Circles of the soul, 60, 72, 77,
        222n49
    cosmic, 127, 137–138, 155, 160,
        241n12
    moral and political, 60, 64–65,
        112, 155, 183–184, 251n35,
        259n49

cosmic soul. *See* world-soul
cosmopolitanism. *See* citizens (of the
    universe)
courage. *See* bravery
craft (*technê*), 34–35, 81, 82–83, 118,
    140, 142–143, 155, 164, 167,
    207n41, 219n3, 225n12, 227n28,
    232n58, 241n12, 246n52
creation,
    of soul, 26, 43, 168–169, 234n76,
        255n21
    of universe/its parts, 30, 31–35, 45,
        132–133, 149–150, 203n16,
        212n83, 244n37
Creator. *See* god, Demiurge
Cronus,
    age of, 124–128, 131–132, 134–145,
        153–154, 158–160, 190,
        242nn15,18,
        243nn24,30,32,34,35,36,
        244nn37,38, 245n39, 246n48,
        247n60, 251nn31,33,34, 253n46,
        see also Golden Age
    as name for Demiurge, 150
cycles, cosmic, 124–145, 147–149,
    151–152, 160–161, 175,
    241n12, 242nn15,18,
    243nn31,34,36, 244n37,
    245nn39,40,45,
    251nn29,30,31,33, 258nn38,39
    See also astronomy; reversals

demiurge (*dêmiourgos*),
    god as, *see* Demiurge
    human being as, 62–63, 112–113,
        122–123
    meanings of, 203n11
    philosopher-ruler as, 8, 52, 122,
        252n36
Demiurge, the,
    as creator, 8, 29–31, 31–35, 43, 45,
        90, 132–133, 149–150, 244n37,
        250n20
    and Forms, 29, 36, 39, 45, 46–47,
        49, 51–52, 57, 69, 90, 151, 202n4,
        208n48, 209n58, 212n84,
        213n87

mythical presentation of, 14, 24, 25–28, 29–31, 34–35, 51–52, 54, 62–63, 78, 96–97, 132–133, 149–150, 194, 204n17, 224n66

and necessity, 35, 36–42, 47–49, 63–66, 78, 87–88, 210n60

and *nous*, 19, 35–51, 98–100, 150–151

as role model, 26–27, 52, 57–58, 63–66, 69–70, 78, 194–195, 217n8, 219n29

and teleology, 19, 28–31, 34–42, 45, 46–48, 49–50, 151, 206n32, 209n58, 262n79

and world-soul, 16, 19, 42–52, 211n70, 214n96, 215n99, 216n107

See also god

Democritus, 5

See also Atomism

Descartes, R., 198n14, 211n68

design, 8, 21, 29, 55, 76, 112–113, 116, 126, 164, 167, 201n64, 240n4, 246n56

See also teleology; rule

desire (*epithumia*), 59–60, 61, 80, 101, 106, 112, 137, 157, 160, 245n40, 251n35

dialectic, 69, 79, 80, 81–84, 118, 119, 120, 123, 143, 220nn35,39, 222n53, 224n4, 239n43, 252n38

dialogue form, 14, 17–18, 79–80, 200n54

dianoia, 63, 200n51, 203nn9,10, 207n41, 219n26

disease, 40, 61–62, 65, 67, 72, 105, 106, 109, 111, 155, 157, 164, 173, 183, 184, 186, 219n24, 248n3

disorder, 13, 21–22, 36–37, 49, 61, 87, 100–101, 137, 141, 146–147, 151–152, 156, 157, 158, 177, 180, 184–188, 203n13, 214n96, 240n4, 248nn3,4,10, 249n12, 258n37

disorderly motion, 60, 88, 147, 148–149, 174, 185, 241n10, 247n61, 249n12

See also chaos

division, method of, 69–70, 79, 81–85, 119, 224n4, 226n23, 235n13

See also dialectic

dualism,

cosmic (good/evil), 147, 152, 176–177, 184, 258n42, 259n43

mind-body, 5–6, 19, 42, 49–50, 97, 98, 167, 168, 169, 194, 198n14, 211n68, 233n67, 255n22, 260n60, 264n9

Earth, 40, 54–55, 56, 149, 159, 182, 220nn38,39

earthborn (*gêgeneis*), 131–132, 134–138, 159, 244nn37,38, 245n40

ecology, 5, 186

See also environment; environmental philosophers

education,

and astronomy, *see* astronomy

and autonomy, 10–12, 68–69, 75, 140–141, 189–190, 253n50

and happiness, *see* happiness

and myth, *see* myth

recipients of, 10, 12, 75–76, 117, 119–121, 124, 155–156, 162–163, 189–190, 198n29, 202n1, 223nn58,59, 253n50, 253n1, 254n7

and virtue, *see* virtue

egoism, 193

See also self-interest

elements (so-called: fire, air, water, earth). *See* bodies

elenchos, 80, 118, 237n25

emotions, 15, 59, 63, 160, 199n43, 256n28

Empedocles, 208n47

environment, 142, 159–161, 164, 261n73, 263n7

environmental philosophers, 5, 194,
    199n34, 263nn6,7
Epicurus, 263n3
eschatology, 181, 182, 259n56
    See also afterlife
eternity,
    of Forms, 33, 73, 83, 90, 221n46,
    226n18
    and time, 33, 226n18
    See also immortality
ethical naturalism, 4, 192, 263n3
Euripides, 242n17
evil, 6, 17, 21–22, 25, 27, 40, 72,
    106, 147, 152, 155, 164, 176,
    178–188, 193, 248n3,
    260nn64,65
evil soul, 163, 170–180, 183–184,
    185–186, 258nn39,42,
    259nn43,51, 260n64
examined life, 7, 117, 118, 190
explanation, 6, 28, 38, 51, 64, 91,
    164–165, 176, 191, 198n17,
    202n8, 209n55, 210n63,
    216n105, 231n54
    See also cause; mechanism
external goods, 64, 67, 241n12,
    246n54
    See also luck

Fine, G., 38, 202n67,
    209nn50,51,53,56,58, 213n87,
    231n53
flux, 80, 95–96, 231nn53,54, 232n57
    See also compresence
Foot, P., 197n11
Forms,
    and being-becoming contrast,
    93–96, 205n23, 225n13, 231n56,
    232n58
    and causation, 39, 46,
    209nn53,54,57, 210n64, 213n88,
    229n38
    and Demiurge, *see* Demiurge
    eternity of, *see* eternity
    and fourfold classification, 20,
    89–90, 91, 224n8, 225n10,
    226nn16,23

and god, *see* god
    knowledge of, 9–10, 12, 43, 47,
    69–73, 82–83, 90, 118, 120, 123,
    158, 214n97, 215n98, 217n9,
    220n35, 222nn54,55
    imitation of, 58, 71, 73, 157–158,
    251n34
    immutability of, 29, 44, 46–47, 49,
    73, 90, 151, 205n23, 212n84,
    250n23, 251n34, 252n42,
    254n12
    participation in, 46, 51–52, 83–84,
    209n58, 213n87
    problems concerning, 46–47, 69,
    224nn3,8, 254n12
    See also dialectic; model/s;
    separation; teleology
fortune. *See* luck
fourfold classification, 84–102, 122,
    191
    See also apeiron; cause; Forms;
    mixture; *peras*
Frede, D., 113, 214n92, 220n35,
    224nn3,6,7,8, 225nn11,13,14,
    226n23, 228n33, 231n53,
    232n56, 234n71, 234nn1,4,5,6,
    235nn10,12, 236nn16,18,
    237n25, 238n29, 239n39
Frede, M., 17, 200nn53,54, 202n8,
    205n23, 230n49, 232n57
freedom, 180–181, 192, 259n53
    See also responsibility;
    self-determination

Gadamer, H. G., 200nn49,52,
    233n70
generation (*genesis*), 29, 31–35, 44,
    81–83, 89, 92, 93–96, 112–113,
    142, 164, 169, 212n83, 215n102,
    222n49, 230nn49,50, 231n53,
    232n58, 234n76
    See also becoming; creation
god/s,
    as cause, *see* cause
    cosmic, 54–57, 73–74, 76, 158, 182,
    218n13, 252n43
    as creator, *see* Demiurge

and Forms, 51–52, 57–58, 69, 73–74, 115, 151, 212n84, 218nn15,16,19, 221n48

goodness/rationality of, 27, 34, 36, 57, 63, 170, 173, 174–175, 177–178, 184, 199n42, 206n30, 210n65, 249n14, 258n39

heavenly bodies as, 40, 54, 55–56, 148, 177, 204n18, 217nn4,5,8, 218nn13,16, 224n66, 249n14, 259nn45,59

imitation of, *see* imitation

immanence of, 6, 42–52, 54, 99–100, 150–151, *see also* separation

as legislator, 65, 180–182

lesser/secondary, 31, 54, 56–57, 139–140, 150, 154, 156, 160, 178, 204n17, 211n67, 217n8, 246nn47,48,56

as living being, 4–5, 57, 62, 115, 122, 239n32

as mediator, 29, 46–47, 49, 57–58, 70, 73–74, 78, 151, 158, 221n48

as model/example, 4, 19–20, 27, 53–62, 63, 65, 68–69, 73–74, 77, 103, 113–116, 123, 142, 153–156, 159, 194–195, 246nn53,54, 251n34, 252n42

and necessity, *see* necessity

as *nous*, 5–6, 19, 35–36, 42–46, 49, 57, 98–100, 150–151, 212nn75,84, 224n66, *see also* intellect

not omnipotent, 27, 36, 63, 261n71

as one-and-many, 31, 54, 56, 150, 204nn17,18, 246n56, 257n31

Platonic vs. Judeo-Christian conception of, 44, 57

and pleasure, 20, 103, 113–116, 123, 234n1, 235n12, 238nn30,31

as principle of motion, 29, 47, 151, 250n25

proofs for existence of, 97–100, 164–170, 170–175, 257n33

as ruler or leader, 36, 49, 133–134, 150–151, 154, 184, 207n36, 239n32, 245n43, 250nn20,25, 257n31, 258n39, 259n59, *see also* rule

as self-mover, 150–151, 180, 239n32, 250n25

and teleology, 19, 28–31, 34–42, 46–48, 49–50, 55, 56–57, 68, 116, 127, 151, 163, 184, 262n79

traditional, 26–27, 54, 57, 114–115, 182, 217nn11,12, 221n48, 256n28, 257n31

universe as, 4–5, 6–7, 49–50, 54, 71, 177, 181–182, 216n104, 217n4, 249n14, 259n45

visible/sensible, 50, 54, 78, 148, 217n5

world-soul as, 28, 43, 45, 49–50, 54, 78, 256n28, 259n59

See also assimilation with god; creator; Demiurge

godlessness, 20–21, 124–125, 126, 139, 143–144, 214n15, 243n36, 245n39

Golden Age, 125–126, 158–159, 162, 243n36, 246n56

See also Cronus, age of

good,
  and beauty, *see* beauty
  and being, 95, 107, 108–109
  and completeness, *see* completeness
  derivative/instrumental, 109, 110, 237n19
  and evil, 1, 24, 40, 60, 147, 152, 176–177, 183–184, 186, 188, 192–193, 198, 258n42, 260nn64,65, *see also* evil; evil soul
  Form of, 10, 52, 91, 203n13, 208n48, 209nn53,54, 220n39, 229n38
  as good life/happiness, 9, 79, 80, 84, 92, 110, 113, 116, 119, 187–188, 238n30
  immanent, 91–92, 102, 208n48, 229n38, 262n79

good (*cont.*)
  intrinsic, 92–93, 96, 102, 104, 108,
    109, 110, 237nn19,23
  and measure/order, 30, 91, 92, 108,
    116, 123, 155, 203n13, 210n65,
    227n28, 229nn38,39,41, 250n26
  and *peras*, see *peras*
  and pleasure, *see* pleasure
  of society, 9–11, 52, 155, 193
  and unity, 30, 95, 203n13
  of universe, 6–7, 13, 29–30, 52, 102,
    163, 179, 187–189, 192, 193,
    208n40, *see also* teleology
Gosling, J., 113, 224nn3,7, 225n13,
  229n38, 230n43, 232nn56,63,
  234nn1,4, 235n12, 236n18,
  238nn26,27,29
greed. *See* overgaining
gymnastics, 61–62, 75–76, 202n1,
  219n26, 222n50

happiness (*eudaimonia*),
  and astronomy, *see* astronomy
  characterised, 9, 65, 72, 79–80,
    84, 103, 187–188, 198n21,
    230n45
  and education, 10, 25, 74–76, 103,
    119, 121, 124, 162, 189–190,
    239n43, 240n44
  elitist vs. populist conceptions of, 7,
    9–13, 20, 53, 68–69, 74–76, 103,
    116–123, 143, 189–190, 194–195,
    239n43
  of god/the universe, 58, 62, 103,
    113–116, 122, 155, 187–188
  and pleasure, *see* pleasure
  of the *polis*, 9–10, 155, 246n54
  and politics, 11–12, 75, 117, 122,
    123, 124, 190, 246n54
  and virtue, *see* virtue
harmony, 8, 15, 30, 54, 56, 58, 61–62,
  67, 71, 72, 76–78, 88, 91, 106, 114,
  155, 203n13, 220n37, 228n34,
  230n46, 251n34
health, 40, 61, 67, 92, 109, 112,
  159–160, 222n50, 230n45,
  237n22

heaven and hell, 180–182, 259n57
heavenly bodies,
  as causes/rulers, 56, 140, 175,
    178–179, 214n95, 217n8, 257n31
  as gods, *see* god
  motion of, 55–56, 77, 129, 148, 157,
    174–176, 217nn6,7, 248n10,
    249n13
  nature of, 55–56, 59, 70–71, 99,
    148, 217nn5,8, 239n32, 240n45,
    257n31
  See also astronomy; planets; stars
hedonism, 20, 79–80, 95–96, 104,
  108, 109, 110–113, 123, 237n25,
  263n3
Heraclitus, 4, 197n8, 263n3
Hesiod, 26, 56–57, 132, 158
heteronomy, 10, 75, 198n27, 246n57,
  247n60
  See also autonomy
holism, 187–188, 193, 203n16,
  261n76, 263n7
Homer, 26, 56–57, 63, 67, 219n29
hubris, 25, 64, 65, 68, 184
Hume, D., 197n10
Hursthouse, R., 198n12
hylomorphism, 5–6, 233n67

illness. *See* disease
imitation,
  of the cosmos, 12, 13, 58–59, 61, 62,
    77, 124, 127, 134, 139, 153,
    157–158, 187–188, 193, 222n49,
    241n12
  of Forms, *see* Forms
  of god, 26–27, 61–62, 73, 154,
    157–158, 217nn8,11, 219n29,
    222n49
  of role models, 27, 58, 62
  See also model/s
immortality,
  of Forms, 71, 218n19
  of god, 218nn15,16,19, 258n39
  and humans, 59, 218n19, 233n67,
    259n56, 263n3
  of soul, 59, 61, 143, 154, 204n17,
    218n19, 233n67

of the world, 31, 58–59, 71, 138, 249n14

immutability. *See* Forms

imperfection,
  and human nature, 59–60, 104–105
  of sensible universe, 36–37, 39–40, 64–65, 87–88, 104, 185–186, 193

indeterminate. See *apeiron*

infinite. See *apeiron*

injustice, 26–27, 58, 61, 67–68, 152, 155, 160, 184, 192, 249n12, 255n22

intellect/intelligence,
  and body, 19, 21, 28, 44–45, 49–51, 59–60, 67, 97, 147, 149, 152, 167, 191, 207n38, 211n68, 212n81, 216n105, *see also* body
  as cause, *see* cause, *nous* as
  of cosmic soul/universe, 5–6, 12, 13, 19, 20, 28, 44–45, 48–50, 57, 59–62, 71, 97, 99–100, 121, 127, 149, 177, 199n33, 214n96, 243n36
  and Demiurge, *see* Demiurge
  dependence on soul, *see* soul
  and Forms, 47, 51–52, 57, 69–70, 75, 90, 151, 212n84, 218n15, 232n58
  and god, 5–6, 28, 44–45, 48–49, 54–58, 58–62, 149–151, 174–178, 210n65, 258n39, *see also* god
  human, 10, 13, 15, 19, 20, 22, 30, 50–51, 58–62, 65–66, 67, 69–78, 101–102, 107, 112–113, 115–116, 121–123, 154, 156–159, 161, 162, 173, 183–184, 193, 197n7, 198n27, 212n81, 216n105, 218nn19,23, 219n26, 222n49, 223n57, 234n79, 239n40, 253nn48,50, 261n76
  motion of, 44–45, 48–49, 73, 151, 174, 212nn75,79,80,81,84
  and necessity, *see* necessity
  and order, *see* order
  and pleasure, *see* pleasure

and teleology, 19, 30, 35–42, 50–51, 60–61, 62, 100–102, 127, 142, 151, 163, 183, 261n76
  theoretical and practical functions of, 35–36, 47–49, 51–52, 150
  See also god; rule; separation

intelligibility, 16–17, 28, 50, 87, 90, 95, 102, 120, 151, 191, 231n54, 232n56, 235n9

interconnectedness, 22, 37, 179, 181, 186–188, 193

Irwin, T., 1, 17, 110, 197n1, 198nn26,27, 201nn55,65, 205n23, 222n51, 225n13, 227n25, 231n54, 234nn1,6, 236n18, 237n24, 238n27

judgement. *See* belief

justice,
  cosmic/natural, 6, 7–8, 65, 68, 179–184, 192, 260n61
  in the individual, 73–74, 185, 192, 237n22
  social, 9–10, 67–68, 155, 184

Kant, I., 10

kinship,
  of all souls, 121, 181
  of humans with animals, 70, 159, 253n48
  of humans with Forms, 73
  of humans with god, 59, 73, 115, 121
  of humans with universe, 22, 73, 162, 187, 189, 192

knowledge,
  broad sense of, 75, 222nn54,55
  and the Forms, *see* Forms
  and happiness, 9–12, 20, 75, 103, 118, 119–122, 123, 239n43
  and intelligibility, 87, 94–95, 119–120, 232n56
  and method of division, 80–81, 83–84, 222n55
  and pleasure, 20, 79, 84, 109, 110–113, 115, 116, 118, 122, 237n23

kosmos,
   meaning/s of, 199n32
   See also order; universe

law (*nomos*),
   and nature, 4, 162–163, 166–167,
      180–182, 191–192, 260n60,
      263nn3,4
   as second best, 11–12, 252n38
life. *See* soul
likely account/story, 16, 25–26,
      147–148, 219n26, 263n8
limit. See *peras*
Line allegory, 63, 219n26
living being/s,
   beauty and, 30, 219n32
   Form of, 36, 69–70, 208n48,
      212n84, 262n79
   god as, *see* god
   and happiness, 114–115, 121–122
   heavenly bodies as, 55, 239n32
   universe as, 4–5, 6, 34–35, 57,
      58–59, 62, 149, 190–191, 239n32,
      249n12
love (*erôs*), 59, 77–78, 115–116,
      232n66
luck, 19, 28, 63–68, 194, 219n31
   See also virtue

MacIntyre, A., 219n29
macro-microcosm analogy, 97–100,
      116, 255n19
marriage, 263n3
materialist theories/materialism, 5, 17,
      34, 164, 168–169, 187, 207n41,
      208n47, 215n102, 240n3,
      260n60, 261n75, 264n9
mathematical structure,
   of body, 30, 46, 216n103
   and intelligibility, 87, 90, 94–95,
      102, 120, 232n56
   peras as, see *peras*
   of soul, 59, 70, 72, 220nn37,38
   of universe, 20, 30, 84, 92, 94, 95,
      102, 203n13, 231nn53,54
mathematics, 76, 87, 118, 119–121,
      189, 200n51, 219n26,

      220nn34,39, 222n50,
      223nn56,57,60
matter,
   intelligible (Aristotle), 224n8
   See also body; traces
measure,
   and beauty, *see* beauty
   god as, 192, 254n4, 263n4
   and good, *see* good
   and *peras*, 88, 91, 92, 106–109, 113,
      119–120
   See also harmony; proportion
mechanism, 8, 19, 37–39, 41, 48, 50,
      165, 208n47, 216n105
mentalism, 168–169
mind, 199n33 (characterised)
   See also intellect/intelligence;
      soul
mind-body balance, 5, 19, 59–62, 67,
      219nn24,26,32, 222n50, 223n56
mind-body relation/problem, 5–6,
      21–22, 42, 49–51, 97–99,
      167–170, 182, 190–191, 198n14,
      211n68, 216n104, 233n67,
      255nn19,22
   See also dualism
mixed life, 75, 79, 84, 91, 92, 110–111,
      113, 123, 229nn41,42, 234n3
   See also mixture
mixture (of *peras* and *apeiron*), 89,
      91–96, 101, 108–109, 112–113,
      207n38, 229n42, 230nn45,46,49,
      231nn53,54, 234n3, 235n13,
      236n15, 237n19
model/s,
   Forms as, 29, 39, 47, 52, 58, 73, 90,
      203n16, 209n58, 213nn87,88,
      251n34, 262n79
   god as, *see* god; Demiurge
   universe as, 8, 12–13, 22, 58, 61, 68,
      72–74, 76–78, 100, 116, 121, 122,
      144, 148, 160–161, 189–191, 193
   See also imitation; role models
moderation, 7–8, 106, 107, 109, 110,
      112, 113, 122, 177–178, 184,
      235n7, 237n20
monads, 81–84, 229n38

Moore, G. E., 197nn10,11
motion,
 of body, *see* body
 circular, 148, 151, 175, 214n93,
  241nn10,11, 243n36, 248n10,
  252n42
 disorderly, *see* disorderly motion
 of heavenly bodies, *see* heavenly
  bodies
 of *nous*, *see* intellect
 presupposing space, 44–45, 49, 165,
  182
 primary vs. secondary, 48, 164–165,
  166, 167, 170–171
 principle of, 29, 46, 47, 50, 151,
  165–166, 209n52, 210n61, *see also*
  god; soul
 rectilinear, 241n10, 247n61,
  254n10
 rotatory, 44–45, 157, 174, 214n93,
  241n10, 254n10, 257n32
 types of, 254n10
 See also self-motion; soul
music, 92, 198n29, 202n1
myth,
 and argument/rational discourse
  (*logos*), 2, 14–16, 24, 25–27,
  45–46, 62–63, 68, 86–87,
  147–148, 199n39, 200nn44,51,
  224n66, 248n5
 and education, 15, 26, 57–58, 63,
  68, 198n29, 219n29, 220n34
 and the emotions, 15, 63, 160,
  199n43
 Platonic vs. popular, 15, 130,
  199n42, 200nn44,49
 and truth, 15, 200n44, 219n27

Nagel, T., 256n24
naturalistic fallacy, 4, 191–192
nature,
 harmony with, 13, 80, 123, 159, 161,
  188, 193
 intrinsic value of, 20, 102, 191–192,
  194, *see also* good, intrinsic;
  universe, sensible, elevated
  account of

 and law, *see* law
 as principle, 164, 254n8
 and soul, 48, 164, 166–167, 182,
  255n18, 260n60
 theories of, 3, 17, 80, 162–165,
  232n58
necessity (*anankê*),
 and *apeiron*, 87–88, 100–101,
  227n27, 228n31, 234n77,
  250n18
 as auxiliary cause, *see* cause
 and the bodily, 37, 149, 152, 240n4,
  245n45, 250n18
 and causation, *see* cause
 and god, 19, 27, 35, 36–42, 47–49,
  58–62, 63–66, 78, 87–88, 210n60,
  223n59
 hypothetical (Aristotle), 208n46
 and imperfection, 36–37, 39–40,
  65, 87–88, 142, 193, 245n45
 instrument vs. obstacle, 36–42,
  60–61, 63–64, 101
 and intellect, 6, 30, 36–42, 58–68,
  74, 101, 141, 149, 152, 154, 158,
  164, 193, 210n60, 240n4,
  245n45, 250nn18,27
 lower parts of the soul and, 65,
  207n39
 in mathematics, 223n59
 and pleasure/pain, 234n79
 and randomness or chance, 64, 101,
  164, 234n77, 240n44, 250n18
 and rectilinear motion, 247n61,
  254n10
 and space, 36, 227n27
 and teleology, 6, 24–25, 30, 36–42,
  61, 68, 101–102, 142, 164–165,
  193
 as wandering cause, *see* cause
norm. *See* law
normativity, 4, 162–163, 191
nous. See intellect/intelligence;
 mind
Nussbaum, M., 198nn14,15,27,
 199n38, 233n67, 234n1,
 236nn14,18, 237n21, 238n27,
 264n12

one-many problem, 81–84, 224n6
opinion (*doxa*). *See* belief
order,
    and goodness, *see* good
    and human soul/life, 7–8, 22, 72,
        75, 77, 80, 101, 112–113, 116,
        144–145, 157–158, 160–161, 180,
        193, 199n32, 262n80
    imposed by god/mind, 35–36, 45,
        47, 48, 51–52, 88, 97, 100–101,
        116, 121, 126, 144–145, 147–151,
        155, 157, 174, 179, 183, 207n36,
        210n65, 240n3, 257n33
    social/political, 8, 51–52, 142,
        153–156, 161, 199n32
    in speech, 35, 207n34
    and time, 33–34
    in universe, 7–8, 12, 22, 30, 51–52,
        75, 80, 88, 97, 100–102, 116, 144,
        150, 158, 174–175, 183, 193,
        199n32
overgaining/greed (*pleonexia*), 13,
    184, 186, 187, 260n67
Owen, G. E. L., 23, 93, 124, 202n67,
    228n32, 230n47, 240nn2,3,
    241n12, 246n57,
    250n23

palingenesis. *See* reincarnation
panpsychism, 191, 256n24
paradeigmatism, 73–74, 89
    See also model/s; Forms
paradigm/s. *See* model/s
participation. *See* Forms
parts,
    of the soul, 61, 172, 218n23,
        258n41, *see also* soul; tripartition
    of the universe, 31, 178–179, 186,
        188, 246n56
    and wholes, 187–188, 193
peras,
    and causation, *see* cause
    and dialectic, 79, 81–84,
        225nn13,15
    and the Forms, 89–90, 95,
        225nn10,13, 228n31
    and the fourfold classification, 84,
        88–91, 225n15, 228n29

    and goodness, 90–91, 92, 95, 96,
        104, 108, 109, 237n19
    and intelligibility, 87–88, 90, 94–95,
        102, 120, 232n56
    as mathematical structure, 87–88,
        90–95, 102, 119–120, 231n53
    and measure, *see* measure
    mixture with *apeiron*, *see* mixture
    and pleasure, 79–80, 82, 104,
        107–110, 112–113, 115, 237n19
    and teleology, 91, 94, 95, 100–102
Philolaus, 87, 224n5, 228n34, 230n46
philosopher-ruler, 8, 9–11, 11–13, 52,
    74–75, 76, 124, 190, 246n57,
    252nn36,38
philosophy, 9, 15, 20, 30, 38, 58, 69,
    71, 72, 73, 74–76, 83, 116–117,
    119–120, 143, 158–159, 189–190,
    198n28, 216n104, 220n35,
    223nn58,60, 239n43, 247n60,
    248n63, 252n38, 253n46
physicalism, 6
    See also materialism
planets, 3, 6, 54–56, 77, 175,
    217nn7,10, 220n38, 248nn8,10
    See also astronomy; heavenly bodies
plants, 30, 121
pleasure,
    and *apeiron*, see *apeiron*
    and beauty, *see* beauty
    and being-becoming contrast, 20,
        104, 107–109, 231nn52,55,
        235n12
    and belief, *see* belief
    and god, *see* god
    and goodness, 20, 81–82, 84,
        108–110, 236n17, 237n19
    and happiness, 20, 75, 79–81, 84,
        86, 103, 113–115, 119, 123
    and imperfection, 86–88, 104,
        252n39
    and intelligence, 103, 110–111,
        115–116, 121, 236n17
    and knowledge, *see* knowledge
    mixed and pure, 104–112, 114–116,
        234n3, 235nn7,8,12,
        236nn14,16,17, 237nn19,20,
        238nn26,28,31

and necessity, *see* necessity
vs. neutral condition, 113–114, 236n16, 238n30
and *peras*, see *peras*
quantitative criterion for, 111–112, 236n18, 238nn26,27,28
and stability, *see* stability
and teleology, 101, 112–113
true and false, 104–113, 235n7
and virtue, *see* virtue
See also hedonism
Plutarch, 177, 204n19, 258n41
politics, 19, 21, 24, 53, 75, 103, 122–123, 126–127, 128, 141, 142, 144–145, 146, 153–156, 159–160, 190, 241n12, 243n35, 246nn50,54, 247n62, 252n38
See also city (*polis*)
Posidonius, 201n64
Presocratics, 4, 208n47, 263n3
Proclus, 204n19, 205n26, 206n28, 217n7, 234n72, 250n27, 258n39
proportion, 30, 46, 61, 72, 73, 87, 88, 90, 91, 92, 94, 95, 102, 104, 106, 107, 108, 109, 113, 120, 148, 174, 203n13, 207n38, 220nn37,38, 221n47, 222n50, 229n38, 232n56, 236n17
See also harmony; mathematical structure; measure; *peras*
Protagoras, 254n4
providence, divine, 16, 18, 128, 140, 141, 150, 155, 163, 175, 180, 185–186, 194, 206n30, 215n98, 245n43, 256n28, 258n39, 259n59, 261n71
punishment, 180–181, 183, 192, 255n22
Pythagoras/Pythagorean, 119–120, 224n5, 233n67

reason. See *dianoia*; intellect/intelligence; mind; rule
receptacle, 209n58, 213n88, 226n23, 227n26
See also space

recollection,
of Forms, 158
of god, 158, 253n43
reincarnation, 51, 74, 135, 233n67, 247n61, 251n30, 259n56
relativism, 163, 254n4
responsibility, 21–22, 60, 64–65, 159, 160, 163–164, 179–184, 185, 186, 187, 192–193
reversals,
of ageing process, 131–132, 134–135, 137–138, 153, 245n40, 247n61, 251n30
of universe, 125–129, 133, 135, 137–138, 147–148, 153, 241nn10,11,12, 242nn18,22, 243n36, 244n37
See also cycles
role models, 4, 27, 52, 53, 58, 62, 195, 219n29, 264n13
See also model/s
rotation. *See* motion
Rowe, C., 127, 130, 197n5, 201nn57,65, 239n38, 241nn6,8,12, 242nn13,15,16,19,20, 243nn23,36, 245n39, 246nn47,52, 247n62, 248n2, 250n23
rule,
of Circle of the Same, 55, 59, 215n98, 217n6
of god's reason in the universe, 21, 29, 35–40, 48–49, 59, 64, 96–97, 100–101, 126, 141, 150, 154, 155, 174–175, 178–179, 180–183, 207n36, 240n4, 261n71, *see also* god
of heavenly bodies, 56, 140–141, 178–179, 257n31, 259n59
of human beings in the universe, 68, 160, 178–179, 183–184, 187–188
of political expert, 9–11, 48–49, 53, 122, 124–125, 127, 145, 155–156, 246n57, 247n62, 252n38, *see also* philosopher-ruler

rule (*cont.*)
  and principle (*archê*), 166, 259n50
  of reason in the individual, 30, 59,
    64–66, 67, 74, 101–102, 110,
    112–113, 158–159, 161, 253n50
  of reason in society, 154, 162
  of soul over body, 48–49, 55, 59,
    166–170, 259n50
  of world-soul, 46–50, 55, 70,
    98–100, 172–178, 217n7, 257n31,
    259n59
  See also autonomy; heteronomy;
    self-rule

Sedley, D., 197n3, 198n20, 200n48,
  202n8, 209n53, 212n81, 215n102,
  216n2, 221nn41,47, 222n49,
  223n60, 239n38, 261n76,
  264n10
self-control/mastery, 80, 157
  See also temperance
self-determination, 180, 192
self-fulfilment. *See* happiness
self-interest, 187, 193–194
  See also egoism
self-knowledge, 4, 75, 106, 118,
  121–122, 188, 239n40, 240n46
self-motion,
  of god, *see* god
  of soul, *see* soul
self-realisation, 190
  See also happiness
self-rule,
  human, 10, 75, 84
  societal, 141–142
  of universe, 139–141, 153, 241n10,
    243n36
  See also autonomy
self-sufficiency, 62, 110, 219n24
  See also Sufficiency Thesis
senses, sense perception, 26, 30, 38,
  70–71, 74, 77, 87, 116, 215n98,
  238n26, 256n25
sensibles, sensible realm, 29, 30, 31,
  46, 49, 82, 83–84, 85–88, 104,
  148, 205n23, 209n58, 213n87,
  226n17, 228n36, 248n10
  See also universe

separation,
  of Forms, 39, 46–47, 49, 69–70, 78,
    81–82, 89–90, 93, 102, 213n87,
    228nn32,36, 231n51
  of god, 5–6, 16, 19, 42–43, 44–45,
    49, 115, 151, 258n39
  of *nous*, 5–6, 19, 20, 42–43, 49–51,
    96, 98–100, 151, 211n68, 224n66,
    234nn71,76, 258n39
Sherman, N., 198n12
similarity (with god). *See* assimilation
  with god
skill (*technê*). *See* craft
sophists, 4, 82, 163, 197n9, 224n6,
  251n31
soul (*psuchê*),
  and corporeality, 49–50, 194,
    215n102, 256n25
  cosmic, *see* world-soul
  dependence on body/space, 21, 28,
    44–45, 50–51, 67, 98–100,
    167–170, 182, 191, 215n102,
    233n67, 255n22, 256n24
  and generation, 26, 43, 168–169,
    234n76, 255n21, *see also*
    becoming; creation
  and god, 164–165, 170–172,
    256n27, *see also* assimilation with
    god; kinship; world-soul
  of heavenly bodies, 55, 59, 99–100,
    177, 217n5, 257n31, 259n59
  immortality of, *see* immortality
  infant, 60, 72, 157, 210n62, 247n61
  and life, 21, 166, 170, 239n32
  as mediator, 47, 70, 73–74, 78,
    254n12
  as necessary for *nous*, 42–44, 51, 97,
    99, 100, 212n84, 231n54,
    234n76
  as primary cause or principle of
    motion, 43, 46–48, 50–51,
    164–166, 167–170, 185, 209n52,
    210n61, 213n90, 216n104, 254n9
  and Principle of Opposites,
    171–172
  priority over body, 21, 164, 167–170,
    191, 259n50
  as ruler, *see* rule

as self-mover, 50–51, 151, 165–166,
167, 169–170, 180, 182, 209n52,
213n90, 214n93, 216n104,
217n6, 233n67, 239n32, 254n13,
255n22
tripartition/subrational capacities
of, 48, 59, 61, 70, 77, 115–116,
172–173, 176–177, 207n39,
218n23, 219n28, 221n47,
232n66, 239n36, 258n41
and visibility, 170, 215n102, 256n25
See also intellect; evil soul
sound-mindedness (*sôphrosunê*), 9–10,
118, 177, 239n40
See also moderation; self-control
space (*chôra*), 36, 44, 49, 115, 165,
169, 227n27, 228n31, 255n22,
261n73
See also receptacle
spirit (*thumos*), 30, 59, 61, 115
stability,
of the Forms, 25–26, 29, 83, 90,
148, 215n98, 232n58, 251n34
of happiness, 80, 101–102, 108, 109,
111, 112–113, 238n26
and *peras*, 88, 90, 108, 113, 229n39,
231n53
and pleasure, 104, 107, 108, 109,
111, 112–113, 236nn14,15,
238n26
and the sensible universe, 26, 80,
87, 88, 90, 94–96, 148, 231n53,
232n58
stars, 6, 7, 54, 55, 77, 217n7, 221n46
See also heavenly bodies
Stoics, 4, 22, 192, 194, 197nn7,11,
215n102, 263n4, 264n9
strangers (in a city), 116–117, 253n1
Sufficiency Thesis, 66–68, 237n23
See also virtue

taxonomy. *See* division
teleology,
vs. chance, 37, 100–102, 163–165,
207n41, 240n4
cosmic, 6, 13, 19, 28, 127, 151,
163–165, 179, 191, 198n20,
206n32, 262n79

and Demiurge, *see* Demiurge
and explanation, *see* cause, primary;
explanation
and evil, 6–7, 13, 40, 60, 65–66,
151–152, 163–164, 170–178,
178–184, 188
and god, *see* god
holistic vs. anthropocentric,
203n16, 261n76
humans as agents of, 6–7, 13,
61–62, 64–68, 112–113, 142, 179,
182–184, 187–188, 192–193,
218n23
and intellect, *see* intellect
and mechanism, 19, 37–39, 41, 48,
50, 164–165, 185, 208n47,
216n105
and necessity, *see* necessity
open vs. closed, 183, 192–193
and *peras*, see *peras*
and pleasure, *see* pleasure
temperance. *See* moderation;
self-control
therapy. *See* astronomy
time, 30, 31–34, 73, 85, 100, 169,
206n28, 226n18
traces (*ichnê*), 37–38, 88, 169, 203n13,
207nn35,38, 209n58, 211n68,
227n27, 250n18, 254n14
transcendence. *See* separation
truth, 15, 22, 71–72, 91, 95, 105, 107,
111, 118, 200n44, 219n27,
229nn38,39, 232nn56,58,
238n26, 248n5

unity,
of the body/world-body, 50, 88, 98
of the Forms, 30, 81–84
of the good human life, 12, 80
of the person, 8
of the state, 160
of the universe, 8, 12, 30, 37, 46, 80,
160, 188, 203n13, 250n18,
262nn79,80
universe,
anthropomorphic description of,
21, 156–158, 161, 249n14,
251n35

universe (*cont.*)
  as battlefield of human good and
    evil, 183–184, 186, 188, 189,
    192–193, 260nn64,65
  and beauty, *see* beauty
  and completeness, *see* completeness
  creation of, *see* creation
  as god, *see* god
  and goodness, *see* good; teleology
  holistic account of, *see* holism
  humans as citizens of, *see* citizens
  imitation of, *see* imitation
  and imperfection, *see* imperfection
  mathematical structure of, *see*
    mathematical structure
  as model, *see* model; assimilation
    with god
  and order, *see* order
  as organism, 22, 179, 181–182,
    187–188, 190–191, 262n79, *see
    also* interconnectedness; living
    being
  rule of humans in, *see* rule
  sensible, elevated account of, 20,
    84, 92–96, 102, 191–192,
    231nn51,54, 232n58
  and stability, *see* stability; flux
  and unity, *see* unity
  See also nature; sensibles, sensible
    realm
unlimited. See *apeiron*

vice, 60, 61, 65, 67, 68, 163, 181, 184,
  186
virtue,
  and education, 26–27, 60, 61–62,
    119, 155–156, 157, 162–163,
    219n29
  environmental/cosmic import of,
    178–179, 183–184, 261n73
  and the Forms, 9–10, 57–58,
    251n34
  god as model of, 19, 28, 58–68,
    72–78, 177, 194–195, 221n47
  as necessary for happiness, 9–10,
    65, 74–75, 80, 220n33
  as sufficient for happiness, 65–68,
    110, 220n33, 237n23

  and harmony, 58, 61–62, 67,
    251n34
  and luck, 19, 63–68, 194, 219n31
  and pleasure, 109–110, 112–113,
    237nn22,33
  and story telling, 26–27, 57–58, 63,
    68, 194, 219n29
virtue ethics, 4, 195, 219n29, 264n13
Vlastos, G., 2, 33–34, 116–117, 202n8,
  204n19, 205nn20,21,23,24,
  206nn28,29, 209n53, 213n90,
  217nn10,12, 220n36, 222n51,
  239n37, 247n62, 249n15,
  254n16, 255n21, 260n68,
  261n70

wandering cause. *See* necessity
war and peace, 136, 159–160,
  220n33
Williams, B., 234n5
wisdom, 10, 74–75, 110, 112, 113,
  143–144, 158, 184, 239n40
world. *See* universe
world-soul,
  as cause, *see* cause
  and Demiurge, *see* Demiurge
  faculties of, 47–49, 59, 100,
    172–178, 212n98, 214n96,
    215n98, 258nn39,41
  as god, *see* god
  nature of, 28, 47, 48, 54–55, 59, 70,
    77, 100, 185, 213n85,
    214nn92,96, 216n103,
    220nn37,38
  as ruler, *see* rule
  See also soul

Zeus,
  age of, 66, 128, 130, 131, 134, 135,
    136, 137–138, 138–145, 153, 154,
    158–159, 240n3, 242nn15,18,
    243nn35,36, 244n37, 246n47,
    247n60, 251nn33,34
  in Atlantis story, 65
  as name for cosmic god, 150,
    232n64, 256n28
  as name for Demiurge, 149–150
  in traditional religion, 54, 114, 129